LANDLORDING

DEDICATION

This book is dedicated to the scrupulous landlady in my life. Ivy, that's you.

ACKNOWLEDGEMENTS

I would like to acknowledge the following good people for their help in one way or another: Robert Armentrout, Bob Bochemuehl, Maynard Briggs, Bob Bruss, Wallace Darling, Bud Ekstrom, Ron English, Fred Felder, Robert France, Herb Frank, Ruth Furey, Dave Glubetich, Al Good, Vernon Graves, David Halbrook, Scotty Herd, Larry Hughes, Tom Javorina, Robert Jones, John Koczan, Carl Lindh, Charles Manning, Robin Maydeck, Oliver McClory, Margaret Miglia, Rita Moore, Connie Nakano, David Patton, Richard Randolph, Jack Reed, Daniel Robinson, Dario Robinson, Nancy Robinson, Ira Serkes, Jo Stender, Paul Warren, Suzanne Wehausen, David Williams, Nancy Williams, Jay Wilson, Jim Woollen, and the hundreds of landlords and landladies who've endured my landlording classes with many suggestions and few complaints.

Without their help, this book wouldn't be in the shape it's in.

THE USUAL CAVEAT

LANDLORDING

A Handymanual for Scrupulous Landlords and Landladies Who Do It Themselves

WRITTEN BY
LEIGH ROBINSON

ILLUSTRATED BY
DAVID PATTON & NANCY ROBINSON

PUBLISHED BY

P.O. BOX 1639
EL CERRITO, CA 94530-4639

FIRST EDITION   September, 1975
SECOND EDITION   May, 1976
   Revised   February, 1977
   Revised   June, 1977
   Revised   March, 1978
   Reprinted   September, 1978
   Reprinted   November, 1978
   Revised   June, 1978
THIRD EDITION   March, 1980
   Revised   October, 1980
   Revised   October, 1981
   Revised   February, 1983
   Reprinted   January, 1984
   Reprinted   August, 1984
   Reprinted   January, 1985
   Reprinted   May, 1985
FOURTH EDITION   January, 1986

COPYRIGHT ©1975, 1976, 1977, 1978, 1979, 1980, 1981, 1983, 1986 by
   Leigh Robinson

COVER AND BOOK DESIGN by David Patton

LIBRARY OF CONGRESS CATALOG CARD NUMBER: 79-57253

INTERNATIONAL STANDARD BOOK NUMBER: 0-932956-08-4

PRINTED IN THE U.S.A.

THE LANDLORDING SERIES™ AND THE LANDLORDING CHARACTER ARE
TRADEMARKS OF ExPRESS and LEIGH ROBINSON

Library of Congress Cataloging in Publication Data
Robinson, Leigh 1940-
   Landlording: a handymanual for scrupulous landlords and landladies who
do it themselves / written by Leigh Robinson; illustrated by David Patton and
Nancy Robinson.—4th ed.—El Cerrito, CA.: ExPress, 1986.
   350 p: ill.; 28 cm.
   Bibliography: p.333-344
   Includes index.
   ISBN 0-932956-08-4: $17.95
   1. Real estate management—Handbooks, manuals, etc. 2. Rental
housing—Handbooks, manuals, etc. 1. Title HD 1394.R62 1986 333.5'068
—dc19 79-57253 MARC

PREFACES

PREFACE TO THE FIRST EDITION (1975)

After I bought my first rental property, I soon learned how little practical information there was to help landlords and landladies through the many tribulations they face day after day after day. So, I took "Landlording" at Hard Knocks College. The tuition was dear, but I learned what I needed to survive.

This book was written to be the text for the course at good old HKC. If you study it carefully, you should be able to make a good grade.

As a landlord who does in fact teach school and who also does all of the bookkeeping chores, some of the maintenance, some of the repairs, and some of the managing of thirty-five rental units, I have indeed spent many years at HKC, but I have had little uninterrupted time to write. These pages bear the marks of many interruptions to fix cold heaters, broken windows, leaky faucets, leaky roofs, dead electrical outlets, wet-bottom water heaters, and so on and so on. Sympathize, if you will, dear landlord or landlady. No one else will.

PREFACE TO THE THIRD EDITION (1980)

Since *Landlording* first appeared in 1975, I have learned much more about the residential income property management business from my tenants, my students at dozens of University of California Extension seminars, and from readers of the first two editions who have kindly taken the time to write.

This new edition incorporates those suggestions made so generously, as well as some new ideas which have occurred to me spontaneously over the past four years. In addition, that information in the earlier editions which was specific to California has been deleted, so that barring certain local laws and regulations, this edition may be used anywhere in the U.S.

The old evictions chapter has been replaced by a new one on getting rid of problem tenants, both because the old one contained information useful only in California and because there are other good ways to "evict" people which you should know about and which you should try as your first resort, good ways landlords and landladies can use anywhere. That old evictions chapter, by the way, is still available, but in a new guise. It has been expanded and now appears separately under the title, *The Eviction Book for California*.

There are other changes in this edition which are equally important. Some, such as the discussion of whether or not you should do a task yourself, have resulted from an increase in the size of my own landlording business. Those 35 rental units my wife and I used to have in 1975 have become 244. With that many tenants to look after, there's no way we can handle everything ourselves. We have had, therefore, to learn more about hiring people to work for us--managers, painters, bookkeepers, gardeners, maintenance helpers, and others. In the process, we learned, surprisingly enough, that some work in this business, no matter how few or how many units you may have, is not worth doing yourself. In fact, doing it yourself may be costing you money rather than making or saving you money.

Other changes in this edition, such as the much expanded chapter on getting good tenants and the new chapter on keeping good tenants, have resulted from a continuing search for methods which work successfully for many people under varying conditions.

One change suggested by a female reader, retitling the book *Landladying*, I have politely rejected. Someone else will have to write that book.

Incidentally, you will notice that various product brand names and suppliers' addresses appear in this book, and you may wonder whether these companies pay for the plugs. The answer is no. Having had first-hand experience with each of these products and companies and having been thoroughly satisfied, I am pleased to recommend them to you along with their names and addresses so you won't have to waste the time hunting for them that I did. If you choose to use any product or company mentioned here and you are dissatisfied for any reason, please write me in care of ExPress stating the nature of your complaint, and I will investigate. Likewise, if you know of any outstanding company or product related to this business which would be of use to other landlords and landladies throughout the U.S., please let me know, and I will consider including it in a later edition.

I hope you find this new edition of *Landlording* useful.

PREFACE TO THE FOURTH EDITION (1986)

A little more than five years ago I last revised and updated *Landlording* from cover to cover. Since then, I've acquired more properties, dealt with more tenants, encountered more problems, made more mistakes, met more people in the business, listened to more battle stories, given more seminars, attended more seminars, heard from more readers, and read more books and articles on the subject. As a result, I have learned still more about how to survive and succeed at landlording.

Much has happened during that time in the world at large to change how we ought to go about this business, too. New laws and new interpretations of old laws have compelled us to make certain changes. Microcomputers have entered our lives in force and abundance. And a wealth of new ideas and materials have appeared on the scene.

With so much having happened all 'round since the third edition appeared, I have felt obliged to produce a completely new edition of *Landlording*.

In this "new and improved" fourth edition, I have retained the best of the rest of the earlier three editions, generally in an expanded form. I have split two old chapters into four, added six new chapters, and dropped two old ones.

Dropped were the two chapters with maintenance and tool information, including information on subjects such as repairing sheetrock holes, locksmithing, using a ceiling access plate, and exterminating abominable pests. One of these days, all of that and much more will appear in a new book.

Added were six chapters on subjects which I hope you'll find of interest: managing the rental house, coping with legal matters, participating in the Section 8 subsidized housing program, fattening the bottom line, counting your assets, and using a computer.

Split were the two old chapters, "Taking Over & Keeping Good Tenants" and "Insurance & Security." Each of these subjects cried out for separate treatment and more space, so I gave it to them.

Although I have been experimenting with singing eviction notices, I haven't quite succeeded in perfecting them yet. I am still trying, but I've been having some problems setting them to the right music, finding the right key, getting them to stand up in court, hogtying tenants so they'll hear the entire message out, and subduing bystanders' laughter. If you think of any ways to solve these persistent problems, please let me know.

Singing eviction notices may not appear here, but a dozen new graphic rent reminders do. I have no conclusive, scientific proof that they work 76.893% of the time. All I can say for sure is that they work pretty well most of the time and that they aren't carcinogenic. I'm as unbiased as a pathologist working on cancer research for a tobacco company when I make that statement, of course. Give them a try sometime and see whether you agree that they can be effective.

Besides the graphic rent reminders, there are lots of other new illustrations here. I hope you enjoy them and this new edition and that you go about landlording with a broad smile on your face. It's the only way!

TABLE OF CONTENTS

INTRODUCTION

Of all the people in the world, who's more detested than the landlord? After all, he puffs big cigars, sneers, wears a black cape, drives a Cadillac car, dallies with divorcees, runs down little kids, drives unfortunates from their homes, ignores all tenant complaints, keeps at least one family of roaches in every unit, loves the fresh air which broken windows provide, and welcomes rodents of all kinds to make their homes in his rentals.

And if that landlord happens to be a landlady—well, then, everybody knows what she's like! She's got a nose longer than Pinocchio's, larger than Durante's. Her ears rival Dumbo's. She's got Big Brother's omniscience, and she blabs every bit of it. She's devised ways to pinch her pennies that Jack Benny never dreamed of, and while there may not be snakes growing in her hair, big pink rollers sure do.

You're a landlord or landlady, aren't you? Don't these descriptions sound just like you? They don't?

Aha! Then you must be a scrupulous landlord or landlady. Wonderful! Thank heavens we found each other! You're pretty difficult to recognize, you know. You're not at all like the characters described above, those weird mythological creatures. You look and act reasonably normal. Well, that's just great because this book was written with you in mind!

Being quite normal yourself, you have probably wondered how landlords and landladies ever got such terrible reputations in the first place and why they get so little sympathy from most people today, no matter what the situation, no matter who's at fault.

They got such bad reputations deservedly years ago because they were largely unfettered by laws (what laws there were, were of their own making) and could easily take advantage of their tenants, and so some did, arbitrarily controlling their tenants' lives like petty dictators. They were feared for the power they wielded and naturally they were hated, becoming folklore villains who were always portrayed as being insensitive, cruel, thoughtless, heartless, and greedy to an extreme.

Although they have been stripped of most of their power, landlords and landladies are hardly liked even today because they provide an essential service (who likes the telephone company or the utility companies?), and they continue in ill repute (tarts are in ill repute, too, of course, but at least they're frequently portrayed as having hearts of gold) because they make such good news stories when they try creative remedies to extricate themselves from seemingly impossible situations. What kind of a story do you think the news media made of the landlord who chopped down the outside stairway to his deadbeat tenant's second-story duplex apartment or the landlady who poisoned her tenant's mongrel pooch which she and the tenant had been feuding over for months? It makes no difference whether the landlord and landlady were really good people at heart who had been driven temporarily crazy when they committed these foolish acts. They committed the acts and thus they unwittingly succeeded in perpetuating the old folklore-villain stereotypes.

Don't be suckered into believing these old stereotypes. They're wrong. Most landlords and landladies today are just like you, decent human beings. It is true that they're more skeptical, more practical, more resourceful, more imaginative, more circumspect, and more intelligent than the average Tom, Dick, and Harriet, but it's not true that they're any greedier, uglier, dumber, or stingier. What happens when Dick and Harriet sell their house for whatever the market will bear? Are they considered greedy? Are they called price gougers? Heck, no! They're considered smart. But what happens when Lester Landlord rents out his apartment for whatever the market will bear? He's never called

smart. He's called greedy. He's an A-Number-1 rent gouger, a scourge of society! Try sorting that one out! The "greed" charge is a bum rap, and don't you forget it! You cannot charge more for anything than someone is willing to pay for it.

Don't overreact to the stereotypes and say to yourself that you're going to be different from your moneygrubbing counterparts, that you're going to win your tenants over by being extra nice to them and giving them cheap rent. You won't succeed, I can assure you. They won't think you're nice. They'll think you're stupid.

Don't go out and buy yourself a hairshirt (if you must wear one, at least make sure it's a designer hairshirt) because you want to atone for the sins of being a landlord or landlady. There aren't any.

Don't be ashamed to admit that you're a landlord or landlady when people ask you the second question they have on their minds upon meeting you socially. Be proud of yourself for doing something so smart and for doing it so well.

Don't be apologetic about this role you're playing in our society. It's not merely important, it's absolutely essential. Be pleased with yourself that you can provide an essential service. You have people depending on you for a roof over their heads. You're keeping them warm and dry and making utilities available to them when they want them. You may be the butt of jokes and you may get worse press than serial murderers, but so what? Regardless of what some people may say or think, nobody provides rental housing better than the private-enterprising landlord or landlady like yourself. Nobody but nobody out there does it better.

Ask yourself what the state of housing in general would be like in this country if you and others like you weren't around to provide rental housing. There'd be a whole lot more people living with outdoor plumbing than there are now; that's for sure. People would be living in tents, lean-to's, caves, cars, and cardboard shanty towns on a permanent basis. Anybody lucky enough to obtain conventional housing would jam two, three, and four generations into it. Each room would become a multiple-family dwelling in itself. Families would be sleeping in shifts. People would be waiting years to get even remotely habitable accommodations.

Take a look at those *National Geographic* photographs showing what life's like in the Third World. Well, that's how people would be living in this country except for you.

Americans wouldn't be happy living that way, you say? Perhaps you're right. Perhaps they would be out there clamoring to that solver of all society's problems, government, to do something about the country's wretched housing conditions. And perhaps government would try to provide residential rental housing for one and all. So how do you think the government would fare as the country's landlord? Well, we happen to have some way of knowing because the President's Private Sector Survey on Cost Control, otherwise known as the Grace Commission, reported not too long ago that the federal government as landlord employs seventeen times the people and spends almost fourteen times as much money on total management costs as a private company. Can you imagine spending that much more on management costs than you already do? I can't either.

What kind of shape would rental housing be in if the federal government were the sole landlord around? That's some question to consider! The federal government would probably have a full-time manager for every fourplex, and those managers would probably be so busy doing their paperwork that they wouldn't have time to fix a faucet themselves. No, I forgot. That wouldn't be the main reason. It would be their 616-page job description which would keep them from repairing a faucet. Management people don't do "maintenance" work, not even minor repairs. So they'd call an $80-an-hour approved plumber who'd either replace the leaky faucet with a pedigreed $350 model or fix the old one with $55 worth of parts. Where would the money come from to pay for seventeen times the people and fourteen times the management? Oh, from the usual sources, a billion from here and a billion from there. Borrow more, tax more, print more. That's how it's done. And that's how it would be done without you.

How about state governments? What kind of a job are they doing? The State of California has done a great job looking after the governor's mansion. It's in perfect shape. The only trouble is that in almost a decade it's never had a tenant. What's the problem? After the place was built, the governor then in office didn't want to live there. So what happened to it? Didn't they rent it out to someone else? Are you kidding? It's still vacant. They don't have to worry about loan payments and property taxes, so why should they worry about generating rental income? What a luxury that would be! Owning rental property and not having to rent it out, not having to deal with tenants! Boy, oh boy! But that's not really landlording now, is it? That's not providing anyone with housing.

How about local governments? How do they fare? Well, the City of San Francisco with its 7,000 units is by far the biggest residential landlord in San Francisco. Are the city-owned rental dwellings kept up? Are the tenants happy? Are the costs kept under control? No, no, and no.

A federal audit revealed that the San Francisco Housing Authority was failing to collect $42,504 in damage charges and $239,000 in rent every year. Its total *monthly* deficit was around $180,000, and "nobody" on the scene seemed to be aware of it. Can you imagine that? Losing $180,000 every month and nobody knowing about it? I can imagine how that much negative cash flow might be possible for a time in some privately operated housing projects with 15% loans to service and high vacancy factors during fill-up periods, but these places had no loans to service and no vacancy factors to worry about.

This deficit was no temporary matter either because the housing authority owed millions of dollars in overdue utility bills to the Pacific Gas & Electric Company alone. How many private landlords could get away with that? The housing authority was receiving almost half of its $24 million annual operating budget from the U.S. Department of Housing and Urban Development (HUD), and yet it was $5 million in debt!

What's more astonishing, though, is that the city's public housing wasn't being properly maintained. According to HUD's regional administrator, the San Francisco Housing Authority was "failing to adequately maintain its housing units in a decent, safe and sanitary condition." The enormous monthly deficits were resulting in "deferred maintenance."

Remember that famous photograph showing a huge St. Louis public housing building being blown to smithereens when it was a few years old? Something similar occurred in my own home town, except that the building there was only 24 units and it was only five-years old. Private-enterprising landlords and landladies had nothing to do with these projects. Perhaps they should have.

So much for the government as landlord. Are we mom-and-pop operations any better at landlording than these faceless, feckless, wasteful government operations? How can we not be? We are so much closer to the problems. We act quickly. We show understanding. We keep our costs in check. We provide our customers with what they want in a place to live for the price they're willing to pay. We are truly free enterprise at work.

Not only are we free enterprise at work, we are, for the most part, true mom-and-pop businesses. Landlording is not the oil business. The sky doesn't darken with Lear jets around the country when politicians discuss rental housing legislation in Washington or Tallahassee, Sacramento or Austin, Albany or Springfield. No, all in all, we're strictly small-time.

People go about lamenting the passing of the corner grocery store and the family farm, but they don't seem to realize that the landlords and landladies in this country are in the same category. We're small-time operators, too, and we're being driven out of business as well. What's driving us out of business, however, is not big-time operators coming in and taking over. It's excessive legislation spawned by do-gooders who still believe in those old stereotypes. They still believe that tenants are noble, that landlords and landladies are greedy. They still believe that government could do a better job of housing people. They still believe in the fairy godmother, Robin Hood, deficit spending, and the resolution of any kind of problem in time for the 11 o'clock news, too. They don't understand that tinkering with the rental housing business makes it less competitive and that less competition creates poorer housing at a higher price to society.

What they do understand is a sobbing welfare mother and her half dozen waifs being evicted in front of a TV camera on Christmas Eve. That news item and others like it provide them with further verification of our terrible reputation. That's what we landlords and landladies are supposed to be doing on Christmas Eve, isn't it? Sure, we've got a past. Sure, we've got a reputation. The fact that few of us live up to that reputation doesn't matter much, though.

Part of the problem is that most people know full well what it's like to be a tenant, but they have never experienced the problems and frustrations of being a landlord or landlady. Never have they been cursed or threatened or cheated or robbed by an unscrupulous tenant. They cannot know the mental anguish and anxiety of waiting out an eviction week after week while some devil-may-care tenant who's being evicted for nonpayment of rent uses free legal aid to contest the eviction, hammers holes in the walls, puts out cigarettes on the carpets, burns the linoleum, plays music late and loud, and hurls insults at all the neighbors. Most people cannot possibly know what it's like to deal with that unscrupulous tenant and to feel so helpless, so wronged.

Another part of the problem is that people love to have someone to hate. We're one of those "someones." We're it.

Don't get too upset about being hated. Don't bother starting a local chapter of the Landlord Anti-Defamation League. Just expect to be hissed and booed now and then, and retaliate by thinking bad thoughts about the unscrupulous people who make the landlording business tougher than it ought to be.

If only the unscrupulous tenants would get together with the unscrupulous landlords and landladies of the world to do business with each other, rent to each other and rent from each other! That would solve most of the problems the rest of us poor folk have in this business. Unfortunately, since that's about as likely to happen as our ever again being able to buy gasoline for 30 cents a gallon, gold for 35 dollars an ounce, or rooms for $6 at Motel 6, we have little choice but to seek help.

To help the scrupulous tenant deal with unscrupulous landlords and landladies, there are pamphlets, books, hot lines, tenant action groups, government-provided legal aid, and publicly funded housing organizations. The scrupulous tenant is hardly alone. Helping hands abound.

We scrupulous landlords and landladies, on the other hand, seem to be so totally alone as we deal with an unscrupulous tenant. Nothing is free to us. We are expected to have unlimited funds available for legal counsel, management, repairs, and services. We shouldn't need any other help.

Well, we do. You know it and I know it. This book is intended for scrupulous landlords and landladies who want to do well by themselves and by their tenants but need some help to do so. I hope it provides you with the help you're looking for.

DO-IT-YOURSELF LANDLORDING

"$82,000? Holy buckets! That's $8,000 less than I paid for the place seven years ago!"

"It may be, but you've had some pretty rough tenants in here, and there's so much deferred maintenance now that you just can't get any more for it."

Sound familiar? I hope not. "Deferred maintenance" is a euphemism for gross neglect in real estate jargon. Those dilatory property owners who ignore their tenants, neglect maintenance, and do slipshod repairs on their property suffer more losses than they realize. They can't get good tenants, they can't get good rents, and they can't get a good price when they sell. Their buildings are depreciating not only on paper at tax time. They're depreciating daily.

Anyone who neglects a business, any business, deserves to lose money at it, and people do lose money at landlording, for it is nothing if it's not a business.

Ah, but you don't have to lose money in this business so long as you take some time to learn the ropes. Here's a look at some of those ropes, together with an overview of this funny business.

LOOKING AT THE BUSINESS

Landlording is a funny business, to be sure. It requires one to know at least the rudiments of the skills of an accountant, appliance repairer, architect, attorney, banker, bill collector, bookkeeper, buyer, carpenter, carpet layer, custodian, diplomat, drapery hanger, electrician, financial analyst, garbage collector, gardener, glazier, insurance agent, interior decorator, lobbyist, locksmith, painter, pest controller, plumber, psychologist, real estate agent, roofer, salesperson, secretary, sleuth, trucker, vinyl tile layer, and wallpaper hanger. In addition, the landlord and landlady must have some business savvy, some common sense, and equanimity by the houseful.

Breathes there a person with all these skills and all these attributes? Hardly! The only people I know of who have every bit as much equanimity as this landlording business requires have body temperatures considerably below 98.6 degrees Fahrenheit, and equanimity is their only attribute. They have none of the other attributes nor any of the skills. And the only people I know of who have all the skills and common sense this business requires are purely fictional. Even if they did exist, these James Bonds and Wonder Women, they wouldn't have any time for a pursuit so mundane as landlording. They'd be out of town a lot, spending most of their time saving the world from villainy.

Where does that leave us real-world landlords and landladies who are very much alive and bent on providing decent housing to decent people at decent prices in anticipation of making a decent profit? It leaves us with lots to learn and lots to do.

It's no wonder so many people neglect their rental properties and fail at landlording! They're overwhelmed by what's required in terms of skills, attributes, and time.

Landlording is not simply an investment opportunity as it is so often regarded, one you sink your money into and forget all about. It's a business, a tough business. You have to work at it. You have to know so much. You have to be so self-sufficient, and you have to understand people so well, too.

You even have to understand that you are an imperfect landlord or landlady dealing with imperfect tenants and that you will make mistakes, mistakes which hopefully will not sour you on the business forever. "We should be careful to get out of an experience only the wisdom that is in it and stop there lest we be like the cat that sits down on a hot stove lid. It will never sit down on a hot stove lid again, and that is well. But it will never sit down on a cold one either," wrote Mark Twain. You will sit on more than one hot seat in this business. Don't abandon the business altogether because of them.

All of us fail at landlording a little bit in one way or another. We can't help it, and we shouldn't let it worry us so long as we learn from these failures and keep them small. After we have failed, we just have to remind ourselves for the thousandth time that landlording is a business which must be operated like any other business and then we must doggedly continue, resolving not to make the same mistake again.

Do-it-yourself landlording is surely more mistake-ridden than the ordinary homeowner variety of do-it-yourselfing, and it differs also because you as the landlord or landlady must repair and maintain your property promptly and professionally. You have contracted with your tenants to provide them with habitable accommodations. That's what the business is all about. You cannot leave messy, unfinished, or neglected jobs if you wish to continue landlording successfully. That might work all right at home, but tenants won't stand for it, nor should they. After all, if they are paying full value for habitable shelter, they have every right to expect full service for their money.

On the other hand, being businesslike when you are handling the maintenance and repairs on your property yourself requires that you do the work as quickly and as well as you can and then leave. Tenants have a knack for finding just one more little job for you to do if you linger around, and you can waste precious time fixing the little things they should be fixing themselves. If you don't have any business there, stay away. Otherwise you tend to develop personal relationships which will hinder your making wise business decisions. Being there too much and getting involved with your tenants is almost as bad for your business as neglecting the place entirely.

Being businesslike doesn't mean you should be austere and avaricious all the time either. Use your common sense. Be flexible when a situation calls for flexibility. If a tenant gives you a six-day notice that he's moving after having been there only two months, and he asks you whether he can get any of his deposits back in spite of his agreement to give thirty days' notice, tell him "sure" so long as he leaves the place clean. Agree to give him back a generous portion of his deposits, even though you may be legally entitled to keep them, and if he does leave the place clean, pay up. Otherwise, what incentive does he have to leave everything in good shape? He might take out his frustrations on your rental property's windows, doors, and walls over your angrily refusing to return any of his deposits. That's being businesslike and using common sense.

Yes, landlording is a funny business, but through many trials, many errors, and much work, you can make it into a good business, one which will be very good to you.

JOINING WITH OTHERS IN THE BUSINESS

It's good business to ally yourself with other landlords and landladies through membership in a rental property owners' association. Such groups offer a wide range of services and benefits to the small-timer as well as the big-timer. Besides distributing a monthly publication, holding periodic meetings, sponsoring seminars, supplying readily available and current landlording information over the phone, and providing access to credit bureau information on rental applicants, these associations advise their members of pending legislation and support lobbying efforts so that not every new landlord-tenant law will favor the tenant. And if all this doesn't seem to you to be worth the basic membership fee of around $75 (the fee varies according to the number of units you have), then consider the advantage of meeting people who can keep you current on rents and vacancy factors in your area, people who will listen sympathetically to your woeful tales of landlording despair because the same thing happened to them only last week, people who can understand the lack of balance in media stories about landlords and landladies, and people who know what choice rental properties are coming on the market even before they're listed. Seventy-five dollars a year is a small price to pay for all that.

If you can't locate a rental property owners' association in your area, call or write the National Apartment Association, 1101 14th Street, N.W., Suite 804, Washington, D.C. 20005, (202) 842-4050. They will provide you with the information you need to contact a nearby association if there is one. And if there isn't one, why not think about starting one?

Do not assume that because you own only one rental house or one fourplex you'd be out of place in such an association. You won't be.

FINDING DISCOUNTS

As a landlord- or landlady-do-it-yourselfer, you use more supplies than the average homeowner do-it-yourselfer does, and suppliers know it.

Your local hardware store may give you charge-account privileges and a ten-percent discount to boot. Ask. Even if you can't qualify for a volume-buyer's discount yet, open a charge account anyway, because it will simplify your bookkeeping to pay only once a month and make only one bookkeeping entry for most of your hardware needs. Many hardware store owners will special-order for you those items which they don't stock regularly, items such as glass-fronted fire extinguisher boxes, apartment house mailboxes, and locksmithing supplies. (My local hardware store owner even found me a portable, hand-cranked Keil key-cutting machine which has proven to be a big timesaver, cutting my umbilical cord to the locksmith.)

Other firms are anxious to do business with you, too, if you let them know who you are and what your requirements are. Sears has a contract sales department in many stores which offers rental property owners special discounts on certain merchandise, like coin-operated laundry machines and other appliances.

Check the advertisements in your rental property owners' association's publication for those firms which are specifically soliciting business from landlords and landladies. They should understand the nature of your business and give you the service and discounts you deserve.

CULTIVATING BUSINESS CONTACTS

There are certain business people in your community who are in a position to help you run a successful landlording business, and you should strive to cultivate personal contacts with them whenever you can. You may have to shop around awhile before you find trustworthy people in these relevant business pursuits, people who suit you and who know their businesses well, but once you find good contacts and you come to know each of them personally, you will find that they will go out of their way to assist you with service, advice, equipment, and supplies. Remember that your relationship should be mutually beneficial, that you are in a position to help your contacts by recommending their services to the other landlords and landladies you know.

At one level, you should seek out and nurture business contacts with an accountant, an attorney, a banker, an insurance agent, a loan broker, and a real estate agent, each of whom has some special expertise directly related to your making or losing substantial sums of money in landlording. These people can help you with specific and knowledgeable answers to your many questions in their fields.

At another level, you should seek out an appliance repairer, a carpet layer, a hardware store owner, a painter, a plumber, and a roofer. While these contacts may save you money with their advice, they benefit you chiefly by coming to your aid with their labor and supplies when you need immediate solutions to your pressing problems.

In addition, and surely as important as any, is that contact you should make with another landlord or landlady who either owns as much rental property as you do or has owned rental property longer than you have and is willing to compare notes. You are in a position to help each other psychologically and physically more than you may ever imagine at first.

How well should you know all of these people? You should know them at least well enough so that you could reach them on the telephone and be greeted familiarly, and then you could pose a question involving their field of expertise, expecting them to give you a direct answer, perhaps free of charge, perhaps not.

Be good to these people. Take them out to lunch now and then and, of course, patronize them.

If you elect to expand your business at all, you will come to rely on these people more and more, and they will become a kind of advisory board for you, absolutely essential to your success.

HANDLING THE BUCKS

It's good business to have a separate checking account for your landlording transactions. Some landlords and landladies even open a separate account for each building they own (if their rentals are single-family dwellings, they have one account for all) and then use that account as their only "bookkeeping system," channeling all of the building's income and expenses through the account, a simplistic but workable approach. Whatever you do, open at least one checking account for your rental properties, and itemize your deposits and checks carefully so your bookkeeping chores will be easier later.

Before you visit the bank, though, select the name you want to use for your property account. This name has nothing to do with how you hold title to your property, how you write rental agreements, who is authorized to write checks, or what street the building is on. It is only the name which your tenants will use as the payee for their checks and money orders.

Presumably to prevent someone else in the area from using the same name you have selected, banks require that everyone opening an account under a business name which does not include the owner's real name has to file a fictitious name statement, a process involving a filing fee and legal advertising.

Whereas your business name would be a valuable asset to you if you were operating the Playtime Tavern or the Capri Motel, it's hardly important in the rental property business, except for large, heavily advertised complexes. Even then, no one else would want to confuse people in the area with a second Sun Garden Apartments if you were using that name already, and it would not likely be used except through an oversight.

You can circumvent the folderol of filing a fictitious name statement by opening your account under your own name and having your checks imprinted in bold letters with your surname followed by the word "PROPERTIES." If your name were Lester Landlord, for example, then your tenants could make their checks and money orders payable to "LANDLORD PROPERTIES," and you could distinguish between accounts for different buildings, if you wanted to, by simply calling them "LANDLORD PROPERTIES ONE," "LANDLORD PROPERTIES TWO," and so on sequentially.

If you want to open an account under a fictitious name like "Sun Garden Apartments," expect to encounter a banker who will insist that you file a fictitious name statement. If you do not wish to go to all the trouble of filing, however, and you want to use the name "Sun Garden Apartments" as payee, merely open the account under the name "Lester Landlord's (use your own name here, of course) Sun Garden Apartments," and you may accept checks made out simply to "Sun Garden Apartments." That's really all you care about anyway, simply getting the rent checks deposited into an account that you can write checks on, an account which is easily distinguishable from your personal account and carries a name easy enough for your tenants to remember.

Don't become so involved with picking a name for your landlording bank account that you fail to familiarize yourself with the bewildering array of checking and savings accounts available nowadays. And don't expect your financial institution to open an account for you which will necessarily be the best for your situation either. Financial institutions make their profit by getting your money at the lowest possible rate (they like it free if they can get it) and lending it out at the highest possible rate (how about 20%?). Ask about the options available. Look out for yourself.

Your checking account should bear maximum interest with the minimum of minimum balances; it should allow you to write without charge as many checks as you'll reasonably need each month; it should provide printed checks at minimum charge; it should not hold the deposits you make to your account until your tenants checks have cleared their accounts; it should charge reasonable fees for stop-payments; and it should have some kind of overdraft protection.

In addition to keeping at least one separate checking account for your landlording funds to flow through, you may want to open one savings account for refundable deposits only. These monies are not taxable when you receive them and should be distinguished as separate from your other landlording income, all of which is taxable. These deposits still belong to your tenants, not to you, and separating them will make them readily available when you need them to use or return. Separating them will also help to remind you to pay interest periodically if you are compelled to do so by law in your area or if you are inclined to do so as a good-faith gesture.

Sums designated as last month's rent belong to you, not to your tenants. They are taxable as soon as you receive them, and they should not be kept in a savings account for refundable deposits. All rents paid in advance, whether they are first month's or last month's or in-between, are designated as rent and nothing else and should be deposited into your property checking account for operations use.

USING BUSINESS CARDS

After you have opened those bank accounts for your rental property, order yourself some business cards.

"Business cards for landlords and landladies you say? Ridiculous! What a waste of money!"

Although you might scoff at the idea initially, consider some of the many uses for business cards in your do-it-yourself landlording business before you reject the idea completely.

• Use them as your "open sesame" for access to many "Wholesale Only" suppliers of appliance parts, plumbing wares, and the like who refuse to sell to the general public.

• Pass cards out to your tenants for handy reference when they need to contact you (designating yourself as owner, manager, or partner on your business cards lends credibility to your adopted landlording role; see Chapter 11, "Should You Own Up to Being the Owner?").

• At rental property owners' association meetings, give your cards to other owners who might be thinking about selling their buildings and might consider a direct sale.

• And when those good business contacts you're cultivating hand you their business cards, hand them each one of yours in return. Then they'll understand that you do know one of the first things about running a business.

Besides being useful, business cards are one of the least expensive purchases you will ever make in your landlording business. Local printers will print up a lifetime supply for around $30, and mail-order firms will print up a sufficient supply for a pittance. Among its many gadgets and gewgaws, the current Walter Drake catalog lists 200 personalized business cards for $2.98. Can you beat that? They're not exactly what you'd want to have printed up if you were trying to project an elite corporate image, but they'll do. Write Walter Drake, Colorado Springs, CO 80940, for a catalog.

While you're ordering cards for yourself, have some printed for your manager, too, if you have one. Personalized business cards show managers that you have confidence in their professionalism and their permanence and are always much appreciated.

---

123 Neat Street
Littletown, CA 91111
(415) 123-4567

LANDLORD PROPERTIES

LESTER LANDLORD
Partner

DANDY PROPERTIES

LESLIE LANDLADY
Manager

453 Sweet Street
Littletown, CA 91111   (415) 123-6789

MASTERING THE TELEPHONE

Much of your landlording business involves communicating with people either face to face, by letter, or by telephone. Of course, there are times when you ought to make a personal visit to talk with someone, and there are times when you ought to write a letter, but there are also many times when you really ought to pick up a telephone and call.

In most cases, telephoning is cheaper all 'round. Business letters, excluding postage, now cost companies an estimated $7.60 apiece if they're handled the conventional way, that is, with a typewriter, or $5.70 if they're done on a desktop computer or dedicated word processor. Each trip you make to your property as an absentee owner costs you something for fuel or shoe leather, too, don't forget, no matter how close that property is to your home or work. Besides, you simply cannot afford the time to go traipsing all over the country looking for hard-to-find parts, wayward tenants, special services, best buys, and so on. For many of these tasks, you can communicate just as well by telephone, while using considerably less of your money and precious time.

Now I know that there are some people who seem perfectly normal in other ways, but they have an irrational fear of the telephone. They have no fear of flying, public speaking, darkness, high places, or their mother-in-law's raw-fish dinners, but they will not initiate a telephone call for any reason. You, landlord or landlady, cannot afford such a phobia. The telephone is one of the tools you must learn to use well in order to succeed; it's as necessary to your business as a garlic press is to an Italian chef. If you find yourself reluctant to use the phone, buy yourself a phone that looks friendly, one that looks like a mutt if you like dogs or Mickey Mouse if you have fond memories of the Mouseketeers. Think of it as a freedom machine enabling you to get a whole lot more accomplished in a whole lot less time. Thumb through the Yellow Pages and imagine how many different kinds of business people you can contact just by punching seven buttons. That's freedom! That's power! That's convenience!

Use your telephone!

Here are some hints which might help you to use it more efficiently for outgoing and incoming calls.

• Keep all your tenants' telephone numbers handy. Because many tenants nowadays have unlisted numbers which no operator or directory could possibly provide you with, having those numbers handy will save you from having to make a visit to inform tenants of minor, but necessary, matters, such as an anticipated utility shutdown the next day. Make up a little directory of your own, or, better still, use the Tenant Record form in the FORMS section of this book to keep track of tenant telephone numbers and other relevant tenant information.

• Keep a categorized list of telephone numbers for all of your landlording business contacts or keep their business cards handy in a small file.

• Use the Yellow Pages to shop locally for product availability and prices. Make appropriate notes right in the book next to the listings of those firms you've called so you'll have some clues to follow the next time.

• If your rental property is located in an area served by a telephone directory different from the one you use at your home or office, secure a copy of that directory from the telephone company so you can shop conveniently from the Yellow Pages for that area. Usually there's no charge for a reasonable number of additional directories. The phone company wants greater exposure for its Yellow Pages advertisers.

• Buy a directory of toll-free 800 numbers from your bookseller and check to see whether the firm you wish to call has an 800 number available.

• When you want to contact people or businesses outside your area-code region and you don't have their numbers, find them quickly by using the telephone company's long-distance information number, 555-1212, preceded by the area code of the region you wish to call. Since the breakup of the American Telephone & Telegraph Company and the availability of alternative long-distance telephone services, access to this long-distance information is no longer "free." The charges are nominal, however, so don't be deterred from using this service when you need it. Make a note of the numbers you inquire about so you won't incur the charge a second time for any one number. Call 1-800-555-1212 for information on toll-free 800 numbers.

• Take advantage of the cheapest rates available by scheduling the calls you make to other time zones for checking tenant references or making business inquiries instead of picking up the telephone and placing your call any old time. During the week, place calls to time zones east of you before eight in the morning, your time, and place calls to time zones west of you after five in the afternoon, your time. On weekends, call anytime. Low rates are available throughout the day.

• Consider installing a second telephone line for your landlording calls, but don't have it installed as a "business phone" unless you crave a listing in the Yellow Pages for some reason or other and unless you also understand that you will be paying the higher fees charged to business users. They pay a charge for every outgoing call, even local ones. Have it installed as a second personal line instead, you know, like an extra phone for the teenager in the family. Besides helping to keep your private affairs separate from your business affairs, this second phone line simplifies your business-call recordkeeping because it saves you from having to prorate your bills and from having to keep track of each business call you make on your one personal line. Instead, make all your outgoing business calls on the second line and expense the entire bill.

• Buy an answering machine, preferably one with a remote access feature so you can call your machine when you're away and find out who's left a message. Use the machine to screen calls you don't want to take right when they come in, and use it to provide an unattended message announcement for the benefit of those people who are responding to your advertisement of a vacancy.

• Get a telephone credit card and use it. Not only are they a real convenience, enabling you to call anywhere from any private-, business-, or pay-phone and have the charges billed directly to you, but they give you a tally of the charges for those calls so you won't forget to expense them. To avoid unauthorized use, memorize your card number and keep it a closely guarded secret.

• Check into call forwarding. It's an inexpensive telephone company service, and it's useful if you divide your time between two locations and want to make sure you don't miss a call.

• Buy a cordless telephone for yourself and/or for your your manager. They're especially handy when you're preparing an empty rental for occupancy, and you have to be near a phone to take calls from prospective tenants.

Whenever you face a landlording task which involves communication, ask yourself first whether Ma Bell can help before you crank up the Volkswagen or get out the old Smith-Corona.

ORGANIZING EVERYTHING

There are many sources of discouragement in this do-it-yourself landlording business, many of which you can do absolutely nothing about, but there is one source you can do something about, and that is disorganization. Disorganized landlords and landladies make the job much more difficult than it already is, and consequently, they become needlessly discouraged time and time again because they cannot find what they're looking for in the chaos of their stacks and piles.

There are tenant records to keep organized as well as receipts, insurance policies, building records, keys, supplies, tools, and spare parts, and you cannot have a memory sufficient to locate all of them when you need them. You have to get them organized or you will fail miserably in this business.

You will find a number of hints and forms in this book to help you get organized. Use them, adapt them to fit your needs, and you will succeed in making your job easier and surely far less discouraging.

CONTINUING YOUR EDUCATION

If you own no rental property at all right now, you are wise ("Wise people learn by other's mistakes, fools, by their own."—old proverb), not because you own no rental property, but because you are taking the time to educate yourself about landlording before you actually become involved. Few first-time landlords and landladies ever have the training necessary to cope with the multitude of problems they will encounter in this business. Some cope well and thrive. Some give up and sell. Some capitulate and commit hari-kari. But most just manage to muddle through.

There's no reason for you to repeat all the same mistakes that others have made so many times before and to pay a high price for making those mistakes again because now there's an abundance of good information available in books, on tapes, in periodicals, in classes, and in seminars, some of which are referred to in the "Sources and Resources" section in the back of this book.

Learn all you can from these sources, but especially take the time to attend classes and seminars. Hard Knocks College no longer has a monopoly on property management courses. Adult schools, community colleges, university extensions, property owners' associations, educational exchanges, and proprietary educational companies all offer sessions for those landlords and landladies who want to know more about this business.

If such sessions are unavailable where you live, ask for them. The people who schedule these sessions try to accommodate local demands, but sometimes they overlook the need for such courses entirely.

New owners obviously profit from attending these sessions, but experienced owners profit from continuing their education, too. Whether you are experienced or inexperienced, you are dealing with large sums of money in this business and you cannot afford to be complacent or uninformed. Times change and laws change and you need to reassess your business operations all the time, picking up one good idea here and another there, and you can do that best by continuing your landlording education both formally and informally. Continuing education offers you the opportunity to spend a little and save a lot.

MAINTAINING YOUR IMAGE

As a landlord or landlady, you are always in the crosshairs, targeted by some ninny or other as one of the banes of society. Be on your guard. What you do, what you say, and how you look, all of these things affect the way your tenants see you and react to you. If you have to have a Cadillac or a Mercedes, don't drive it anywhere near your rentals. Your tenants know that you paid for it in cash with their rent money. No matter how warranted any rent adjustment is, if your tenants think of you as a wealthy owner, they will resent the increase and resent you, too. Give them little cause to resent you. Don't brag to them about your country club or your cruise around the world. Don't show them your gold Rolex or your full-length mink. Sure, you've worked hard for these trappings of success, but save the display for your in-laws. Keep a low profile around your tenants. Drive your oldest car or pickup truck around to your rental properties. Make your tenants think you need the rent money to pay the mortgage and the other expenses, whether you do or not.

WEARING PROPER ATTIRE

Not every rental property has them—busybodies who thrive on buttonholing the manager or owner and babbling on interminably. If you do have such tenants, however, you know they're more of a nuisance than hemorrhoidal tissues. They're usually model tenants otherwise and you hate to offend them, but you also hate to waste your precious time lending them your ears.

Take courage. You can avoid these gossipmongers by wearing overalls that are all speckled with paint when you set foot on your rental property. You may have just showered or awakened from your afternoon nap, but they won't think so. Those overalls clothe you with a certain busy-worker mystique and give you license to do what you came to do and then leave without having to make or listen to small talk.

PRIORITIZING YOUR WORK AND KEEPING SANE

Don't expect spontaneous remission to remedy many of your tenants' complaints for repairs, but do give it a try sometime by prescribing the tardy treatment for certain piddlin' problems. Since no one has yet found a way to fix a leaky roof over the telephone, you must make a visit for that kind of thing, but if the problem's of a lesser magnitude, you should reassure the tenant with a gentle voice that everything will be taken care of in due time and then jot down the job on a priority list. Don't rush over to your properties for every little thing. You'll soon need a new spouse and a shrink if you do. Accumulate the little repair jobs until they warrant a fixit visit themselves or until you need to go there for some other reason. You'll be surprised how often the little problems will have taken care of themselves in the interim.

Just because you don't leap up immediately to respond to every tenant's complaint doesn't mean you should discourage your tenants from reporting the little repair problems they notice. On the contrary, you should be encouraging them to report these problems because you will pay dearly for postponing repairs on your rental property too long.

Linoleum which is just beginning to pull loose at a seam is so much easier and cheaper to fix than when a piece has torn away and been lost. A water leak under a kitchen sink will eventually cause wood decay in the cabinetry if it's neglected, decay which certainly won't be overlooked by the termite inspector.

Use your good common sense to determine when you should make a visit to your property and when you should stay away.

EQUATING YOUR TIME WITH MONEY

Remember that all your landlording expenses are tax deductible as business expenses and that there will be times when you'll have to pay extra for something you need in a hurry, or times when you'll have to call for professional help because you can't do a job, because you're fed up and shouldn't do it, or because you don't have the time to do it. Call for the help and think of the bill as a business expense. That's what it is. Don't get frustrated because you couldn't do it yourself and save the money. Sometimes it pays you to do it yourself and sometimes it pays you not to (see Chapter 11, "Should You Do It Yourself"). You're not the ordinary do-it-yourselfer, remember, and you don't have that kind of time to case creation for what you want at the price you want to pay. Let ordinary do-it-yourselfers boast about how they spent long hours scrounging for something and then got it for little or nothing. You have no time for that. You have a business to tend to, a business in which time translates into money.

NOTING STORE HOURS

Your spare time, more specifically that portion of your spare time given over to maintaining your rental property, hardly coincides with normal business hours. You likely work at your properties in the evening, late at night, in the morning, and on weekends. Because these times are all on the fringes of most stores' normal hours, you have undoubtedly experienced the frustration of scurrying off to the paint store at 6:15 on a Sunday evening to buy that last can of paint needed to complete redecorating a dwelling which a new tenant wants to more into the next day, and when you arrive, you find that the paint store closed at 6.

How can you avoid a repetition of this frustration? The next time you go on your buying errands, write down the hours for each store you visit. Keep these times in that wallet, purse, or glove compartment which usually accompanies you on your landlording tours of duty. One quick glance at this information will tell you which store is still open at 9:12 on a Tuesday night when you need to buy the parts to replace an old toilet valve that came apart in your hands. You can spare yourself more spare time for plotting rent raises and smoking noxious-smelling cigars if you aren't waiting around for stores to open in the morning or driving wildly about town looking for any supplier who's open late at night.

DOING IT YOUR WAY

Some people prefer their toilet paper to roll off the front of the roll, some prefer it to roll off the the back, some prefer it to roll off sideways, and I'm sure there are those who prefer no roll at all. They like their toilet paper in separate sheets. No preference, no way is "right." Likewise, there is no right or wrong way to do every little thing in landlording. You have to decide what's right for you, what you're comfortable with, and then continue in that direction. There are many ways to collect rents promptly, for example, and though I do give more than one way here, I don't give them all. In truth, I don't know them all.

Use what you read in this book as starting points for developing your own ways of doing things. Don't suppose that there are no other ways. Be creative. Find your own way. You'll enjoy landlording more when you do.

SOME LAST WORDS

Some of the things involved in landlording may be tough to do. No landlord or landlady ever said this business was easy, but if you practice sound business methods, use your common sense, keep a level head, learn enough skills to do some things yourself, and know enough to call for help when you need it, you won't find your property declining in value. It will actually be increasing in value, making money for you while you sleep. Indeed it will!

And when you buy yourself mixed nuts to munch on, you'll be able to buy the ones without the peanuts. You deserve 'em!

TAKING OVER
AS THE NEW OWNER

"I have to pay for the privilege of being those people's landlord because the rent they pay me doesn't nearly cover all my expenses, and still they expect me to hotfoot it over there day or night to unplug the toilet which they stopped up. What kind of a business is this anyway?"

"I felt like maybe I'd died and gone to hell!"

"My landlording bloopers that first week were enough to start a whole new TV series."

"I felt as lonely as a flatulent sheep dog."

"Never before had anybody called me up at 3 A.M. demanding that I come right over and kill a monster roach."

"I never realized how many tenants were street lawyers."

Yep, taking over as the new owner of a rental property can be pretty traumatic for some people. At the very least, it's an eye-opener for most people. You may find yourself wondering what ever possessed you to get involved in this funny business in the first place. Take heart; it's not all that bad, and there's a lot you can do to make things run pretty smoothly right off the bat.

Let's say that you have just purchased some residential income property and you are anxious to get started as the new owner. You have already bought a copy of *Landlording*, a most commendable beginning. You have joined your local rental property owners' association and have bombarded all the people there with your questions. You have secured a copy of the local housing code from the powers that be and have familiarized yourself with the basic services and amenities which you must provide by law. You have notified the appropriate utility companies about the property's change in ownership so the bills will be sent directly to you. You have decided already how you're going to do the banking and bill-paying for the property. You have decided to handle the off-site management yourself. You have thought about the building and about what needs to be done there, having made several inspections before you ever bought the place, and you have lined up some workers to help you take care of the property's obvious deficiencies. But, because the former owner kept such abominable records, you have no information whatsoever about the tenants you have inherited, and, what's more, they have none about you. They're now wondering what to do with their rent, whom to call about their roaches, when the rent's going up, what's happened to their deposits, and how soon they're going to get the new carpets which were promised to them last Christmas.

MAKING CONTACT: THE LETTER

The very next thing you should do is communicate with them, for communication is the lifeblood of this business. Send them a letter or, better still, for establishing good rapport with them all the more quickly, take a letter around to each one of them and meet

September 16, 1986

Dear Mr. & Mrs. Renter,

You probably know already that the building where you live has changed hands. Because tenants usually feel some apprehension every time such a changeover occurs, we would like to take this opportunity to clear the air by letting you know just what you can expect in the future about a few things.

DEPOSITS...One special concern you must have is your deposits. We are concerned, too, and we want to make absolutely certain that all of your deposits are credited to you. To avoid any misunderstandings about your deposits and other matters related to your living here, we would like you to answer the questions on the sheet attached. They are questions which you should be able to answer quickly from memory or by referring to information readily available to you. Please do so as soon as possible and return your answers to us in the envelope provided.

PAYMENT BY CHECK OR MONEY ORDER...Since it is unwise for anyone to keep or carry cash around in quantities, we request that you pay your rent by check or money order (made payable to us exactly as underlined below). You will be protected and so will we.

PROMPT PAYMENT...You are expected to pay your rent within three days after the due date. For example, rent due on the first must be paid by the fourth at the very latest. If you anticipate being late beyond that for any reason whatsoever, please let us know beforehand. If you don't, we will assume that you are deliberately avoiding payment, and we will immediately serve you with the notice which starts eviction proceedings.

MAINTENANCE...We expect you to pay your rent promptly, and you can expect us to respond promptly to maintenance problems. Sometime within the next week, we will visit you to inspect for any building maintenance work that should be taken care of. You can help by starting now to make a list of such work which you notice around the house.

RENTAL AGREEMENT...We will also stop by soon to explain to you the standard rental agreement we use, and we will leave you with a copy of your own.

We are reasonable people and we will try anything within reason to make living here enjoyable for you, but naturally we need your cooperation. If we have it, we will get along well together and we can all take pride in this place that you call home.

Sincerely,

Leslie Landlady (123-6789)
DANDY PROPERTIES
453 Sweet St.

these people who are now your tenants. Advise them in the letter that the building has indeed been sold, just as they suspected, and that you are (pick one) the owner, one of the owners, or the manager (determine now whether you intend to stop the buck or pass it-- see Chapter 11). Allay their fears about their deposits, inform them about your rent collection procedure, tell them you do want to hear about their maintenance problems, and mention that you expect to come calling soon with a rental agreement.

The letter given here includes all of these elements and more, and like the other forms shown in the text, you will find a full-sized copy of it in the Forms Section in the back of the book. It may be photocopied as is, or you may adapt it to fit your own circumstances. If you do plan to use the letter as is, make sure you intend to follow through with all that you are promising to do in it, visiting your new tenants within a week or two to check for maintenance problems, and so forth. Don't say you're going to do anything unless you can and will do it, especially not now when people you've never done business with before are looking at you with a "show-me" eye. Prove yourself to be a person of your word and not a flim-flammer.

GATHERING TENANT INFORMATION

Besides telling your new tenants about their building's new management, you need to gather some information on them as well, so along with your letter, provide a tenant information sheet and include a stamped, self-addressed envelope for its return. This information is intended to supplant most of what you would already have in your files on tenants you select yourself, information normally available from the Rental Application and the Condition and Inventory Checksheet. Neither the application nor the checksheet is really appropriate to use when you have inherited new tenants whom you know nothing about, however, for then you are trying merely to establish some basic facts

about them and their tenancy. The Tenant Information form shown here is specifically designed for gathering the information needed in this particular situation.

Give your new tenants two weeks to return the information sheet to you. Then, whether they have returned it or not, arrange to meet with each of them face to face to discuss your policies and go over the written rental agreement you intend to use.

Some tenants are inclined to be stubborn and secretive when asked to reveal anything at all about themselves which they consider to be none of your business. Like some primitive people who are afraid to be photographed lest their inner spirit be robbed of them, they imagine that you are snooping into their private lives so you can lay them bare to some big-brother intelligence gathering agency.

To counteract this paranoia, try to be as delicate and inoffensive as possible if they don't volunteer to provide you with the information themselves. Be neither offensive nor

Tenant Information:

Your Name _Jeremy Youngster_

Your Address _432 Chestnut, Apt. 6_

Your Home Telephone Number _535-0012_ Your Work Phone _535-2332_

Who lives with you? (Include ages of the children, please) _Nobody_

_____

What pet(s) do you have? _no_

Do you have a waterbed? _no_

What vehicle(s) do you have? Make(s) _Buick_ License(s) _442-701_

Where do you work? (Company name) _Sears_

Where does your co-tenant work? (Company name) _NA_

When did you move in? _March 01, 1984_

What is your current rent per month? _$545.00_

What date is your rent paid up to right now? _Sept. 30_

When is your rent due each month? _1st_

What refundable deposits have you paid? Keys $ _Ø_ Security $ _210_

Cleaning $ _Ø_ Other (please explain) $ _Ø_

When you moved in, you paid your first month's rent. Did you also then pay your last

month's rent? _no_ If so, how much was it? $_____

Which of the following furnishings belong to the owners of the building? (Please give room locations where appropriate.)

Carpets _✓_ Drapes _____

Shades _✓_ Blinds _____

Stove _✓_ Refrigerator _✓_

Other appliances? (Please list) _none_

Other furniture? (Please list) _none_

Do you have a rental agreement or lease in writing? _Yes_

If so, what is the date of the latest one? _March 01, 1984_

In case of an emergency, what friend or relative of yours should we contact?

Name _Mrs. Amy Youngster_ Telephone Number _333-0210_

Date _9/18/86_ Your Signature _Jeremy Youngster_

defensive about gathering it. After all, there are sound, logical reasons why you need every bit of it, so you may want to stress that their own best interests are being served by their divulging it to you.

If need be, explain why you are asking for each item on the Tenant Information form. You need to know their home telephone number in case there's an emergency, perhaps someone noticed lurking about their dwelling, and you need to get in touch with them in a hurry. You need to know their work number for pretty much the same reason. You need to know who lives with them so you will be able to help keep unauthorized people from entering their dwelling. For example, you want to know what you ought to do if an unfamiliar face asks you to let him in, if he says he lives there and forgot his key. Emphasize especially the concern you have for determining precise sums and dates, both of which you need to establish in order to prevent misunderstandings later. You need to know exactly how much they paid in deposits to the previous owner so you will know exactly how much to set aside for them when they move out.

If they won't cooperate with you in providing the information, there's nothing you can do to force them, and you shouldn't bother getting upset about it yourself or getting them upset with harsh words and threats. Consider them to be ignorant, foolish, mentally unbalanced, generally uncooperative, or any combination of these possibilities. Then rely on others to supply the information. Use the deposit figures provided by the previous owner, and ask him what else he knows about that tenant. It shouldn't be too difficult to uncover the few facts needed to complete the Tenant Information form from other sources.

Remember that part of your effort to communicate with your new tenants involves proving yourself to be a reasonable person. Don't allow yourself to be drawn into an argument. Don't talk about other tenants. Don't talk much about yourself. Find out what's on these new tenants' minds, what's troubling them. Let them talk if they want to, and listen carefully to what they have to say. Be concerned, be polite, and be more ready to smile than a Miss America contestant at a press conference.

COMING TO TERMS USING YOUR RENTAL AGREEMENT

Before you ever bought the property, you should have found out what kind of rental agreements or leases were being used there, but if you didn't, during this visit you will want to establish how your relationship with these new tenants is governed. You should ask to see a copy of the tenants' rental agreement, if any. You may be awestruck when they actually produce one whereas the previous owner couldn't, so do ask. Look it over carefully, understanding full well that you as the new owner are bound by it.

When you have inherited tenants, your business relationship with them is governed by one of four possibilities, the same as it might have been if these tenants had been yours from the start of their tenancy:

1) Current lease
2) Expired lease which has become a month-to-month agreement
3) Written month-to-month agreement
4) Verbal agreement

No matter what kind of contract governs your relationship, you are governed by it for at least thirty days, that is, unless the previous landlord and the tenant had specifically agreed upon a shorter or longer period. Generally the contract period coincides with the rent period, so if the tenants pay on a weekly basis, they're probably on a weekly contract. If they pay on a fortnightly basis, they're probably on a two-week contract. If they pay on a monthly basis, they're on a monthly contract or a lease. If there is a lease

NOTICE OF CHANGE
IN TERMS OF TENANCY

TO ___BOB BALKER___, Tenant in Possession

___12 CHANCELLOR AVE., NO. 3___

___BIGCITY, CALIFORNIA___

YOU ARE HEREBY NOTIFIED that the terms of tenancy under which you occupy the above-described premises are to be changed.

Effective ___MAY 3___, 19_87_, there will be the following changes:

___the terms of the Rental Agreement attached, which you___
___have refused to sign, shall take precedence over any___
___written or verbal agreement which you may have had___
___with a previous owner.___

Dated this ___1st___ day of ___April___, 19_87_.

___Sarah Newsome___
Owner/Manager

This Notice was served by the Owner/Manager in the following manner (check those which apply):
☑ by personal delivery to the tenant,
☐ by leaving a copy with someone on the premises other than the tenant,
☐ by mailing,
☐ by posting.

involved, you're bound by its terms, whatever they happen to be, and for whatever period it covers, six months, one year, or even more, like it or not. In any case, you may not shove a new agreement at them and tell them they have to sign it right away and abide by it from that day forward. You have to give them time. That is their due.

You may give them a new agreement any time you want to, of course, but you may not enforce it until they have signed it and have had some period of time to get accustomed to it. How much time do you have to give them? Barring any especially restrictive local ordinances, before you can change the terms of their existing contract you have to give them the same amount of time as the length of their existing contract. When tenants have an existing contract covering periods shorter than a month, you ought to give them 30 days' notice of a change. That's only fair. When they have only a verbal agreement and nothing in writing, give them 30 days, too. In fact, you ought to give thirty days to everyone except those on leases. Give a contract to those tenants who have valid leases at least thirty days before the lease expires so it will take effect the very day the lease actually does expire.

Spend some time with each inherited tenant and explain the various terms of your Rental Agreement just as you explained the Tenant Information form to them. Listen to their objections and make adjustments if warranted.

What do you do if they are contrary and refuse to sign? Can you have an enforceable written contract signed by only one of the two parties involved? In most cases involving rental agreement conditions, when the tenant already occupies the premises, you certainly can. If they won't sign, explain to them that you will then simply go ahead and prepare a Notice of Change in Terms of Tenancy and attach it to a copy of the Rental Agreement. This notice is very much like the one you use to increase rents. Their signature is not required for a notice of this sort to take effect in thirty days, and take effect it will. By refusing to sign, they gain absolutely nothing. They label themselves uncooperative. That's all. Tell them that you would like to have their cooperation in your mutual business dealings but that you will go ahead and manage the property your way, which you feel is quite a reasonable way, whether you get their cooperation or not.

The conditions in your new agreement must be legal, of course, and they ought to be sensible as well. You can't make your inherited tenants tolerate elephants upstairs or rats underfoot any more than you can make any other tenant tolerate such things. You can do such things as set quiet hours, require them to pay their rent by a certain day of the month, limit the premises to personal use only, and restrict motor vehicle repairs if you want to.

If your conditions are much different from the ones under which your inherited tenants have been living, especially if you initiate a no-pets policy when the tenants already have a pet, understand that you will have a fight on your hands. People won't give up a pet without a fight. Under those circumstances, you might be wise to adopt a no-pets policy for all new tenants and a policy of no-new-pets for existing tenants. After all, the old pets have probably already done as much damage as they're going to do to the inside of the building.

Be as resolute as an Afghan freedom fighter about imposing a reasonable rental agreement on your new tenants. This may be your first test as the new owner. Be firm. Stand up to them now, and they will be easier to deal with later.

HANDLING TENANTS' DEPOSITS

The only time I've ever been hauled into court for failing to return a tenant's deposit was when I acquired a small property and hadn't received any of the deposits from the previous owner. That owner always collected $50 upfront and never returned any of it. He thought of the money as a cleaning "fee" rather than a cleaning "deposit." He assumed that none of his tenants would leave their places clean enough to get a deposit back anyway, so he gave his manager the money as compensation for cleaning the apartments before the tenants moved in. The tenant who was suing me had assumed in the absence of a written agreement that the $50 was a cleaning deposit, not a fee. He left his apartment clean and, as far as I was concerned, he deserved to get the money back, but because I had never received it from him or the previous owner, I didn't think that I was the one to return it.

Don't get caught in a squeeze like that. If possible, get all the tenants' deposits sorted out and credited to you at closing. In order to do it the right way, you should know precisely what the seller *and* the tenants believe those deposits to be before you ever take over. Then you'll be able to take care of any discrepancies while you still owe the seller money. You won't have to take him to court to collect.

Besides worrying about whether they're actually getting the correct deposit amounts, new owners frequently worry about whether the deposits they do get are going to be enough to compensate them for future difficulties. Worry about it if you want to; just don't do anything about it. Don't even consider raising your tenants' inadequate deposits at this time or at any other time unless you want to precipitate a building revolt. Most tenants will simply refuse to give it to you. Then what do you do? Evict them? Take them to small claims court? Forget it. You'll look toothless and inept trying to collect higher deposits, and you'll spend too much energy trying. Don't undermine your position as a non-nonsense landlord or landlady by attempting to accomplish that which none but a Mafia capo could accomplish.

RAISING THE RENT

Don't raise the rent immediately upon assuming possession. You have enough else to do. If you feel that a raise is definitely warranted when you take over, don't give it out until you have begun to establish yourself and have become better acquainted with the situation you have acquired or until you are ready with your new rental agreements, whichever comes first. Those are the "right" times. If the former owner raised the rents within the previous twelve months, make your rent raise coincide with the anniversary date of that rent raise. Raising rents any more frequently than once a year, whether during a change of ownership or in the normal course of events, causes tenants too many anxieties. If you know the rents are too low, though, don't wait much longer than a month to raise them. Not only will you be losing income, but your tenants will come to think of you as soft in the head.

HANDLING THE LAST MONTH'S RENT

For the various reasons given in Chapter 5, I don't recommend that you collect last month's rent as such, but you may acquire a property where the previous owners have been collecting it all along. It may present a problem, and then again it may not.

So long as the last month's rent as turned over to you by the previous owners is the equivalent of the current rent, there is no problem. But a problem does arise should you inherit a tenant whose last month's rent has never been increased to the current level. Why? Tenants generally assume that the last month's rent which they originally paid when they moved in ought to be the same as the last month's rent when they actually do move out. They may have paid $400 in rent when they moved in, and over the years let's say that their monthly rent's gone up to $625. When they give notice that they're going to move, they think that their last month's rent has been paid in full with the $400 which they paid when they moved in. They're wrong. They actually owe an extra $225.

If they won't pay it, you're going to be out the money yourself unless you can find out where they're moving to and you can take them to small claims court.

With each rent raise, the former owners should have increased the amount they were holding to be used as the tenant's last month's rent. Then there would have been no confusion about whether the full last month's rent had been paid or not.

When you take over as a new owner and encounter this situation, you might want to give your new tenants a choice so as to avoid needless conflict. Tell them that they may increase their last month's rent to the equivalent of the current rent or they may convert it into a deposit, augmenting the other sums already designated as such. The first choice would require them to part with some funds; the second would not. Either choice would eliminate the confusion.

No matter what you decide to do, no matter what choice your tenants make, be sure that you spell out in writing what you've all decided.

SORTING OUT THE KEYS

At the same time you're sorting out all the paperwork for your newly acquired rental property, you ought to take the time to sort out the keys for the property as well. A handful of keys given to you by the previous owner can be so mixed up that they're virtually useless when you try to find a particular key to open a particular lock.

Almost anything might have happened to mix them up. Tenants may have changed their own locks and neglected to give the previous owners a duplicate copy of the key. A maintenance person may have mislabeled some keys. A set of locks that were installed on one place may now be on another, but the installer overlooked changing the label. Some may have been misplaced. Others may have been lost for good.

Take all the keys you have for the property with you when you make your maintenance rounds and try to match up each unit with the right key. If you can't make a proper match, ask to borrow the tenant's key for a time so you can have a copy made, and then try the copy when you get back to make sure it works.

Because some tenants insist on being the only ones with keys to their rental dwellings, you may have to approach the matter of obtaining copies with strong resolution. If they are insistent, tell them that they have no right to withhold keys from you, that you, in fact, have every right to have copies of all the keys for all the locks restricting entry to the premises, no matter who installed

them. Tell them that you recognize they have a right to privacy and that you have no intention of violating that right. Tell them that you will use the passkey only when you are legally entitled to do so, that is, in four situations—1) in case of an emergency; 2) in order to make repairs after giving appropriate advance notice; 3) in order to make repairs with the tenant's consent; or 4) in order to show the property to prospective tenants or buyers after giving appropriate advance notice. Tell them that you want to be reasonable and cooperative and that you expect them to be the same.

After all this, most people realize that you're being reasonable and they will cooperate. If they flatly refuse, stay calm and leave. Don't fight them. Don't take it upon yourself to change their locks in retaliation. Merely treat them coolly from then on.

SOME LAST WORDS

Make the transition of ownership as smooth as possible by giving every indication that you are businesslike and reasonable and that you sincerely want to improve the operation of the property.

ADVERTISING

You don't know them yet and they don't know you yet, but out there somewhere are some very nice people searching for a suitable place to live and a nice landlord or landlady like you. They may have placed an ad in the "Rentals Wanted" column of your local newspaper (look there), they may have posted notices in public places (look around), they may be pumping their friends for information (keep your ears open), or they may even be out pounding on doors (open up).

Of course, they may not be doing any of these things either, because they may not be so enterprising and because they may be able to find vacancies aplenty without taking any such initiatives. Since you can't count on every good prospective tenant to find you so easily, you may have to take the initiative yourself when you have a rental dwelling available or coming available. Spread the word out there to reach those nice people you want as your new tenants. In other words, advertise.

There are lots of ways. You might put the word out to your tenants, friends, and acquaintances that you have a place available for rent, or you might let people know with a card on a community bulletin board, a handbill in local circulation, a sign on the premises, an ad in a newspaper, or a listing in a rental guide, or you might list your rental with a housing office or a real estate agent.

You might try any one or any combination of these methods, but first, whatever you do, pay especially close attention to the exterior appearance of your building, for no matter how skillful, how costly, or how comprehensive is your advertising approach, you will never get your place rented to those desirable tenants who are out there looking for you if they are repelled by the exterior of your rental property. Any rental dwelling's foremost "advertisement" is a well-kept, neatly painted exterior which looks so inviting to good prospective tenants that they will take the time to inspect the inside. That exterior is the packaging for your "product," and you know how much care and money most companies put into the packaging of their products. Puh-len-ty!

Once, shortly after my wife and I purchased a fixer-upper sixplex with two vacancies, we prepared one of the apartments for rent, advertised it in the local paper, and found that we couldn't get a single good prospect to stop by and inspect the interior of the apartment itself, even after the people had called and promised to show up at an appointed time. We would notice cars slowing down and necks craning, and then off they'd go. What a disappointment! We had redecorated this one apartment beautifully, and we were already working on the second, but because the exterior of the building looked so dilapidated, and everyone who responded to our newspaper ad saw that exterior first, no one except the truly undiscriminating would venture further. Faced with the dismal prospect of renting only to leather-faced transients chugging through the neighborhood in their battered Ford stationwagons, which appeared to levitate on clouds of exhaust smoke, and towing trailers piled high with distressed furniture and even more distressed kids, we reacted in a hurry. We fixed up the exterior. We hadn't planned to do anything to it quite so soon, but as soon as we did, the quality of our prospects improved dramatically.

People do judge a rental by its exterior. And why not? They intend to live there and invite their friends to visit them there, and they want themselves to be identified with a building which projects the kind of image they have of themselves.

A building with a well-kept exterior advertises to one and all that the living is better there than it could possibly be in a dilapidated building. It shows that the managers have carefully selected good tenants and that everyone takes pride in the property.

Remember, whenever you have a vacancy and you're trying to interest prospective tenants in the place by using any of numerous direct advertising methods to spread the word, you will attract all kinds of tenants through your advertising, but you won't ever attract good tenants unless you give your building curb appeal.

Here are the eight advertising methods most commonly used by do-it-yourself landlords and landladies, together with some of the advantages and disadvantages of each, and a listing of the various factors affecting the decision to choose one method over another, all of which may assist you first in selecting the best advertising methods for your rental property and then in making them work well for you.

ADVERTISING METHODS

• WORD OF MOUTH—Existing tenants in your multiple-family dwellings have as much of an interest in whom you select to be their new neighbors as you do, perhaps more. That rental building of yours may be your business, but, after all, it's their home twenty-four hours a day, and you can't blame them for wanting to have compatible neighbors.

No matter who they are, what they do for a living, or where they live, above all, they want to feel safe and secure where they live, and they hope that you will select new neighbors for them who will assure their safety and security, not jeopardize it. They might even hope that their new neighbors would be pleasant, accommodating people with a cup of milk or a bottle of brew handy when they run out, if it's not too much to ask.

Because of this common interest in securing good new tenants that you and your existing tenants have (neighbors around a rented single-family dwelling have this same common interest and should be included in any word-of-mouth advertising you do, too), you are wise to advise them of any impending vacancy as soon as you know about it, and, if warranted, even to offer them a finder's fee of, say, forty or fifty dollars for finding the new tenants.

You need not include all of your tenants in your word-of-mouth advertising campaign. If you wish, approach only those tenants who, you believe, would most likely solicit the kind of prospects who would fit in well. Make your offer verbal rather than written so you can direct it to your good tenants more discreetly and casually shrug off any accusations of favoritism.

If you do elect to offer a finder's fee, forestall any misunderstandings over your obligation to pay by insisting that the finders accompany those whom they have interested in the place on the first visit or, at the very least, that they call you and give you the person's name before the first visit. You don't want a tenant claiming a finder's fee unless that tenant was directly responsible for the prospect.

Besides approaching those who, because of where they live, would be affected by the selection of the new tenants, approach others who meet and talk with the public in the course of doing business in the area, people such as Avon ladies, barbers, beauticians, corner grocers, insurance agents, mail carriers, neighborhood pharmacists, service station managers, motel managers, and apartment house managers. They are certainly in positions to pass the word along.

Whenever you enlist anyone in your word-of-mouth advertising campaign, apprise them of at least these relevant facts about your vacancy—rent, size of building, size of unit, location, and availability, and then give them your business card so they'll know how to get in touch with you when they do find someone. There should be no confusion in these matters.

No matter who the referral is, even a relative of someone you know well, reserve judgment on that person to yourself, and, by all means, complete the full procedure outlined in "Getting Good Tenants." Sometimes the friends and relatives of finders are not up to your standards, and you may be the only one discriminating enough to understand why you shouldn't rent to them. Make that decision the same way you make it concerning anyone else who applies to rent from you.

Advantages—inexpensive, targeted, usable anywhere for any kind of rental.

Disadvantages—uncertain, inclined to be slow, time-consuming, awkward if you have to refuse unqualified prospects.

• BULLETIN BOARDS—Most supermarkets and some other stores provide community bulletin boards as a service to their customers, just as general stores used to provide community forums around their pickle and cracker barrels years ago, but the exposure, and hence the efficacy, of bulletin board advertising varies widely. Some boards are prominently located within busy stores, while others are almost hidden from view by stacks of merchandise and rarely ever discovered. Some boards are well organized and well maintained by the management, and others are just a jumble of flyers, business cards, 3" x 5" announcements, posters, and small lost-and-found items. For best results, select the busiest boards which are within the trading area surrounding your rental.

```
┌─────────────────────────────────────┬──────────────┐
│  ★ FOR RENT ★                       │  123-4567    │
│                                     ├──────────────┤
│  350 BOONDOCKS LANE                 │  123-4567    │
│                                     ├──────────────┤
│  Spacious 3 bedroom house,          │  123-4567    │
│                                     ├──────────────┤
│  fireplace, carpets, drapes,        │  123-4567    │
│                                     ├──────────────┤
│  built-in stove and                 │  123-4567    │
│                                     ├──────────────┤
│  refrigerator  $450                 │  123-4567    │
│                                     ├──────────────┤
│  3/15   CALL: 123-4567              │  123-4567    │
└─────────────────────────────────────┴──────────────┘
```

To make your bulletin board rental ad most effective on any bulletin board, whether it be a community board or a more specialized board such as one where you work or where others work (schools, fire departments, bus "barns," county offices, and the like generally have their own bulletin boards for employees and will gladly post your ad if you mail or take it to them), prepare your ad at home on a 3" x 5" card with a large "FOR RENT" at the top, list all the particulars as you would in a newspaper ad, add color or a simple eyecatching design to make it stand out, and date it. Because you are advertising something perishable, a vacancy, the date is important to anyone who is looking for a rental and sees your ad. Therefore, you should try to replace the card every week with one bearing a more current date.

One danger with this kind of advertising is that without your knowing it, your ad card may simply disappear into the hands of someone who is interested in responding but has forgotten to bring paper and pencil. To accommodate these people, you might make a few cuts into the card at the side and put your telephone number on each removable tab so the entire card won't be removed, just bits of it.

Advantages—inexpensive, localized.

Disadvantages—time-consuming to prepare and post, limited in exposure.

• HANDBILLS—Handbills are a time-honored advertising method for a variety of things, and today with transfer lettering, computers, photocopying, and "instant" printing all readily available, you can prepare professional-looking handbills faster and cheaper than ever before, but preparing them isn't everything. You have to distribute them as well. Aye, there's the rub. You have to make certain that they reach the kind of people you're looking for.

When you do put them before the public, you have to make certain that your handbill distribution doesn't cheapen the image of your rental, either. To keep from cheapening your rental, avoid plastering handbills "everywhere." Avoid stapling them to telephone poles and fences, for example, both of which should be left to political messages and lost-pet handbills. And avoid hiring kids to pass them out on street corners. Instead, use handbills primarily to extend and reinforce your word-of-mouth advertising campaign within the community. Give them to the local businesspeople you patronize and ask them to display the handbills by their cash registers or in their store windows. Give them away as reminders to people you know who appear interested either for themselves or others. And post them on those bulletin boards which allow handbills. You'll be reaching the public you want to reach in ways which won't turn them off.

When you distribute any handbills, keep a list of their locations so that when you do rent your dwelling, you will know exactly where to go to retrieve them. If you leave them hanging about for more than a few weeks, people will begin to wonder what's wrong with this rental that won't rent.

Advantages—relatively inexpensive, localized.

Disadvantages—time-consuming to prepare, distribute, and retrieve; suitable primarily for less expensive rentals; dependent upon your personality and contacts.

• THE SIGN—You might be surprised by how many people there are who will pick an area where they want to live and then scout that area for vacancies. Believe it or not, more than half of all tenants do it this way, and some of them don't even wait for signs to appear before knocking on doors. When they see any indication that someone is moving, they begin making inquiries about the dwelling's availability. These super-sleuths aren't always around hunting U-Hauls, though. Most people who are looking through a neighborhood for places to rent look for a "For Rent" sign.

The "For Rent" sign you use reveals to the public something about the kind of business you're running and should be consistent with the exterior image of your rental building. A cheap-looking sign indicates a penny-pinching operation run by amateurs, and whereas such a sign will do all the advertising you'll ever need during periods of high occupancy, when everyone becomes a super-sleuth, it's just not good enough during periods when you're competing with everyone else for good tenants.

There's no reason to skimp on a sign purchase anyway, no matter what the vacancy factor in your area happens to be, because, unlike the classified ad, which costs you a few bucks every time it appears, the sign is a one-time expense, and that one-time expense is actually quite reasonable. One professionally painted sign cost me the same as two newspaper ad insertions and has lasted for years.

Mine is a two-sided 20" x 30" sign painted in three colors on 5/8" plywood, and it is designed to hang at any of my buildings from a yardarm positioned at right angles to the street so that people passing in either direction can see it readily (the hardware used to attach the sign consists of eye bolts, clevis hooks, and harness snaps). The "2" in the "2 BDR" is painted on the board itself because most of my apartments happen to be two-bedroom units, but this number may be covered with another one painted on sheet metal which bolts right to the board. If necessary, a similar provision for changing "unfurnished" to "furnished" could be added. The telephone number painted on the sign  is my own, of course, so prospects may call me directly if the manager is unavailable at the site.

Create your own sign design to look as good as your rental units and say whatever you require, and then hire someone to paint it for you. You'll like the image this combination projects and so will your discriminating tenants.

Advantages—inexpensive, orthodox.

Disadvantages—dependent on traffic exposure, inviting to troublemakers when used at vacant single-family dwellings.

• CLASSIFIED ADS—For some people, classified ads are their first resort for information when they're looking around for a rental dwelling, and because tenants are so conditioned to consulting the classifieds, no one would begin to question this kind of advertising's effectiveness. Many landlords and landladies would question their cost, however, and since they can be expensive, you should make the dollars that you spend on classified ads pay off.

Here's how.

Be certain, first of all, that the people you want to reach are among the paper's readers. There's no need to pay the higher rates of a widely circulated daily newspaper's advertising when a smaller readership daily will do, that is, assuming you do have a choice. Look also at special-interest newspapers and periodicals which carry classifieds. They're especially useful for advertising vacation rentals.

And don't overlook the local weekly newspapers or those free shoppers which carry classifieds. Because they are so localized, they frequently draw more responses than dailies, and you'll find that their advertising rates are more reasonable than mass-circulation dailies. If you do plan to advertise in a weekly, though, be certain you know when the deadline for ad copy is, and if you miss it, by all means, don't keep your available rental off the market for a whole week while waiting for the next issue's deadline. Advertise it somewhere else.

Because many people prefer to rent from small-time landlords and landladies, avoid the appearance of a big-time operation in your classified advertising. Restrict each ad to a maximum of two vacancies with different addresses or descriptions. One vacancy per ad is preferable, of course. That way you can avoid classification complications if the two properties would normally appear under different headings, you can emphasize the features of each rental, and you also get greater flexibility for cancelling the ads as each property is rented.

To write effective ads for rental property, you don't have to think like a Madison Avenue copywriter. You're not trying to sell a billion cans of still another underarm deodorant. Those people who are looking for you have a definite need for housing. All you have to do is direct their attention your way.

Word your ad succinctly, but make sure it's descriptive and appealing as well. Take a look at these two ads.

3-BEDROOM APARTMENT in
Boyle Heights. Wall-to-wall carpets,
stove, refrigerator, drapes. Close to
transportation and shopping. $370
per month. Deposit required.
Available now. For more
information, call 123-4567.

CLOSE-IN 3 BEDROOM. Carpets,
stove, refrigerator, drapes. $370.
123-4567.

Just look at all the wasted words in the first ad! The second ad conveys in two lines the same message that the first one does in six.

Because classified ads are arranged under distinct headings, which already tell the readers a few things about the ads appearing there, you do not need to duplicate the same information in words you are paying good money for. The ads above would be printed in the "Unfurnished Apartments—Boyle Heights" section of a city paper, and they need not specify any of this information again in the body of the ad. Many of the other wasted words in the first ad express ideas which the reader takes for granted anyway. "Deposit required," "Available now," "For more information." Such expressions are completely unnecessary when you're trying to say as much as you can in as few words as possible and still attract attention.

Besides avoiding unnecessary verbiage, consider carefully the first word or two you plan to use. Think of your ad as a billboard which must catch the reader's eye immediately or be missed completely, and you'll understand the importance of your ad's beginning words. Since you can't include a picture of the place in your ad, the descriptive words you use must conjure up the most appealing picture possible. Words like "sparkling," "just painted," "quiet," "superclean," "cozy," "superbig," and "quaint" all create positive, pleasant pictures in readers' minds. They'll want to take a closer look. If your newspaper arranges its ads alphabetically under its various classifications, you may want to make sure that your first word begins with one of the first letters in the alphabet. How about "A-1" or "beautiful"? If you have trouble selecting words appropriate for your own rental, scan the ads in several daily newspapers and you'll find enough good words to last for years. You're not trying to win some prize for creativity in advertising, so don't be afraid to appropriate other people's good ideas and incorporate them into your own ads.

Include in your ad just enough information so you or your manager won't be bothered with lots of calls inquiring where the place is, how much it rents for, and the like. Here are the kinds of things you might want to include if they apply: number of bedrooms, carpets, drapes, laundry hookups, garage, carport, fireplace, dining room, utilities, stove, refrigerator, child ok, adults, pet ok, yard, storage, and pool. Include the size of the building only if it is favorable, that is, if it is relatively small, below five units (some people prefer the community feeling of smaller buildings over the institutional feeling of larger ones). These other items to include are marginal, depending upon the rental area: water, garbage, air conditioning, hardwood floors, and steam heat. Include price, for sure, along with the exact address and your on-site manager's telephone number, if any, followed by your own. An ad with these elements will create a favorable impression and tell readers what they need to know before calling.

Keep your ad readable by using only those abbreviations which are commonly understood in your area. Spell out "bedroom" rather than "BR"; use "kitchen," not "kit"; "dishwasher," not "D/W." Abbreviations commonly understood are A/C, St., Ave., and OK. Aren't they?

Study the way your newspaper charges for its ads. You might find that an ad running only Saturday and Sunday will bring enough responses all during the week while costing you just half as much as an ad running every day, or you might find that an ad running only one day, no matter what day it is, will do the same. Experiment. Your newspaper's classified rate schedule may be such, however, that your ad could run the whole week for slightly more than the cost of shorter insertions. If so, take advantage of these discounted rates, and cancel the ad when you are certain you have the place rented. Watch also the minimum number of lines, the abbreviations allowed, the size of type used for the first word or first line, and the number of spaces per line. You can always dictate your ad to the ad taker, ask for a quote on that number of lines, and then add or subtract words to suit yourself and your pocketbook.

Here's an ad for placement in an expensive metropolitan daily which has a one-line minimum and allows any and all abbreviations—

6 Rms Riv Vu. 123-4567

This kind of ad is all right for a tight rental market and for those readers who are savvy about all the arcane abbreviations used in rental advertising, but just think of all the questions such an ad raises! Why, you could write a play about them!

Here's an attractive ad for placement in a community daily with a four-line minimum and a prohibition against abbreviations—

> Quaint two-bedroom in four-plex.
> Carpets, drapes, stove, carport,
> water, garbage. By bus. 858 Sweet St.
> $485. 765-4321; 123-4567

Once you have devised a well-worded ad that suits you and yields a good response, make a copy and keep it on file so you can use it over and over again or at least have a model to follow, and you won't have to waste time making up a new one from scratch each time you advertise.

When your ad first appears in the newspaper, check it out yourself to verify that it's in the proper classification and that it's worded exactly the way you want it to be. Ad takers do make mistakes, you know, and you might find that you're waiting around for calls that never come because your ad was misclassified or had an incorrect telephone number. After you've verified that the ad is correct and you're still not getting any calls, you ought to reassess other factors and consider making adjustments.

Advantages—well-exposed, simple, time-saving, orthodox.

Disadvantages—relatively expensive.

• RENTAL GUIDES—Rental guides, if available in your area, provide yet another medium for reaching tenants who are searching for new accommodations. These guides, which are simply mimeographed, photo-copied, or quick-printed lists of places for rent, tend to flourish mostly in areas with low vacancy factors, where finding that right place to live is such a tiring, time-consuming task that some weary searchers will pay around $40 for the convenient and detailed listings of rentals which may not otherwise be advertised as available.

The guides may be useful to you, landlord and landlady, because they cost you absolutely nothing and because you can be expansive in your praise and specific in your details about your rental, and consequently, you may save time by not having to answer call after call from those who are merely seeking more information. The guides are good for tenants, too, because they are more current and more detailed than newspaper ads tend to be. Before pounding the pavement or telephoning, tenants have a pretty good idea what each listing is like and whether it's still available.

This is the kind of information likely to be included in a rental guide listing—

listing date	pool
date available	sauna
rental location	spa
cross streets	garage
no. bedrooms	carport
no. baths	off-street parking
home	fenced yard
cottage	patio
flat	balcony
studio	deck
apartment	view
size of bldg.	other features

lower/upper unit	number of children
furnished	infant only/OK/negotiable
unfurnished	cat only
gas stove	other pets/OK/negotiable
electric stove	amount of pet deposit
refrigerator	other restrictions
garbage disposer	utilities included:
dishwasher	water, garbage,
carpets	gas, electricity,
hardwood floors	heat, hot water
drapes	rent per month
shades	length lease required/
blinds	negotiable
hook-up for washer/dryer	first and last month's rent
laundry room	required/negotiable
den	security deposit
family room	cleaning deposit
fireplace	other deposits/fees
wood-burning stove	agent fee
dining room	person to contact
breakfast area	phone number
basement	best time to call

A newspaper ad running every day with all that information would cost half a month's rent!

Remember, though, that rental guide firms earn their only income by selling these listings to tenants. To attract paying customers to their service, they will sometimes place misleading ads in the regular classifieds, offering swanky penthouses at basement rents. To find out where these bargains are, tenants have to buy the guide, and when they do, they all too frequently learn that these come-ons have "already been rented." Such flimflam may have alienated those who learn of your available rental through a guide, and they may be chagrined at having been duped, but there is a way you can give them some preferential treatment. Because this advertising is free to you anyway, even over a long period of time, use a rental guide to advertise an upcoming vacancy several weeks before it's actually available, thereby giving the rental guide customer an exclusive, a genuine advantage over everyone else. That way, everyone profits. Then, if you haven't rented your place as the vacancy date approaches, continue using the rental guide, by all means, but begin supplementing that listing with other advertising as well.

To find out whether rental guides exist in your area, contact your rental property owners' association, check the Yellow Pages under "Real Estate Rental Service," or scan the classified ads in your local daily newspaper, looking for numerous ads that list bargain rentals all without addresses and all with the same telephone number.

Advantage—inexpensive, time-saving, fully descriptive.

Disadvantages—limited in exposure to those willing to pay for the service.

• HOUSING OFFICES—Many college campuses and military installations, as well as large public and private employers, maintain their own housing offices to assist their students and staff in finding local housing. These offices are subsidized as a convenience and hence charge neither the renter nor the landlords and landladies who use the service.

Once you have established which of these local housing offices you wish to use, you may use them repeatedly for only the cost of a telephone call, but do remember to call and cancel your listing as soon as you have come to terms with a new tenant, so the housing office can keep its records up to date.

Advantages—inexpensive, targeted, simple to use.

Disadvantages—slow and inefficient at times.

• REAL ESTATE AGENTS—Not every real estate agent will help you find a renter, but those who will, generally list themselves in the Yellow Pages under the same classification as rental guides, "Real Estate Rental Service." The range of services they provide in this context varies widely from simply advertising your vacancy in their window free of charge to advertising it actively in newspapers to fully managing the property, including advertising the vacancy, showing it, and screening the prospective tenants.

Seldom do real estate agents make any money by providing these services. Mostly they are just trying to build a dedicated and obligated clientele who will bring them more lucrative business later when old properties are disposed of and new properties are acquired.

Agree in advance on the exact services your agent will provide, including the kinds of advertising to be used, and agree upon the charges for those services as well. You should have to pay only if your agent secures a renter and only if that renter stays at least six months. Shorter tenancies should entitle you to more services without additional charge. Get the arrangement down on paper.

Advantages—based on commission (no results, no payment), helpful to owners living out of the area.

Disadvantages—obligating, expensive in comparison to other kinds of rental advertising.

ADVERTISING FACTORS

Now that you know something about the advertising methods commonly used by landlords and landladies and something about the various advantages and disadvantages of each, you might wonder how to select the best methods for advertising your $950-per-month rental house. Should you break with tradition and advertise it with a 30-second TV spot on the six o'clock news? The answer to that question is an obvious "no" because your rental doesn't need that much exposure and because you'd have to sell, or at least mortgage, the property to pay for the ad, but the answer isn't so obvious if you're considering which of the eight methods you should use to advertise your rental house next door. All kinds of factors affect that advertising decision. Here are fourteen of them:

• NUMBER OF UNITS—Is the rental a house, a fourplex, or a twenty-five unit complex? Use on-site signs at multiple-family dwellings for maximum exposure, but avoid using them at single-family dwellings unless the old tenants are still in possession and agree to cooperate in showing the house to anyone who stops by. As a rental house owner, you do not want people tramping through the roses to get a peek in the windows, and you definitely do not want vandals or squatters to suspect that the house may be empty.

• LOCATION—Is it in a high, medium, or low traffic location, that is, Main Street, Middle Road, or Boondocks Lane? Rely upon on-site signs more at high and medium traffic locations. If enough people pass by your rental property, a sign might be all the advertising you'll ever require.

• RENT—Does it rent for a song or an aria, $195 or $1950? Pull out all the stops to advertise the expensive rental because you stand to lose so much more every day the place is vacant and because it has a much smaller number of potential renters to reach than the $195-a-month dwelling has.

• RENTAL'S AVAILABILITY—Is the rental vacant and available now or have your tenants just informed you at Christmas time that they're moving by Easter? Before your rental becomes vacant, try the less expensive methods.

• AREAWIDE VACANCY FACTOR—Are available rentals scarce or in ample supply? The appearance of outward-bound furniture will suffice for advertising during scarcities, while searchlights and sideshows may be insufficient during high-vacancy periods. Prepare to spend more on advertising and be more creative when the areawide vacancy factor increases. If a major employer leaves the area and tumbleweeds begin to litter the streets, you may need to change more than your advertising. A changeover to allowing pets and encouraging nudists might save you. Then again, you might consider advertising in motorcyclists' magazines. You won't find many other landlords and landladies advertising there.

• DISTANCE FROM MANAGEMENT—Are you managing a rental property seventy miles from where you live or do you live in the building? Find a local contact, perhaps another tenant, a real estate agent, or a next-door neighbor, to take phone calls and show your rental if you live at some distance from the property. Few people will dial a number with an unfamiliar prefix unless they have to. I remember well buying a fourplex with three vacancies from a fellow who lived twenty miles away from it. He had been trying to rent them himself without much success, and he practically gave me the place. I tried nothing different from what he'd already been trying, but I had it fully occupied within ten days because I was located nearby and had a local telephone number.

• EFFORT—How much effort do you or your manager wish to devote to your advertising campaign? Very little or whatever it takes? Remember that advertising through classified ads, rental guides, signs, real estate agents, and housing offices all take less effort than full-scale word-of-mouth, bulletin-board, and handbill advertising campaigns.

• TIME OF YEAR—Is there a seasonal nature to rental accommodations in the area? Vacation and student rentals have obvious seasons, but, surprisingly enough, so do other rental properties. The most active periods for permanent rentals precede the beginning and ending of summer as identified by the Memorial Day and Labor Day holidays. People like to be settled in by then. Advertise during those periods with the less expensive kinds of advertising and add the more expensive kinds only in the final week before Memorial Day or Labor Day.

• TARGETED CLIENTELE—Are you looking for little old ladies with Harleys, students with Moog synthesizers, newlyweds with round waterbeds, municipal bus drivers with tabbies, or Mother Hubbards with umpteen urchins? To appeal to a particular clientele, select certain people as contacts, certain housing offices, certain bulletin boards, or certain newspapers. Post-secondary schools have housing offices which should attract students aplenty every September. Some senior centers, businesses, and union halls have bulletin boards and news organs which should appeal to the precise type of renter you seek.

• EXPOSURE—Should your advertising reach 1 or 100,000 people? Naturally each of your rental dwellings can accommodate only one living group at a time and you need to find only that one, but you may have to expose your rental to many people in the general population to find that one, especially if it's an expensive rental. Do not pay for exposure to people obviously too distant to be interested. Renters, even those who don't live in the area where they plan to locate, consult local sources after deciding where they plan to make their homes.

• ADVERTISING AVAILABILITY—Are rental guides, housing offices, bulletin boards, and real estate agents who list rentals all available in your rental's area? Make some effort to discover all the locally available advertising sources and use those which suit your needs.

• ADVERTISING COST—How much are you willing to spend? Nothing or whatever it takes? Take full advantage of inexpensive advertising: word-of-mouth, bulletin boards, handbills, signs, rental guides, and housing offices, but weigh the cost of eschewing more expensive advertising with the loss of rents you are sustaining so long as your rental remains unoccupied.

• EXPERIENCE—Have you had previous good experience with a local newspaper shopper, a particular bulletin board, a certain rental guide, or a cooperative real estate agent? Conduct your own advertising survey by asking those who come to look at your rental how they learned about it, and then continue using whatever works for you. Whenever you notice the effectiveness of your old reliable methods diminishing, try others.

• ORTHODOXY—Are rental housing seekers accustomed to using this advertising method? Advertise in ways and places that rental seekers expect you to use so they'll be looking for you there. Whereas skywriting, TV spots, searchlights, and helium air bags will undoubtedly yield some results, the eight methods mentioned in this chapter are more orthodox and will yield more results per dollar than unorthodox methods ever will.

AN APPLICATION

Applying these fourteen factors to your own particular vacancy, you might construct a scenario like this:

If your available rental is a four-bedroom house located on Boondocks Lane, if it rents for $950 and is one among several similar houses for rent in the area, if you are looking for a professional's family of five or fewer, if you are willing to spend between $50 and $100 on advertising, if it's around the middle of July, if you live next door to your rental house, if the house is now ready for occupancy, if you have little time yourself to spend on advertising, then you would be wise to take a two-method approach, place a "For Rent" sign on the property and put a classified ad in your local daily newspaper for one week. If there are no nibbles at all, reconsider very carefully the rent you are advertising and reword the ad to expand on the best features of the house, but be prepared to have a vacancy for a few weeks until the market becomes very active again around Labor Day.

SOME LAST WORDS

Whichever method of advertising you prefer, whichever you use, be sure you keep word about the availability of your rental dwelling before the public, for if nobody knows it's vacant, it can't possibly get rented. It might as well be off the market altogether or even, perish the thought, occupied by a nonpaying renter. You're not collecting any rent while those fixed expenses of yours continue unabated. Hustle the place. Lace up your black plastic shoes, wax your moustache, slick down your hair, practice your business card tricks, shell out a few bucks, and get the place rented.

Somewhere out there are some very nice people searching for a suitable place to live and a nice landlord or landlady like you. Help them find you.

GETTING GOOD TENANTS

Vacancy times are times which try landlords and landladies. They're working times, loss-of-revenue times, doubtful times, and if you're a small-time landlord or landlady whose every vacancy represents a high percentage of all your rentals, you are likely to be especially anxious to get that vacant rental filled. Be anxious, but don't be hasty. You want a smooth operation, one which won't continue to be trying when there's no vacancy at all.

The most important factor in the smooth operation of rental properties is getting good tenants. If you become adept at this, all your landlording troubles will be little ones, and you may skip the whole of Chapter 8, "Getting Problem Tenants Out." How lucky you are, getting to skip a whole chapter! How shrewd you are, knowing enough to "evict" bad applicants in the first place, before they ever have a chance to become your problem tenants. You practice prevention when you should. Good for you!

No matter what procedure you follow for selecting tenants, if it's working for you, keep at it. No one can argue with success. But if you should have reason to doubt the effectiveness of your tenant selection procedure, consider making modifications until you hit upon a successful combination which does work well for you.

Just as anyone can pick a horse to bet on in a race, anyone can pick a tenant, but picking winners ain't easy. It requires lots of diligence and patience, as well as a little luck and some intuition. Fortunately, though, the odds are somewhat better for picking good tenants than they are for picking winning horses, and the odds improve geometrically if you follow the ten steps which are arranged here more or less chronologically—

   1) Prepare the dwelling for occupancy.
   2) Prequalify the prospects.
   3) Show the dwelling.
   4) Take and scrutinize all applications.
   5) Check references.
   6) Visit applicants' current home.
   7) Review your rules, requirements, and policies.
   8) Fill out and sign the Rental Agreement.
   9) Request rent or a deposit.
 10) Fill out and sign the Condition & Inventory Checksheet.

You may skip all of these steps except the ninth one if you're remiss about your business, and you may actually get good tenants. Who knows, you just might get lucky! But you might as well be buying a used car from Slick Tawker at Kurt's Kar Korner without so much as starting the engine or kicking the tires. Sooner or later you'll get a lemon for a tenant, and then you'll learn the hard way that getting rid of a lemon tenant is considerably more difficult than getting rid of a lemon automobile. You can always park the car in a tow-away zone, play stunt man and drive it off a cliff, or take a sledge hammer to it if you get stuck with one that's a lemon, and after your catharsis, you can forget all about your car troubles. But you cannot park and forget lemon tenants. You can't even get some cheap satisfaction out of pummeling them or, at the very least, depriving them of electricity and running water, much as you'd like to. Once you get bad tenants, you're stuck with them for some time to come, and when you finally do succeed in getting rid of them, they'll likely leave a few remembrances, and I assure you, you won't forget them.

Cull out the lemons among your applicants. Follow the ten steps religiously, steps which any landlord or landlady can follow, and you'll never rent to them. Leave the lemon tenants for those unscrupulous landlords and landladies you hear and read about. They deserve each other.

These ten steps are hardly what one might call difficult, but they do require time and attention, some of them more than others. Take the time and give them the attention they require, for when you consider the dreadful alternatives to getting good tenants, the time and the attention spent on all ten steps are well spent indeed.

After any of the initial seven steps, you might choose to reject the prospective tenants, and you shouldn't be afraid to do so. You are not obligated to rent an available rental dwelling to the first person who expresses an interest in renting it. I repeat, you are not obligated to rent an available rental dwelling to the first person who expresses an interest in renting it. Surprised? Read on.

You're looking for a good tenant, right? Right! So keep on looking until you are thoroughly satisfied that you have found an applicant who will be a good tenant for your building and for you, someone with whom you might have a reasonably friendly and enduring relationship. Maybe the first person who wants to rent from you and has the means to rent from you will be a good tenant, and then again maybe not. You never know straightaway. Just remember that nobody can force you to rent to that person, not the government, not the applicant's mother, not the mayor of your town, and not the applicant's motorcycle gang. You get to make the selection yourself, and in doing so, you must be very, very discriminating, legally discriminating, of course.

Be as discriminating as you can possibly be in your selection, but by all means, do not be discriminating about race, color, religion, sex, marital status, national origin, or ancestry. Such discrimination is illegal throughout the U.S. That's federal law. In most areas it's also illegal to discriminate against those who are physically disabled. In addition, many areas have specific laws prohibiting discrimination regarding age (applies to children as co-tenants), sexual orientation, source of income (occupation), personal appearance, political affiliation, place of residence, place of business, matriculation (student status), and family responsibilities. Other regions have less specific but more encompassing anti-discrimination laws which prohibit discrimination in rental housing unless it is based on legitimate business grounds.

Now that might sound as if you do have to rent to the first person who expresses an interest in your vacant rental dwelling and is willing to plunk down the money. The truth is that you don't.

What is left that you may be discriminating about? Quite a bit, believe it or not. You may still be discriminating about the tenant's ability to pay, willingness to pay, pets, waterbeds, number of vehicles, type of vehicles (motorcyclists you may not be allowed to discriminate against, but noisy motorcycles are another matter), recommendations, number of co-tenants (even though you may not discriminate against children in some areas, you may still limit the number of people you will allow to occupy the premises), intelligence, honesty, attitude (use care with this one; I measure their attitude by whether they laugh, or at least smile, at my jokes), smoking or drinking habits, permanence, noisiness, cleanliness, and the like.

Those should be sufficient criteria for tenant selection, shouldn't they? Although in the areas with the strictest anti-discrimination laws, you may not refuse to rent a two-bedroom apartment to an applicant on the grounds that she is a lesbian who collects welfare, wears black leather hotpants and frizzy pink wigs, solicits tricks at the local tavern, lives with her seven-year-old bastard son and a succession of painted ladyloves, and is an anarchist student twenty-one years old, you may refuse to rent to her if she smokes cigars, and you rent only to non-smokers. That's the equivalent of the government's pursuing an underworld character for tax evasion when they don't have enough evidence to nail him on any other charge even though they know he's running gambling, prostitution, toxic-waste-disposal, and drug operations. Refusing to rent to someone who's undesirable on many counts only because she smokes cigars is perfectly legal, and it's perfectly just. There is a legitimate business reason for doing so. Furthermore, you'd have to be totally indifferent to the matter if you couldn't find some reason to refuse to rent to her.

Don't despair about anti-discrimination laws. They mean well. A great many people have been unfairly discriminated against in finding housing only because they were old or mongoloid or Mormon or black or female or Irish or Jewish or divorced. The laws merely declare that those are no longer valid reasons by themselves to refuse to rent to someone. You may not discriminate arbitrarily. That's all. You should always be able to find a valid legal reason not to rent to those who are obviously objectionable. Set your own standards well within the law, and then set about getting good tenants you can work with.

Your standards for a particular rental might look like this—

Gross income: four times rent
Income stability: at least six months with same source of income
Assets: five times rent (bank account and/or automobile equity)
Credit: nothing negative
Rent punctuality: prompt
Pets: none
Waterbed: one queen-size OK

Vehicles: one auto, no motorcycles
Personal recommendations: one available (preferably local)
Number of tenants: maximum of three
Intelligence: average or above
Attitude: cooperative
Smoking: no
Drinking: moderation (maximum of two drinks daily)
Permanence: at least six months in each of last two residences
Cleanliness: average

Naturally some of the standards you use are relative to a given dwelling, some are relative to you, some are relative to a particular state or municipality, and some are relative to commonly accepted rules of thumb. Be reasonable in determining those standards because if they are overly restrictive, you may well find that no one who wants to live in your rental can possibly qualify. For most standards, you will have to determine yourself what is reasonable and what is overly restrictive (see Chapter 11 for ideas about accepting pets and waterbeds), but there are some rules of thumb you might want to follow for two of them—gross income and number of tenants.

For gross income, the commonly accepted rule of thumb is *four times rent*, though some landlords and landladies lately have even reduced that to three. If an applicant's gross income is less, then you may accept or reject him. The decision is yours. The point is that you don't have to accept any applicant who grosses less regardless of his other qualifications. You may if you want to, say, if that applicant comes with sterling recommendations from two previous landlords and landladies, but you don't have to.

Moreover, just as the Equal Rights Amendment, were it ever adopted, would be a two-edged sword for women, so, too, are laws prohibiting housing discrimination based on marital status. If you may not inquire into an applicant's marital status (you will notice later that the rental application included in this book makes no mention of marital status), then you have every right to require each adult occupant to have a gross income equal to three or four times the rent. After all, the living arrangements, whether sanctified by marriage vows or not, may break up, and you, dear landlord or landlady, may get stuck with the one tenant who has no income and can't pay the rent. (You don't have to be so restrictive if you don't wish to be, but you may be that restrictive legally if you do wish to be.) Note that if you choose to separate the income of two unmarried adults, then you must separate the income of married couples as well. Likewise, if you combine the income of unmarried adults, you must combine the income of married couples. Apply your standards to one and all alike. That's all that anti-discrimination laws require you to do.

Regarding an acceptable number of occupants, the rule of thumb is *one fewer than the number of rooms*. In other words, a studio or efficiency dwelling (2 rooms) should accommodate one occupant; one bedroom (3 rooms), two occupants; two bedrooms (4 rooms), three to four occupants; and three bedrooms (5 rooms), four to five occupants.

Exceeding these numbers increases the population density to a point where maintenance and repair costs increase considerably. Floors show more wear. The toilet flushes more frequently. The doors swing open and closed more. Faucets, switches, outlets, windows, heaters, garbage disposers, and all the other parts to a rental dwelling just get a lot more use and hence wear out more quickly. Besides, when the place begins to resemble a rabbit warren, exterior maintenance increases as well.

Some people may fudge on these numbers, either increasing or decreasing them. As you might expect, the United States Department of Housing and Urban Development (HUD) increases them. Its minimums and maximums for rental occupancy are as follows: efficiency (no bedrooms), one to two occupants; one bedroom, one to three occupants; two bedrooms, two to five occupants; three bedrooms, four to seven occupants; and four bedrooms, six to nine occupants.

Fortunately, you don't have to agree with HUD. Unless local housing regulations say otherwise, you are free to adopt your own guidelines for occupancy so long as you apply them consistently to all the applicants who are interested in a particular vacancy. You may limit efficiencies to one person, one-bedrooms to two, two-bedrooms to three, and so on. You may also require that children of the opposite sex be housed in separate bedrooms. On that basis, a husband, wife, son, and daughter would not fit into anything smaller than a three-bedroom place.

What does all of this mean to you? It means simply that you cannot be discriminating in certain prejudice-oriented ways when you are selecting tenants, but you can be, and should be, discriminating in a great many other ways, business-oriented ways, if you wish to protect your property investment.

The truth is that you have to be discriminating when you're selecting tenants because you will find that some people are completely incapable of selecting their own living accommodations prudently themselves. They think that a family of five, soon to be six, one dog, one cat, and a pet crocodile will fit comfortably into one of your one-bedroom apartments. You have to instruct them in the folly of their thinking.

Now let's take a closer look at how you can be discriminating in selecting tenants. Let's examine individually each of the ten steps for getting good tenants.

1) PREPARE THE DWELLING FOR OCCUPANCY.

This first step in getting good tenants would appear to be totally unrelated to the overall task, but it is, in fact, just as important to getting good tenants as their payment of rent is to their staying on as tenants.

Your job at this point is to fix up, paint up, clean up, and dress up your rental dwelling to make it attractive enough so that a good prospect will want to rent it from you for the rent you want to charge. You will always attract the best tenants and get the most rent from that dwelling which shows well and smells good. (Give vacating tenants an incentive to clean well and hope that they do, but don't bank on it.)

Even so, don't become overly concerned about sanitation or perfection when you are preparing a dwelling for occupancy. Remember that you are appealing primarily to the senses of sight and smell. In this context, clean the appliances, stove hood, and cabinets (under the sink, too) both inside and out. Remove all non-adhesive shelf paper. Clean the showers, tubs, toilets, sinks, mirrors, and medicine cabinets (inside as well). Dust the ceilings (for cobwebs), baseboards, window sills, miniblinds, and closet shelving. Wash the kitchen and bathroom walls, and spot-clean the walls in other rooms. Dryclean the draperies. Wash the light fixtures and windows inside and out. Vacuum and steam-clean the carpets. Scrub and wax the floors. Sweep the entry, patio, storage enclosure, and garage. Remove all personal belongings of the previous tenants (including clothes hangers and cleaning supplies). And dispose of all trash.

One landlady I know who takes this business very seriously took her preparation cues from motels. She asked herself how motels manage to make their rooms appear clean every day when they can't possibly clean every square foot of those rooms every day. She noticed that motels spend extra effort in the bathroom, wrapping the glasses, supplying new bars of soap, sanitizing the toilet bowl, wrapping a paper band around the seat, folding the next sheet on the toilet paper roll carefully, and sometimes providing shower caps and shampoo. Now she prepares her rentals in somewhat the same fashion. She bought a supply of those paper bands, and she wraps one around each toilet seat after it's been thoroughly cleaned. She leaves a new dispenser of liquid soap at the sink, and she mounts an unwrapped roll of toilet paper in the paper holder. Needless to say, the people who look at her vacancies are impressed. Then, on the day her new tenants move in, she leaves a small box of chocolate-covered mints on the kitchen counter with a welcome note.

Do a good job of cleaning overall, but do not do such a good job that you get callouses on your knees from crawling all over the floors scrubbing them laboriously and polishing them to a mirror-like finish. Do not work your fingers to the bone by scrubbing the tile grout with a toothbrush. That's wasted effort.

Remember this one very important truism about each of your rentals: *You, landlord or landlady, are not going to live there.* Remind yourself. Remind your partner. Say it out loud while you're cleaning, "I am not going to live here." Do not give way to excessive cleaning. Clean your rentals well, but don't try to clean them any better than a maid would clean a room in a motel which is part of a nationwide chain. Your new tenants may be as fastidious about housekeeping as Felix Unger is in *The Odd Couple*, and if they are, they will probably clean everything again themselves anyway. Your thorough housecleaning efforts are a waste of time and energy in that case, and they're definitely a waste if your new tenant is an Oscar Madison.

In addition to preparing the place for occupancy by cleaning, perfume it as well. No, not with Chanel No. 5. That's for people, not dwellings. Perfume the place by cleaning the kitchen and bathroom with a lemon or pine-oil scented cleaner. Or allow the new paint odor to prevail. Use a commercial air freshener to make the place smell of honeysuckle, limes, or new-mown hay. Or make it smell of grandma's baking by heating two tablespoons of imitation vanilla extract on the stove.

The sense of smell is very important. Those who study such things say that smell revives memories more than any of our other senses. Remember the wonderful aroma of homemade cookies and all the pleasant memories that go along with them? Who doesn't! Well, those boutique cookie shops which have become so successful in shopping malls around the country are trading on those very memories and, of course, on your weakened sales resistance once your salivary glands start reacting to the fresh-baked-cookie aromas. That's how they snag you as a customer. Good odors conjure up pleasantries and help to sell products. Likewise, they can help to rent residences. If prospective tenants are charmed by agreeable odors of one kind or another, they become more willing to pay good rent for a place. You know what new cars smell like, don't you? Can you imagine someone ordering a new car to be delivered without that new car smell? Give your vacant rental dwelling a fresh, clean, pleasing odor, too.

2) PREQUALIFY THE PROSPECTS.

This step is based mostly upon your tenant standards, whatever they happen to be, and consists of five or more determinations which can and should be made rather quickly, even over the telephone, and will save you untold time, gasoline, shoeleather, and grief. This step serves to eliminate those people who are interested in renting from you but fail to qualify. Here you are prequalifying them before you ever take the time to show them the rental or have them fill out an application, so you won't be exasperated to learn late in the process that they really didn't qualify to rent from you in the first place.

You can't very well determine at this stage whether someone will qualify according to all of your tenant standards. That questioning would be much too tedious to go into right now, and, besides, it wouldn't yield useful information anyway (certain things you must observe in people, not ask about; can you imagine asking callers straightaway about their cleanliness and intelligence?), but you can certainly select a few important items and prequalify callers with them, devising questions suitable for this kind of situation.

To avoid wasted time, wasted effort, and possible embarrassment later on, then, you might prequalify prospects when they first make an inquiry by determining these five circumstances about them—

1) when they are ready to move in;
2) whether they have enough money to move in;
3) whether the number of people who intend to live there falls within your limits;
4) whether they have pets; and
5) whether they have a waterbed.

If the prospects are not ready to move yet and your dwelling is ready for immediate occupancy, look for someone else. If you require $735 to move in and they have only $400 to commit right now, what's the sense of talking to them; look further. If they are a family of four, and you're looking for a maximum of three people, tell them so. If they have a huge heart-shaped waterbed for themselves and a twin-sized waterbed for their four-year old, and you have decided against allowing any liquid-filled furniture in this house you inherited from your favorite uncle, well, then, that's that.

Unless you have a lie detector handy, though, establishing the truth regarding these particulars may take some doing. Certain people will tell you exactly what they think you want to hear. They will move in whenever you want; they have $1000 in cash to cover move-in costs, no kids, no pets, and no waterbed, and besides, they will tell you with a smile, "We're nice people." That's what they may say, but where does the truth lie? Who knows?

How do you get at the truth? At this stage, without being omniscient, all you can do is phrase your questions whenever possible in such a way that you give few clues to the answers you're looking for.

Because people seldom dissemble in answering questions about their readiness to move and their ability to pay the move-in costs, however, you can be pretty direct about the first two questions. State whether the place is available now or will be in three weeks, and ask whether the prospects' moving plans might coincide with that time frame.

Regarding move-in costs, state flatly what sum you require to be paid before they move in so much as a bag of groceries or a stick of furniture, and ask them whether this is within their means right now.

The next two questions are the ones which generally involve the most deceit—people and pets. These are the ones to be most wary about. To learn the truth, simply ask the prospects disarmingly how many kids they have or how many people will be living with them. Do not say, "We take only one child. How many do you have?" That approach will only elicit this response, "One's all we have." (Remember that in most areas which have laws prohibiting age discrimination, it is perfectly legal to limit the number of people you will allow to occupy your rental. There is no law anywhere which compels you to accept three people in a one-bedroom dwelling, but there are a very few local areas which have laws compelling you to accept as many as two people per bedroom. If your local area has no laws about age discrimination, chances are it has none about occupancy limits, and you are free to choose your own.)

After establishing that the prospects fall within your definition of acceptable numbers, ask them point blank, "Do you have any pets?" Don't reveal your policy on pets before asking the question, of course, or you will likely be able to predict their answer. Reveal your policy only after you hear their answer.

Finally, now that you have prequalified the prospects on four counts, and they pass, ask whether they plan to keep a waterbed in the place they are seeking to rent. Again, reveal your policy only after you hear their answer.

With all of these matters settled to your mutual satisfaction, invite them to take a look at the place.

3) SHOW THE DWELLING.

This step requires no great talent or skills, but you might wisely employ a number of ideas to make it less troublesome and more beneficial for you.

• After you have prequalified those who phone and express an interest in renting your available dwelling, answer whatever questions they may have while they're still on the phone, and explain exactly where the rental is located so they aren't astounded by the neighborhood if it's not quite what they had expected. Also, give them clearly understandable directions so they won't lose their way trying to get there.

• If you're one of those much maligned absentee landlords or landladies renting out a house or other dwelling located at a distance from where you live, you'll want to refrain from making repeated trips over there. Do this by encouraging people to drive by the building first and then call back for an appointment to see the inside, or do it by holding an "open house" for showing your vacancy at designated hours (should be one to two hours long). Tell those whom you have prequalified just when you intend to hold this open house and then make certain that someone is there to show the place. You will save yourself many wasted trips and hours of waiting around for a specific caller who may or may not even bother to show up.

By the way, if you do make appointments to show the dwelling to specific callers, get their names and telephone numbers so they'll feel a little more responsible about showing up and so you can call them back in case something happens and you can't keep the appointment yourself.

• Never rent out a dwelling sight unseen. Some prospective tenants will tell you over the phone that they want to rent your place without even looking at it. If they're that eager, don't insist that they see it, but don't rent it to them either. Something's sure to be suspect if they're that undiscriminating.

• If a dwelling which will soon be available is still occupied and you know it's in such poor condition that it won't show well, don't show it. Instead, show another one which is similar and is occupied by a clean, cooperative tenant. Before you do, however, be absolutely certain that the prospects are well qualified and very interested in renting from you. In other words, you should feel reasonably certain that the prospects are not really well dressed burglars casing the joint.

• Always accompany your prospects on their tour of the premises. Don't hand them a key and tell them to look it over by themselves. Consider the showing as something of an opportunity to talk with the prospects and size them up.

• When you are actually showing prospects through the dwelling, you'll want to make a little sales pitch. Point out all the features of the place, including the special features of the building and the neighborhood. Be honest, though. Don't say it's quiet in the evening when, in fact, right next door there's a fundamentalist church which shakes and rolls to loud gospel music every Tuesday, Friday, and Sunday night. If you ignore the drawbacks, you may have to contend all over again with another vacancy very soon. The prospective tenants have a right to know what the place is really like, and you should tell them. Of course, you may want to speak of the drawbacks as if they were advantages: "One thing I really like about this place is the great gospel music they play next door three evenings a week. It's such a joyful sound, don't you think?"

• The first impressions you have of prospects while you show them around may tell you all you need to know to reject them outright, but there's no need to alienate them by telling them right now. Do what small claims court judges do when they don't want to anger a losing party in court. They take the matter "under submission," which simply means that to avoid fistfights in the corridors, they will render their decision at a later time. Offer all your prospects applications, and tell them that you will be accepting applications over the next few days. After that, say you will check them all out and pick one. That way you avoid potential arguments over your grounds for refusing to rent to them, and everyone saves face.

• If possible, avoid mentioning whether any one prospect is the first person to submit an application. Many people believe erroneously that landlords and landladies have to check rental applications by sequence of submission. Perhaps one day we will have to, but that day hasn't arrived yet. The process is really quite similar to selecting someone for a job opening. Employers may not discriminate illegally in hiring any more than you may discriminate illegally in renting. An employer interviews a number of people for an available position and considers each one equally over a period of time or until the person best suited for the job appears on the scene. The first person to be interviewed is certainly considered for the job but rates no special consideration for having shown up first.

• Get applications from everyone who wishes to submit one and don't commit yourself to rent to any of the applicants until you have checked them out. Not only is the information on applications essential to the selection process, but also because you have more information to base your selection on than just the obvious things such as sex, race, or color, the chances of your being considered culpable of illegal discrimination on the basis of these criteria are substantially reduced. Face it. You are less vulnerable to charges of illegal discrimination if you solicit applications than if you do not. Without applications, you have little information to base your decision on, and the deciding factors may more easily be construed to be discriminatory.

4) TAKE AND SCRUTINIZE ALL APPLICATIONS.

Your rental application should be simple to read, simple to follow, brief, and yet thorough. You don't need applicants' entire life histories to help you decide whether to rent to them. You might satisfy your idle curiosity by reading those life histories, but

Rental Application

for (address) 456 Sweet Strut

Name Richard Renter

Home Phone 555-1988   Work Phone 535-9686

Social Security No. 423-45-6789   Driver's License No. A0987677

Present Address 1510 - 12th Street

How long at this address? 10 mo. Rent $ 240—   Reason for moving Want to be closer to work

Owner/Manager Leslie Landlady, Manager   Phone 555-3210

Previous Address 1 View Circle, apt. 105

How long at this address? 2 yrs. Rent $ 200—   Reason for moving Got married, too small

Owner/Manager Joe Littleshoes, owner   Phone 555-1000

Name and relationship of every person to live with you (include ages of minor children)
Mary Renter, wife

Any pets? NO   Describe —   Waterbed? Yes

Present Occupation operator   Employer Bi-Lift   Phone 123-4440

How long with this employer? 1¼ yr.   Supervisor B. B. Jones   Phone 123-4441

Previous Occupation operator   Employer Upstate Lift   Phone (200) 112-1160

How long with this employer? 6 yrs.   Supervisor Lou Smith   Phone (200) 112-1160

Current Gross Income Per Month (before deductions) $ 1655—

List sources of income (other than present employment listed above) None

Savings Account: Bank Safe Savings   Branch downtown   Acct. No. 111-11-0011

Checking Account: Bank Big Bank   Branch Main   Acct. No. V04039586

Major Credit Card None   Acct. No.

Credit Reference A-Z Furniture   Acct. No. R-1345   Balance Owed $ 650—   Monthly Payment $ 79.50

Credit Reference —   Acct. No. —   Balance Owed —   Monthly Payment —

Have you ever filed bankruptcy? NO   Have you ever been evicted? NO

Vehicle(s) Make(s) Volkswagen   Model(s) Rabbit   Year(s) 1979   License(s) 222-123

Personal Reference Donna McGillicutty   Address 1516 Marina Way   Phone 555-1763

Contact in Emergency Eula Renter   Address 498- 15th St, Bigtown   Phone 544-3061

I declare that the statements above are true and correct, and I hereby authorize verification of references given and a credit check.

Date 1/10/86   Signed Richard Renter

they likely wouldn't be any more useful to you in determining whether you ought to rent to somebody than would the information contained in a simple one-page application.

The application you use should have sections with information on the applicant's current and previous tenancies, current and previous jobs, fellow occupants, pets, financial status, vehicles, and driver's license. If this information is complete, you will have plenty to consider and check in the next step.

Notice that among other things the application included here asks for the name of a person to contact in an emergency. This name would not likely appear on an application unless specifically requested. Yet, this information may prove vital if a tenant disappears without a trace, as some are wont to do, fails to show up to pay rent, or dies on the property. Such things do happen, you know, and you ought to be prepared for them if they do.

As mentioned before, because landlords and landladies may no longer refuse to rent to someone on the basis of marital status, you should ask every adult who expects to occupy your rental dwelling to fill out an application. Husbands and wives should fill out separate applications, and adult roommates, regardless of their relationship to one another, should each fill out an application as well. You'll use a great many applications this way, but you'll be well protected against accusations of unfair discrimination and you'll have plenty of good information for later reference.

Some landlords and landladies require applicants to submit deposits along with their rental applications. I do not. A deposit involves too much of a commitment too soon. You know nothing about the applicants and yet they assume that you are "holding" the rental for them, that it is as good as theirs already. If you accept deposits from applicants and you later reject their applications, then you have to face the unpleasantness of returning their deposits and explaining why you decided not to rent to them. Too often such an explanation precipitates an argument.

If you follow my practice and don't take deposits with the applications, you do run the risk of wasting your time checking out applications submitted frivolously and even losing good prospective tenants who make deposits and commitments elsewhere, but you can always keep in touch with the best prospects by telephone. I much prefer this freedom to look over a number of applications without making any commitments, either expressed or implied. Then I can pick the best applications to pursue further, regardless of when they were submitted. There are times, to be sure, when one applicant looks good from start to finish and you won't want to wait for more applications. That's no problem. You can complete all the steps in short order if you wish, and you'll still have the tenant committed with a deposit in the end.

When applicants hand you their completed applications, look them over quickly for legibility and completion, making sure that they're

signed, too. Their signature authorizes you to conduct a credit check. Without it, you're invading their right to privacy if you begin snooping into their affairs. Then ask to see their driver's licenses and credit cards for identification. Ask non-driving applicants for some other form of "official" identification with their picture on it, such as a passport, military ID, or other government agency ID card. Compare the pictures on the identification with the faces you see before you, and say something kind or droll about the likenesses if you can. Then compare the numbers on the identification and credit cards with those given on the applications to verify the information as given. If they don't match up, ask why they don't. You have no way of knowing otherwise whether the person whose name and references are listed on the application is the same person who wishes to rent from you.

Remember that whenever you rent out a dwelling, you are entrusting a valuable piece of property to a stranger. You must know whether that stranger is a proper stranger. You must know what that stranger's true identity is. Automobile rental agencies ask for identification before they will rent you a motorcar. Merchants even ask for identification before they will cash a five-dollar check. Yet your rental property is many times more valuable than an automobile or a check for a paltry sum. Shouldn't you check your applicant's I.D.? You stand to lose plenty if you rent to an unscrupulous tenant, not to mention all the grief and aggravation you could suffer. Be cautious. Check the applicant's identification for certain.

If, for one reason or another, you fail to check an applicant's identification while you are looking the application over initially, don't despair. You can still check it when you visit the applicant's home. I prefer to check it at the first opportunity, however, so I don't waste any more time than I have to if an applicant proves to be impersonating someone else, such as a friend or relative who has impeccable references.

Unless you already know more about the applicants than what's on their applications, look at each application as if you were trying to collect an eviction judgment. If applicants have no job, no automobile, and no bank accounts to attach, then how will you be able to get any money out of them if they stop paying their rent and you have to take them to court? Many applications may be rejected at this step without further checking. You can "evict" now at the lowest possible cost. (On the backs of all applications you reject, write the reasons for your decisions and then file away each application for at least three years as proof of your fairness in tenant selection.)

Once you have scrutinized the applications to check for internal inconsistencies and obvious disqualifying factors as measured by your tenant standards, you should act promptly. Other landlords and landladies are looking for good tenants, too, and your prospects may be filling out applications for more than one dwelling.

5) CHECK REFERENCES.

Some people know that because few landlords and landladies bother to check out the information given on rental applications, they can lie and probably get away with it. I know it's a revelation to you that anyone would ever lie on a rental application. It isn't? Good, then you should be able to hold your own in this business. Be suspicious of the information given on every rental application submitted to you. Check the references, especially those regarding tenancy and income and maybe the credit references, too.

   • TENANCY—Call the current landlord or landlady to learn whatever you can about the applicants' tenancy, but be careful. Since it is relatively easy for anyone to impersonate a landlord or landlady over the telephone, you may be talking to someone else. Say something like this when you call to check the reference: "Hello, I'm Lester

Landlord, a landlord in Littletown. Richard and Mary Renter have given you as a reference on an application they made to rent a house from me. Can you tell me how you came to know them?" If you had indicated that the woman at the other end of the phone line was supposed to be the one renting to Richard and Mary, then she might have suspected that the Renters were trying to use her as a managerial reference and would string you along, giving you just the kind of information you'd like to hear. By not indicating that you know what their relationship is, you give her no clues about what you already know, and you will more than likely learn what their true relationship is. Maybe they're just personal friends. Who knows? String her along instead of being strung along yourself.

Should you still have doubts about whether you're talking with the applicants' real landlady, tell the woman you're telephoning that the rent is substantially higher or lower than what's given on the rental application and ask for a verification. The real landlady will know right away what the correct rent is. A phony won't.

One other pitfall you might encounter when asking an applicant's current landlord or landlady to say a few words about a departing tenant is that the current landlord or landlady may be so anxious for the tenants to move that they may be recommended to you even if they are being evicted. Be especially wary, therefore, of glowing recommendations made by the current landlord or landlady, and weigh them cautiously against whatever else you have learned about the applicants. Compare the reasons for moving given by the tenants on their applications with the reason given by the current landlord or landlady, and if there's even a hint of discrepancy in their stories, check with the previous landlord or landlady given on the application. That person no longer has an interest in whether the tenants stay or move and would be the most likely one to give you an unbiased appraisal.

When you have exhausted your own good specific questions about the applicants (Do they pay on time? Do they bother the neighbors? Are they clean? Are they cooperative? etc.), close your conversation by asking, "If you had the opportunity, would you rent to these tenants again?" The answer to this question will give you a good final clue about them.

• INCOME—After checking into the applicants' current and previous tenancies, call the employer to verify employment, length of employment, and income. Sometimes firms are reluctant to divulge such employee information, so be sure you state who you are and why you're making the inquiry. Your call might go something like this: "Hello, my name is Lester Landlord. I'm a landlord in Littletown. Richard Renter, who says he works for you, has made an application to rent a house from me, and I'd like very much to verify some information about him so I can qualify him and his wife to move in as soon as possible." In effect, you are saying that your inquiry will benefit the employee. Smaller firms will assent to this reasonable request because they know their people individually and they want to help their employees obtain housing and because you have said that you are only verifying information you already have. Large firms will switch you to their personnel departments, and you'll have to repeat your speech from the top, but they, too, will generally verify the information you give them. Continue by saying, "Richard Renter says he has been working there for a year and three months. Is that about correct?" If they answer in the affirmative, say, "He has indicated that he earns a gross income of $1,655 per month. Is that about right?" Phrasing your questions in this way, so they may be answered affirmatively or negatively, relieves employers of the anxiety they sometimes feel about divulging information they shouldn't.

• CREDIT—Regarding credit information, you have three choices: 1) Choice one is to rely solely on the tenancy and income references already obtained to provide good clues about the applicant's ability and willingness to meet the financial obligations incurred in renting from you. 2) Choice two is to check with some or all of the credit references listed on the application. Finance companies and merchants with customer charge accounts will usually give you the information you need over the phone, but banks will rarely release any information to you unless authorized to do so by the customer, and even then, it may take a few days. A letter of authorization which you might use is included here. It must be signed by the tenant-customer first and will be returned to you by mail unless the people at the tenants' bank know you and will hand it back to you in person. You may, of course, do a "quick-and-dirty" financial resources investigation by calling the bank and inquiring whether a fictitious check for a certain sum of money would clear the applicant's checking account. 3) Choice three is to call your rental property owners' association and request a credit report on the applicant. Almost every association belongs to a credit reporting agency and provides its members with credit reports for a nominal charge. These reports generally take just a couple of hours to obtain and can reveal information on bad debt collections that you wouldn't otherwise learn about.

If you don't belong to a rental property owners' association, you may be able to call on your bank's resources and get them to run a credit check for a small fee. Some will accommodate you if they value you as a customer; some won't, no matter what. You may also get a credit report directly from a credit reporting agency (see your Yellow Pages under "Credit Reporting Agencies"). The drawback in dealing directly with an agency yourself instead of indirectly through your association is the high cost of securing a single credit report every so often. Agencies charge annual fees and then a fee for each inquiry. If you make only one inquiry a year, it could cost you $50 directly through an agency because you'll have to pay the annual dues plus the inquiry charge, while it might cost $5 to $10 through a rental property owners' association.

How much credit information you should obtain on applicants depends on the amount of rent involved, the percentage of their income that will be paid out in rent, and the difference between the old and new rents. If the new rent is high or if it's equal to more than a third of the applicant's gross monthly income (rent, together with monthly credit obligations, should total around 40% of gross income) or if it represents a considerable increase over what they have been paying, you should check the credit thoroughly. Even though you know how much they make and that they have been paying their rent on time, you know very little about their current financial obligations and their previous credit experience. The increased cost of an improvement in their housing may prove to be too great a financial burden for them right now, and you should have some clues in advance so you can advise them against renting too expensive a place. If the new rent is relatively low and amounts to less than a quarter of their income, and represents little, if any, increase over what they have been paying, then rely on the tenancy and income references alone or call just one of the credit references given. You'll have to decide upon the right amount of credit information you need in each instance.

There's a lot of information available, but you have to spend money or time to obtain it, and only you can determine how much information would be helpful to you in making your decision whether to rent to them. All the information available to you on applicants is merely a supplement to your good judgment. You alone must decide whether they will make good tenants.

BANK INFORMATION AUTHORIZATION

BANK: This request to report your direct experience and transactions is for the purpose of establishing your customer's ability to pay rent to the landlord or landlady whose name appears below. It is understood that this report is a business courtesy and is strictly confidential. Its authorship will not be disclosed nor will your bank assume any obligation for errors, omissions, or changes in this information.

	Savings	Commercial (Checking)		Loans
Date Opened	_____	_____	No Experience	_____
High	_____	_____	Date Opened	_____
Medium	_____	_____	Open Balance	_____
Low	_____	_____	Date Closed	_____
Date Closed	_____	_____	How Paid	_____
			Satisfactory____ Unsatisfactory____	

Remarks _____

Authorized Signature _____   Bank Stamp:

TENANT-CUSTOMER: Please complete all information in this section and forward to your bank along with a stamped envelope addressed to the landlord or landlady whose name appears below.

Renter	Richard	Mary
Last Name (Print)	Husband (First Name)	Wife (First Name)

Address   1510 – 12th ST, Littletown

Bank   Big Bank   Savings Account No. _____

Address   101 Main St.   Checking Account No. **V04039586**

Littletown   Loans _____

Richard Renter   *Mary Renter*
Tenant-Customer Signatures (His & Hers)

LANDLORD/LANDLADY: Print your name and address in the blanks provided, sign your name as acceptance of the above statement to bank, and give this form to the tenant who has applied to rent from you.

Name   Leslie Landlady

Address   453 Sweet St.

Littletown   *Leslie Landlady*
Signature

Co-Signer Agreement

Dated___*June 16, 1987*___
(Addendum to Rental Agreement)

This agreement is attached to and forms a part of the Rental Agreement between ___*Vernon Graves*___, Owners, and ___*Dana Levno*___, Tenants, which is dated ___*June 1, 1987*___.

My name is

_____*Ellen Levno*_____.

I have completed a Rental Application for the express purpose of enabling the Owners to check my credit. I have no intention of occupying the dwelling referred to in the Rental Agreement above.

I have read the Rental Agreement referred to above, and I promise to guarantee the Tenants' compliance with the financial obligations of this Agreement.

I understand that I may be required to pay for rent, cleaning charges, or damage assessments in such amounts as are incurred by the Tenants under the terms of this Agreement if, and only if, the Tenants fail to pay.

Signed:

_____*Ellen Levno*_____

• HANDLING A SPECIAL SITUATION—Your rental applicants may have good credit, poor credit, or no credit established at all. You'll want to eliminate those with poor credit, of course, but you may want to consider renting to those who have never established credit before. Let's say your applicant is a twenty-one-year-old registered nurse who's always lived at home before and has just taken a new job in the area. She hasn't had the time or the opportunity to build a credit, tenancy, or employment record yet. Should you refuse to rent to her for lack of credit reference? You may, certainly, but you may be wise to consider renting to her if everything else checks out satisfactorily, and you feel inclined to give her a chance to prove herself. For your own peace of mind, however, you could request that she secure a co-signer, someone who already has an established credit rating which you could check by having the co-signer fill out a separate rental application. Be as careful in checking the co-signer's credit as you were with the applicants's. If everything checks out satisfactorily, ask the co-signer to sign the Co-Signer Agreement in your presence, and make sure the co-signer understands the responsibilities involved.

With this additional agreement in hand, you reduce the risk involved in renting to someone who lacks established credit. If the tenant turns out to be a deadbeat, you have someone of substance to pursue.

• HANDLING ANOTHER SPECIAL SITUATION—Every so often you will want to check the references of applicants who look outstanding both on paper and in person, but because it's a holiday weekend at the end of the month and you can't get a credit check or verify either their tenancy or employment, you're stymied. The information you need to make your decision is simply unavailable for a few days. What might you do? Here are three possibilities—

The first is to tell the applicants to wait until you can check all their references as you normally do. Apologize that you're unable to check their references immediately, but assure them that you will check everything as soon as the holiday weekend is over. The advantage of this option is that you run little risk of renting to someone who may be a professional deadbeat. You will know with some certainty when you check them out whether they are what they appear to be. The disadvantage of this option is that you risk losing good tenants who will likely continue looking around until they find another suitable place which they can rent without having to wait for clearance.

The second possibility should also protect you from deadbeats, but it does have its price. Tell the applicants to find accommodations for the weekend if necessary and tell them you will deduct, say, $35 from their first month's rent for every night they have to sleep at a motel, provided, of course, that their references do check out and that you do rent to them. If you have to pay for two or three nights' lodging in order to secure good tenants, the expense is well worth it compared to the loss you would sustain if you had to evict problem tenants.

The third possibility is a little more creative and requires some special shrewdness to carry off, but it is almost as cautious as the other two, and it usually settles the matter quite sufficiently. Ask the applicants to show you their latest rent receipts and their latest payroll stubs. If current, a rent receipt will verify an applicant's tenancy, and a payroll stub will verify both employment and wages. Since few people carry these two items around with them and since the rent receipt could be forged pretty easily if the applicants were to leave your sight after you made the request, refrain from requesting the rent receipt unless you are visiting the applicants at their current residence in the next step. A payroll stub, on the other hand, is more difficult to forge, so have no qualms about asking to see one when you first decide to try this option. If the applicants claim to have stubs at home, tell them you'll meet them there shortly. When you arrive, follow the procedure outlined in the next steps and ask to see both their payroll stubs and rent receipts. Be sure to check driver's licenses and credit cards at some point and make no exception to your normal method of payment for move-in costs. In other words, accept only cash, gold, silver bars, money orders, or cashier's checks for payment. Accept no personal checks for the first rental payment from this or any other new tenants.

6) MAKE A VISIT TO THE APPLICANTS' CURRENT HOME.

If everything about the applicants checks out satisfactorily so far, call them on the phone and arrange to visit them shortly at the place where they are currently living. Much as you might like to show up without letting them know you're coming, you'll find that calling them first will insure that they're home and save you a wasted trip. You are not trying to catch them completely off guard, only slightly off guard. You might want to invent an appropriate pretext for the visit, perhaps that you need more information about the credit and personal references given on their application, but the main reason for this visit is to see how the applicants live and to meet all those who would become your tenants.

If the applicants presently live too far away for you to make a visit, you may have to skip this step, but do so reluctantly. On your arrival, say a few pleasantries and then begin asking questions such as these: "I see here that you work at Dario's Pizza Parlor. What are your hours there? Do you receive any commissions in addition to your regular salary? How long have you been banking at Midtown Bank? Is Cash Kramer still the manager there? Did you attend school in this area? How long have you lived around here? What keeps you living in this area?" and so on.

While you're conversing, strain your peripheral vision so hard that you'll need peripheral-vision glasses on your temples some day. Look around for various indications of how well these prospective tenants care for this place where they currently live. Is there a half-assembled motorcycle in the living room? How many holes are there in the walls and doors? Are there burns in the carpets? What shape is their furniture in? How's the housekeeping? How closely does this place resemble the dwelling they wish to rent from you? The closer the resemblance, the better they will be as your tenants.

Also, look and listen for pets and people likely to make the move with the household. You might expect that the springer spaniel asleep on the sofa will make the move. If he doesn't appear on the application, ask why he doesn't. If they say they're planning to get rid of old Rufus, make a note of their answer and judge for yourself whether they're telling the truth or not. If you hear two kids raising Cain somewhere out of sight and it appears to be the kind of dispute that siblings usually have, you can assume that these offspring will both probably be accompanying their parents in the move. If only one kid appears on the application, inquire into the matter. If the parents say they're trying to get rid of one of the kids, try to contain yourself and make a note of their answer. Who knows, maybe they have sold one already and the purchasers just haven't taken delivery yet.

At some time during your visit, if you haven't done so before, say that you'd like to see the applicants' driver's licenses, or another form of identification bearing their photographs, and some major credit cards so you can verify the numbers. When you have them in hand, check to see whether the numbers match those given on the applications, note down the full names (including middle names), and verify the birth dates.

Rental Agreement

Dated <u>January 12, 1986</u>

Agreement between <u>Lester Landlord</u>, Owners, and <u>Richard H. & Mary L. Renter</u>, Tenants, for a dwelling located at <u>456 Sweet Street, Littletown, Calif.</u>

Tenants agree to rent this dwelling on a month-to-month basis for $ <u>428</u> per month, payable in advance on the <u>1st</u> day of every calendar month to Owners or their Agent, <u>xxxx</u>. When rent is paid on or before the <u>4th</u> day of the calendar month, Tenants may take a $ <u>20</u> discount.

The first month's rent for this dwelling is $<u>550</u>.

The security/cleaning deposit on this dwelling is $ <u>720</u>. It is refundable if Tenants leave the dwelling reasonably clean and undamaged.

A deposit of $ <u>3</u> for <u>3</u> keys will be refunded after the keys have been returned.

Tenants will give <u>15</u> days' notice in writing before they move and will be responsible for paying rent through the end of this notice period or until another tenant approved by the Owners has moved in, whichever comes first.

Owners will refund all deposits due within <u>7</u> days after Tenants have moved out completely and returned their keys.

Only the following persons and pets are to live in this dwelling:

<u>Richard & Mary Renter xxx</u>

Without Owners' prior written permission, no other persons may live there, and no other pets may stay there, even temporarily. It may not be sublet or used for business purposes.

Use of the following is included in the rent: <u>Carpets, drapes, shades and stove. Refrigerator on loan temporarily.</u>

Remarks: <u>Water and garbage paid. Tenants pay other utilities. Parking in space 2. Occupancy contingent upon existing tenants' vacating premises.</u>

Tenants agree to the following:

1) to keep yards and garbage areas clean.
2) to keep from making loud noises and disturbances and to play music and broadcast programs at all times so as not to disturb other people's peace and quiet.
3) not to paint or alter their dwelling without first getting Owners' written permission.
4) to park their motor vehicle in assigned space and to keep that space clean of oil drippings.
5) not to repair their motor vehicle on the premises (unless it is in an enclosed garage) if such repairs will take longer than a single day.
6) to allow Owners to inspect the dwelling or show it to prospective at any and all reasonable times.
7) not to keep any liquid-filled furniture in this dwelling. *LL MR RR*
8) to pay rent by check or money order made out to Owners. (Checks must be good when paid or Owners will not grant discount.)
9) to pay for repairs of all damage, including drain stoppages, they or their guests have caused.
10) to pay for any windows broken in their dwelling while they live there.

Violation of any part of this agreement or nonpayment of rent when due shall be cause for eviction under appropriate sections of the applicable code. The prevailing party shall <u>not</u> recover reasonable attorney's fees involved.

Tenants hereby acknowledge that they have read this agreement, understand it, agree to it, and have been given a copy.

Owner <u>Lester Landlord</u>   Tenant <u>Richard Renter</u>

*By_____   Tenant <u>Mary Renter</u>

*Person authorized to accept legal service on Owners' behalf

pg 1 of 3

If you have any doubts about the applicants after this interview, say only that you want to check the applications further and leave, but if everything meets with your approval, proceed at once with the next three steps.

7) REVIEW YOUR RULES, REQUIREMENTS, AND POLICIES.

Before you finally commit yourself to accept any applicants as your tenants, review your rules, requirements, and policies with them in order to avoid possible ambiguities and prevent later misunderstandings. Remember that at this time, while you are talking with the tenants before they move in, you can get them to agree more readily to strict terms than you can at any later time.

Discuss your rules, requirements, and policies regarding the following: deposits, rent collections, rent payment, first month's rent, last month's rent, guests, parties, quiet hours, parking, utilities, garbage, pets, waterbeds, hanging things on the walls, changing locks, painting, maintenance, emergencies, window breakage, drain stoppages, lockout, and insurance. Add to this list any other special considerations which may apply to your situation. Mention, for example, that these new tenants renting is contingent upon the existing tenants vacating, if they still occupy the premises. Mention that the pool is heated only by the sun's striking the surface of the water (it's unheated). Be candid. You want your new tenants to have realistic expectations about living there.

Indicate that you are especially concerned that they keep the dwelling clean, that they be relatively quiet, and that they pay their rent promptly. Tell them that you are quick to evict tenants who do not abide by the rules and ask them whether they think they can live there in your rental under those circumstances. If they agree, and you believe them, then commit yourself to rent the place to them.

8) FILL OUT AND SIGN THE RENTAL AGREEMENT.

Now put in writing most of what you have already agreed upon verbally. Use a simply worded rental agreement (see "Searching for the Right Rental Agreement" in Chapter 10), one which most tenants can easily understand. In fact, you should use agreements written not only so they can be understood, but also so they cannot be misunderstood.

Explain every bit of your agreement to your new tenants, word for word. Give them blank copies and read everything to them as you are filling in the blanks. Many adults cannot read, and many others won't read anything thrust at them for their signatures. Because the rental agreement is so important to your future relationship with these people, read it to them now in order to avoid misunderstandings later.

If you decide to give tenants a discount for paying on time instead of adding a late charge when they're late, explain that the monthly rental figure used in the agreement is higher than what you advertised because this gross rent includes an amount, usually between $10 and $20, which is deducted as a discount when the rent is paid on or before the late date. Tell them you advertise the net rent because that's what most people pay. Make sure they understand this discounted rent policy before you continue.

Explain that the first month's rent is higher than the usual rent because it is supposed to cover some of the many costs connected with a new tenancy, costs such as cleaning the carpets and drapes (tell them they won't have to clean the carpets or drapes or wax the floors when they move out; tell them that move-in costs are borne by those who cause them, new tenants; otherwise the rents would have to be higher for everyone), advertising, showing the dwelling, checking credit, and changing locks. Tell them that the difference between the first month's rent and the rent for succeeding months is in no way

Lease

Dated *April 26, 1986*

Agreement between ___*Leslie Landlady*___, Owners, and
___*Tina Oldtimer*___, Tenants, for a dwelling located at
___*350 Boondocks Lane*___
Tenants agree to lease this dwelling for a term of *one year*, beginning
May 1, 1986 and ending *April 30, 1987* for $*470* per month, payable
in advance on the *first* day of every calendar month to Owners or their Agent,
___*x x x x*___. When rent is paid on or before the *fourth* day of
the calendar month, Tenants may take a $ *20* discount.

The first month's rent for this dwelling is $*560*.

The entire sum of this lease is $*5730*.   (*see Pet Agreement*)

The security/cleaning deposit on this dwelling is $ *715*. It is refundable
if Tenants leave the dwelling reasonably clean and undamaged.

If Tenants intend to move at the end of this lease, they agree to give
Owners notice in writing at least 30 days before the lease runs out. Otherwise
they will be regarded as automatically switching over to a month-to-month tenancy.

A deposit of $ *2* for *2* keys will be refunded after the keys have
been returned.

Owners will refund all deposits due within *10* days after Tenants have
moved out completely and returned their keys.

Only the following persons and pets are to live in this dwelling:

___*Tina Oldtimer and Fang x x x x*___
Without Owners' prior written permission, no other persons may live there, and
no other pets may stay there, even temporarily. It may not be sublet or used for
business purposes.

Use of the following is included in the rent: *Carpets, drapery rods,
built-in stove and built-in refrigerator.*

Remarks: *Owner pays water and garbage. Tenant responsible
for all other utilities.*

Tenants agree to the following:
1) to keep yards and garbage areas clean.
2) to keep from making loud noises and disturbances and to play music and
   broadcast programs at all times so as not to disturb other people's peace
   and quiet.
3) not to paint or alter their dwelling without first getting Owners' written
   permission.
4) to park their motor vehicle in assigned space and to keep that space clean
   of oil drippings.
5) not to repair their motor vehicle on the premises (unless it is in an
   enclosed garage) if such repairs will take longer than a single day.
6) to allow Owners to inspect the dwelling or show it to prospective at any and
   all reasonable times.
7) not to keep any liquid-filled furniture in this dwelling.
8) to pay rent by check or money order made out to Owners. (Checks must be
   good when paid or Owners will not grant discount.)
9) to pay for repairs of all damage, including drain stoppages, they or their
   guests have caused.
10) to pay for any windows broken in their dwelling while they live there.

Violation of any part of this agreement or nonpayment of rent when due shall
be cause for eviction under appropriate sections of the applicable code. The
prevailing party shall —— recover reasonable attorney's fees involved.

Tenants hereby acknowledge that they have read this agreement, understand
it, agree to it, and have been given a copy.

Owner *Leslie Landlady*   Tenant *Tina Oldtimer*

*By_____   Tenant_____
*Person authorized to accept legal service on Owners' behalf

Pg. 1 of 4

to be considered deposit. That it is not. It represents an all-inclusive charge to new tenants only for the services which they alone require.

I should mention here as an aside that landlords and tenants have done battle for years over move-in costs. Landlords have always maintained that new tenants should pay for the extra costs involved in a change of tenancy, and tenants have always maintained that these costs are nothing more than ordinary costs of doing business, and as such, they should be absorbed into their regular rent. Personally, I feel that tenants who stay put should not be subsidizing those who don't. Tenants who come and go are more expensive to deal with, and consequently, they should pay something more. In times past, some landlords have collected this "something more" in devious ways, most notably by withholding deposits, and tenants have screamed loudly enough so that laws to curb these devious ways have come into being.

My own way of charging new tenants something more to offset costs is to charge a higher first month's rent, just as tool rental yards charge one hourly rate for the first four hours and another hourly rate for the balance of a 24-hour period. I explain my reasons to my tenants at the outset so there won't be any confusion about refundability and so it cannot be considered the least bit devious. It works quite well for me.

You should know, however, that some California tenants have challenged the legality of charging a higher first month's rent, arguing through some pretty tortuous reasoning that the extra rent is in reality a deposit and therefore refundable. They have lost one court decision and they have won one. I am not deterred. In the absence of any clear-cut reason not to, I am continuing to use this technique. You will have to decide for yourself whether you want to do so as well. Either put a higher sum in the rental agreement's blank for first month's rent and explain why you're doing it, or put the regular month's rent in the blank. The decision is yours.

Next, explain that there is a deposit of one dollar per key which is refundable after the keys have been returned to you. The purpose of making this deposit separate from the others is to underscore the importance of returning the keys. The return of the keys represents the transfer of possession. Tell them that when they leave, you want those keys back so you can go ahead and prepare the rental dwelling for re-renting as soon as possible. Those keys entitle you to possession and relieve them from the obligation to pay more rent so long as they have given proper notice. Turning them back to you is important.

Tell them how much notice they should give you before they plan to vacate. Thirty days is most common, but I use fifteen because that's all the time I really need to prepare for a vacancy, and fifteen days is much more realistic for tenants. It has another important side benefit for you as well, one which is explained in step nine.

Ask for the names of all persons and pets who will be living in the dwelling, and write them into the agreement by name. Explain that nobody else may live there without your written permission. Tell them that their "guests" become tenants after two weeks (in some areas, laws may set the guest limit for a longer period, up to one month, and may allow any one person to be a guest twice in one year; check the applicable law for your area) and will have to be approved and added to the agreement at a slight increase in rent. Tell them what your pet policy is (see "Should You Accept Pets?" in Chapter 11). If it's a no-pets policy, tell them exactly what you mean by "no pets." Point out the words "even temporarily" in the contract. Tell them that those words mean what they say. You do not allow pet-sitting for even five minutes.

List briefly the appliances and furnishings which are included in the rent and indicate whether any of them are on "loan" (see "Should You Furnish the Major Kitchen

Appliances?" in Chapter 11). Explain that you and they together will make a complete on-site survey of the dwelling using the Condition & Inventory Checksheet as a record.

Explain which utilities you pay for and which parking space or garage the tenants may use, and indicate this information under "Remarks." Also, if the rental is still being occupied, stipulate here that the agreement is contingent upon the other tenants vacating the premises.

Review once more the other requirements in the agreement just as you did in Step 7. Remind them that they are responsible for any drain or sewer blockage which they cause themselves. Tell them that you don't use their drains and you aren't going to unclog the drains or pay to have them unclogged unless the tenants can prove to your satisfaction that the building was at fault. Remind them that they are responsible for any windows broken in their rental dwelling regardless of who breaks them. And remind them that they shouldn't expect you to provide lockout service 24 hours a day free of charge. Explain that the regulations will be strictly enforced and that after fair warning, you will evict them for any violations.

Read in Chapter 10 about the pros and cons of asking for attorney's fees, and decide whether to put the word "not" in the blank to indicate that you do not want the prevailing party to recover reasonable attorney's fees or whether to put a horizontal line in the blank to indicate the opposite.

If applicable, complete a Pet Agreement and a Waterbed Agreement at this time.

Finally, sign the Rental Agreement yourself and have the tenants sign, too.

9) REQUEST RENT OR A DEPOSIT.

Think back for a moment to Step Two, Prequalification, and remember two of the questions you asked then to determine the following: when the prospects would be ready to move in and whether they would have the money necessary to move in. These two considerations become very important now that you are preparing to conclude this initial phase of your rental relationship.

At this point you have a signed agreement in hand and you have taken the dwelling off the market, so as far as you are concerned, the place is now rented and the rent should begin the very next day, but if the tenants cannot move in for a week or so, you might consider splitting the rent with them for this short period as a goodwill gesture. For example, if you come to terms with them on Monday, March 10th, and they can't move in until Wednesday, March 19th, you might begin their rent from March 14th. Whatever you do, though, don't split rents for more than two weeks, don't do it if the tenants are going to be moving in immediately, and don't do it at all around the first of the

month. Above all, don't come to terms with prospective tenants, tie up the place for a week or two while they are preparing to move, and then begin the rent from the day they actually move in. That's not a goodwill gesture at all; that's a foolish gesture, for you suffer the full loss of rents due to circumstances which are beyond your control. It's their problem that they can't move in, not yours. You're ready for them to move in now. Share the loss, if you're inclined to, but don't assume it all yourself.

If you and the Richard Renters agree that their rent should begin March 14th, then their rental period for that first month is March 14th through April 13th. Since you probably want their rent to be due on the first (see Chapter 5 for the advisability of having rents due on the first) of the month, prorate their rent the second month, not the first. Request the full month's rent when they move in as a full commitment from them and a kind of insurance for you. On April 1st, collect rent to cover the period April 14th through April 30th. Make a point of telling them that the prorated rent for the balance of April is due on the first of April, not on the fourteenth, the same as it would be if they owed rent for the entire month. Keep them a full month ahead during this crucial early period of tenancy when you are just getting to know them and you don't know yet how dependable they are.

Be careful when you prorate rent. You can cheat yourself quite easily doing proration calculations. Consider the period of April 14th through April 30th, for example; is it 16 days or is it 17? It may appear to be 16 because the difference between 30 and 14 is 16, as every sixth grader knows, but it's not. It's not because this period includes both the 17th *and* the 30th, as well as the days in between. To calculate the number of days correctly, you have to subtract 14 from 30 and add one. If that doesn't make much sense to you, count the days on your fingers and toes, and you'll see that 17 is correct. Once you know the correct number, divide the monthly rent by the total number of days in the month and multiply that figure, which is the rent per day, by the number of days the tenants are going to be occupying the premises. Tell them what this amount is even before they move in so they will know how much to set aside to pay you on the first of the following month.

You should request as much advance money as you can get from new tenants. How much is enough? Whatever the market will bear and the laws will allow. Some local laws restrict advance money for unfurnished dwellings to the equivalent of three months' rent and for furnished dwellings to four months' rent. That should be sufficient; all told, that would work out to the first month's rent and combined deposits for security, cleaning, pets, waterbed, and keys equal to two months' rent.

Unless the laws in your area specify exactly what you may require tenants to pay in the categories of first month's rent, last month's rent, and combined deposits, do not require any last month's rent at all. Instead, add that amount to the deposits. Make the deposits much larger because you can use them to offset repairs, cleaning, or rent, whereas whatever sum is designated as last month's rent must be used for last month's rent and nothing else.

There is, of course, always the problem of tenants who want to use all or part of their deposits for last month's rent, and there's not much you can do about it except to require high deposits in the beginning and stress that these deposits are *not* to be considered last month's rent. So long as you hold a deposit significantly higher than their last month's rent, you won't have too much cause for concern if tenants do want to apply their deposits to the last month's rent.

Another solution to this problem is to require less than thirty days' notice to vacate. If you require only a fifteen-day notice, the tenants' rental period and the notice period do not coincide, and tenants are less likely to think about using their deposits for rent. In most cases, when they do decide to give notice, they will already have paid their last month's rent two weeks before and won't be tempted to use their deposits for rent.

You can't always get the equivalent of three months' rent before tenants move in, however, so you should have a minimum, too. The minimum amount to request before letting tenants move in under a month-to-month agreement, no matter which day of the month they do so, is the sum of the first month's rent, a security/cleaning deposit equal to one month's rent plus $50, and a one-dollar deposit for each key. Consider that the minimum. In those bygone days when anybody could buy a new tract house for no money down, I used to request less than this minimum in order to be competitive, but I wound up losing too much to unscrupulous tenants. That's Lesson Number 2116 at Hard Knocks College— *Require plenty of upfront money.* For some strange reason, the greater the deposit, the harder tenants try to get it back. Of course, the more advance money you require, the better you are protected, but the harder it is to find new tenants with a large advance sum. To help you decide how much to require, you might inquire into the prevailing practice in your rental area and then follow suit.

Few people keep much money lying around the house, so it would be understandable if Richard and Mary Renter did not have on hand all the money they need to move in. If they cannot pay you all the rent and deposits immediately, accept a minimum of a half month's rent. Do not hold the dwelling without receiving some payment at this time, and under no circumstances should you issue keys or let them move a "few things" in until every last cent has been paid. Too many landlords get burned by allowing tenants to move in some belongings without their having paid the full amount owed. Once they're in, the tenants pay not a cent more and have to be evicted. Don't get burned with this little ruse, and don't accept anything but greenbacks, gold, silver bars, money orders, or cashier's checks from brand-new tenants without first verifying it. Only when you know their money is at least as good as what the government prints should you issue keys.

Be sure to issue a receipt for whatever money they pay. If you don't have a receipt book with you, use the back of the Rental Agreement to write up an itemized receipt, making at least an original and one copy.

10) FILL OUT AND SIGN THE CONDITION AND INVENTORY CHECKSHEET.

"The palest ink is better than the most retentive memory," states an old Chinese proverb. Because you and your nice new tenants will surely differ in your recollections of the rental dwelling as it was when they moved in compared with its condition when they finally do move out, you should have a written record (if you want a photographic record, too, take some Polaroid pictures in the tenants' presence) of its condition and contents to protect both yourself and them.

To fill out the checksheet properly, show them the smoke alarm paragraph, take them to where the smoke alarm is located, demonstrate how it works, and get them to initial the paragraph to indicate that they know how to look after it. Then go through each room of the dwelling with the tenants, circle the applicable rooms, and fill in the "condition" and "item" columns with the appropriate abbreviations. Do not put anything in the "charges" columns. They're for you to fill in after the tenants have moved out. Now add up the tenants' security/cleaning, pet, waterbed, and key deposits and write down that sum as the total deposits. Date the checksheet, sign it yourself, and have the tenants sign it as well. Keep the original and one copy and give them one copy.

Then when the tenants have moved out and are demanding their deposits back, take your original and your copy and make a comparison inspection of the dwelling, marking the charges for broken shades, dirty carpets, etc. (see Chapter 7).

Only after you and your new tenants have signed the Rental Agreement, filled out the Condition & Inventory Checksheet, and settled all your accounts, should you issue keys

Condition & Inventory Checksheet

Dated _January 15, 1986_

Tenant Name _Richard & Mary Renter_   Address _456 Sweet St., Littletown_

Date Moved In _1/15/86_ Date Notice Given_____ Date Moved Out _____

Abbreviations:

Air Conditioner, A/C	Clean, Cl	Drapes, Drp	Hood, Hd	OK, OK	Table, Tbl
Bed, Bd	Cracked, Cr	Dryer, Dry	Just Painted, JP	Poor, P	Tile, Tl
Broken, Brk	Curtains, Ctn	Fair, F	Lamp, Lmp	Refrigerator, Ref	Venetian Blinds, VB
Carpet, Cpt	Dinette, Din	Good, G	Lightbulbs, LtB	Shades, Sh	Washer, Wsh
Chair, Ch	Dishwasher, Dish	Heater, Htr	Linoleum, Lino	Sofa, Sfa	Waxed, Wxt
Chest, Chst	Disposer, Disp	Hole, H	Nightstand, Ntst	Stove, Stv	Wood, Wd

Circle applicable rooms; enter abbreviations	Walls, Doors		Floors		Windows		Light Fixtures		Inventory: Appliances, Furniture		
	cond.	chgs.	cond.	chgs.	cond.	chgs.	cond.	chgs.	Item	cond.	chgs.
(Living Room)	ok		cl. cpt		Wind cr scrn ok cl drp		ok LtB g		⊘		
Dining											
(Kitchen)	ok		wxt lino		scrn ok Sh G		ok LtBg		stv, Hd Ref (on loan)	cl cl	
(Bath 1)	JP		wxt Tl		scrn ok Sh G		ok LtBg				
Bath 2											
(Bedroom 1)	ok		cl cpt		scrn ok cl drp		⊘		⊘		
Bedroom 2											
Bedroom 3											
Other											

Charges   ____   ____   ____   ____   ____

Total Itemized Charges _____

Other Charges Not Itemized
(Broken Locks, Dirty Garage, etc.
Explain on Backside) _____

Deduction for Improper Notice _____

Deduction for Missing Keys _____

Total Deductions _____

Total Deposits _$723_

Less Total Deductions _____

Deposit Refund or Amount Owed _____

RR
mr

☑ Tenants acknowledge that the smoke detector was tested in their presence and found to be in working order and that its operation was explained to them. Tenants agree to test the detector at least every other week and to report any problems to the Owner in writing. If the smoke detector is battery operated, Tenants agree to replace the battery as necessary (unless laws require otherwise).

Tenants hereby acknowledge that that they have read this Condition & Inventory Checksheet, agree that the condition and contents of the above-mentioned rental dwelling are without exception as represented herein, understand that they are liable for any damage done to this dwelling as outlined in their Lease or Rental Agreement, and have received a copy of this checksheet.

Owner _Lester Landlord_   Tenant _Richard Renter_

By_____   Tenant _Mary Renter_

pg 273

and change the mailbox label. Both of you are then completely committed to each other, having created that special landlord-tenant relationship.

Even after you have completed all ten steps with Richard Renter and have created that special relationship, you and he will still be conjuring up strange mental images of each other, but you will have done all you can do to assure yourself of a good tenant. Give him a chance to prove that he is what he seems to be, at the same time you're proving to him that you are what you seem to be.

REJECTING APPLICANTS

Rejecting those applicants you believe would be poor tenants for one reason or another is a corollary to this whole process of getting good tenants. Rejection is hard for some people to take, and it is still harder for others to give. Some landlords rent to the first person who expresses an interest in renting their place because they just can't say "no." That kind of timidity you can ill afford. You have to get used to saying "no" in this business every so often, and one of the most important times you'll ever say it is when you refuse to rent to an applicant.

The trick is to say "no" in a kindly way. If you have more than one applicant for a vacancy and you have decided to rent to the one you consider the best, saying "no" is relatively easy, for you are merely informing the unsuccessful applicants that you have rented the place to somebody else. In that case, you might call them and say something like this, "Hello, Gulley Jimson, I just wanted to let you know that somebody else rented the house on Sixth Street that you were interested in. We had four applications for it, and I sure do wish we'd had four places to rent because all four applicants would have made fine tenants, but unfortunately we had only the one vacancy and we could accommodate only one tenant. We'll certainly keep your application on file in case something else comes up, and we'd like to wish you good luck in finding something else even more suited to your needs." This kind of rejection sounds sympathetic enough to be acceptable to practically anybody. It's inoffensive and it's entirely plausible. It works well.

If your dwelling has not been rented, however, such a rejection would be both foolish and risky. Never say a place has been rented unless it actually has been. Never say it has been rented in order to dissuade a persistent inquirer or anyone else, for that matter. Such a simple-minded ploy will only cause you trouble. Even when you are not actually discriminating against someone illegally, this falsehood, if discovered, could be construed to be a sign of blatant discrimination, and it could be all the evidence needed by those who thrive on suing unsuspecting landlords and landladies for discrimination.

Be more cautious than that. Even when you have yet to find a suitable tenant and you are being pestered for acceptance by undesirable applicants, don't ever resort to saying the place has been rented just to get them off your back. Stall if need be. Say that you turned the applications over to a tenant-checking service and that they are a little slow at times in notifying you of the results. It's not the best approach, but it will suffice for a few days while you pray for good acceptable applicants to come along so you can rent to them and then use the kindly rejection approach on the others.

Sometimes the best approach, though, is one which is honest and direct. It may not appear to be kindly on the surface, but it is, because it deflates the applicants' high hopes for your rental so they can realistically assess their prospects and won't waste any more time waiting to hear from you. Tell the applicants by phone, if possible, that you're sorry they just don't fit your tenant guidelines and that they should begin looking further for housing. If you want to, give them the precise reason for the rejection (do not reveal the details of a negative credit report; simply give them the name of the credit reporting agency), and be as polite as you can be while they argue their case, recount their sad story, bang the receiver in your ear, or string together a few profanities. Don't budge from your decision, no matter what they do or say. You know you don't want them to be your tenants. Let them rent from someone else who has different standards.

Endure the few unpleasantries right now that your rejection might cause, and you won't have to cope with them later as unsuitable tenants.

SOME LAST WORDS

Throughout this whole selection process, be as conscientious and organized as a first-grade teacher with 31 fidgety little charges to look after, and you will find that your "luck" in getting good tenants will improve as if by magic.

RENTS

"What do you think your landlady does with the rent money you pay her?"

"Oh, I suppose she buys fancy clothes, makeup, and stuff, and she goes on trips every summer, love-boat trips, I think someone told me. The rest of it she probably sews inside her mattress or puts in the bank. She's a rich lady to own this building. That's for sure!"

Many tenants believe that you pocket either their entire rent payment or a substantial portion of it. They cannot understand what else you might do with it, for they are mostly oblivious of loan payments, property tax bills, garbage bills, utility bills, advertising bills, maintenance bills, repair bills, vacancy losses, replacement reserves, and insurance bills, not to mention management costs (your time included). They regard rent as a kind of legal extortion or a tax levied by the rich directly on the poor, and thus, some of them feel justified in depriving you of the rent money or, if that's not possible, in depriving you of the prerogative to charge more rent to meet your increasing expenses (rent control).

Short of turning over the property completely to your tenants and letting them try to pay all the bills themselves out of what rent they are able to collect, you may find that convincing them that their rent money pays bills directly related to their tenancy is just as hard as convincing them that their daily lottery ticket is a sucker's bet. Old, old notions about landlords and landladies and rents are deep-rooted indeed.

Try educating your tenants little by little whenever you have the opportunity, though. Sometime when you're out collecting the rent, ask them what they think the rent money goes for, and be prepared for some very astonishing answers. Tenants haven't a clue what you do with their rent money. Of course, you might not know yourself exactly what percentage of a $450 rent check goes to pay utilities, what to insurance, and so on, and you should certainly calculate those percentages (use expenses for the previous tax year and include as an expense at least 5% of the income to represent your own time contribution for overall offsite property management alone) before you ever broach the subject to your tenants. (On an average, the percentages are as follows for multiple-family dwellings: insurance, maintenance, repairs, and utilities, 25%; taxes, 25%; interest, 35%; debt retirement, 2%; vacancy factor, 5%; overall property management, 5%; and cash flow, 3%.) Once you have calculated your own percentages, you may be quite surprised by how little of their rent you do pocket (positive cash flow) or, more likely, by how much you have to contribute (negative cash flow) to keep a roof over your tenants' heads. Like any teacher preparing a class lesson, you may learn much more about rents while preparing to teach your tenants than you ever knew before.

Don't be too hopeful that your students will learn their lessons, however, for you have some very reluctant learners. Neither these informal discussions nor formal disclosures with copious explanations will enlighten your tenants about their rent so thoroughly that they will volunteer to pay their "fair share" of the expenses, but at least through such attempts, you *might* find them a *little* more understanding about rent collection, rent raises, and rent control, all subjects of this chapter.

COLLECTING RENTS

You may have your tenants trained to pay you their rent two weeks before it's due. If so, skip this section and the next. Everyone else, read on.

Collecting rents on time requires persistence, consistency, and firmness. You can't expect tenants to pay their rent promptly if you aren't trying to collect it from them, or if they never know whether you will be coming on the third or the tenth of the month to collect, or if you give them the impression that you're an old softy. Be persistent. You earn that rent money, and you shouldn't be the least bit timid about collecting it. Keep after those tenants who haven't paid. Be consistent. Rent collecting is so important to landlording that you must learn to subordinate everything else when rents are due so you can pursue rent collection in the same way month after month, year after year. Be firm. Convince your tenants that their rent money is your top priority.

Remember that paying rent is just as unsatisfying to tenants as paying taxes is to you. Neither rent nor taxes pay for anything that the payer didn't already have before, or so it would seem. Few would pay if they didn't believe that they would be penalized somehow. You have to establish yourself, therefore, from the very beginning as a threat, like the I.R.S., a landlord or landlady who expects the rent to be paid promptly, no matter what. When it isn't, you become menacing, a force to contend with.

All too frequently it is easier not to pay the landlord or landlady than it is not to pay the bookie, the dentist, the grocer, the utility company, the haberdasher, the finance company, the barber, the gasoline company, the insurance company, or even the news carrier. Who then gets paid last, if at all? You, that's who! Why? You're not firm enough when you should be. Be like the family dog that is faithful and loving except when anyone tries to take away his food. Then he growls and bites. There's no reason you can't be considerate to your tenants either, except where rents are concerned. Then you have to be menacing. After all, you and your rental properties live on rent money just as dogs live on Alpo.

Make it more difficult for your tenants not to pay you than for them not to pay anyone else. Explain precisely what your policy is regarding rent collection. Tell them before you ever rent to them that your rent is due on the first, it is late on the fifth, and if it's not paid by the fifth, you'll give them just three days to pack up and leave. Talk tough. Be tough when you collect rents. You won't be understood otherwise.

Besides persistence, consistency, and firmness, collecting rents on time requires a reasonable, lucid, and strict rent collection policy more than anything else, a policy which should include a mutually agreed upon collection procedure, a specified form of payment, set due and late dates, and a definite penalty for late payment.

• COLLECTION PROCEDURES—Which collection procedure you use will depend upon what kind of tenants you have, where you live in relation to the units, how many units you have, how much you want to be involved, and whether you have an on-site manager. Some landlords prefer to have the tenants visit them or the manager to pay the rent in person, some collect it by mail, some actually go themselves to their tenants' dwellings to collect rents, and some annoint a rent collector. There are merits to each procedure.

Having the tenants come to you or to your manager, if either of you lives close by, is surely the most common collection procedure. It's personalized and it's pretty efficient, but it may make you feel confined to one place while you wait for tenants to come to you. To eliminate this confining feeling, consider making a mail slot available where they can put their checks when you're not around. Also, consider combining this procedure with the others.

Collecting the rent by mail is certainly the easiest and most efficient for you. To make it easy for your tenants as well, you might consider sending them a self-addressed, stamped envelope on the 15th of each month and asking them to send you by return mail a check postdated on the first for that next month's rent. Then, when the first rolls around, you will already have their check in hand, and neither you nor your tenants need worry about whether it will reach you on time. What's more, you don't have to waste time going to the tenants' dwelling or waiting around for the tenant to come to you. You don't have to listen to the latest gossip about the neighbors, and you don't have to listen to the inevitable complaints. It's quick and it's easy, but it's also impersonal, and it separates you from your source of income to the point where you may lose touch and eventually control. If you keep in touch with your tenants at other times and in other ways, by all means, have your tenants mail their rent to you, but if rent collection day is the only chance you have all month to see your property, then maybe you'd better collect the rent on the spot. You might see something that should be remedied, and you might see it while it still can be remedied easily.

Despite some very real disadvantages to the third procedure, its inefficiency and its placing of the burden for the transaction on you, there are advantages to collecting rents on the tenant's doorstep or inside the tenant's dwelling itself. It's as personalized as possible. It shows that you care enough to take the time to look after your property. It shows that rent collection is important to you. It lets you know straightaway whether a tenant will be late and, if so, what the tenant's excuse for late payment is, and it allows you more freedom of movement because you don't have to wait around for anybody to call on you.

There's one more rent collection procedure you might think about trying if you happen to be an absentee owner with no manager on the premises of a reasonably small multiple-family building. It involves selecting the oldest tenants you have in every building and giving them, say, $2.50 for every rent they collect including their own. Older tenants like the responsibility involved and they appreciate the opportunity to earn a little extra income. They're also more conscientious in their rounds than you would ever be. The other tenants are less likely to give the usual excuses to one of their neighbors, especially an elderly one. You save yourself from having to make trips over to the property and having to spend time dealing with many people separately. At $2.50

apiece, the collection at a six-plex would cost you only $15 a month, money well spent. Be sure that you have workers' compensation insurance if you try this procedure. An elderly tenant who breaks a hip while collecting rents for you would qualify for compensation.

No matter which collection procedure you use, you should be absolutely certain that your tenants understand how you expect to collect their rent. You don't want them to be waiting around for you to knock on their door to collect it when you're expecting them to send you a check.

• PAYMENT, RECEIPTS—Since you want to be certain that your rents will reach the bank intact, stipulate in your rental agreement that all rents are to be paid by check or money order. If you don't, you could be carrying large sums of cash around with you at rent collection time and be a tempting mark for a mugger. (See "The Little Old Rubber Stamp Trick" in Chapter 16 for another safety precaution.)

And since you want to keep good income records which brook no argument, take the precaution of receipting all rents in duplicate if you collect the rents yourself or in triplicate if you have someone else collect them (one copy for the tenants, one for the rent collector, and one for you). The negligible expense and trouble involved in writing receipts for every rent collection, even for those paid by check or money order, have paid off for me more than once. Neither you nor your tenants should have to rely on your memories to verify dates, amounts paid, and rental periods. Put it in writing.

Whoops, I almost forgot. There is one more form of rent payment I ought to mention here. It's a natural extension of our society's penchant for charging everything now and paying for it later. Charge rents? You heard right. Instead of paying you by check or money order or in cash, your tenants could charge their rents on their Visa or MasterCard. While it does have a certain few drawbacks, it can work reasonably well.

The main drawbacks, as far as you are concerned, involve getting yourself established as a credit card merchant and being charged a fee for accepting payment by credit card. You didn't think Visa and MasterCard offered this service for nothing, did you? They don't. They exact a percentage of every dollar charged. Out of $400 in rent charged to a tenant's card, they would commonly take 3% or $12. You would net $388. To ensure that you would get the same amount of rent no matter how it's paid, you could do what some merchants do, give tenants a discount for paying by cash, check, or money order similar to the discount you give for paying on time. Juggle the numbers so they come out right.

The incentive for you here is not the same as it is for a regular merchant, to entice the customer into buying more. No, the reason you might want to consider accepting bank cards is so you would know the rent would be prompt. The only circumstance which would prevent you from getting paid would be where a tenant has exceeded the card's credit limit. You could find that out easily enough, of course, by calling the bank card company. They know and they tell, too.

The main advantage for tenants in paying their rent by bank card is that they can postpone payment until later. They're able to use their own money longer.

• DUE DATE, LATE DATE—You may have noticed I mentioned before that rent is due on the first. My rents all are. Why the first? There are several good reasons. Rents traditionally are due on the first. Tenants are in the habit of paying on the first. They associate the first of the month with rent payments, and consequently they are more likely to remember to pay without having to be prompted. Busy as you are, you remember, too, that rents are due on the first and late on the fifth. You can then concentrate all your energy on those tenants who haven't paid by the fifth. You can identify and handle the delinquencies more readily if the rents are all due at the same time and late at the same time.

Once I bought a 41-unit residential income property which had rents due all throughout the month. This interminable series of rent due dates confused the tenants as much as it did the manager and me. So we changed all the due dates to the first. Collections immediately became easier, and delinquencies declined. The tenants remembered to pay, and we remembered to collect.

Just as important as a realistic due date is a realistic late date. This is the day when rents are considered delinquent and penalties are assessed. I give my tenants a four-day grace period, considering their rent late only if it's paid on the fifth or thereafter. Why? There are two good reasons, one legal and one practical.

Some places around the country have a law which specifically requires that the rent due date be a banking day, that is, a weekday when the banks are open. According to the thinking behind the law, tenants must have had an opportunity to visit their bank to cash a check, buy a money order, or withdraw funds to pay the rent. If the rent due date falls on a Saturday, Sunday, or holiday, days when they cannot get to the bank, you may not consider the rent late until the day following the next available banking day. If the rent due date falls on the Saturday of a three-day weekend, for example, the rent may be paid on the following Tuesday without penalty, and it is not considered late until Wednesday. Now if that Saturday were the first, and the first were your normal rent due date, that Tuesday would be the fourth of the month. Four days would be the longest possible legal

period of time that tenants would ever have in which to pay their rent without incurring a penalty. In my opinion, there's some common sense behind this law. Tenants aren't known for their adherence to the Boy Scout motto. So in order to be entirely consistent, I use this same grace period throughout the year. There are no exceptions.

In practice, this four-day grace period works well. You no longer have to listen to those hackneyed excuses tenants have for not having paid their rent on or before the first. You know and they know that if the rent hasn't been paid by the fourth, there's either a serious excuse or there's a conscious attempt to avoid paying altogether. You save innumerable calls and trips on the second or third or fourth of the month to inquire after the rent, and you can feel entirely justified collecting more from a tenant who's missed the due date by at least four days.

While I was still requiring tenants to pay on or before the first of the month, I would feel guilty about charging a late paying tenant $20 more if that tenant were only a day or two late. Sometimes I'd just tell the tenant to forget it, or I'd allow some tenants to get away without paying the additional sum and not say anything about it because I knew that collecting it from them would be well nigh impossible anyway. Such inconsistency in my collections made the whole process too subjective, too open to negotiation, and it made me uneasy. On the one hand, I wanted to be reasonable, and on the other hand, I wanted to be tough and collect rents promptly when due. My first-of-the-month due date became as well enforced as the 55-mile-an-hour speed limit. So I changed my definition of lateness and adopted a policy that the tenants and I could live with. It sure does work!

• RENT DISCOUNT—To encourage prompt payment, I use a discounted rent policy. My gross rents are set $20 higher than the advertised rent. If tenants pay on or before the third day following the due date, that is, by the fourth of the month, they may take a $20 discount from the gross rent. In other words, they pay the net advertised rent. This method is legally defensible and it works.

Late fees, which you assess tenants if they pay their rent after a certain date, work almost as well to encourage prompt payment as the discounted rent policy, but some fees of even $15 have been challenged as excessive in the courts, and some judges have ruled that rent late charges must not exceed the damages you sustain when tenants pay late. This is a gray area, subject to too much interpretation. Since the discount for paying on time represents a reduction in rent rather than an addition to it, you may deduct whatever you please if tenants pay on time without having to prove what your damages are. The approach you take makes the difference.

The one other late fee you may find in some agreements stipulates that tenants are to pay so much a day for each day of delinquency. Although penalizing late payers more and more for each day they are late sounds like a good idea, it may work against you, for at least one judge has held that so long as tenants have agreed to pay the accumulating penalty, they must be allowed to retain possession even though they are in arrears. I don't claim to understand such convoluted legal thinking, but I prefer to avoid the difficulties it could cause. Instead of chalking up increasing penalties against nonpaying tenants, penalties which you have a slim chance of collecting anyway, you might as well use one penalty tied to one late date, and beyond that, you should use the various means described in Chapter 8 to get nonpayers to move.

• LATE RENTS—Collecting rents requires an effective, pragmatic rental policy with teeth in it and someone to carry it out who is both firm and quick. You are in business and you should mean business when you are collecting rents.

Always treat late rents with gravity, but also treat late payers with understanding, depending upon your past experience with them as tenants. Sometimes the unexpected will cause even the most diligent of tenants to pay a few days late, and they will advise you voluntarily in advance just why they expect to be late and when they will have the money to pay. Such tenants deserve your patience while they cope with a calamity or a disruption in their income, and you would do well to accommodate them if you believe their explanation for the delay and if you believe the rent will be forthcoming in a couple of weeks.

If, however, by the third day after the rent due date, normally the fourth of the month, the tenants have neither paid you their rent nor have advised you that the rent will be delayed for some good reason or another, you should make plans to visit them the very next day to deliver a Notice to Pay Rent or Quit. Listen to their explanation sympathetically; talk with the about rental assistance programs available, if appropriate; and then have them make a definite commitment to pay on or before a certain date, not over two weeks hence for the best of tenants and within just a few days for those doubtful ones. Tell them that you will sue for eviction if they do not pay by the promised date.

NOTICE
to Pay Rent or Quit

TO __CHESTER & CATHY CAREFREE_____, TENANT IN POSSESSION:

You are hereby notified that the rent is now due and payable on the premises now held and occupied by you, being those premises situated in the
City of __LITTLETOWN_____, County of __SADDLEBACK_____,
State of __CALIFORNIA_____, commonly known as
__460 SWEET ST._____

Your account is delinquent in the amount of $___506°°___, being the rent for the period from __MARCH 1__ to __APRIL 1, 1985__.

You are hereby required to pay said rent in full within __3__ days or to remove from and deliver up possession of the above-mentioned premises, or legal proceedings will be instituted against you to recover possession of said premises, to declare the forfeiture of the Lease or Rental Agreement under which you occupy said premises and to recover rents and damages, together with court costs and attorney's fees, according to the terms of your Lease or Rental Agreement.

Dated this __5TH__ day of __MARCH__, 19__85__.

Lester Landlord
Owner/Manager

PROOF OF SERVICE

I, the undersigned, being at least 18 years of age, declare under penalty of perjury that I served the Notice to Pay Rent or Quit, of which this is a true copy, on the above-mentioned Tenant in Possession in the manner(s) indicated below:

☑ On __MARCH 5__, 19__85__, I handed the Notice to the tenant.
☐ I handed the Notice to a person of suitable age and discretion at the tenant's residence/business on _____, 19_____.
☐ I posted the Notice in a conspicuous place at the tenant's residence on _____, 19_____.
☐ I sent by certified mail a true copy of the Notice to the tenant at his place of residence on _____, 19_____.

Executed on __MARCH 5__, 19__85__, at __LITTLETOWN, CA__.

Lester Landlord

Have the notice already filled out so you can hand it to them before you leave and tell them, "We give everybody one of these notices if the rent isn't paid by the fifth, regardless of who it is. We treat everyone the same way."

Giving them the notice on the fifth strengthens your case should you have to go to court later because you would have waited a reasonable period before giving the notice and you would have waited longer than required before filing the court papers. You would not appear hasty to the court, but more importantly, you would already have begun your court case. If you fail to give the tenants a notice on the fifth, and they don't pay on the appointed day, you'll have to deliver the notice then, and you'll have to wait the required number of days following service of the notice before you can file your papers with the court. That wastes precious days; whereas, if you deliver the notice on the fifth and the tenants don't pay on the appointed day, you can go right ahead if you wish and file your court papers that very same day because you have already served the notice and you should already have waited the required number of days.

What's that? Did I hear you say that you'd rather not give your delinquent tenants a Notice to Pay Rent or Quit the very first time you go after them about their late rent? Okay. That's somewhat understandable. Although a whack on the side of the head in the form of an "official" notice, along with the threat of a full-scale eviction, may be the only thing sufficient to motivate some tenants to pay, others may be motivated better through a tap on their funny bone in the form of a light-hearted rent reminder.

Displayed here are two of the twelve reminders in the Forms section, all different, and all designed to remind tenants in a half-humorous, half-serious way that their rent hasn't been paid yet and that you are going to do something about it unless they pay up.

Use these reminders sparingly, and vary them. Because each particular one loses its impact if used a second time, don't give the same one twice to the same tenants. Better tenants shouldn't need reminding that often anyway. There are plenty here to last a tenancy's lifetime.

Remember that these reminders do not take the place of Notices to Pay Rent or Quit as far as legal eviction proceedings go. They're a human-to-human approach intended to keep your relationship with your tenants from becoming too adversarial. They're a friendly nudge. That's all.

The reminders shown on these text pages are much reduced versions of the ones given in the back of the book. Those are sized to accommodate copying on either half or full-sized sheets of paper. Select the one you want, copy it, insert the appropriate names, deliver it, and expect to get your rent with a smile.

Sometimes your tenants won't have all that they owe you, so they will offer to pay you part of the rent and promise to pay the balance before the month is out. If they do, hesitate a little just to be dramatic, and then take the money. Tell them you prefer not to accept part of the rent but that you will do it this time under the circumstances, provided they understand that they must pay the balance within a specified time frame. Much as I dislike the extra bother involved in collecting partial rent, I would much rather get some of the rent money than risk getting none at all.

Whenever you accept partial rent, give the tenants a receipt which does not cover a specific rental period. The second receipt you write, the one for the balance, should include the rental period covered by both payments. Trying to calculate exactly how many days in a 31-day month are covered by 56% of the rent money is too confusing. Don't bother.

Writing receipts for past-due rents can be every bit as confusing as writing them for partial rents. Just remember that you should never write a receipt for a current rental period if the tenant is in arrears for an earlier period. All rent monies paid should apply to the earlier period first. Here's why.

Suppose some tenants are one month behind in their rent and you sue them for nonpayment. Suppose also that on July first they pay June's rent, but you give them a receipt covering the month of July. In court the tenants produce your receipt for the current month of July and tell the judge they lost the receipt for June. The judge has to assume that they are telling the truth because you can't prove conclusively that they didn't pay for June. Your not having a copy of their June rent receipt doesn't prove anything. It's only what you have with you that counts. How can you prove that you don't have something? How can you prove that their June rent receipt never existed? And your stating under oath that they didn't pay for June doesn't prove anything either. It's your word against theirs. So the judge has to base his decision on the existence of their July rent receipt. It suddenly becomes important because it does prove that they paid for July, and if they paid for July, then they probably did pay for June. They win. You lose one month's rent.

Losing one month's rent can be very important, can't it? So I repeat—*Never write a rent receipt for a current rental period if the tenant is in arrears for an earlier period.*

When tenants do get behind on their rent, the chances are good that they're behind on their other bills as well, and they'll be shaping up a list of payment priorities mentally or on paper. See that yours is on top. Pressure them. Become a physical and psychological presence in their lives.

Credit experts rank most people's priorities for paying their bills in descending order as follows—

1) Rent/mortgage	7) Heating fuel
2) Utilities	8) Cleaning/laundry
3) Telephone	9) Schools
4) Car payments	10) Doctors
5) Insurance	11) Dentists
6) Taxes	12) Club dues

Surprising, isn't it? You're right up there on the top of most people's bill priority list. Even so, remember that landlords and landladies are fair game to some people. They think there's nothing wrong with trying to beat you out of your rent money. They think they can string you along with one promise after another and that you'll just be so beguiled by their ruses that you will neither collect rent from them nor evict them for a long time to come.

What do you wish to allow your tenants to get away with? It's up to you. I have seen a middleaged schoolmarm, 4 feet 10 inches tall and all of 90 pounds, keep supposedly incorrigible, hyperactive high school boys under her complete control. Another teacher, marveling at the situation, asked one of the boys why he never misbehaved in Miss Cheever's class. The boy replied, "Oh, she doesn't allow it." You can allow your tenants to pay late if you want to, but you'll be the one who pays in the long run. Don't allow it!

If tenants don't have one month's rent when it's due, they're surely not going to have two months' rent in thirty days. The longer they stay without paying, the harder it is for them to pay and the less desire they have to pay. Staying without paying becomes easier and easier. Why should they pay for time they have already spent under your roof? By allowing them to stay rent free, you are only postponing the inevitable.

Remember, too, that tenants who aren't paying their rent are actually stealing from you. They might as well be picking your pocket or snatching your purse, but the law doesn't quite see it that way. The law gives you no immediate recourse. You can't call the cops for help. You have to rely on your own self to get them to pay up or move out, and if you do something drastic, you're the one who'll be in trouble just like a homeowner who harms a burglar with a booby trap. Only after you have resorted to a legal eviction procedure can you get the law behind you to settle the matter.

In all my experience as a landlord, I have never been pleased with myself when I have allowed any tenant to stay more than fifteen days beyond a missed rent due date. Dealing with them has always cost me extra money, extra time, or both. Even so-called good risks, teachers, preachers, police officers, apartment managers (yes, even them), and college student body presidents, have moved out owing me money when I have permitted them to get more than fifteen days behind. I have collected lots of promises and a sheaf of letters. In some cases I did manage to collect the past-due rent in full, but it always required more of my time, and I had to become a bill collector to do it.

Bill collectors generally charge 50% of whatever they are able to collect. They know how much time and effort such work requires. You aren't charging enough rent to include bill collecting among your many services, and you really do become a bill collector when you have to scurry about collecting late rents. Your rents should be paid promptly and voluntarily. Each collection shouldn't require more than ten minutes' worth of your time per month. That's all. That's plenty.

Collecting your rents swiftly and doggedly on a scheduled basis will prevent evictions for nonpayment of rent more than anything else. Your tenants will know full well what to expect of you. They may test you once, but they won't do it again. It's too costly. If they have to, they will borrow the money from someone else to pay their rent rather than risk your wrath and risk being evicted.

LOWERING RENTS

"Are you crazy? Lowering rents is un-American! It's communistic! It's ludicrous and idiotic! Why, everybody knows that rents are supposed to go up, not down! Did the soft drink bottlers raise their prices when sugar skyrocketed? You bet your sweet closet auger they did. Did they lower their prices when sugar costs plummeted? Not on your paint-speckled spectacles they didn't. Well, I won't lower my rents either! I'd leave my places vacant before I'd ever lower my rents."

This subject tends to animate some landlords and landladies, those who think they have some sacred duty to society to raise rents whenever they can. Whether we like it or not, this is a competitive business. When somebody builds a new housing tract close to where your vacant rental house is, and investors snap them up and start renting them out for a hundred dollars less than what you have been renting your place for, you've got a problem. Either you lower your rent accordingly, or you become accustomed to having a vacancy on your hands. The same holds true when the overbuilding of apartment houses increases the vacancy factor in an area.

Some landlords and landladies cope with an areawide high-vacancy situation by reducing the move-in costs, giving away premiums like television sets and microwave ovens, or offering a month's free rent, all with the express purpose of getting the occupancy rate up, as if occupancy is the name of the game. The one thing they'd never consider is lowering the rents.

Let's stop to consider the costs and implications of these various incentives, though, and compare them with lower rents. Let's say that a standard 2-bedroom unfurnished apartment in our Sampletown is going for $350, and let's say, too, that each one of the three incentives being tried is reasonably successful in attracting tenants.

Reducing the move-in costs to, say, one month's rent, the first of our incentives, is certain to attract the kind of tenants who don't have savings, and you have to imagine that such people are likely to be irresponsible. At the end of one month's residency there, they have possession of your $35,000 apartment unit, and you have nothing of theirs, no prepaid rent, no security deposit, and no cleaning deposit, nothing to insure that they will live up to their obligations to you. If they choose to stay there until evicted and tear the place apart, which they might conceivably do, you're going to lose a bundle. You may even wind up buying them out with their original $350, and still you'd have a devastated apartment on your hands. This incentive is too risky for me. It's strictly for high rollers. What can you possibly hope to gain by filling a building with tenants who haven't complied with the time-honored requirement made of tenants, that they put up a deposit in case there's a problem later? Not getting a deposit is an invitation to trouble, big trouble, for it puts you at the tenants' mercy. They can leave their rental in any condition they want to and at any time they want to, and there wouldn't be a thing you could do about it. The cost to you of this incentive is an unknown, too. My advice is this—*Do not reduce your move-in costs in order to attract tenants.*

How about the second alternative which some owners seem to love, the free TV or microwave oven? This one may work, but it's going to cost you cash dollars up front, don't forget. Nobody who moves in to get a free television set is going to wait a day, let alone a year, for the payoff, and what do you do when the tenants give notice after three months that they're leaving? Ask for the merchandise back? What do you do when they decide to move at the end of a year so they can get a new bedroom set offered as a move-in premium at another apartment complex? My advice on offering premiums in order to attract tenants is this—*Don't.*

How about offering a month's free rent as an incentive? After all, everybody likes something for nothing. Free rent should attract tenants the way free love attracts shore-leave sailors. Yes indeedy, but the trouble is that neither the tenants nor the sailors tend to stay around very long. And good long-term tenants are the real name of the game in rental housing, aren't they? Then there's always the question about which month should be free. Should it be the first? the sixth? the twelfth? And again, what do you do when tenants move out immediately after they get their free month? Should those who stay longer than twelve months get an extra month's rent free? They'll want it, you know. Another problem with free rent is that it interferes with the smooth flow of your income. You could have some months with no income at all or at least much less than normal. My advice on free rent is this—*Don't open the store every Monday and give away the product.*

All right, how about lowering the rent? Lowering your rent $25 below everybody else's will bring you all the tenants you can handle, and it will cost you $25 per month; that's $300 spread out evenly over a year's time, *but* it will likely gain you tenants who will still be around after a year, at which time you would be reassessing Sampletown's vacancy situation and resetting the rent. My advice on lowering rents is this—*If you feel you have to do something in order to be competitive and keep your occupancy rate up, then, by all means, lower your rents. It can actually increase your income.*

If lowering rents makes sense as a marketing ploy, you have to wonder why there's so much resistance to it. The answer isn't hard to find. Owners are reluctant to lower their rents because they think that they're devaluing their property. Rents affect the value of a multiple-family rental property more directly than any other factor. If an owner were going to put the property up for sale, a buyer would want to know how much rent he could expect the property to produce. A seven-times-gross property would be worth $2100 less if the rent on only one unit were reduced $25 per month. A ten-times-gross property would be worth $3000 less. So most owners in high vacancy areas prefer to concede anything but rent. They think of the cost of lowered rent in terms of property devaluation rather than annual rent loss. They'd much rather give away a $300 TV set or a month's rent to preserve the illusion that the property is worth thousands more. What they're really doing, though, is setting up an unsuspecting buyer for a sting. They're thinking in terms of bailing out of the investment for the most they can possibly get rather than holding onto it until the vacancy situation changes. Such people aren't going to take my advice on lowering rents. That I know. They're flim-flammers who're always chasing the fast buck, but their strategy doesn't make any sense for an investor who's content to wait out an adversity. If you're that kind of person, a tortoise of a landlord or landlady, you'll profit more from lowering your rents than you will by giveaways. Try it if you have to and see.

SETTING RENTS

Because rents used to be tied fairly closely to property values, setting rents was simple. The rule of thumb for an unfurnished house or duplex was that the monthly rent should equal one percent of its fair market value. A $25,000 house, for example, would rent for $250 a month, and the tenant would pay for all the utilities and tend to the minor repairs. For multiple-family dwellings larger than duplexes, the rule or thumb was that the monthly aggregate of rents would approximate 1.2% of the value of the property, a figure which is the reverse of the common yardstick that the value of multiple units should equal seven times their annual gross rents. Each apartment in a $40,000 fourplex, then, would normally have rented for $120 per month.

Those old rules of thumb, which took into account a decent cash flow return on the investment, simply do not apply now as much as they once did, for property values have outstripped rents significantly in most areas. Today, an $80,000 house may rent for any sum of money, from $400 to $800, from one-half of one percent of the property value to a full one percent, and a multiple-family dwelling may rent for as little as one-half of one percent to as much as 1.4% of its value. In this business, your costs bear no relationship to the prices you can charge. This is strictly a supply-and-demand business. You cannot simply add up what you are paying for utilities, maintenance, financing, bookkeeping, taxes, and management, and then add a percentage for your profit and say that you're going to rent out your property for that sum of money. It would be nice to be guaranteed a profit, but it can't be done. Rents no longer guarantee owners a cash flow return, and setting them is no longer a simple calculation using percentages and multipliers.

Since the residential real estate market, which is measured by property values, and the rental housing market, which is measured by rents, have diverged appreciably over the past fifteen years so that they no longer are bound together by time-honored rules of thumb for setting rents, you must look to the rental housing market itself when you set rents today. In other words, with rents no longer contingent upon the value of your investment or upon your costs for maintaining the property, you have to familiarize yourself with what people are willing to pay for a place to live like the one you have available for rent, and then charge accordingly. You can't expect to get $800 a month for your $80,000 house if other owners are renting similar houses for $500, and some of those are going begging.

Setting rents nowadays involves learning about the rents being asked for vacant dwellings similar to yours in location, amenities, and upkeep, for those vacant dwellings are your competition. You needn't concern yourself with the rents being charged for occupied dwellings. Those places are no longer available to the public. They are currently off the market and can't be rented by applicants at any price. Only when they come back on the market do they become your competition. That's when supply-and-demand factors come into play.

Whenever I think about how supply and demand affects rents, I think about the housewife who goes to the meat market to ask the butcher for a 5-pound, cross-rib roast. He shows her a beautiful one, well-marbled and well-trimmed, and as he puts it up on his scale, he says, "Let's see, at $2.79 a pound, that'll be $13.95." She looks at him wide-eyed and exclaims, "$2.79 a pound! Mr. Crump down the street sells me his cross-rib roasts, which are just as nice as this one, for $1.99 a pound." So the butcher asks, "Then why don't you go down the street and buy one from Mr. Crump?" And she replies, "I'd like to, but he doesn't have any!"

Prospective tenants can only compete with each other to rent unoccupied rental dwellings. And likewise, you are competing only with other landlords and landladies who have places available for rent. Those rents are the ones which are important to you now.

To find out what your competition's rents are, do a market survey of sorts. Check newspaper advertising, ask people at your rental property owners' association, ask other owners you know, and inspect other vacant properties yourself in the area. If you want to go further, check the classified ads for rental property similar to yours in a newspaper which is several weeks old. Call about a number of them and ask if the dwellings are still for rent. If they are, you know the rents are too high. If they have been rented, the rents are either too low or about right. When you have done all that, you will know what constitutes a competitive rent for your dwelling, and you won't have to wonder after it is rented whether you could have charged more.

Remember that when you set any rent, you are virtually fixing it at one level for a 12-month period, so do treat this process with the seriousness it deserves. Don't be afraid to set your rent high, because anyone who looks at the place will tell you if the rent really is too high, whereas they won't say a word if it's too low. You can easily lower the rent any time you want, but you can't always raise it so easily.

The decision to charge a certain rent is yours, and if it is a deliberate, informed decision, you can trust yourself to find the right rent.

RAISING RENTS

If you are at all like most landlords and landladies, you dislike rent raises more than any other aspect of this business because of the tenant dissatisfaction and resentment they frequently cause. In spite of what you see in the media, statistics show that landlords and landladies have a real aversion to raising rents, for not only have rents failed to keep pace with percentage increases in property values over the years, they haven't even kept pace with the consumer price index. In other words, no matter what people in general think about rent levels, no matter how shrill their cries for rent control, landlords and landladies have actually been both lax and restrained in raising rents. Consequently, the profitability of rental property is shrinking perceptibly, and residential income property is becoming less attractive as an investment.

There's no good reason for you to stop disliking rent raises, but you should come to accept them as a necessary element in the conduct of your own landlording business, an element made absolutely necessary by the impact of inflation on your expenses. Since your very business survival depends upon your being able to meet these increased expenses with increased revenues, you have no choice but to raise rents or go out of business.

You must expect that any raise may expose you to charges of profiteering and may precipitate a whole host of tenant complaints, but you must learn to cope with these problems unless you have some perverse desire to subsidize your tenants, in effect, for the dubious privilege of serving them as their landlord or landlady, or unless you wish to invest your money and time in a business venture which only loses money. You are in this business to make a profit, aren't you? It certainly is not worth the worry, the risk, the trouble, the time, or the expense otherwise.

To have the desired effect, raising rents requires a policy as carefully outlined as your rent collection policy, one which is calculated to minimize tenant dissatisfaction and resentment. Rent raises under this policy should occasion neither a mass revolt nor a mass exodus of your tenants because they should come to understand that your rent raises are fair, and therefore, acceptable. This policy should involve five elements—careful preparation, proper timing, reasonable increments, amicable notices, and personal delivery.

• CAREFUL PREPARATION—Careful preparation for rent raises consists of much more than merely preparing the notices to change terms of tenancy. That's the most visible, most mandatory part of the preparation, but it's really the smallest part and the least time-consuming,too. Actually, careful preparation should continue year-round. As soon as you give one increase, you should already be preparing for the next one. Here's what you ought to be doing to prepare—

Richard and Mary,

Sorry we have to raise your rent. We want to continue maintaining your place as best we can, but with our costs going up the way they are, we just have to raise it. I am giving you two months' notice, to give you an opportunity to look around at other places. I hope you'll stay here, of course.

— Lester

NOTICE OF CHANGE
IN TERMS OF TENANCY
(Rent)

TO ___RICHARD & MARY RENTER___, Tenant in Possession

___456 SWEET ST.___

___LITTLETOWN, CALIF.___

YOU ARE HEREBY NOTIFIED that the terms of tenancy under which you occupy the above-described premises are to be changed.

Effective ___April 1___, 19_87_, your rent will be increased by _#33_ per month, from _#478_ per month to _#511_ per month, payable in advance.

Dated this ___1st___ day of ___February___, 19_87_.

___Lester Landlord___
Owner/Manager

This Notice was served by the Owner/Manager in the following manner (check those which apply):
- ☑ by personal delivery,
- ☐ by leaving a copy with someone on the premises other than the tenant,
- ☐ by mailing,
- ☐ by posting.

✻ When rent is paid on or before the 4th day of the calendar month, you may take a $20 discount.

Prepare by keeping up with your bookkeeping every month so you know how much your expenses are and how much you need to raise the rents to operate profitably and also so you can refer to your expenses knowledgeably whenever you must discuss with your tenants your reasons for raising the rent.

Prepare by keeping track of market conditions in your area so you know what current rents are for other similar rentals.

Prepare by beginning a rumor that the rent will increase to a level higher than what you anticipate, so the tenants are relieved when they learn later how small the increase was in comparison to what they had expected.

Prepare by telling your tenants exactly when they can expect the rent to increase.

Prepare by charging new tenants at the anticipated higher rents so that when the rents are raised for everyone else to those market levels, or close to them, you can indicate to your old tenants that new tenants have already been paying higher rents (because good, long-term tenants are hard to find and cost you far less in many ways than do short-termers, give them special consideration when you're raising rents; keep their rents $5 to $20 below market levels).

With such preparation, you should be able to forestall most charges tenants might make that your increase was unfair and irresponsible.

• PROPER TIMING—The proper time to raise rents is always when tenants are expecting an increase. More than at any other time, they expect increases when there is a change in ownership, so give them an increase then if one is justifiable, but take a few weeks first to become acquainted with the property and determine whether an increase is, in fact, justifiable.

Once when I was a new student of landlording and reluctant to raise rents at all, I waited twenty months after buying a building before making a well-warranted increase, from $165 to $185, and when I did so, one irate tenant called to complain. She said that she had expected me to raise the rents when I bought the building almost two years before, but coming when it did, the increase was a complete surprise to her and therefore totally unfair. How do you argue with that kind of reasoning? You don't. Clearly, I had done things wrong even though I hadn't done her wrong. I had assumed that an impersonal increase notice and all that elapsed time since their last increase would be sufficient for the tenants to accept a new rent raise unquestioningly. Of course, that wasn't sufficient because the tenants simply were not expecting an increase right then. I had failed to condition them.

You should raise your rents when tenants expect increases, and you should condition them to expect increases like clockwork one year after the rents were last raised. Following this policy, you might want to stagger the increases throughout the year by scheduling them to coincide with the anniversary of each tenant's arrival; that way you manage to spread the repercussions.

If possible, time your rent increases to coincide with some improvements you are making to the property so the tenants will believe they are getting something more for their money and will complain less at having to pay more.

Proper timing refers to the cycle of increases and to tenant conditioning, and it also refers to the actual moment when the official written rent increase notice will reach the tenants. That best time is just after they have paid their rent, at least thirty days before the increase goes into effect, or, if possible, sixty days before (give lessees similar notice before their lease expires). Your tenants will appreciate sixty days' notice, for they will feel far less threatened when you give them that much time to consider their alternatives.

They will have a whole month to look around before they have to give notice that they intend to move. Such a strategy will lessen the tension and win as much of their cooperation as you can possibly expect at this time.

• REASONABLE INCREMENTS—Having carefully prepared for the increase, you will know what rents are reasonable for your rentals and you will also then know approximately how much the raise should be. Because you have to take many factors into consideration when you calculate any rent increase and because your final figure will usually be the result of numerous compromises, you may want to select an increment which is psychologically more acceptable to your tenants. The more acceptable numbers are those which are not multiples of five. $12, for example, is better than $10, and $18 is better than $15. Such figures lead tenants to believe that their increases have been carefully calculated to match actual increases in operating expenses rather than to include still more arbitrary profit for the owners rounded up, of course, to the nearest $5.

You are taking a calculated risk of creating vacancies with any raise you give, but that risk increases somewhat if the rent increase exceeds either 10% or the consumer price index, whichever is greater. If you have timidly lagged behind the marketplace and you now have to raise your rents higher than those guidelines to approach a reasonable rent schedule, you may want to do so even knowing full well that some tenants are going to vacate. Wish them well, and then don't get yourself into the same bind again.

Raise your rents on an annual basis from then on.

• AMICABLE NOTICES—Besides preparing carefully, timing properly, and calculating reasonable increases, you should announce your raises officially in writing using honest, sympathetic notices. The notice itself is the culmination of all your work, and it should reflect the great care you have put into all the preparation thus far. The notice should soften the blow with some reasons for the raise and an expression of your personal concern about the possible hardships the increase might cause.

Use a cold, impersonal legal notice like the Notice of Change in Terms of Tenancy if you want, but add to it your own personal message. Mention the tenant by first name in a handwritten aside and apologize for the increase, saying that you are trying to maintain the tenant's dwelling as best you can, but that it is impossible to do so unless you raise rents.

Or you might want to type up your own complete notice using personal wording like this—"As you know, we are living in inflationary times, and even though I do my best to keep costs down, there's no way I can reduce the expenses of this building back to what they were a year ago. I have absorbed these increases as long as I could, but not I am forced to increase your rent by $_____, or _____%, from $_____ per month to $_____ per month, effective _____, 19_____."

Remember that if you use any rental agreement or lease form which has a discount provision, the increase should be based on the gross or non-discounted rental figure and not on the discounted amount that you are accustomed to collecting when the tenant pays on time. You might want to remind the tenant of this situation by stating it directly on the notice, asterisking the rental figures and explaining below as follows—"*When rent is paid on or before the third day following the rent due date, you may take a $20 discount."

Remember also that if you or a previous landlord collected your tenants' last month's rent when they moved in, the sum you originally collected will be insufficient to cover the increased rent which will be in effect during their last month of tenancy. To avoid misunderstandings later, advise them that they should pay the increase for that last month's rent as soon as the new rent becomes effective. Otherwise you will have a difficult time collecting the difference between what they paid as last month's rent when they moved in and what the rent happens to be when they move out. Their having paid their last month's rent when they moved in does not entitle them to get their last month's rent at that lower amount. They owe you the difference, and you should collect it whenever you raise the rent.

• PERSONAL DELIVERY—You may deliver a rent increase in person or by mail, but personal delivery is certainly preferable because it provides an opportunity to discuss the reasons for the increase with your tenants on a personal level. If you can't serve it personally, send them the notice, and post one on their door, too. You must rest assured that they have received at least the minimum time provided by law for such notices, and your sending them a copy by first-class mail won't give you that assurance.

CONTROLLING RENTS

Can you imagine any politician proposing wage controls without price controls (trade unions might bicker among themselves about some matters, but this would unite them like iron filings on a magnet)? Can you imagine any politician proposing ceilings on the prices which homeowners are allowed to sell their single-family dwellings for (homeowners would take up their Saturday-night specials to defend their right to sell their castles at fair market value)? Both are such absurd proposals that any politicians espousing them today would be stripped of their brown shirts and whisked off to asylums to babble and cavort with the other lunatics.

Yet, how many politicians are there who seriously propose rent control as the solution to rising rents, a scheme every bit as illogical as controlling wages without controlling prices and as utterly ridiculous as putting a ceiling on the prices of houses? In effect, rent control does both. It limits the landlord's and landlady's "wages" without affecting their expenses, and it artificially limits the value of their rental property. That's what I call "landlord bashing."

Politicians who support rent control don't see it that way, however, and they don't see themselves as fascists either. They see themselves as Robin Hoods, championing the cause of impoverished, victimized renters in the interminable and righteous struggle against wealthy landlords and landladies. That's you, remember. They hear the caterwauling of their tenant constituents lamenting the hardships of living on a fixed income and decide that the simplest way to appease these people is to limit the obscene profits, fix the income, of the monopolistic property owners. You again. Although do-gooder politicians are only greasing the squeaky wheels in their communities when they act to control rents and are ignoring the long-term ramifications of what they are doing, they are in truth attempting to silence those noisy tenants the only way they can, with a specious solution to a large and complex problem.

The problem we all face, tenants, politicians, and rental property owners alike, is not constantly increasing rents, and the solution to constantly increasing rents is not rent control. The real problems are a shortage of housing and an increase in the many expenses involved in landlording, from toilet parts to interest rates. The only real solutions are to build more housing, control inflation, and subsidize the housing of those who are truly poor. Obviously these are formidable solutions, ones which local politicians cannot effect easily or inexpensively, if at all. Rent control, on the other hand, is easy to enact and relatively inexpensive to administer, and it provides immediate relief. So what if it does exacerbate the real problems. So what if it does victimize those who own rental property. So what if it does favor all tenants regardless of their financial need. It appeases the people with the votes. Therefore, it is an ideal political solution for harrassed politicians struggling to cope with what appears to be a local problem they feel they can handle, and it is a solution which appears to be gaining more and more vocal proponents. Why not? It offers something for nothing. It appeals to people's greed.

Whenever it becomes an issue in your area, you would be wise to become involved in the political process which will determine whether rent control will be adopted, and if so, what form it will take. Any talk of rent control should bring you to your feet before rent control itself brings you to your knees. Support the political efforts of your rental property owners' association. Attend hearings. Ask the reference librarian at your local library to help you find some of the many studies on the subject. Write letters to your politicians and to the editor of your local newspaper citing certain rent control case studies and outlining your own views relative to the local situation. If, at last, you sense that some form of rent control is inevitable, become involved with the shaping of the measure so it will be easier to live with. Face the fact that we live in a world which is more consumer-oriented than ever before, and expect to have to give a little.

Odious as rent control sounds to us landlords, conjuring up images of abandoned properties and bankruptcy, it may be written as a compromise to everyone involved. Tenants fear quantum leaps in their rents, increases of 30% and 50% a year, and you can hardly blame them. Landlords and landladies fear being forced to maintain rents at certain base levels *ad infinitum* and eventually losing their buildings. But some form of rent control might assuage both those fears.

Would you balk, for example, at rent control which would apply only to buildings with six or more units and would allow owners to pass through all increased expenses and prorations of improvements, as well as to increase rents by 15% per year? That wouldn't be hard to live with, would it? Well, that is rent control just as much as is a measure which requires you to roll back your rents to what they were twelve months ago and then keep them there forever. Compromises are possible, even desirable at times, in order for everyone involved to save face.

Finally, if rent control is adopted in any area where you own rental property, take the time to learn all you can about it. Are certain sizes of rental dwellings exempt from controls? Under what circumstances may you raise rents? What procedures are there for grievances? How are evictions affected by the controls? The rent control regulations and the bureaucrats who administer them will answer these and other pertinent questions you might have. Be more familiar with these regulations than your tenants are. Be cooperative with the authorities, work within the law, and seek to change it whenever possible.

Don't panic. Don't give up. Shrewd owners study such predicaments thoroughly and learn how to profit from them. There's usually a way.

But do not invest any more of your money in rent control areas. Invest it elsewhere.

SOME LAST WORDS

Your raising rents doesn't suddenly metamorphose you into a greedy, unscrupulous monster of a landlord. Rather, it means that you are a good business person who understands the nature of the business you are in. You understand that you can lose money in this business if you want to, just as you can in any other business, and that no one will care, least of all your tenants. You understand that no one is going to nominate you for the "Landlord of the Year Award" just because you leave your rents low and that no one is going to tell you that your rents are too low either.

When was the last time one of your tenants told you the rent was too low and offered to pay more? Don't wait for it to happen. It won't. Tenants who offer to pay higher rents are as rare as one-armed violinists. Just because they don't volunteer to pay more, however, doesn't mean that the dwellings they occupy aren't worth more rent and that they can't pay more rent. You are the only one to judge, and you alone must take the initiative necessary to raise your rents.

KEEPING GOOD TENANTS

Although some high fallutin landlords and landladies like to think of themselves as manor-born lords and ladies, while at the same time they think of their tenants as serfs and underlings, people born to be kicked around, they are utterly wrong in that persuasion, just as wrong as those high and mighty tenants are who think of landlords and landladies as their natural-born enemies.

You, landlord or landlady, are a businessperson. Your tenants are your customers. Never forget that. Your tenants are your customers. They're not serfs. They're not underlings. They're not people to be stepped on. And they're not merely one-shot, single-purchase customers either. They're repeat customers, loyal customers, the very best customers any businessperson could hope to have. Month after month, they pay you good money to occupy the shelter you own.

When was the last time you heard the businessperson's credo, "The customer is always wrong"? No, I've never heard it either. Yet that's the way some landlords and landladies treat their very best customers. They act as if their tenants were always wrong. They act as if they would be better off without having any tenants at all. Bunk, balderdash, bull, and baloney! There's no doubt that we would be better off without certain tenants, the sneaks, the complainers, the deadbeats, the gossips, the noisemakers, the pigs, the crazies, but that doesn't mean we'd be better off without having any tenants at all.

Tenants are important to this business. In fact, they are crucial to this business. Perhaps you've never stopped to consider just how crucial your tenant-customers really are. Let me explain.

You probably already know from your reading about real estate that there are four ways in which you as an investor can make money in the residential income property business. First, there's appreciation, also known as capital gain (as a result of the natural inflation caused by the government's busy printing press or the forced appreciation caused by the property's having been improved somehow, your property should be worth more when you sell it than when you bought it); second, there's equity buildup (your loan principal decreases each time you make an amortized loan payment, and as a consequence, your equity in the property increases); third, there's tax shelter, sometimes called depreciation (at tax time you deduct a portion of your property's improvements and consider them paper losses to offset your income); and fourth, there's cash flow (this is the money left over from rental income after you have paid off all the bills). Although one or several of these four ways might be more significant than others for a certain property, all of them are important to the overall business we are in.

Of these four ways, however, only one of them will keep working for you regardless of how you treat your tenants. Only one of them will work for you if you neglect tenant matters to the point where tenants stop paying you their rent and start tearing the building apart, window by window, door by door, wall by wall, toilet by toilet. That one way is tax shelter.

Sometime after you first acquire your residential income property, you or your accountant will set up a depreciation schedule for that building, and each year you will depreciate the building for tax purposes using whichever method of depreciation is most advantageous to you. You will continue depreciating the building on paper regardless of whether the building is shipshape or dilapidated, occupied or vacant. It makes no difference whatsoever. As far as tax shelter is concerned, tenants are as unimportant to an owner as bag ladies are to a fashion designer.

But things are very different for the other three ways to make money: appreciation, equity buildup, and cash flow. In order for appreciation to work for you, you and your tenants together have to keep their places livable, even attractive, so the property will increase in value. In order for you to pay off your loan every month and take advantage of equity buildup, your tenants have to keep paying you their rent so you can make those loan payments. And if you are ever to have any cash flow, it will have to come from your tenants. They are the ones who pay you the money that pays the bills and accumulates in your wallet, purse, or bank account.

Can you afford to cut yourself off from three of the four ways to make money in residential income property? If you can, then go ahead and neglect your tenants all you want to. That's your prerogative. But you should be asking yourself why in the world you're in this business anyway. You really ought to be enjoying yourself clipping your bond coupons, fondling your gold coins, stroking your minks, being seen in your Rolls, and taking cruises through the sunny climes of the world. You ought to think about getting out of the landlording business altogether or at least delegating the management of your property to someone else with landlording savvy. You're giving the rest of us a bad name.

If, on the other hand, you cannot afford to cut yourself off from three of the four ways to make money in residential income property, you should, by all means, not neglect your tenants. You cannot really succeed in this business if you do unless, perhaps, you decide to invest in that one kind of residential income property where tenant problems are minimized, cemeteries. Those tenants you could neglect. They don't complain. They don't plug toilets, break windows, mark up walls, hold noisy parties, or refuse to pay their rent. No matter what you did, you'd have them for keeps, and you could concentrate most of your energies on keeping the property itself in perfect condition.

Come to think of it, running a cemetery isn't the only way to avoid tenant problems entirely and keep your rental property in perfect condition. You could simply not rent it out at all just as the great state of California has done with its governor's mansion. You'd have no tenants to worry about. You can get along perfectly well without tenants, can't you? So why not let your building age and weather gracefully without subjecting it to all that tenant abuse and subjecting yourself to all those tenant problems? Sound interesting? It is, except that without any tenants at all you'd lose out on one of the most time-honored ways to make money in this entire business. You wouldn't have any positive cash flow. There would be cash flow all right, but it would be flowing in the wrong direction, out of your bank account and into the property instead of out of the property and into your bank account. Of course, you would get the old standby, tax shelter, and you would get some appreciation, but not as much as you would be getting if you had good tenants occupying your rentals. What about equity buildup? You'd get some, naturally, but because the loan payments would be coming entirely out of your own funds every month, the equity buildup couldn't be considered a way to make money. You'd merely be robbing Peter to pay Pauline, taking money from one of your accounts and putting it into another. That'll never make you rich. All things considered, then, renting to good tenants and keeping them content enough to stay where they are a long time is surely the best way to run a landlording business. You need them and they need you.

Besides, good tenants also help to determine the value of every rental property you can possibly imagine, that is, with one exception, the house or duplex which buyers want to occupy themselves. And even in that case, although the buyers want to displace the tenants and don't care about rental values, they'll pay more if good tenants have been keeping the property in good condition. Prospective buyers who have no intention of displacing existing tenants will always pay more for a rental property which already has good long-term tenants living there, tenants who pay their rent on time, respect the property of others, and respect other people as well. Such tenants are prime assets. You cannot get along without them. Treat them well, these good customers of yours. They are the layers of your golden eggs.

Recognizing that good tenants are indeed important to you and that losing them will cost you hundreds of dollars, if not thousands, you are wise to consider various ways to keep those tenants living right where they are as long as you possibly can (on an average, almost half of those renting unfurnished dwellings will move during any given year). You can increase your chances of keeping your good tenants longer by being friendly with all of them, though friends with none, by being reasonable at all times, and by making an extra effort to please them at certain times.

Here are some specific things you can do.

• When tenants first move in, change all the door locks right before their very eyes (see Chapter 16 for hints on changing locks; usually the best time to change locks is when you're reviewing the Condition and Inventory Checksheet).

• Continue to provide your tenants with that same sense of security during their tenancy by changing their locks again whenever they reasonably request a change, after a roommate moves out or they lose their keys or their home is burglarized. (Because you are responsible to each tenant who has signed your rental agreement, you may not change the locks to exclude any of them singly. If you do, you will have to provide access to that person later anyway so long as his or her name appears on the agreement. Before you go to the trouble of changing the locks, therefore, advise the remaining tenant of this responsibility you have. Of course, if the excluded tenant has not signed the agreement, you have no responsibility to him or her whatsoever.)

• Provide them with useful written information for coping with some of life's little emergencies and for doing various things around their home. Here's a form which you might want to use for this very purpose. It has space for your name (as manager) and telephone number along with other important telephone numbers, numbers which should all be readily available in one place. There's also space you may use to indicate where the utility shutoffs are and how to shut them off, and there are some suggestions for coping with such problems as plugged toilets and ice-jammed refrigerators. Many times you will assume that your tenants understand how to use, say, a garbage disposer or a fire extinguisher when, in truth, they don't have a clue because nobody has ever taken the time to explain how to use one before and they themselves are too embarrassed to ask. Whether you make this information part of your move-in procedure or distribute it later is up to you.

• Make available to your tenants both a plumber's helper (plunger) and a garbage disposer wrench. They're so low on burglars' requisition lists and they're so inexpensive

FOR YOUR INFORMATION:

Important Numbers:

Police _911_	Telephone Co. _555-1010_
Fire _911_	Gas Co. _535-1660_
Ambulance _911_	Electric Co. _535-1885_
Paramedic _911_	Water Co. _535-1937_
Doctor _555-2845_	Manager _555-9140_

The best time to contact the manager is _8 AM - 6 PM - Mon - Fri._

In an emergency, when you cannot get hold of the manager, call _555-3987_ .

Helpful Hints:

1) A fire extinguisher is located _Under kitchen sink_ . Use short bursts aimed at the base of the fire. Never use water on a grease fire; either use the extinguisher provided or throw baking soda on it.

2) The electrical shutoff for your dwelling is located _Just outside back door_ . Check there to see whether a fuse has blown (have an extra on hand) or a circuit breaker has tripped. Restore service by replacing any fuse which appears to be blown (use one with the same number on it) or by flipping the circuit breaker switch back and forth once.

3) The gas shutoff for your dwelling is located _N.E. Corner of building_ , but there may be an individual valve on the line supplying each appliance as well. Shut off the gas by turning the valve 90 degrees, that is, so it crosses the direction of the supply line.

4) The water shutoff for your dwelling is located _Just outside back door_ , but you may be able to shut off the water to an individual faucet by turning off the supply valve below your sink or toilet (not your tub or shower). If hot water is leaking anywhere, shut off the valve on top of the hot water heater.

5) Whenever you defrost the refrigerator, turn it off or set the control knob to defrost. Place a pan to catch the water and empty it when necessary. Do not try to break up the ice with any implement like a knife or an ice pick. Let it melt on its own or speed it up by placing a pot of hot water in the freezing compartment. Dry the floor thoroughly when you have finished.

FOR YOUR INFORMATION - Page 2

6) Whenever you use the garbage disposer, if you have one, feed garbage in gradually along with lots of cold water, and let the water run for half a minute after you turn off the switch. Use the disposer only for those things which are edible, but don't put either cooking oil and grease down it; put them and everything else except toxic liquids in the trash. Keep metal objects out of the sink while using the disposer and turn off the switch immediately if you hear any loud metallic noises. Do not put your hand into the disposer (use tongs to retrieve objects) and do not use any chemical drain openers. If the disposer stops running on its own and you haven't heard it make any strange noises, something may have gotten stuck. Try turning the blades with a disposer wrench. Then push the reset button. After you have tried all this and you find that it still doesn't work, call the manager.

7) Whenever you want to dispose of any liquids which aren't edible, please see the manager. Many liquids are toxic and should not be put down the drain or in the trash. They must be disposed of carefully so they will not contaminate the soil or the water supply in this area. Included in this list of hazardous household wastes are the following: oven cleaners, ammonia-based cleaners, drain cleaners, floor wax, furniture polish, deodorizers, spot removers, medicines, paint, thinners, paint removers, wood preservatives, art supplies, photographic chemicals, antifreeze, car waxes, crankcase oil, fuels, radiator flushes, rust inhibitors, engine cleaners, insect sprays, weed killers, and swimming pool chemicals.

8) Whenever water rises in the toilet bowl, do not try flushing the toilet again. The bowl can hold just one tank of water at a time. More water from the tank will only cause the bowl to flow over. Use a plunger first, and then try flushing it again. Do not try to flush feminine napkins or paper diapers down the toilet. They may disappear from the toilet bowl, but that's no guarantee they'll clear the sewer pipes completely. They could require a plumber's visit, and that'll cost you money.

9) Whenever you have showered or bathed, please take a moment to mop up the excess water on the bathroom floor. A dry floor is a safe floor.

10) Whenever you want to hang anything from, or stick anything to, the walls or ceilings in your dwelling, please ask the manager to explain how to do it acceptably.

11) Whenever you want to remove the screens from your windows, please ask the manager how to do it properly. Some screens have to be removed from the inside and some from the outside. The manager will show you how.

that you needn't worry much about whether they'll disappear from an accessible location. They're handy, easy-to-use tools, and their availability to your tenants may save you some maintenance trips.

• Recognize as certainties that the heaters at your rental properties will malfunction only on the coldest Sunday of the year and that the air conditioners will malfunction only on the hottest holiday. Naturally there will be neither parts nor repairers available to fix the heating or cooling equipment right away, and your tenants may tend to believe that you are somehow to blame. Keep cool. Anticipate that such problems will occur regardless of how good your preventive maintenance is, and prepare for them. Buy a good portable electric heater which the building's electric circuitry can reasonably accommodate and lend it to those freezing tenants until their broken heater has been repaired. Likewise, buy a portable cooler or large-bladed fan and lend it to your tenants until their air conditioner is back in service. Such thoughtfulness will convince your tenants that you care about whether they are freezing or sweating and that you are attempting seriously to remedy the problem.

• Memorize all of your tenants' names, even the pets' and kids', and try to remember a few specific things about each tenant which you might use later in conversation. Everyone responds better to the personal touch, and what's more personal than a name?

• Give an ear to your tenants when they come to you with their concerns. Unless they're talking while you've got your head under their sink, look them straight in the right eye and concentrate on what they're saying. To show them you've been listening, ask them questions every so often and express some agreement. Always let them do more talking than you do. Take time to listen to the bores as well as everybody else. After a while you'll know which tenants have the sense to limit their own talking themselves and which ones you'll have to limit. If you've been reasonably patient in listening to your tenants all along, they will listen to you more readily when you come to them with your concerns.

• Whenever possible, hire tenants to work for you, doing such things as cleaning, yardwork, and painting. Tenants appreciate the opportunity to pick up some extra money without having to travel any distance from their home, and they take more pride in the place where they live if they have contributed some of their own labor to make it look more attractive. My best groundskeepers have always been tenants who lived on the premises. My best vandalism deterrents have always been those troublesome teenager tenants I've hired to do odd jobs for me (be advised that teenagers working for you do require supervision).

• Become familiar with the various kinds of rental housing assistance available through public agencies and other charitable organizations. Help your tenants who might qualify for this assistance to apply for it and run the bureaucratic maze to get it. Many tenants who should be getting assistance are totally unaware that it exists or are too timid or too proud to apply. There may be some tenants you'll encounter who cannot read or write well enough to fill out even the simplest of the necessary forms and are embarrassed to admit their handicap. Your help could make the difference between their remaining as your good tenants and their moving to less expensive and less desirable quarters.

• Sometime during the holiday season, send your tenants holiday greetings, express your gratitude for their having been your good tenants for whatever length of time they have lived there, and enclose a check which equals the bank interest earned during the year by their security/cleaning deposits. Some states and municipalities have laws on the books requiring owners to pay interest on tenants' deposits. In those places your payment is no more than compliance with the law rather than a good-will gesture. When the payment is made voluntarily, however, you will find that it makes a pleasing, long-lasting impression on the recipients. Remember, too, that the interest on a $500 deposit at 6% is only $30, and that $30 will pay a bigger dividend when paid to your tenants than it would if it were to remain in your own bank account.

• Remember your tenants' special days with greeting cards. People in service businesses have known for years the public relations value of sending personal greetings on special occasions, and you'll find that tenants like to be remembered by their landlords and landladies as well.

• Order a catered platter of food or some other token of your concern delivered to those tenants who are mourning the death of a loved one they have been living with. Times of death are awkward times. They're also times when hordes of people suddenly descend upon the survivors with their condolences, hungry people they are, too. A platter of food materializing out of nowhere is always welcomed, and you will find yourself welcomed later when you pay a visit to express your sympathy once again and learn how the death will affect the survivors' tenancy.

• Include your good tenants in your efforts to secure other good tenants. Enlist them in your word-of-mouth advertising campaign (see Chapter 3), for they have as much of an interest in who their new neighbors will be as you do. Generally they welcome the opportunity to participate in the search for new tenants and make a conscientious effort to find good ones.

• Offer to redecorate their dwelling if it hasn't been done in three or more years and the place is beginning to look shabby. All too frequently good tenants feel compelled to move because their landlord or landlady expects them to tolerate living in a dwelling which needs new linoleum in the bathroom, paint in the living room, drapes in the bedroom, and carpeting in the hallway. When they decide not to tolerate such conditions any longer and they move away to a dwelling which has been completely redecorated by a new landlord or landlady, their former landlord or landlady is forced not only to redecorate but to lose rent while the

place is vacant and then to bear the expense and suffer through the process of finding new tenants who may or may not be as good as the old ones. That former landlord or landlady would actually have saved money by redecorating to keep the good old tenants instead of redecorating to attract good new ones. You cannot afford to be oblivious of the condition of your occupied rentals any more than you can afford to be oblivious of the condition of your vacant rentals.

SOME LAST WORDS

You may be a greedy, myopic, misanthropic landlord or landlady if you want to be, one who pooh-poohs any act of cooperation or kindheartedness, but your tenants will move out more frequently than will those of benevolent, circumspect landlords and landladies who value their good tenants and cater to them whenever possible, while still being formidable enough, when need be, not to permit any tenant to kick sand in their faces.

Remember that as a landlord or landlady you are managing both buildings and people. Buildings are easy. Any simpleton can manage them. People are not so easy. They require management with care, loving care mixed with caring discipline.

HELPING TENANTS
MOVE OUT

Tenants come and tenants go with some degree of frequency every year (throughout the U.S., turnover averages 45% for unfurnished rentals), and when they do either, you as the landlord or landlady involved have certain responsibilities you should be aware of and be prepared to carry out. You know pretty well what those responsibilities are when tenants move in and you probably pay close attention to them then, but chances are good that you know only superficially what your responsibilities are when tenants move out, and furthermore, that you pay little attention to them.

Except in the most perfunctory ways, we all tend to neglect helping tenants when they move out because we are generally disappointed at their moving and regard it as a desertion of sorts and also because their moving is overshadowed by our simultaneous preparation for new tenants, something we regard as much more important. While the pitfalls you face when tenants move in may indeed be more momentous than those you face when they move out, pitfalls do exist when they move out, too, pitfalls which can cause you unnecessary aggravation and cost you plenty of wasted time and money.

Ask a sampling of small claims court judges about the landlord-tenant cases they hear, and they will tell you that almost all such cases involve disputes which arise when tenants move out. Sometimes the landlord or landlady is bringing the case, and sometimes it's the tenants, but almost always the cases are related to the tenants moving out. Either the deposits weren't refunded as they should have been or the deposits were insufficient to cover the charges owed for damages and cleaning or there were misunderstandings about the condition of the dwelling before the tenants moved in as compared to its condition after they moved out or there were misunderstandings about the meaning of the expressions "reasonably clean and undamaged" and "normal wear and tear" or there were misunderstandings about the ownership of certain contents of the dwelling or there were misunderstandings about whether the deposits could be used for last month's rent. That's altogether too much misunderstanding, if you ask me, and even though it cannot all be avoided, much of it can be with some preparation and some pointed communication.

You may lessen the chances of misunderstanding every time tenants move out merely by following these six steps—

1) Prepare at move-in time for the move out.
2) Provide a written "Notice of Intention to Vacate" form for your tenants to fill out, sign, and give to you when they decide to move.
3) Advise your departing tenants what they can do to get their deposits back.
4) Inspect the dwelling and itemize its deficiencies.
5) Calculate the charges fairly.
6) Return the deposits promptly, but not too promptly.

NOTICE OF INTENTION TO VACATE   Date 9/13/86

TO: *LESTER LANDLORD*

FROM: *RICHARD AND MARY RENTER*

Please be advised that on *SEPTEMBER 30, 1986* we intend to move from our residence at *456 SWEET ST., LITTLETOWN* .

We understand that our rental agreement calls for *15* days' notice before we move and that this is *17* days' notice. We understand that we are responsible for paying rent through the end of the notice period called for in the rental agreement or until another tenant approved by the management has moved in, whichever comes first.

We understand that our deposits will be refunded within *7* days after we have moved out completely and returned our keys to the management, so long as we leave our dwelling reasonably clean and undamaged.

Reasons for leaving: *WE BOUGHT A DUPLEX!*
_____

Forwarding address: *1610 DURANT, LITTLETOWN*

In accordance with our rental agreement, we agree to allow the management to show our dwelling to prospective tenants at any and all reasonable times.

Tenant *Richard Renter*
Tenant *Mary Renter*

Received 9/13/86 ll

Those don't sound difficult, do they? They're not. You probably know enough already to be doing many of them automatically. Still, let's look at each one more closely.

1) PREPARE AT MOVE-IN TIME FOR THE MOVE OUT.

Avoid this kind of misunderstanding:

"Mrs. Lilliput, we're going to be moving to Houston next Tuesday, and we'd like to use our deposits to pay for the balance of the rent we still owe you from last month, plus whatever else we'll owe you when we leave. That'll just about balance everything out, won't it?"

"I can't believe what you're saying, Mr. Runfree! You give me five days' notice that you're moving and you want me to apply your deposits to the rent? I can't do that. You're supposed to get your deposits back after I've inspected your place and found it to be acceptably clean and undamaged. Right now you owe me $65 on last month's rent, and since you're giving notice today, you owe rent for a full one month from today as well."

"Oh, don't you worry your little head about it. We'll leave everything spic 'n' span. You'd be refunding our money anyway. We'll save you the 22 cents postage you'd have to pay to send it to us."

When your tenants moved in, you were already preparing for them to move out, whether you ever thought about their moving out at some future time or not. You stipulated the notice period necessary for them to advise you when they were moving; you asked for proper notice in writing; you inspected the dwelling with the tenants before they moved in, and you noted its condition and its inventory in writing; you collected adequate deposits; and you informed the tenants that those deposits were not to be considered as last month's rent. You did each of these things for one very good reason—to avoid misunderstandings when they were about to move out.

Should you fail to establish these things at the very beginning of your relationship, you will have to expect misunderstandings later, for you cannot expect tenants to know what they should and should not do when they move out unless you inform them. Isn't it logical for them to think that their deposits should cover their final rent payment, especially if the two are identical sums? Isn't it logical for them to expect all of their deposits back as soon as they move out, without having to wait two weeks? And why should they have to give you any notice at all? You'll only re-rent it the very next day anyway, won't you? Discuss the end-game rules with tenants before you ever rent to them and put those rules in writing.

2) PROVIDE A WRITTEN "NOTICE OF INTENTION TO VACATE" FORM FOR YOUR TENANTS TO FILL OUT, SIGN, AND GIVE TO YOU WHEN THEY DECIDE TO MOVE.

September 13, 1986

Dear *Richard and Mary,*

Moving time is always a busy time, and you will have lots of things on your mind now that you have given notice you are moving. One of those things undoubtedly is how to get your deposits back promptly. In your case, they amount to $ *228.00* .

Contrary to what some tenants believe, we WANT to return your deposits, and we WILL return them to you so long as you leave your place "reasonably clean and undamaged." That's what your rental agreement says and that's what we will do. You're probably wondering, however, what "reasonably clean and undamaged" means, so we'd like to tell you how we interpret it and tell you also what you should do to get your deposits back.

"Reasonably clean" to us means as clean as you would leave your dwelling if you knew your best friend or favorite aunt were going to move in after you. To get it that clean, we expect you to clean the appliances, stove hood, and cabinets (under sinks, too) both inside and out; remove all non-adhesive shelf paper; use an appropriate cleanser on the showers, tubs, toilets, sinks, mirrors, and medicine cabinets (inside as well); dust the ceilings (for cobwebs), baseboards, window sills, and closet shelving; wash the kitchen and bathroom walls, and spot-clean the walls in other rooms; wash the light fixtures and windows inside and out; vacuum the floors; scrub the floor tile or linoleum; sweep the entry, patio, storage enclosure, and garage; remove all personal belongings (including clothes hangers and cleaning supplies); and dispose of all trash. PLEASE DO NOT CLEAN THE DRAPERIES, SHAMPOO THE CARPETS, OR WAX THE FLOORS. We prefer to do those cleaning chores ourselves, and you will not be charged for our doing them.

"Reasonably undamaged" to us means that items which we have supplied should not be missing (including light bulbs) or broken; that there should be no new burns, cracks, chips, or holes in the dwelling or its furnishings; and that the paint on the walls should be sufficient to last at least two years from the time they were last painted. PLEASE DO NOT REMOVE ANYTHING YOU HAVE ATTACHED TO THE WALLS OR CEILINGS WITHOUT FIRST TALKING TO US, and please try to avoid nicking the paint in the halls and doorways as you move things out.

After you have returned the keys, we would like to inspect your dwelling with you to check it for cleanliness and damage, and unless we have to get prices on special work or replacements, we will refund all deposits owed to you at that time.

We expect you to have moved out completely by *September 30, 1986* . Because we are making arrangements for new tenants to move in soon after that, we would appreciate hearing from you immediately if your moving plans should change.

We hope your moving goes smoothly, and we wish you happiness in your new home.

Hate to lose you!

Sincerely,

Lester Landlord

Avoid this kind of misunderstanding:

"Hello, Lester? This is Richard Renter. I just called to tell you we're all moved out and we'd like to get our deposits back."

"That's news to me, Richard. You never gave me any notice."

"Come on, man! I did, too! Don't you remember last month when I told you we were planning to move before school started? Isn't that notice enough?"

"No way! I remember you telling me you might be moving sometime soon when I saw you last, but you never said exactly when you'd be moving. How was I to know you'd be out today?"

The primary reason for requiring written notice from your vacating tenants is to tie them down to a specific moving date so that you can get busy making preparations to re-rent the dwelling without delay. Verbal notice may be satisfactory in some cases, but written notice is always better. It's definite, it's incontestable, and it's useful in those cases which wind up in court.

Some tenants will take the time to compose a letter of their own to advise you dutifully of their plans to move out. Accept it so long as it includes the anticipated moving date, the address of the place they're renting from you, and the signatures of those who signed the rental agreement. But because few people remember how to communicate in writing anymore, you should be prepared to provide a ready-made form for your tenants to fill out in order to make your written notice requirement easier to satisfy. When they give you verbal notice, supply them with one of your forms and ask them to fill it out.

The form provided here includes space for the necessary information plus space for tenants to indicate why they are leaving, information which might prove useful to you in case there's something you might do to get the tenants to stay, should you be so inclined. It's also information which may enable you to improve your landlording operations in general.

3) ADVISE YOUR DEPARTING TENANTS WHAT THEY CAN DO TO GET THEIR DEPOSITS BACK.

Avoid this kind of misunderstanding:

"What do you mean you're going to deduct $85 from my deposit? The place is spotless. I spent $15 on cleaning supplies and cleaned in there myself for six hours!"

"I admit that on the whole it's clean, but just look at those drapes! They were new only last year, and now they look so threadbare I wouldn't even wear them to a toga party! You weren't supposed to wash them. They have to be dry cleaned."

"Well, how was I supposed to know? You never told me what to do."

Some of the conditions you impose on your tenants for the return of their deposits are necessarily subjective and open to interpretation. You may have explained what those conditions were way back when the tenants first moved in, but since time tends to muddle recollections and since the tenants were hardly thinking then about moving out, you should review your conditions once more while they are thinking much more specifically about moving out and are more concerned about getting their deposits back.

Discuss your conditions with them in person or send them a letter like the form shown here outlining the conditions or, better yet, do both. Whatever you do, remind them of the amount of their deposit which is at stake and convince them that you will refund it promptly. Even if they have failed to meet certain conditions already and you are legally entitled to keep most of their deposits, you should establish some amount they will receive if they return the place to you reasonably clean and undamaged. Give them an incentive to do just that.

Because tenants will seldom clean the draperies, shampoo the carpets, wax the floors, or remove their wall and ceiling attachments to your satisfaction, you would be wise to give them very precise instructions for performing these jobs or tell them not to bother at all. Well-meaning tenants may attempt a job and bungle it so badly that you will have to spend extra time and money setting things right, and the tenants, for their part, will expect a full refund regardless of the extra work they have caused you. That kind of situation frustrates everyone involved and can easily be avoided.

4) INSPECT THE DWELLING AND ITEMIZE ITS DEFICIENCIES.

Avoid this kind of misunderstanding:

"That oven was dirtier when I moved in."

"I know it was clean, Mary Renter, because I remember cleaning it myself. It was a two-cans-of-Easy-Off job."

"Well, I cleaned it after I moved out and I say you aren't going to charge me for a dirty oven! I'll take you to court! You can't prove anything anyway. It's your word against mine."

If you can possibly arrange for the vacating tenants to accompany you as you inspect their dwelling to determine deposit refunds, do so. You can then explain precisely what is wrong with the place, and you can give them the choice of correcting those deficiencies themselves or paying for the corrections.

Tenants' conceptions of what their dwellings looked like when they moved in are as likely to be mistaken as yours, but from quite the opposite perspective. That's why a proper move-out inspection requires a record of a prior inspection attested to by the tenants. If one is lacking, there is no standard for comparison. Did the vacating tenants put twelve burns in the carpet or only nine? Did they break the toilet tank lid or did their predecessors do it? Were the lightbulbs working in every fixture when they moved in or were the bulbs mostly burned out?

There are two quite adequate ways to prove whether the current tenants are at fault. One is to take an extensive array of "fat-farm" (before-and-after) photographs and then to play "hocus focus" with them, and the other is to use a form like the Condition & Inventory Checksheet which lists the defects and contents of the dwelling when the tenants moved in and can be used again when they move out to determine the final reckoning.

If you decide to use photographs for comparison, take enough of them at move-in time, at least two per room, date them, and have your new tenants initial them to indicate that they acknowledge these photographs to be authentic and properly dated. Then repeat only those shots which show evidence of damages after the tenants move out. If they leave the place in good condition and you expect to return the deposits, don't waste film taking any more photographs.

Condition & Inventory Checksheet

Dated _January 15, 1986_

Tenant Name _Richard & Mary Renter_   Address _456 Sweet St., Littletown_

Date Moved In _1/15/86_ Date Notice Given _9/13/86_ Date Moved Out _9/30/86_

Abbreviations:

Air Conditioner, A/C	Clean, Cl	Drapes, Drp	Hood, Hd	OK, OK	Table, Tbl
Bed, Bd	Cracked, Cr	Dryer, Dry	Just Painted, JP	Poor, P	Tile, Tl
Broken, Brk	Curtains, Ctn	Fair, F	Lamp, Lmp	Refrigerator, Ref	Venetian Blinds, VB
Carpet, Cpt	Dinette, Din	Good, G	Lightbulbs, LtB	Shades, Sh	Washer, Wsh
Chair, Ch	Dishwasher, Dish	Heater, Htr	Linoleum, Lino	Sofa, Sfa	Waxed, Wxt
Chest, Chst	Disposer, Disp	Hole, H	Nightstand, Ntst	Stove, Stv	Wood, Wd

Circle applicable rooms; enter abbreviations	Walls, Doors		Floors		Windows		Light Fixtures		Inventory: Appliances, Furniture		
	cond.	chgs.	cond.	chgs.	cond.	chgs.	cond.	chgs.	Item	cond.	chgs.
(Living Room)	ok		cl. cpt		Wind cr drp. scrn ok rod cl drps torn		ok LtB 2		Ө		
Dining											
(Kitchen)	ok		wxt lino		scrn ok Sh G		ok LtB g		stv, Hd Ref (on loan)	cl cl	
(Bath 1)	JP		wxt Tl		scrn ok Sh G		ok LtB g				
Bath 2											
(Bedroom 1)	ok		cl cpt		scrn ok cl drp		Ө		Ө		
Bedroom 2											
Bedroom 3											
Other											
Charges	Ө		Ө		$16		Ө			Ө	

Total Itemized Charges ___ $16 ___

Other Charges Not Itemized
  (Broken Locks, Dirty Garage, etc.
  Explain on Backside) ___ Ө ___

Deduction for Improper Notice ___ Ө ___

Deduction for Missing Keys ___ 1 ___

Total Deductions ___ $17 ___

Total Deposits ___ $723 ___

Less Total Deductions ___ 17 ___

Deposit Refund or
Amount Owed ___ $706 ___

RR
mr

☑ Tenants acknowledge that the smoke detector was tested in their presence and found to be in working order and that its operation was explained to them. Tenants agree to test the detector at least every other week and to report any problems to the Owner in writing. If the smoke detector is battery operated, Tenants agree to replace the battery as necessary (unless laws require otherwise).

Tenants hereby acknowledge that that they have read this Condition & Inventory Checksheet, agree that the condition and contents of the above-mentioned rental dwelling are without exception as represented herein, understand that they are liable for any damage done to this dwelling as outlined in their Lease or Rental Agreement, and have received a copy of this checksheet.

Owner _Lester Landlord_ Tenant _Richard Renter_

By _____ Tenant _Mary Renter_

pg 273

Whereas you really ought to use the photograph-comparison method selectively, in those situations where you suspect that the tenants might prove to be "difficult" later on, you should always use a written accounting.

The Condition & Inventory Checksheet should have been filled out in triplicate before the tenants moved in, one copy for the tenants to keep, and two for the landlord or landlady to use at move-out time. Retrieve those same two sheets from the tenants' file and itemize in duplicate all the various deficiencies you notice this time around during your tour of inspection, from holes in the screens to holes in the walls. Then you can make direct line-by-line comparisons of the condition previously with the condition currently, and you can analyze the discrepancies.

5) CALCULATE THE CHARGES FAIRLY.

Avoid this kind of misunderstanding:

"How come you kept $30 from my deposit? What was it for?"

"You didn't leave the place clean."

"I did so."

"No, come to think of it, you did leave it pretty clean. Well, you must have broken something then."

"Why should I pay you $30 for something when you can't even remember exactly what it was? Don't you have a receipt or anything?"

Having itemized the rental's deficiencies, you can begin calculating approximately how much to charge the departing tenants to restore their dwelling to its original splendor, minus normal wear and tear, of course. These calculations will be estimates, naturally, but they should suffice for determining deposit refunds in most cases, especially since you are trying to expedite the refunds. Those tenants who request calculations based upon actual, rather than estimated, expenditures will just have to wait longer for their refunds.

Most of the time you will be able to calculate what the deductions and charges should be without ever having to contact a contractor or supplier. You'll have a pretty good idea how much things such as towel bars and lightbulbs will cost and you'll know approximately how long chores like cleaning an oven will take.

Be reasonable with your estimates. Lightbulbs don't cost $2 apiece just yet, and oven cleaning, no matter how dirty the oven, shouldn't take anyone twelve hours to do. Remember, too, that you should charge tenants only for the useful life remaining in an item which is broken or missing, not for its replacement cost. If two-year-old draperies are missing, charge tenants for only half, rather than all, the cost of the replacements. Likewise, because interior paint jobs should last two years when people are moving in and out, charge for just half of a new paint job when tenants move out leaving their walls, which were painted one year before, looking like the walls in a New York City subway. After all, you had half the use out of those drapes and that paint job before they were ruined.

6) RETURN THE DEPOSITS PROMPTLY, BUT NOT TOO PROMPTLY.

Avoid this kind of misunderstanding:

Scene 1. Telephone conversation.

"Where's our deposit, Les? It's been three days since we moved out."

"I've been so busy I haven't had a chance to check your apartment. Is everything all right there?"

"Everything's perfect."

"OK, I'll send you the money tomorrow."

Scene 2. Courtroom.

"But, your honor, I sent them back their deposit right away, and later I found all this damage."

"Mr. Landlord, you are to be commended for returning your tenants' deposits so promptly, but you should have inspected the apartment first. I can't possibly award you a judgment because when you refunded your tenants' deposits, you actually acknowledged that you were accepting the condition of their dwelling and were settling all debts with them, whether you understood that or not. Be more careful next time."

Do not return tenants' deposits until you are absolutely certain that you have calculated everything that might be deducted. If you have already returned the deposits and you later learn that the tenants have broken a $25 refrigerator door shelf, you have no legal grounds for collection, and as a practical matter, you might as well forget it, too. Once you have inspected the dwelling, however, and have subtracted all the deductions and charges, there's no sense in procrastinating about the matter any longer. Return the balance of the deposits. Even though most laws which govern rental deposit refunds allow you a very reasonable 14 days' time to return and account for the deposits after tenants move out, you should try to return them sooner if you can. Tenants who are moving most likely need the money more than you do, and they appreciate receiving it without delay.

Remember that all those tenants' deposits you hold are not yours. They have been entrusted to you in good faith to insure tenants' compliance with the terms of their rental agreements. If they have indeed complied, then there's no reason to keep the money any longer. Refund it promptly. Whenever possible, combine the inspection calculation and the refund steps together, and do them both at the same time so long as you feel absolutely certain that you have inspected the dwelling carefully and can make a proper accounting.

SOME LAST WORDS

You'll have to forgo an acquaintance with your local small claims court judge if you follow these six steps for fulfilling your responsibilities when tenants move out, but you'll be well compensated. You'll be saving yourself a great deal of aggravation, as well as both time and money, and you'll be earning yourself a reputation as a fair landlord or landlady, too. That's good business. People will remember your fairness and will recommend your rentals to others, and the tenants who remain with you will feel relieved of any worry about their own deposits.

GETTING PROBLEM TENANTS OUT

Problem tenants are the bane of the landlording business. They are always testing you. They're the last ones to pay and the first ones to gripe. They're the ones who change their own locks, paint their walls flat black, adopt stray animals, report you to the health department, and invite their latest friends to move in with them, all without ever saying one word to you. They can be noisy, contrary, destructive, malevolent, or hypocritical all at the same time or at various times. They enjoy their music one way, loud, especially between midnight and sunup, and they can cuss as well as any guttersnipe, but what they seem to enjoy most of all is misquoting landlord-tenant laws to you. They love those incredulous looks on your face when they tell you what your legal responsibilities are as their landlord or landlady and what their rights are as your tenants.

Have you ever encountered such people? Let's hope not. Still, plenty of them are around out there, that's for sure.

Unless you inherit them from a previous owner, you'll never have the displeasure of encountering them yourself if you practice prevention whenever possible, if you select tenants carefully, enforce agreements assertively, and collect rents promptly. Remember that in landlord-tenant relations, an ounce of prevention is worth many pounds of cure, for cures are costly, agonizing, time-consuming, crisis-oriented, and sometimes downright dangerous to life, limb, and property. Prevention methods, on the other hand, are not cheap either, but neither are they costly. They may cause dyspepsia at times, but they are hardly agonizing. They do take some time to do, but they save much time in the long run. What's most important, though, is that they serve to eliminate crises altogether, and they never endanger anyone or anything.

When you recognize that you do have problem tenants with some of the characteristics mentioned above, however, you cannot think in terms of prevention. You have to think in terms of cures. You have no choice really. Either you get rid of them or you'd better begin preparing yourself for complaints from the neighbors, deterioration of your property, departures of your good tenants, your bankruptcy, your capitulation, or all five. Humor these problem tenants, ignore them, pacify them no longer. Marshal your forces, steel your will, and think in terms of getting them out. You can get them out, you know, and while you're doing it, be mindful of the following:

• Be more interested in getting problem tenants out than in teaching them a lesson. They don't learn.

• Be pragmatic and businesslike with nonpaying tenants rather than feeling wronged and challenged. You will either lose their challenge or pay a big price to win. Suppress your feelings. This is purely a business matter.

• Try to stop losing rent money as soon as possible instead of relying solely on the certainty of an eviction to cut your losses later. Be relentless. Hound those tenants.

NOTICE
to Perform Covenant

TO _HENRY & GLADYS ANGEL_, TENANT IN POSSESSION:

PLEASE TAKE NOTICE that you have violated the following covenant(s) in your Lease or Rental Agreement:

TENANTS AGREE NOT TO PAINT OR ALTER THEIR
DWELLING WITHOUT FIRST GETTING OWNERS'
WRITTEN PERMISSION

You are hereby required within _3_ days to perform the aforesaid covenant(s) or to deliver up possession of the premises now held and occupied by you, being those premises situated in the City of _LITTLETOWN_, County of _SADDLEBACK_. State of _CALIFORNIA_, commonly known as _460 SWEET STREET_

If you fail to do so, legal proceedings will be instituted against you to recover said premises and such damages as the law allows.

This notice is intended to be a _3-_ day notice to perform the aforesaid covenant. It is not intended to terminate or forfeit the Lease or Rental Agreement under which you occupy said premises. If, after legal proceedings, said premises are recovered from you, the owners will try to rent said premises for the best possible rent, giving you credit for sums received and holding you liable for any deficiencies arising during the term of said Lease or Rental Agreement.

Dated this _5TH_ day of _APRIL_, 19_87_.

Lester Landlord
Owner/Manager

PROOF OF SERVICE

I, the undersigned, being at least 18 years of age, declare under penalty of perjury that I served the Notice to Perform Covenant, of which this is a true copy, on the above-mentioned Tenant in Possession in the manner(s) indicated below:

☑ On _APRIL 5_, 19_87_, I handed the Notice to the tenant.
☐ I handed the Notice to a person of suitable age and discretion at the tenant's residence/business on _____, 19____.
☐ I posted the Notice in a conspicuous place at the tenant's residence on _____, 19____.
☐ I sent by certified mail a true copy of the Notice to the tenant at his place of residence on _____, 19____.

Executed on _APRIL 5_, 19_87_, at _LITTLETOWN, CA_.

Lester Landlord

• Heed the adage, "Spare the evictions, spoil the tenants," but recognize that "evictions" can be alternative eviction methods as well as the conventional ones which use the judicial system full-strength.

CONSIDERING THE LEGAL ALTERNATIVES TO EVICTION

You can always hope that a Notice to Pay Rent or Quit (used when tenants are in arrears—see Chapter 5), a Notice to Perform Covenant (used when tenants break their rental agreement), or a Notice to Terminate Tenancy (used when you wish to terminate a rental agreement for any reason at all—check its legality in your area) will precipitate the response you desire, but don't bet any big money on it. Like all consumers nowadays, tenants are better informed than ever before, and many know that you simply cannot legally put them out on the street in just a couple of days. Consequently, they tend to linger beyond the period specified in the notice, and you then seemingly have only one alternative—a full-scale eviction.

Even if you handle an eviction yourself the legal way, it will cost you somewhere between $60 and $110 in out-of-pocket expenses for filing and process-serving fees, not to mention what the lost rent will amount to. It will take you time to prepare all the papers and time to present the papers to the court, too. Finally, when it's all over with, after you have painstakingly followed every single obligatory legal step, from serving the proper notice to accompanying the sheriffs or marshals as they put the widows and orphans out on the street, you begin to believe that you and your tenants have been duped because all of you have wound up as losers in one way or another.

Take heart. There are other perfectly legal alternatives you might try when you want to get problem tenants out without ever going to court, alternatives which might seem to be unreliable at first because they follow neither a clear-cut procedure nor a precise timetable and, in addition, require a somewhat artful approach. Some might even say they require a bit of chicanery. Yet, they usually work surprisingly well, and, what's more, they don't make losers of everyone involved. These other alternatives you might try are talking, bribery, intimidation, and throwing a temper tantrum. On third thought, forget the last one. It's legal all right, but generally it's not very effective. Let's consider just the first three: talking, bribery, and intimidation.

Remember that with any of these methods you are trying essentially to convince your tenants that it is more advantageous for them to leave than to stay put. After all, if it *is* more advantageous for them to stay put, they will do exactly that. Wouldn't you?

TALKING—All right, how do you convince tenants to vacate merely by talking to them? Go to their dwelling. Do not summon them to yours like some pompous potentate and do not talk with them by telephone. Make sure when you arrive that the decision-maker of the group is there. Ask them to explain first of all what has happened, why they have broken their agreement with you, and give them plenty of time to talk without interrupting them. Then outline the situation matter-of-factly as you understand it and suggest some alternatives. After that, ask them what they would do if they were in your shoes. If they offer up some unacceptable solution, tell them frankly why it wouldn't work and pose your own. Try to be understanding and try to reach an agreement that allows them to save face. Give a little, take a little, all the time being both reasonable and businesslike.

If you simply cannot reach an agreement which you consider fair, tell them you are left with no alternative but to evict them through the courts. Tell them you are loathe to go to that extreme because they will then be identified to the local property owners' association as having been evicted, and it will be all the more difficult thenceforth for

30-DAY NOTICE
to Terminate Tenancy

TO _____ERNEST PEABODY_____, TENANT IN POSSESSION:

PLEASE TAKE NOTICE that you are hereby required within 30 days to remove from and deliver up possession of the premises now held and occupied by you, being those premises situated in the
City of ____LITTLETOWN____, County of ____SADDLEBACK____,
State of _____CALIFORNIA_____, commonly known as
_____462 SWEET STREET_____.

This notice is intended for the purpose of terminating the Rental Agreement by which you now hold possession of the above-described premises, and should you fail to comply, legal proceedings will be instituted against you to recover possession, to declare said Rental Agreement forfeited, and to recover rents and damages for the period of the unlawful detention.

Please be advised that your rent on said premises is due and payable up to and including the date of termination of your tenancy under this notice.

Dated this ____31ST____ day of _____MARCH_____, 19__87__.

_____Lester Landlord_____
Owner/Manager

PROOF OF SERVICE

I, the undersigned, being at least 18 years of age, declare under penalty of perjury that I served the 30-Day Notice to Terminate Tenancy, of which this is a true copy, on the above-mentioned Tenant in Possession in the manner(s) indicated below:

☑ On ____MARCH 31____, 19__87__, I handed the Notice to the tenant.
☐ I handed the Notice to a person of suitable age and discretion at the tenant's residence/business on _____, 19_____.
☐ I posted the Notice in a conspicuous place at the tenant's residence on _____, 19_____.
☐ I sent by certified mail a true copy of the Notice to the tenant at his place of residence on _____, 19_____.

Executed on ____MARCH 31____, 19__87__, at ____LITTLETOWN, CA____.

_____Lester Landlord_____

them to rent in the area. Their credit rating will suffer because you report all such matters to the credit bureau, and the bill collecting agency will begin hounding them. In addition, they will never again be able to answer honestly on rental applications that they have not been evicted. After stating these consequences candidly, see if the tenants still persist in being unreasonable. If so, depart and say, "I'm disappointed that you have left me no choice. I had very much hoped we could work something out." Don't get into an argument. Don't leave in a huff. Just go.

Your success or failure in using this maneuver will depend upon the kind of relationship you have already developed with your tenants, as well as upon your skills of persuasion. Tailor the appeal to the people you are dealing with. Above all, be firm and polite. Don't antagonize them. Don't call them names or impugn their ancestry. You may believe strongly in your heart of hearts that they are doing you wrong, but remember that your doing them wrong will only make you feel better. It won't help matters in the least. In fact, it will make matters worse, much worse. So resist all of your basic urges to punch them out. Keep your head. Swallow your pride. Keep the dialogue open-ended. If you cut off the dialogue, your impending eviction suit will be all the more difficult to pursue. You want the tenants to be available to be served with court papers as the case progresses. You don't want to alienate them so much that they will fight you at every step, avoiding service and delaying your case in any way they can.

Talking can work well for some people. I know a landlord who successfully convinced a motorcycle gang leader and his savage-looking retinue to vacate a house they had rented under false pretenses. That's right, he did it with talk. How? One evening the landlord brought over a case of beer and gingerly persuaded them that he was entirely sympathetic with their wanting to remain but that he was being harrassed so much by the neighbors who were telephoning at all hours to tattle about what was happening at his rental house that he was falling asleep at work and was in danger of losing his job. He apologized about asking them to move out, but he said that he just couldn't see any other way to end the neighbors' wee-hour phone calls. The gang moved out the following weekend. When the neighbors called to report that the motorcyclists were actually moving their things out, he rushed right over there with two more cases of beer and gave his thanks. They left the place spotless. Of course, talk alone didn't do the trick; the beer helped.

Perhaps you have already tried talking your tenants into leaving, or you feel that talk just wouldn't work. Well, how about bribery?

BRIBERY—Some people gasp and then start whispering at the mere mention of the word, as if it were illegal or somehow wrong. In some situations it may be both, but not here. Here it's a motivating factor, nothing more. It's a motivating factor because it appeals to one very basic human instinct, greed, an instinct which problem tenants seem to be so richly endowed with. The more your bribe excites their greed instinct, the quicker they'll react.

Besides being quick, bribery can be inexpensive as well. It might even be free! That's right! It might not cost you anything! If you required enough in deposits from your tenants before they moved in, you would, if you were to act fast, have money enough available from these deposits to pay the tenants for leaving. This possibility that they might stop paying you their rent was one of the reasons for requiring a deposit in the first place, wasn't it? Obviously, should you succeed in suing to evict them, the money judgment, including court costs, would be subtracted from their deposits, and they could expect to receive little or no money back. In fact, they'd probably owe you some money. An offer to return what's left of their deposits after you deduct for the rent they owe you might be enough to get them moving in more ways than one, and it wouldn't cost you anything!

Calculate approximately how much a full-scale eviction and the rent lost during the eviction would cost you (especially if you hire an attorney to handle the case) before making your offer, and you'll likely find that a bribe will cost you far less. Even if you do have to sweeten the offer somewhat out of your own pocket because you have delayed so long that there's only a paltry deposit balance remaining of, say, less than $100 (few tenants will move for less), you will come out way ahead by bribing them to leave, and so will they.

Greed triumphs again! Oh, who cares? Each of you wins, wouldn't you say? Your tenants get a few bucks, and you get your rental back.

There are some good variations on the bribery gambit, too. You might offer to store the tenants' goods in one of your garages or pay the rent at a miniwarehouse for a few months. The tenants would then be free to stay with friends or relatives until they are able to get back on their feet, and you'd have a dwelling available for a paying customer.

You might offer to arrange and pay for a U-Haul van and a small crew to move the tenants' possessions anywhere within fifty miles or so.

You might cut a $100 bill in half right before the tenants' eyes, give them half, and keep half yourself until they have moved out completely on or before a designated date, or you might leave the entire $100 bill with a neutral party who has instructions to give it to the tenants if they move by a certain date. This ploy is dramatic enough to work, and it also circumvents many tenants' natural skepticism about whether you will really pay off or not. Naturally, you should never pay off until you have verified that they have, in fact, vacated.

You might offer to buy the tenants' TV, stereo, appliances, and furniture if they have fallen on hard times. This would unburden them enough so the move would be easier and so they would have the funds needed to pay their other wild-eyed creditors. Before consummating your purchase, however, you would be wise to determine whether the tenants' possessions have been paid for or whether they're still being paid for and are being used as collateral for a loan. If you're convinced that they have been fully paid for, ask for a bill of sale.

INTIMIDATION—Another maneuver which is perfectly legal and ofttimes prompts tenants to vacate without your ever having to resort to the courts is intimidation. I don't mean hiring gorillas to scare your tenants out. I mean hiring the sheriff, marshal, or constable to scare your tenants out. How? Have the local law-enforcement officer serve your notices. Sure, you can serve the notices yourself, but you're too familiar a face to your tenants. You're simply not intimidating enough. You cannot possibly impress them with the gravity of the matter as much as can an armed and uniformed law-enforcement officer who's handing out a notice signed by you stipulating that the tenants have a fixed number of days to clear out. That is quite intimidating to most people. They simply do not want to get mixed up with the law if they can help it, and they frequently will mistake your notice for one from a court which actually sets a positive date for their eviction. It all seems so official and imperative. That's precisely the impression you want to leave with them.

For $15 or $20 you can arrange to have a notice served by the law-enforcement officer who customarily serves process papers in your area. The officer will understandably take a few days longer to get around to serving the notice than you would if you were to do the serving yourself, but official service is more effective in getting action out of most tenants, and the nominal delay may be worth it.

A variation of this method involves the direct hiring of an off-duty law-enforcement officer to serve your notices. In many areas, officers may wear their uniforms while off duty and may act as process servers on their own. Inquire whether officers can and will moonlight doing this in your area. If you can find someone who does perform this service, your notices will be served more promptly than they will if you have to hire a bureaucracy as well.

In those situations involving tenants who are breaking their rental agreement, you may find that you can intimidate them and gather evidence to build a case against them all at the same time. Here's how. Make a sound recording or take some photographs of the tenants or their dwelling, and do so openly. Try to be seen in the act of recording their loud music or photographing their messy yard and prohibited pet. Do everything possible to arouse their interest in what you are doing, and once you have it, tell them that you are gathering evidence for the court case you are preparing against them. You may find them more cooperative after that, and then again you may not, but even if this activity does not serve to intimidate them into changing their ways, you still would have managed to gather some pretty incriminating evidence to introduce into court should you have to go to the mat with your case.

RECOGNIZING WHICH ALTERNATIVES ARE ILLEGAL

In some respects, it's fortunate that there are laws to keep us landlords and landladies from acting rashly when we're trying to force problem tenants to move out. After being frustrated repeatedly, some of us might be driven to near distraction and feel compelled to take the law into our own hands. We might lock tenants out, toss them out, turn off their utilities, barge in and take their belongings, poison their animals, threaten them with bodily harm, harrass them, or even damage the dwelling we own so as to render it uninhabitable.

Why do laws keep us from carrying out such "perfectly reasonable acts"? These acts disturb the peace. That's why. They enrage tenants and endanger the lives and limbs of everyone concerned, yours too, to say nothing of the possible property damage they might cause. People get hurt when they're being tossed out on their ears without due process. People become infuriated when their belongings are peremptorily confiscated. People become incensed when someone locks them out of their homes. They strike back blindly. Tempers flare. Problems grow out of all proportion, and the police have to be called in to quell the disturbances.

Self-help eviction methods are to be avoided. Do not resort to them. The penalties can be extremely severe, resulting in horrendous fines and even imprisonment. Some states fine headstrong landlords $100 per day for every day tenants remain in their dwellings with the utilities shut off. Fines of $15,000 and more in these cases are not unheard of, and naturally, there's no rent accruing during such times either. The electric company can shut off the electricity if tenants aren't paying their bill, but you can't, not even when the utilities are included in the rent.

Once more then, please, what may you not do on your own initiative to force problem tenants out?

You may not lock them out or lock them in.

You may not toss them out on their ears and throw their belongings after them.

You may not turn off their water, electricity, or gas.

You may not take their belongings.

You may not petnap their Fido or give arsenic to their pets.

You may not threaten to break their kneecaps or their skulls.

You may not disturb their peace and quiet in order to make life there so unpleasant that they'll move.

You may not remove a door, a window, a staircase, or a toilet, or do anything else to violate their "warranty of habitability."

These eviction methods are all illegal. They can get you into big trouble.

Yet, I know some landlords and landladies who do resort to such methods when they believe the circumstances are right for self-help to work, that is, when they anticipate no complications. Generally they're street-wise people dealing with other street-wise people, people who don't use the courts to settle their disagreements anyway. The secret to using self-help methods successfully, they say, is to keep a low profile, know exactly what you're doing, and be utterly canny.

When it was all behind her and she felt she could talk about it, one landlady confessed to me how she had locked out a tenant some time ago, seemingly a dangerous and illegal act. Maybe it would have been dangerous under other circumstances, but she thought otherwise. You be the judge.

It so happened that one of her tenants was two weeks in arrears, and at great inconvenience to herself, she had been trying several times a day for the previous ten days to find him. Upon making inquiries, she learned that none of the neighbors had seen him during that period and she was unable to reach any of the contacts listed on his rental application. To determine whether he had indeed flown the coop or whether he was just being evasive, she peered through the windows, and seeing what appeared to be little but trash inside, she decided to enter with her passkey. Strange to say, from what she saw in this house which she had rented out unfurnished, she couldn't tell whether he was, in fact, still living there or not. There was a mattress on the floor in the bedroom and a table and one chair in the kitchen. That's all there was for furniture. On the back porch was a fair-sized heap of trash, and the usual junk one finds in a recently vacated rental was scattered throughout the other rooms. The place looked pretty much abandoned. With her own eyes she had seen places vacated with more stuff inside them than this; she had cleaned them up herself.

It was then that she decided to change the locks, using old replacements exactly like the originals so her locking out the tenant would not appear obvious to him if he did return. His key would fit into the keyway, but it wouldn't turn. That night at 2 o'clock the tenant called to let her know that he couldn't get his key to work. Apologizing for the "defective" lock, she let him in after pretending to have trouble opening the lock herself. They talked cordially. He apologized for not having contacted her earlier about the rent. All kinds of things had happened to him lately, he said, and he had just forgotten, but he promised to move out within two days, and he did.

She believed that he had been eluding her all that time, coming in late and leaving early, and that he would have continued playing cat-and-mouse, occupying the premises rent-free much longer, if she had not forced him to meet with her. Her stratagem had worked. She had managed to outsmart her tenant. She had recovered possession of her house, and she had done it quickly, much more quickly than she would have done had she gone to court.

Do the ends justify the means? It's an age-old question. This landlady believed that they did in her case. Otherwise she would never have gambled and she certainly never would have won. You will have to decide for yourself whether you might use certain pragmatic, quasi-legal (quasi-illegal?) methods to accomplish your objectives in a given situation quickly, cheaply, and painlessly. I do not advocate the use of any methods which violate or skirt the law because they can be dangerous, they must be carefully chosen and carefully executed, they require extra-careful judgment, they don't always work, and they may actually backfire, but I think you should be familiar with them and their drawbacks nonetheless, just as you should be familiar with the applicable legal eviction procedures in your area.

TAKING LEGAL STEPS

When you have tried and failed to rid yourself of problem tenants by hook or by crook, you have no alternative but to try an eviction by the book. You need legal clout to get them out.

Before you begin, however, you should know that in most areas evictions are handled in small claims courts as well as in other courts, but small claims courts have one major disadvantage. In a word, they are slow. Whenever you hear of a case involving a landlord who has been trying to evict a tenant for three months or more, chances are good that the case was filed originally in small claims court.

Each day tenants spend in your dwelling costs you money. Figure it out. A house renting for $720 a month is costing you $24 a day in lost rent, money you might as well forget about ever seeing again. Four days of that rent would easily pay all your costs in those courts which expedite evictions. If it's summary justice you want, don't go to small claims court. Go instead to whatever other court acts on such cases in your area, be it municipal court, justice court, county court, or circuit court.

You should also know before you begin that you may represent yourself in an eviction case or you may be represented by an attorney. Most of the time you'll be able to handle everything yourself because evictions are little more than a formality requiring that certain forms be filled out properly and that certain time limits be observed carefully. Attorneys seldom do this work themselves anyway. They delegate it to their secretaries, and their secretaries select the appropriate form from a form book which, by the way, you may consult free of charge in your court's law library, and then they fill in the blanks. That's all they do, and you can surely do the same (California landlords and landladies who want to do their own evictions may use *The Eviction Book for California*; see the order form in the back of this book).

Besides, you will devote more attention to your own eviction case than will attorneys who may have some 50 to 150 other cases vying for their attention. You will certainly get the tenants out sooner yourself because you have an incentive which they don't. You are losing money every day a non-paying tenant remains. Attorneys aren't. Regardless of how long an eviction action takes, attorneys will charge you the same sum for their services. In fact, if your eviction takes longer and presumably takes more of your attorney's time, he will charge you more. He ought to charge you less the longer it takes, but that's not the way the system works.

Be shrewd enough, though, to recognize when you do need to engage the services of an attorney. Generally you need one when your tenants have hired an attorney themselves, when your tenants in an apartment house have organized against you, when your tenants have filed a written answer to your complaint or affidavit, or when there are any complications you don't understand. That's when you should hire yourself an attorney, and remember that even though you have begun an action on your own, you may always hire an attorney to assist you whenever you feel you need one as the case progresses.

Because the procedures and time limits for evictions vary considerably from area to area, here is some information on evictions which should prove useful to you as you wend your way through the legal maze to get problem tenants out, no matter where you live.

NOTICES—Every legal eviction must begin with a notice advising the tenants of your intentions. It must be properly filled out and properly served. The notice should include the number of days the tenants have in which to comply (minimums are set by laws governing such matters in the area where your rental property is located), the tenants' names and the names of any other adults living there; if you don't know their names, call them "Does I through X" until you can discover who they are), the address of the rental dwelling, the amount of rent due through the current rental period (applicable only in evictions for nonpayment of rent), the period for which this rent is due, and your signature.

Personal service is better than what attorneys call "nail and mail" (affixing the notice to the door and mailing a copy) because longer waiting periods apply in such substituted service situations. You may serve the notice yourself if you want to, but you may be smart to have someone else do it if you think you may be dealing with a perjurer. Some tenants will deny under oath that they ever received the notice, and the judge then has to weigh your word against theirs. Of course, you can always hire an intimidator to do the job for you.

WAITING PERIODS—In some areas, you may count weekends and holidays when determining the waiting periods in an eviction, but the final day for the tenants to pay the rent, vacate, or answer the complaint must be a day when the court is open. Find out from the court clerk whether you may count weekends and holidays. If you may count them, you will save quite a bit of time in expediting your case.

BEST TIMES TO SERVE—Whenever weekends and holidays may be counted in determining the waiting periods, there are certain especially good days for serving 3-day notices in order to take advantage of weekends and holidays in the count. Those best days are Sunday and Monday. Delaying service of a 3-day notice until Tuesday will, believe it or not, cost you at least five extra days in the whole process.

In those areas where weekends and holidays do not figure into the count, there are no "best" days for serving 3-day notices. They're all good.

The best time to serve a Notice to Perform Covenant or a Notice to Terminate Tenancy is always right after rent has been paid. After being served, the tenant's will to pay rent diminishes drastically, and you may actually create an eviction-for-nonpayment situation if you serve the notice at a "wrong" time.

COPIES—Spend a few cents more to produce enough extra copies of all your eviction papers, including the notices, and you will avoid much disappointment and aggravation later. The copies needed will vary, depending upon the type of form and the number of defendants you have to serve. If you produce an original and three copies of each, though, you will be reasonably certain to have enough of every form to go around.

ACCEPTING RENT—You must accept rent offered to you by someone who is responding to your Notice to Pay Rent or Quit within the period specified in your notice. After that time you may accept rent if you want to, but you don't have to. If you accept so much as one dollar at any time following service of the notice, you may have to begin all over again from the beginning by serving another notice. For this reason, you should not accept any rent after you have spent the money to file your complaint or affidavit, unless the tenant agrees to pay the entire back rent plus your out-of-pocket filing expenses as well.

Should your tenant offer to pay you a substantial sum which is still only part of the total rent owed, and should you want to take it without risking the loss of your court case in the future after all the time and money you've spent on it, secure a formal court agreement with the tenant. Stipulate in the agreement that you may obtain a court judgment for eviction if the tenant fails to pay the balance of the rent or vacate by a certain date. This way you get some rent money at least, and you retain your priority for evicting the tenant.

RECORDS—Whether or not you expect the tenant to appear in court, take with you into court all the records you possess on the tenant you are evicting. These should include whatever is applicable from the following list: rental agreement or lease, pet agreement, condition and inventory checksheet, waterbed agreement, correspondence, certified mail receipts, invoices covering repairs of damage, collection records, notices, photographs, and even a chronology of the events in your deteriorating relationship.

Such records will strengthen your case much more than anything you are likely to say in court. Judges don't really want to hear you and the tenant vent your spleens. They want hard-and-fast evidence.

LESSONS—A final eviction notice on one door of an apartment building serves as a convincing lesson to other tenants that you know how to evict and will evict when necessary. Leave the notice on the door long enough for at least one other tenant to see it and then remove it yourself. The word will spread quickly. Don't leave the notice up longer than an afternoon, however, because you don't want other owners in the area to see it. They will wonder what's wrong with your building and will depreciate its value in their minds.

The final eviction notice on the door of a single-family dwelling should be removed as soon as the tenants' belongings are cleared out. It serves no useful purpose after that.

SOME LAST WORDS

Remember that not getting rid of problem tenants is much more aggravating than all the aggravations of actually getting rid them. Go on. Get it over with. Then get on with your business.

MANAGING
THE RENTAL HOUSE

The rental house business as described in Dave Glubetich's *Monopoly Game* and Robert Allen's *Nothing Down* is a little like the Rent-A-Wreck used car rental business, which enables used car dealers to realize a steady income from cars in their inventory which haven't been sold yet.

Any car sitting on a used car lot is only costing the dealer money because he has money tied up in it which is no longer earning him interest, because he has to provide space to store the car, and because he has to look after the car to keep it from deteriorating. The longer he keeps it, the more it costs him to carry it, so he tries to buy cars which will sell quickly and sell for considerably more than what he paid for them. His profit is the difference between what he paid for the car and what he sold it for, minus his various expenses. By renting the car out while it's waiting to be sold, the used car dealer increases his income. His expenses increase a little, but his income increases a lot. That's good business.

Most rental houses are waiting around to be sold, too. The longer their owners hold onto them, the more they cost to hold, but presumably the more they will be worth down the road as inflation drives up the price of housing in general. While the house is "in inventory," the owner rents it out so he doesn't have to bear all the costs of holding onto it until it is worth more. The problem is that even when rented out, most houses still saddle their owners with negative cash flow.

The rental house business hasn't always been this way. Rental house investors used to be able to buy new or nearly new houses in good neighborhoods and rent them out to the traditional unitary family in the traditional way, with a year's lease perhaps and then a month-to-month arrangement. They'd keep their tenants for years, and they'd get a little cash flow, some attractive tax benefits, lots of equity buildup, and maybe a little appreciation. After twenty years they'd own the house free and clear and keep it for retirement income. Rental houses then were sure things, solid gold investments.

Anyone buying houses at market prices on market terms and renting them out today at market rents is going to be losing money every month. That's not good business.

Rental house investing can still be a good business today, however. The houses themselves have to be more carefully considered than ever before, though, because they don't automatically yield a cash-flow return.

Of all the problems in rental house investing and management, that's the biggest, negative cash flow, but there are some solutions to it, and there are some solutions to other rental house management problems, too.

HANDLING THE NEGATIVE-CASH-FLOW PROBLEM

People who, for any number of reasons, prefer to invest in rental houses rather than multiple-family dwellings have grappled with the negative-cash-flow problem for some time now and have come up with some solutions worth examining. Here are eight, most of which are a combination of investment and management strategies—involving tenants as "partners" through lease-options, actually sharing the space with a number of tenants, creating a duplex out of a house, building more houses on the same lot or buying property with more than one house on a lot to begin with, sharing the ownership with silent partners who want a tax writeoff but don't want to be directly involved with rental property themselves, tinkering with the financing, investing in the least expensive housing available, and stealing the house to begin with.

Let's look at these solutions more closely.

• INVOLVE TENANTS AS "PARTNERS."

Many rental house tenants would like to buy a house but don't have the necessary funds to make the down payment or the necessary expertise to find a good low-money-down deal themselves. The short-term lease-option is perfect in those situations for both you and them. It's perfect for you because the tenants pay a little more in rent every month, enough to cover the house's negative cash flow, and it's perfect for them because they get the right to buy the house at a later time for a fixed price or for an appraised price discounted by something more than the amount of their extra monthly contributions.

Of course, there's another benefit in short-term lease-options. Tenants tend to think of themselves more as owners than as tenants, and they take better care of the property.

See Robert Bruss's book, *The Smart Investor's Guide to Real Estate*, for the in's and out's of lease-options.

• SHARE THE SPACE.

In her book *Managing Your Rental House for Increased Income*, Doreen Bierbrier explains precisely how she rents her houses to perfect strangers (mind you, perfect strangers are not necessarily perfect tenants) and collects more aggregate rent from all of them combined than she would if she were renting to a single household.

Perhaps you shared a house or apartment with a group of friends when you were younger. Five of you might have rented a house with each one of you responsible for paying an even 20% share of the rent and utilities. When one of you got married and moved out, that left the remaining four to pay 25% shares of the rent and utilities. That's the traditional way for groups to rent a commodious dwelling and share the space.

Bierbrier has come up with a variation, one which has advantages for the rental house owner and single tenants alike. She sets up what resembles a rooming house operation although she does not live on the site. She rents out the individual rooms herself and assumes the responsibility for filling them all. Her tenants like the arrangement because they don't have to pay more during vacancies and because they get to help select the new tenants. She likes the arrangement because she gets higher rents and a positive cash flow while still getting all the other benefits of rental house ownership.

• CREATE A DUPLEX OUT OF A HOUSE.

A good friend of mine fixed up the trunk of his car and was living in it during his college days. One day another student knocked on the trunk lid and inquired about rentals in the area. They struck up a deal. My friend rented out the trunk of his car and moved into the back seat. He had created a duplex out of a car, possibly a first in recorded American history!

When that friend started investing in rental property, he specialized in creating duplexes out of houses. With minimal renovation work and and minimal expense, he was able to increase his cash flow in just a few years to a point where he could leave his job and retire. Poor guy, he never got a real baptism in rental house ownership. He'd never knew what negative cash flow was. To him, all cash flow was positive. Isn't that what it's supposed to be?

Lest you be concerned about the legality of creating duplexes out of houses, check your zoning laws. You may be amazed to learn that because of today's housing shortage they're more lenient now than ever.

Almost every time, divided space will yield greater rents than the same space will when it hasn't been divided.

• PUT MORE HOUSES ON THE LOT, OR BUY PROPERTY WHICH ALREADY HAS MORE THAN ONE HOUSE ON THE LOT.

When you want to increase your income playing Monopoly, you build more houses. Right? Many times you can do the same thing in the rental housing game. The only difference in real-life rental house investing is that you build the additional houses on the same lot, not on another lot on Ventnor Avenue.

Two or more houses on one lot require no more land investment than one house on that lot. Yet each one of them adds again as much rent as the one house. Those additional houses help to generate positive cash flow.

• SHARE THE OWNERSHIP WITH A SILENT PARTNER.

People with sizable incomes and no writeoffs are keenly aware of the income tax bite. Yet they're so busy doing what they're doing to make their sizable incomes that they don't want to take the time to look after any rental property.

In exchange for all of the tax benefits and a portion of the capital gain, they may agree to pay your rental house's negative cash flow every month.

Sounds good, doesn't it? Everybody would like to have a sugar daddy. Be well aware, though, that silent partners who have to continue making cash contributions to an investment month after month may decide to stop making those contributions after a while and jeopardize your own ownership position.

Make the payments as painless as possible for your silent partner, so the partner doesn't even think about them. Automatic bank transfers or a year's supply of post-dated checks will work to keep the payments coming.

• TINKER WITH THE FINANCING.

The largest percentage of the rental house owner's expenditures goes to the loan payment. Reduce that loan payment, and you brighten the cash flow picture considerably.

There are many ways to reduce a loan payment, but unless they involve a longer term or a lower interest rate, they will increase the amount of the loan principal. You'll be eliminating the negative cash flow all right, but you'll be creating negative amortization. In effect, you'll be taking out a small loan every month to help with the expenses. You get positive cash flow at the expense of having to pay off a larger loan balance later.

There's nothing wrong with taking out a small loan every month so long as you understand that that's how you're creating your positive cash flow. If the value of your rental house is appreciating more than the loan principal, you'll do well. If it doesn't, be prepared to suffer the consequences later.

• INVEST IN THE LEAST EXPENSIVE HOUSING AVAILABLE.

Mobilehomes, known to some people as trailers and to others as manufactured housing, are the least expensive housing to build and to buy. Because they compete in the rental market with much higher priced housing stock, however, these inexpensive investments can and do command good rents. Rental mobilehomes don't have negative cash flows, not when they sell for $10,000 and rent for $200 a month over and above the space rent.

Sure, there are drawbacks. Financing them, maintaining them, and dealing with mobilehome park management are some of the drawbacks. But there are benefits other than the cash flow they generate. Mobilehomes are 100% depreciable. They're depreciable over a period of ten years, and because they're inexpensive, they're relatively easy to sell.

• STEAL THE HOUSE.

Some rental house investors spend far more of their time shopping for property than they ever spend managing it. They're as close as any investors come to being used car dealers. They try to buy at wholesale from anyone who wants to get rid of a house in a hurry at any price; they hold onto it awhile until the profit from the sale becomes long-term capital gain; and then they sell it for as close to the retail price as they can get.

Now if you can buy $80,000 houses for $60,000 with reasonable terms and rent them out for $650 per month, you'll have solved the negative cash flow problem all right, but you're going to be working mighty hard looking for those deals. They're not available at the sales office of every new housing tract. You'll have to hunt them down.

If stealing houses sounds to you like a good way to eliminate negative cash flow and you'd like to try it, just be sure that you don't neglect management so much that you rent your wholesale houses to people who turn you into someone who wants to get rid of a house in a hurry at any price.

HANDLING THE VACANCY PROBLEMS

Vacancies are more worrisome to the rental house investor than they are to the multiple-housing investor. One vacancy in a fourplex means that the building is 75% occupied whereas one vacancy in a rental house means that the building is 0% occupied. As the owner of that rental house, you're quite aware of the income implications of not having any tenants on the property, and you're going to be trying whatever you can to increase the occupancy level from 0% to 100% as soon as possible, but there are some other implications, too. You need to do more than hunt for new tenants during your rental house vacancy.

• SAFEGUARD YOUR VACANT RENTAL HOUSE.

Take special pains to make sure that your rental house is well looked after during any vacancy period. You want to make it attractive enough to prospective tenants, while at the same time you want to keep it from deteriorating.

Transfer the billings for all the utilities into your own name. Having utilities available when you're repairing, cleaning, or showing is convenient, to say the least. What's more, it saves potential breakdowns in gas-fired space and water heaters, and it enables you to keep up the exterior of the property properly.

Make it look occupied. Keep the lawn mowed and watered, keep newspapers and advertising circulars picked up, empty the mailbox if it's located someplace where the accumulation of mail could advertise that the place is unoccupied. Keep window coverings on the windows. Install a timer to switch on a lamp at night. Do everything you can to discourage the vandals, thieves, burglars, squatters, and buzzards who prey on properties which appear to be unoccupied.

• BE SURE YOU'RE FULLY INSURED DURING EXTENDED VACANCIES.

Whenever any dwelling is totally uninhabited, it becomes more vulnerable to some of the various calamities which owners insure their places against. Insurance companies know this. They know that the risks of fire, flooding from burst pipes, and vandalism, for example, all increase when there's no one around to discover such disastrous developments in their early stages and when there's no one who can act to contain the damage.

They understand that their exposure to property loss is greater during vacancy periods so they are sometimes careful to exclude themselves from certain losses if a single-family dwelling is vacant for an extended period.

Check your insurance policy to be sure. Look for clauses lurking somewhere which exclude coverage during vacancies.

If you'd rather not tax your eyes and addle your brain by reading the small print in your policy, discuss the matter with your insurance agent. Be frank. Don't hide a thing.

Don't ignore the possibility that your insurance policy might contain such a clause and then plead ignorance later if you should have a claim. Discuss the matter with your insurance agent in advance. That, after all, is what you're doing when you secure insurance in the first place, isn't it? You are anticipating that you might conceivably have a problem in the future.

If you are supposed to contact your insurance company every time you have an extended vacancy so you can buy additional insurance, then do so. Buy the added insurance whether your lender requires you to or not.

• TAKE SPECIAL PRECAUTIONS WHEN SHOWING YOUR RENTAL HOUSE.

As a rental house owner, you are by definition an absentee owner, not living on the premises, so whenever you have to show a vacancy, you have to cover some distance to reach your rental house and show it off to prospective tenants. Dropping whatever you happen to be doing and going over there to meet people who want to look at it becomes a bother after a few times. Do what any other landlord or landlady might do. Schedule the showings at a particular time when you will open the house to any and all lookers, or else tell those who answer your classified ad to drive by the place first before you schedule a showing for their eyes only.

What else might you do to cut your involvement in showing the place to a minimum? Ask a cooperative neighbor to keep the keys and either unlock the door for anyone who wants to see the place or else take the people through. Many neighbors are delighted to help, some just to get a good look at their prospective neighbors, some just to get a courteous "thank you," and some just to earn a few dollars.

You can also ask those who are interested in seeing the place to come over to your house or place of business, leave a $30 deposit for the house keys, and show themselves through the house. This do-it-yourself showing may work smoothly in many situations forever, but there's always the danger that the people won't return the key, that they will copy the key so they can gain access later, or that they will brazenly move into the house without your ever getting another dollar out of them. If they did move in, they wouldn't be considered trespassers either, because they had your permission to enter, so you'd have a hard time getting rid of them. For these reasons, I do not recommend giving the key to prospective tenants.

If you choose to do so anyway, make sure that you change the keyed locks on the outside doors just before your new tenants move in. That way, nobody who had access to the keys during the vacancy will have easy access to the house during the tenancy, and you will protect yourself from a potentially damaging lawsuit brought by tenants who claim that your lax handling of the keys to their home enabled a criminal to get in and commit a crime there.

Even if you know a veteran landlord or landlady who's always given housekeys to prospective renters, has never changed the locks, has never had any trouble, and thinks you're a fool for being so cautious, I'd risk being called a fool rather than risk an expensive lawsuit, one which may not even be covered by the insurance policies you have. Be cautious about this sort of thing.

HANDLING THE NEIGHBOR PROBLEM

Many times people go out of their way not to become involved with their neighbors. They try to remain as aloof as possible so they won't be bothered by people who are always close by physically.

As a rental house owner, you're in a somewhat different position because you aren't going to be around much to bother the neighbors in person. You lack the potential to become a 24-hour nuisance. The neighbors think of you differently, and you should think of them differently. Don't think of them as a problem. Think of them as a solution. Without the usual fears neighbors have of each other, you can become friendly with them, and you should.

You should go out of your way to establish a relationship with the neighbors. Knock on their doors and meet them. Tell them who you are, and tell them a little about yourself. If they don't understand that they have a stake in your operation, then enlighten them. Tell them that even though you don't live in the neighborhood, you are still concerned about keeping it up because the condition of the neighborhood affects your property value, too. Tell them that you may want to enlist their help now and again when you have to pick new tenants. Be sure you give them your telephone number so they can be your "first alert system" in case your tenants try to pull any shenanigans.

In other words, "employ" the neighbors who live around your rental house. Keep them abreast of what's happening from your end and ask them to keep you abreast of what's happening from their end.

HANDLING THE RESTRICTIONS PROBLEM

Before you ever rent out any dwelling in a condominium complex, planned housing development, co-operative apartment project, or mobilehome park, apprise yourself of what's been written to govern the tenancy and conduct of anyone living there, owner or tenant. This written word might be called rules, regulations, bylaws, conditions, restrictions, or covenants. They're all "restrictions."

You can usually get away with paying scant attention to these restrictions in a complex when you're planning to live there yourself, but when there are tenants involved, you have to pay heed. Both you and your tenants are bound by them, and you may be held responsible for things that your tenants do against the restrictions unwittingly.

These restrictions can vary widely, too. Some mobilehome parks allow no renting of mobilehomes at all. Others don't care. Some co-operative projects allow unlimited renting. Others allow renting for a limited time but only if the renter satisfies a screening committee. Some places won't admit ex-presidents or rock stars as owners, let alone truck drivers or hairdressers as tenants. Some planned developments have restrictions about animals, landscaping, business uses, satellite dishes, paint colors, recreational facilities, and the like, any of which might affect your tenants. You can't know what's allowed and what's not unless you read up on these things.

Having become familiar with the restrictions yourself, you must inform prospective tenants of their responsibilities to the development, park, or homeowners' association. They cannot be held responsible unless they are informed. You'll be the one held responsible instead. That can become a real problem.

By the way, always inform the "powers that be" in one of these restricted living environments that you have tenants occupying your dwelling. They may need to know in order to extend recreational or parking privileges or somesuch to your tenants.

HANDLING THE BOOKKEEPING PROBLEM

As far as bookkeeping goes, you have an important option. Handle each rental house separately or lump them all together. You have to decide.

Why would you want to handle them separately? Because you would then be able to determine exactly how each house is doing, so you could decide whether to keep or get rid of a particular house.

Why would you lump them all together? Because lumping them together is easier than keeping them separate. Instead of prorating purchases for all of your properties, you merely list things once. Instead of hassling with a number of ledger sheets, one for each property, you hassle with only one.

Unless all the properties are the "same," such as a number of mobilehomes or a number of houses on the same lot, I would recommend that you keep your single-family houses separate. Sure, it's more work to begin with, but it gives you the numbers you need to analyze and control what's going on in your business. Whereas it may seem a trifle ridiculous to have three entries on one house's ledger sheet for the entire month, those entries mean something.

Lumping all of your single-family houses together would be like lumping the statistics for an entire college football season together and not keeping track of the individual games. That wouldn't please the fans, the coach, the players, or the conference.

There's nothing wrong with having only one checking account for a number of rental houses. That makes good sense. Each time you write a check, merely identify in the checkbook register which house's expenditures it should be posted to. Then post it separately later.

HANDLING THE MAINTENANCE PROBLEM

Rental house tenants expect less maintenance service than apartment house tenants, and they will do more things for themselves without bothering the owner. You can encourage them even more in that direction by offering either some sort of ownership-participation arrangement like the lease-option already mentioned or some sort of remunerative arrangement like a cash discount on their rent.

Some owners give their tenants a flat $50 rent discount every month so long as the tenants take care of all the minor maintenance and repairs ("minor" means less than $50), pay their rent promptly, don't call the owner unless there's a major problem, and tend to all the gardening themselves. In a sense, those owners are hiring their tenants to manage the property in the same way a property management company would. It's a good idea, but it has the same primary drawback that hiring a property management company has. It distances the owner. To make it work right, you should require a large enough deposit to begin with so that any maintenance the tenants defer during their tenancy will cost them, not you, when they move out.

HANDLING THE GARDENING PROBLEM

Did you know that there's a vegetarian cult on this planet which sincerely believes that lawn mowing causes grass to suffer pain? Well, there is. Tell your tenants that you have a list of all known members of this cult and that unless you can find their names on that list, they'd better keep their grass mowed or you'll be forced to hire a gardening service and raise their rent to pay for it.

That's one way to handle the "gardening problem" at your rental house. There are others.

Consider using the discounted rent policy mentioned above.

Consider installing low-maintenance landscaping. Don't expect a rental house tenant to look after a rose garden. It may be beautiful to look at, something anyone might enjoy, but it's not a practical landscaping choice. It's high maintenance. Study the low-maintenance possibilities and try them.

Consider providing the proper tools and supplies for your tenants to keep the yard weeded, fertilized, and trimmed.

Consider installing an automatic sprinkling system which will keep the landscaping watered without any effort on your tenants' part. They can't have much of an excuse for not watering if there's a sprinkling system available to do it effortlessly.

At least consider yourself lucky that you do have some gardening choices. Owners of multiple-family housing have none. They simply supply gardening service. For them, it's "master metered." In most complexes it can't be done any other way for there's no practical way to divide up the gardening so that each tenant would look after a plot of lawn or a few shrubs.

SOME LAST WORDS

If someone driving down the street where you own a rental house can pick out that one house of yours from all the others which are themselves owner-occupied, then you're doing something wrong. You're not managing the place properly, and the value of your investment is deteriorating. Keep looking for ways to instill a pride of tenantship in your tenants while at the same time you put some money into your own pockets from the property.

LEGAL MATTERS

You may have thought that window screens were supposed to keep out pesky mosquitos, horse flies, gnats, and moths. After all, screens are pretty flimsy things, especially the plastic ones with the aluminum frames used so widely today. They would hardly challenge a charging elephant, a sharp-clawed pussy cat, a wily cat burglar, or even an errant baseball.

Don't be so naive. In these days of the "Twinkies Defense," when people get away with murder, common sense doesn't count for very much. Not long ago a court decided that window screens were supposed to keep out rapists. That's right; a plastic netting less than a sixteenth of an inch thick was supposed to have been sufficient to keep out a man with rape on his mind. Because the landlord had neglected to replace the screen on the very window that the rapist gained entry through, the landlord was negligent and therefore responsible for the rape. The landlord was to blame for the tenant's misfortune. The landlord had to pay.

Was the landlord really to blame for what had happened? Not in my book he wasn't. Others were to blame, but they weren't available for prosecution and if they had been available, they wouldn't have had the assets or the insurance to compensate the victim with. The landlord was both available and capable of compensating the victim. So the landlord became the target of the suit.

People today have been led to believe that there is no such thing as an accident or a misfortune which is nobody's fault. There has to be somebody to blame, somebody with the means to pay off, even if that person is only a teensy-weensy bit at fault.

You are especially vulnerable to lawsuits because you have what lawyers call "deep pockets," which presumably contain plenty of money to pay off the injured party and, of course, all the lawyers involved. People no longer harbor dreams of striking it rich in the gold or oil fields; today they dream of striking it rich by winning either a big lawsuit or a big lottery. The media trumpet these wins across the land. People listen to and read about them and dream of making their fortunes this new-fashioned way. You can hardly blame them for trying to seize their share of the winnings, especially when it costs virtually nothing to get into the game and it's so easy to play.

Unfortunately there is another side to those dreams of gaining wealth through litigation and that is losing wealth through litigation. You, landlord and landlady, are among those people who have to worry about losing their wealth through litigation. You have to take special precautions to protect yourself and your assets from lawsuits.

A lawsuit is like a breath of stale air. Lawsuits are stultifying, time-consuming, costly, tedious, and unnerving. Except for clear-cut eviction matters, you aren't going to win anything in a courtroom. Don't bother trying. Tenants have little or nothing that you can hope to win from them. Most of them are "judgment-proof." They don't have the resources to pay a judgment which does go against them. Yet, they'll bring liability suits,

habitability suits, contract suits, statute violation suits, wrongful eviction suits, security deposit suits, and just plain old nuisance suits against you time and time again because they think that you have plenty to lose and they have plenty to gain.

You're at a double disadvantage in a courtroom as a defendant because you have assets to lose and an unsympathetic reputation as a greedy landlord or landlady to contend with. As if that's not bad enough, you're also going to have to spend time and money defending yourself and you're going to be worrying yourself sick about the uncertainty of it all. Those are not pleasant prospects. Since you cannot hope to gain any advantage over your tenants in court, you can only hope to keep yourself from being taken full advantage of, nothing more.

Here are some steps you can take to reduce your overall legal difficulties and to keep yourself from being taken full advantage of.

TAKING STEPS TO REDUCE LEGAL DIFFICULTIES

• BECOME AWARE OF THE LAWS RELEVANT TO LANDLORDING IN THAT PART OF THE COUNTRY WHERE YOUR RENTAL PROPERTIES ARE LOCATED.

Lawmakers at the federal, state, and local levels have been busy for a long, long time passing law after law to help keep society running smoothly and peacefully, and they haven't neglected landlording.

There are laws at the federal level, including the Fair Housing Act (sets anti-discrimination standards); the Occupational Safety and Health Act (commonly known as OSHA, this act sets standards for safety on the job); the Fair Credit Reporting Act (sets standards for credit information and availability); the Soldiers' and Sailors' Civil Relief Act (sets special leasing provisions for military personnel); and the Truth-in-Advertising Act (sets advertising standards).

There are laws at the state level which govern tenancies at every stage, from the creation of the tenancy through the duration, termination, and aftermath. State laws tell you what your rights and responsibilities as a rental property owner are and what your tenants' rights and responsibilities are. They outline the proper procedures for evictions. They expand the federal anti-discrimination standards. They go into contracts, deposits, notices, employer/employee relationships, liens, vehicle towing, maintenance, subletting, abandonment, bad checks, retaliation, health, safety. In short, state laws cover almost every conceivable aspect of landlording.

There are laws at the local (county or municipal) level, too, which affect what you do as a landlord or landlady. They generally add further restrictions to federal and state laws and can be the most hobbling of all. Some zealously pro-tenant communities have doomed their stock of rental housing by making landlording practically a criminal activity.

Most laws affecting this business appear to have been drafted by the same folks who write the instructions for income tax returns. Laws do not make for easy reading, and they are not something you want to read all the way through or commit to memory. Lawyers don't even do that. Don't you do it either. Do become generally familiar with them, though, so you will know just enough about them to be able to consult specific laws whenever you have a specific question.

How can you consult them? Call your local rental property owners' association and ask for suggestions. Some state associations have done their members the service of gathering all the applicable federal and state laws together into a single volume. Buy a copy. If such a convenient source isn't available, your association can probably direct you to several books which include the applicable laws, the same books lawyers and judges use. You may not want to buy them if they're expensive. Don't. Call your public library and ask whether they have copies. If they don't, call your county law library. Most every county courthouse has one. They're not always so conveniently located as public libraries, but they'll have the books. Lacking an association to call upon for information about the laws you must follow, try asking your local public housing agency what they would recommend. Even though they're public agencies, they have to follow the same laws governing rental housing that you do. They'll know.

To give you some idea how ignorance of the law can affect your business, I remember full well one tenant I was evicting for nonpayment of rent a few years ago. He answered my court-filed complaint stating that I wasn't providing him with enough heat in his steam-heated apartment. The law stated that I had to provide a minimum of 60 degrees of heat three feet above the floor twenty-four hours a day. Yes, the law was that specific! I hadn't been aware of the law at all. Fortunately, my ignorance didn't cause me to lose the eviction because the tenant had made a mistake. He had never complained to me or to any public agency of this deficiency as he was supposed to. The judge saw through this transparent ploy to gain more days of free rent, and the tenant lost. After that scare, though, I decided that some knowledge of the laws affecting me as a landlord was important.

• KEEP INFORMED.

Laws are one thing. How they're interpreted is quite another. No matter how hard lawmakers try to draft unambiguous laws and enough of them to circumscribe every possible situation, there's always something they didn't think of. They're human, too. Court decisions which settle the disputes arising out of these overlooked or unclear situations affect us as much as laws do. Court decisions interpret and amplify the laws on the books and become the authority for later decisions in other courts.

Interpretation of these laws can differ markedly from state to state, from court to court, and from time to time. In New York, there was a case regarding a landlord who refused to rent to someone for one reason only, because that person was a lawyer. The lawyer-applicant sued, arguing that wholesale discrimination against lawyers was illegal. The landlord responded that lawyers eat landlords for breakfast, that as a whole they are more argumentative and more likely to sue than other people; hence they're more likely to make bad tenants. Amazingly enough, the court sided with the landlord in that case and that decision made national news (perhaps the case merely showed that lawyers cut even less sympathetic figures than landlords).

As a landlord or landlady yourself, you might have thought after hearing about the New York case that you could discriminate against an applicant only because he was a lawyer, counterfeiter, minister, or ballet dancer, in other words, on the basis of occupation alone. After all, you already know that you may not discriminate on the basis of race, color, religion, sex, marital status, national origin, or ancestry. That's made clear by federal law. So you might think after hearing about the New York case that you could discriminate legally according to someone's occupation because that's not one of the illegal discrimation categories in the federal law or in your state or local laws. Why not? If it's not specifically prohibited, then it should be all right, eh? Wrong!

The next thing you know, the California Supreme Court rules that its state's Unruh Act, which is about discrimination in business, must be construed to mean that discrimination is prohibited against any classification of people when that classification has nothing to do with the business at hand. Wow! That really changes things! Because being a lawyer in itself has nothing to do with whether someone will be a good or a bad tenant, landlords and landladies may not discriminate on the basis of occupation. Wages, assets, negative recommendations, and the like do have something to do with whether someone will be a good tenant. They are categories of legal discrimination; occupation is not.

Had you read nothing about the California decision and had you attempted to refuse to rent to a lawyer applicant on the basis of the New York decision, you could have been in trouble. Had the case gone to court, you likely would have lost.

This is all interpretation, remember. You're not going to find a law which specifically prohibits you from discriminating against applicants by height, weight, shoe size, or handwriting, but you may find a court decision which has interpreted some other law as prohibiting you from discriminating in these ways. When you think about these as criteria for tenant selection, they sound pretty illogical, don't they? To refuse an applicant on the basis of shoe size? Come on! That doesn't really have anything at all to do with being a good tenant, does it?

In that window-screen rape case mentioned earlier, there was no law cited which required window screens or else. That case involved interpretation, too. By keeping informed of what's happening in the courts, you will know better what you can do to stay out of trouble yourself. You'll make sure your windows have screens. Right?

Read all the relevant, up-to-date information on rental housing that you can possibly get your hands on. The following are good sources of legal information: daily newspapers (more to make you aware of what's happening than to provide accurate information); rental property owners' association periodicals; and the *Landlord-Tenant Law Bulletin* (see "Periodicals" in Sources and Resources), which is published monthly and summarizes significant cases from throughout the country.

Attend seminars which focus on the legal aspects of the rental property business. These seminars may be sponsored by property owners' associations, a particular attorney, the state bar association, or a local institution of higher learning. Some may be intended for attorneys in general practice (these are generally open to anyone interested in the subject and not just to attorneys); some may be intended for landlords.

Seek out several gurus in the business and ask them questions to clarify fuzzy matters and to relieve specific doubts you might have.

You're in a changing business which requires that you keep informed.

• DO YOUR PAPERWORK PROMPTLY AND PROPERLY.

Act as if it's inevitable that you're going to be dragged into court on some tenant matter or other, and start building your case in advance. Reduce all of your tenant relationships to writing. Use written rental applications, written rental agreements, and written condition-and-inventory checksheets. Make an entry in a logbook each time you respond to a tenant's complaint or call for assistance. Put your own complaints about tenants in writing instead of merely talking with them. Insist that your tenants use a written notice to advise you that they're moving.

If your tenants turn out to be lawsuit-happy, if you have to evict them, or if they leave owing you money, this paperwork will be more essential to you than a figleaf in a nudist camp. Judges tend to be "paper slaves" themselves, and they look kindly on good documentation.

• INSPECT YOUR PROPERTY AND ENLIST OTHERS TO HELP.

Most people consider a site inspection of their property by their own insurance company as an imposition at the very least. They think that the company is spying on them, that it's trying to find some reason to cancel their policy. So they're inclined not to cooperate and even to conceal whatever's faulty.

That's not the right attitude. First of all, remember that your insurance company is for you, not against you. It's on your side. It wants your business. It doesn't want to cancel you out. It doesn't make any money by canceling your policy. It simply doesn't want excessive risk. That's all. Second, any company which is concerned enough about its own exposure to send an inspector to look at your property is a company you want to do business with. They're trying to keep their expenses down. Lower expenses for them translate into lower premiums for you. Third, if they don't send an inspector out, ask them to. You should know what you can do to make your property as safe as possible.

If you can't get your insurance company to send out an inspector, inspect your property yourself, especially the common areas. Look for anything which might possibly trigger a liability lawsuit. Look for exposed electrical wiring, uneven walkways, missing or broken railings, slippery floors, potholes in the parking lot, inadequate lighting, faulty locks, sharp protrusions, poorly ventilated heaters, rotted footings, loose toilet seats, and the like.

By inspecting your property yourself and enlisting the aid of your insurance company to do the same, you'll find most of the obviously hazardous conditions around your property, but you're not going to find all of them, and you're not going to be giving your tenants and their attorneys second thoughts about suing you. That's why you should involve your tenants in your inspection. "Deputize" them to be alert at all times to hazardous conditions. Make them responsible for advising you whenever they notice something which just might be hazardous.

An attorney who frequently represents tenants injured in slip-and-fall cases told me he would have a difficult time winning many of his cases if rental property owners would send their tenants a letter every year asking them to report hazardous conditions. Tenants would be hard pressed to argue that their landlords and landladies were negligent if the tenants themselves didn't notice a particular hazard.

Here's the letter he wouldn't like you to use. Use it once a year, and follow up on it. Keep copies of your tenants' responses together with their applications, agreements, and checksheets. They're important, very important.

April 10, 1986

Dear *Hank and Gladys Angel:*

We want to make the place where you live as safe as it can be. We are constantly on the lookout for anything around your home which might prove hazardous to life, limb, or property. But hard as we try, we cannot uncover every potential danger all by ourselves. We need your help.

Because you are around your home much more than we are, you have a greater opportunity to notice hazards. Please report to us anything you notice which you think might prove hazardous to you or anyone else. We promise that we will investigate the hazardous condition and remedy it if we possibly can.

Please complete the bottom section of this letter and return it to us with your next rent payment.

Thank you for your cooperation in making your home a safer place to live.

Sincerely,

Lester Landlord

- -

☑ We know of nothing which appears to be unsafe in or around our home, but we will alert you whenever we do notice something.

☐ We would like to call your attention to the following unsafe conditions in or around our home:

_____

_____

_____

_____

We suggest that you take the following corrective action:

_____

_____

_____

Signed _*Hank Angel*_____   Dated *April 28, 1986*

• MAINTAIN YOUR PROPERTY.

Whenever you become aware of anything on your property which might be considered unsafe, take care of it as soon as possible. As long as you allow a hazardous condition to continue, you are exposing your tenants to injury and yourself to lawsuits, and at the same time you could be allowing the situation to worsen. You know that you'll have to fix it sometime. Why not fix it now?

• USE COMMON SENSE.

Common sense may not seem to count for very much in a court of law nowadays, but it still counts for something. Laws frequently acknowledge the thoughts and actions of "reasonable people," and they mention "reasonable care" again and again. These are other ways of saying that laws cannot cover every eventuality, and when something arises which they don't cover, judgment will be based on whether the people involved acted reasonably. Did they use the good common sense which reasonable people are supposed to have?

Tenant relations require you to use all the common sense you can muster. Be as reasonable as you can be when tenants are being unreasonable. Don't show anger. Don't act rashly. Don't be stubborn. People get hurt and court cases get filed when you take leave of your common sense.

• IDENTIFY ATTORNEYS SUITED TO YOUR VARIOUS PROBLEMS.

Whenever I think about hiring an attorney, I remember the little old lady who was overheard saying, "I don't want an attorney. I want to tell the truth."

Attorneys do have to contend with a reputation as truth benders. They have been known to speak with forked tongues at times. Yet, representing clients in court in the best possible light is a small part of what they do. They can help you with their good advice, intercede for you when you seem to be getting nowhere with an adversary, review your contracts, and otherwise keep you from getting into trouble.

The day appears to be fast approaching when we will have no choice but to consult an attorney before we advertise a vacancy, reject an applicant, say hello to a tenant, repair a broken window, or pick up a scrap of paper. I don't look forward to that day myself, and I'm sure you don't either. To try to change this impending state of affairs, think about joining HALT (Help Abolish Legal Tyrrany; see "Associations" in Sources and Resources). In the meantime, you'd better come to know those attorneys who can help you with the problems which plague you now and probably will tomorrow.

HALT publishes a useful manual called *Shopping for a Lawyer*. It and a handful of publications like it will assist you in finding the right kind of legal counsel for your particular needs.

Like many other professionals, attorneys have specialties. One might know divorces from the husband's point of view, and another might know them from the wife's. One might know landlord-tenant law from the landlord's viewpoint; another from the tenant's. Find an attorney who specializes. One who doesn't may be legally qualified to represent you but actually know less about landlord-tenant matters than you do. Don't pay for that attorney's education.

• INSURE YOURSELF ADEQUATELY.

No matter how conscientious you are about following the previous suggestions for preventing landlording's legal difficulties, you cannot eliminate the risk of lawsuits entirely. You cannot become a Teflon landlord. That's why you have to have insurance.

There's no law requiring you to have any insurance at all except workers' compensation, and you don't need that unless you employ someone to work for you, but you could be very, very sorry that you didn't protect yourself with insurance when you get summoned into court to defend yourself on some matter or other. Because lawsuits are expensive, and settlements are expensive, insurance is expensive, but not having it can turn out to be more expensive still. It can precipitate financial disaster, your financial disaster. You can't afford that.

Chapter 15, the insurance chapter, describes various types of insurance which will pay for your defense in case you're sued and will pay your judgments in case you lose. There's another kind of insurance which is available as a way to keep you from having to pay high legal bills. It's similar to health maintenance plans which keep people from having to pay high medical bills when disaster strikes. It won't pay any judgments against you, but it will pay your attorney's fees in case you're sued for any number of reasons. It will pay your attorney's or accountant's fees in case you're audited by the IRS. And it will pay for legal check-ups as well. For landlords and landladies, who are so exposed to lawsuits so often, it bears looking into. It's available from Pre-Paid Legal Services, P.O. Box 1680, Ada, Oklahoma 74820, 1-800-654-7757.

SEARCHING FOR THE RIGHT RENTAL AGREEMENT

Some poor souls kept searching for the Fountain of Youth as long as they lived. You'll be searching for the right rental agreement as long as you're in this business. Laws change, practices change, locales change, your property mix changes, and your tenant mix changes. You have to adapt your business practices to these changes or suffer the consequences. The rental agreement you use is at the very center of your business. You must feel comfortable with it. You must feel that it covers everything you want it to cover. And you must feel sure that it's perfectly legal.

As you keep searching for this "right" agreement, you're going to have questions, plenty of questions. The following questions will keep coming up again and again, and you're probably going to change your answers more than once. That's all right. There are no right answers.

• SHOULD YOU USE RENTAL AGREEMENTS OR LEASES?

You'll notice that there are only two choices given in the question above—rental agreements and leases. In truth, there are four choices—oral rental agreements, written rental agreements, oral leases (leases for any period longer than a year must be written), and written leases, but oral agreements and oral leases, while they may be binding, are seldom used anymore because people don't trust their memories or each other as much as they once did. Forget about making oral contracts altogether yourself (after all, some people nowadays even put their nuptial agreements in writing to remind their spouses of certain obligations), and you'll avoid the many misunderstandings which can be caused by people's foggy recollections of what was agreed upon initially. Consider only whether you should use a written agreement or a written lease, here called simply "rental agreement," and "lease," and keep in mind the difference between the two.

Basically the difference is a simple one, but it is an exceedingly important one. Rental agreements cover time periods which are either indefinite (month-to-month) or short (a day), whereas leases cover a definite and longer period of time (generally a year for residential property). Although they may be written to contain rent escalation and thirty-day termination clauses, in which cases they are essentially rental agreements anyway,

leases bind both parties to the terms of the agreement so that no changes may be made by either party until the lease expires or unless one party breaks it.

Lease breaking occurs every day and you don't have to think too much about the matter to figure out who usually breaks them. Tenants do. In theory, if tenants move before their lease expires and they do not have good cause, that is, they have not entered active duty with the U.S. Military or taken employment in another community or lost the main source of income used to pay rent, then they are responsible for paying rent covering the entire lease period, so long as you have been unsuccessful in a reasonable effort to find new tenants at the best rent possible. In practice, however, even if you do make a reasonable effort to rerent the place and find nobody, you would have a difficult time collecting all that rent owing on the lease unless the tenants had sufficient assets, and even then you'd probably have to sue them every month in separate small claims actions to recover.

Leases are like those treaties which the U.S. so naively signs with Russia every so often. They bind the U.S., just as leases bind landlords and landladies, while Russia and tenants do exactly as they please, impudently enjoying the limitations they have placed upon their foolish adversaries.

Leases bind only those who have some assets and want to be bound. Tenants generally have little to lose by breaking a lease, but woe be unto you, landlord or landlady, if you should ever try to break a lease! That "Clark Kent of consumerism," Ralph Charell, in his book, *How I Turn Ordinary Complaints into Thousands of Dollars*, boasts of collecting a $25,000 payoff from his landlords for dispossessing him before his lease was up, and his was a lease which new owners inherited.

Remember that any and all rental agreements, leases included, which are in effect at the time of a property transfer become the responsibilities of the new owners to uphold. Covering extended periods of time as they do, leases can affect the transfer of property substantially if the new owner wants to assume possession of the dwelling or change the terms of an agreement. If you are renting out a house, for example, on a one-year lease which has four months to run, and you have found a buyer who wants to move in upon close of escrow, you may lose the sale entirely unless you can somehow convince your buyers to wait four months or your renters to move before their lease expires.

All of these considerations appear to reflect so negatively on leases that you may wonder why any landlord or landlady would ever use one. There are a few circumstances, precious few, where leases may prove favorable to the landlord or landlady, and even then they should be limited to periods of a year or less (except for commercial properties, which vary according to area and market conditions). Those circumstances include student rentals (to assure year-round occupancy), luxury rentals (to encourage tenant improvements), established tenancies (to ease good, long-term tenants' fears), high vacancy areas (to offer security from rent increases as an incentive), Section 8 subsidized housing (to participate at all), rental houses (to promote greater tenant commitment; only if you feel certain that you won't be marketing the house during the lease period), and commercial properties (to facilitate business cost projections and encourage stability and improvements).

Unless you can conceive of some obvious advantage to you for using leases, use written month-to-month rental agreements instead, and you'll stay out of trouble.

• SHOULD YOU THROW THE KITCHEN SINK INTO YOUR AGREEMENTS?

The one-page Rental Agreement introduced in Chapter 4 does not include the proverbial kitchen sink. Nope, it is simple and understandable, and it includes only the essentials needed to formalize a landlord-tenant relationship involving a residence. It is much better than a verbal agreement, that's for sure, but it is not as good in some ways as a comprehensive umpteen-page agreement drafted for your particular rental property by a lawyer familiar with all the pertinent laws and practices in the locale where the property happens to be. Naturally, such an agreement would include the kitchen sink and a whole lot more.

The trouble with most lengthy agreements, however, be they custom-made or "standard" forms, is that they tend to be repetitive and incomprehensible. They're so full of legal jargon that they don't make much sense to the parties they're supposed to make sense to, and they're so lengthy that you can't possibly review them word by word with new tenants unless you spend half the day pouring over them. Try reading over a lengthy agreement with a new tenant sometime, and you'll barely be able to keep from stifling yawns and rolling your eyes.

Don't you read and try to understand any agreement you put your signature to? If you're not in the habit, you should be. Well, why should you require your tenants to sign a rental agreement which neither they nor you can understand?

Don't use any agreement, long or short, unless you are able to explain it to your tenants as you read it over with them. Anything else, especially if it has lots of fine print, may appear to them to be sneaky, whether it is or not. (One landlady I know goes to the trouble of writing her rental agreements out by hand. She claims that her tenants trust handwritten documents more than those which are typed or printed.)

A rental agreement must communicate the particulars of what you and your tenants have agreed upon, and it must be legally enforceable. That's all. It needn't repeat every last detail of the applicable landlord-tenant law as some agreements do, and it needn't be written so that only someone with a law degree is able to interpret it.

If you feel somehow vulnerable unless you use a rental agreement lengthy enough to cover almost everything in your landlord-tenant relationships, that is, unless it includes the proverbial kitchen sink, get a long-form agreement from your local property owners association. You can be sure that it has been reviewed by lawyers who are familiar with the applicable landlord-tenant laws and that it will include every essential element plus a whole lot more. But don't stop there. Read it over carefully. If it doesn't make perfect sense to you, translate it yourself into a meaningful document so that you'll understand it well enough to be able to help your tenants understand it also.

Another good agreement is available from Professional Publishing Company, publishers of the useful *Realty Bluebook*, 122 Paul Drive, San Rafael, CA 94903. Send them $5 and they will send you samples of all their forms including a rental agreement, a lease-option agreement, and a combined purchase agreement and deposit receipt.

No matter what agreement you use, check it for legality, and keep checking it all the time. As you know, slavery is now against the law in this country. Were someone to agree voluntarily to become your slave and were you to draw up a slavery agreement which was then signed by your slave without any coercion whatsoever, you could not enforce that agreement through any court in the land. When your "slave" wants out of those shackles, you'd better let him go. Don't try to argue that the shackles are foam padded. He has an inalienable right to liberty. That's a right he cannot sign away under any circumstances. So, too, tenants cannot sign away their rights even if they are willing to. Your agreement should not include any provision which deprives them of their rights, such as their right to privacy, their right to quiet enjoyment, their right to minimum notice periods, or their right to the prompt return of their deposits. Such clauses would be unenforceable and would cause a judge to look askance at your entire agreement.

Keep unenforceable clauses and needless repetition of the law out of your agreement and keep it reasonable enough so that when tenants win more new rights, you won't have to revise your agreement completely. Use an agreement with a long "shelf life," one which won't sour after each new law passes.

• SHOULD YOU ASK FOR ATTORNEY'S FEES IN YOUR RENTAL AGREEMENT?

Most rental agreements include a provision which awards attorney's fees to the prevailing party in any litigation between the landlord and tenant which involves the agreement. Without that provision, a landlord who wins such a suit cannot recoup his attorney's fees. That sounds like an unpleasant prospect, doesn't it? But what happens if your tenant wins a long, drawn-out suit claiming that you failed to maintain his rental house adequately and that's why he hasn't been paying you any rent for six entire months? Here's what would happen. You'd lose all or most of the rent for six months. You'd have to pay your own costs and attorney's fees. And you'd have to pay the $3,000 or $4,000 for your tenant's costs and attorney as well. You'd be triply penalized for losing, and it wouldn't matter one whit that you knew full well the tenant was lying in court. His prevailing in court would entitle him to the fees because of that provision in your rental agreement.

You cannot know exactly how this provision or the lack of it is going to affect you at some time in the future. An attorney who's advising you on your rental agreement isn't going to know for sure either. Only in retrospect will you know whether you made the right decision.

You should certainly think about the matter, though, and here are some of the points you should consider.

Do not ask in your agreement that attorney's fees be awarded to the prevailing party if:
—the kind of tenant you generally rent to is "judgment proof" anyway, that is, he wouldn't have the money to pay you if you did get a court judgment against him.
—your tenants generally use legal-aid attorneys to represent them.
—the courts in your area tend to favor tenants in their decisions.
—you generally handle your own evictions (attorneys who represent themselves in court may not charge their defeated opponent any fees for their time nor may you when you represent yourself).

Do ask in your agreement that attorney's fees be awarded to the prevailing party if:
—your tenants tend to have enough money to pay a judgment.
—the courts in your area appear to be relatively impartial in landlord-tenant cases.
—you always hire an attorney to do your evictions.
—you are confident that you will be the prevailing party forty-nine times out of fifty.

After thinking about these various points, look your rental agreement over and see that it reflects your thinking on awarding attorney's fees.

SOME LAST WORDS

An attorney recently told me that there are only two kinds of landlords and landladies—those who have been sued and those who will be. That may sound pretty pessimistic to you. It's not. It's more realistic than you might think. You should be pessimistic about lawsuits. Resign yourself to the inevitability of your being sued for something or other sometime and you won't get too upset when it happens. If you're doing most of what is outlined in this book, you will be reducing your exposure to lawsuits and other legal hassles drastically. Unfortunately, you cannot eliminate them entirely, no matter what you do, no matter how careful you are.

DECISIONS, DECISIONS

Solomon's decisions may have been more momentous, but they were certainly no more numerous than the landlord's or landlady's. There's always some decision or other to be made, and there always seems to be so little time and help available when you have to make them that you might as well be plucking daisy petals or flipping nickels to help you make up your mind. I can only hope that the alternatives presented in this chapter will contribute something toward helping you make a few of those many decisions more sensibly, so you'll be able to improve your profitability and perhaps even begin to enjoy landlording.

SHOULD YOU DO IT YOURSELF?

Do-it-yourself books never discuss whether you ought to consider hiring someone else to do "it" for you. Why should they? That's a subject beyond their province, and besides, they're too involved with explaining *how* you can do things yourself to discuss *whether* you ought to be doing them yourself at all. They assume that doing things yourself is more enjoyable and less expensive than hiring help, and such an assumption will generally prove correct for most do-it-yourselfers unless they botch a job so badly that they only add to its complexity and have to pay that much more for professional help or unless they cut off an ear or a toe and have to pay big medical bills.

This do-it-yourself book is different, however, because landlording is different. In landlording it is often good business, for a variety of reasons, *not* to do everything yourself. You can even ask yourself a few questions when you are trying to make the decision. Here are some of those questions, some obvious and some not so obvious, which take into account the special nature of this business and may help you decide whether you ought to do certain things yourself or hire them done.

• ARE YOU ABLE AND KNOWLEDGEABLE ENOUGH TO DO IT YOURSELF? You know what expertise you have, and you know what you're capable of doing both physically and mentally. Can you do this job? It may necessitate climbing up the side of a two-story building on an extension ladder that sways in the wind. Are you afraid of heights? It may involve knowledge of the latest tax laws about exchanging. Have you been keeping abreast of the field? It may mean testing electrical connections with the power on. Do you know enough about electricity to avoid electrocuting yourself?

If you suspect that you can't do the work properly or at all yourself, hire it done.

• DO YOU WANT TO DO IT YOURSELF? Some jobs, like cleaning ovens, painting bedrooms, mowing lawns, and unplugging toilets, are tedious or repetitious or mundane or loathsome, and you may have no desire to do them yourself even though you know that you are able to do them.

If you simply don't want to do them yourself, hire them done.

• DO YOU NEED SOME COMPANY WHILE YOU DO IT YOURSELF? You may be knowledgeable, ready, willing, and able to do certain work all by yourself, but if you tend to work rather slowly when you work alone, perhaps you should consider hiring someone else to work along with you. You may find yourself becoming more productive when there's a high school or college student working alongside you because you are trying to set a good work example and also to compete with the student's work pace.

If you suspect that you would work better and faster working alongside someone else, hire a helper.

• DO YOU HAVE THE TIME TO DO IT YOURSELF? There are only 168 hours in a week, and even though you may at times think you're superhuman, you still cannot cram any more hours into your week.

If you don't have the time to do a job, hire it done.

• RELATIVE TO THE OTHER LANDLORDING WORK YOU HAVE TO DO, HOW MUCH WOULD THIS JOB COST IF YOU WERE TO HIRE IT OUT? You can figure the relative cost of a job by the type of work involved. Plumbing generally costs more than painting, and painting costs more than housecleaning. If you have a kitchen gusher on a Sunday morning, don't call the plumber and pay his $45 per half hour minimum for weekend work, fix it yourself, that is, unless you figure your own time is worth more.

Sometimes the work you do yourself and the work you hire done should be determined strictly on the basis of cost so long as you are able to do both and have the time to do one or the other. Painting, gardening, yard maintenance, and housecleaning are all relatively inexpensive to hire done, whereas work such as plumbing, electrical, and appliance repair are relatively expensive.

If you have a choice, do the expensive work yourself and hire the inexpensive work out.

• DO YOU HAVE THE MONEY TO PAY FOR HIRED HELP? In the beginning of your landlording career you will have more time than money and you will have to do much more work yourself.

If you don't have the money available to hire work done, do it yourself.

• WILL YOU LOSE ANY ADDITIONAL RENTAL INCOME BY DOING CERTAIN WORK YOURSELF? Some landlords and landladies refuse to hire any help at all because they think "it costs too much" or "you can't trust workers nowadays," or they think of some other reason that suits their fancy. There are plenty.

That kind of attitude sometimes winds up costing them plenty because they haven't considered one very important factor—the rent penalty (lost rent). If preparing a vacated unit for renting will take you three weeks to do yourself in your spare time and the rent you may expect for the place is $300 per month or $10 a day, then your rent penalty for doing the work yourself is $210. If, on the other hand, you hire the work done for $192 (labor only) and it takes three days, your rent penalty is only $30. Adding the rent penalty to the labor costs in each case yields sums of $210 and $222, a difference of $12. In other words, you would be spending three weeks of your spare time, say, 48 hours approximately, and you would be earning all of $12 or 45 cents per hour for your efforts. Why, that's below the minimum wage! You'd better report yourself to your state's employment department and go directly to jail! Do not pass GO! Do not collect a savings of $192! Collect all of $12!

The advantage of hiring help would vary somewhat, of course, if there were no immediate demand for your rental, if the rent were more or less than $300, if the work took more or less than 48 hours, or if your helpers demanded more or less than $4 per hour. Be that as it may, this example serves to illustrate just how shortsighted some landlords and landladies can be when they ignore the rent penalty and try to do everything themselves only to save themselves a few bucks.

If your rent penalty approximates the cost of hiring help, then hire the help.

• IS THE WORK TAX-DEDUCTIBLE? Every expense related to your landlording business is tax-deductible, naturally. If the labor for a landlording job will cost you $200, and you're in a 35% tax bracket, you might say that the job is really costing you the equivalent of $130 in taxable dollars.

Well, let's suppose now that you have two jobs to do, one involving some exterior painting at your rental property and the other involving some exterior painting at your own home. You have a $550 bid on the rental property paint job and a $450 bid for the paint job on your home, but you know you have enough time to complete only one. Which one should you do?

Do the one at home. Why should you? Even though it appears on the surface to cost $100 less, the paint job at home would actually cost you more if you were to hire it out because it's not tax-deductible. The home paint job would cost you $450 in pre-tax dollars and in after-tax dollars, while the rental property job, because it is tax-deductible, would cost you around $550 in pre-tax dollars but only $360 in after-tax dollars if you happened to be in the 35% bracket.

If you must choose between doing several jobs, then, be sure you calculate what their tax consequences are before you decide whether to do them yourself or hire them out.

• IS THERE ANYONE AVAILABLE TO DO THE WORK? Sometimes you will have decided to hire help, but because it's the first day of elk season, Big Game Weekend, New Year's Eve, or Mardi Gras time, there's just no one available to work for you.

If there is indeed no one available, you'll just have to cry, stall until someone is available, or do it yourself. What other alternative is there?

• IS THERE MUCH TRAVELING REQUIRED? Those rental properties you own which are located at a distance from your home require a certain amount of time and expense to reach, and you should calculate approximately what both of them are.

If they are anywhere near the sums necessary to hire a job done and if you have no other good reason to visit the property, pick up the phone, hire it done, and save yourself the travel expense and the bother of doing it yourself.

• ARE PERSONAL RELATIONSHIPS GOING TO SUFFER IF YOU DO IT YOURSELF? A divorced landlord once told me that no marriage could survive more than ten rental buildings, be they houses or high rises. His number may or may not be accurate, I don't know, but he knew from firsthand experience that his own marriage couldn't survive the fourteen rental houses and two sixplexes he and his wife had accumulated. It couldn't survive because he was trying to do everything himself. Looking back on his own experience, he felt that ten would have been the magic number to keep his own marriage intact. Ten may be the correct number for some people, and it may be two or twenty-six for others. The number is relatively unimportant. What is important are the demands which you allow your rentals to place upon your time. Spending all your spare time and energy on your rental properties would strain any personal relationship to the breaking point and would probably strain you, too, even if you could draw your family into the business to help.

If you persist in accumulating rental properties, you must begin to hire help in order to preserve your personal relationships and your own sanity as well. Don't try to do it all yourself. You'll succeed only in becoming a lonely millionaire.

SHOULD YOU HIRE A PROPERTY MANAGEMENT COMPANY?

Country folk have a saying which goes, "Ain't no fertilizer like the farmer's shadow." Landlording is no different. Nobody can do the job of looking after your rental property that you can; absolutely nobody. You knew that already, didn't you? Sure.

But when you start swearing at your tenants more than you feel you should, and you know that you want to hang onto your rental property because you're convinced that it's a sound investment, you start thinking about hiring a property management company to relieve you of the headaches and get you to stop swearing so much. The ads for property management companies certainly do sound enticing. They promise to take care of everything for you, and that they can do.

In fact, property management companies are set up to handle management on three different levels. At the most detached level, they can handle asset management, which involves fact-finding and decision-making about the acquiring, holding, and disposing of properties. It might be characterized as year-to-year management. Then there's off-site management, which involves the hiring and supervision of on-site employees, contracting of work with independent contractors, purchase of larger items, checkwriting, bookkeeping, and the handling of evictions. It's pretty much month-to-month or week-to-week management. And last, there's on-site management, which involves showing vacancies, selecting tenants, purchase of smaller items, minor maintenance, tenant relations, collecting rents, and banking deposits. That's day-to-day management.

Most individual investors reserve asset management for themselves because it involves consequential decisions which can make or break those whose assets are involved. It's the other two which they hire property management companies to take care of, the off-site and the on-site management.

The charge for off-site management generally ranges from a low of 3% to a high of 10% of the gross; 3% for the largest complexes on up to 10% for single-family dwellings. Of course, this doesn't include the on-site manager's wages. It's extra.

A charge of 5% for looking after a twelve-unit apartment building doesn't sound exorbitant, does it? It's not. That's just what I figure I'm earning when I do my own off-site management. Don't forget, however, that no company is going to look after your property the way you would. That percentage of the gross may be all you're paying the property management company, but it may not be all that their service is going to cost you. It'll cost you extra if they create problems which have to be remedied. It'll cost you extra if they don't shop for good prices. It'll cost you extra if they receive kickbacks from certain service companies and suppliers. It'll cost you extra if they write checks for supplies and then get refunds in cash. It'll cost you extra if they collect rent for units which they're reporting as vacant. Situations abound for property management companies to blunder; temptations abound for them to siphon off funds.

And you thought that a property management company would relieve you of your worries! The truth is that some of them can. Some of them are indeed forthright and honest, but you must be careful in picking a property management company, just as careful as you would be in picking a surgeon for your heart transplant. Select one recommended to you by more than one satisfied client who stands to gain nothing from the endorsement. Select one that is sworn by rather than sworn at.

After all this, the question still remains—Should you hire a property management company? Yes, you should if you are too disinterested, too busy, too wealthy, too distant, too exasperated, too decrepit, or too haughty to look after your property yourself.

As for me, the answer is no. I shouldn't hire a property management company, and I won't, no matter where I'm investing, no matter how much I'm worth. I want control. I want to be able to hire an on-site manager I can trust instead of having another layer of management between myself and the property. I want the on-site manager responsible to me. I want to have my bookkeeper handling the disbursements and income reports. I want to see the bids for painting the outside of the building and for trimming the 29 palms. I want to have my finger on the property's pulse. I want to know what's going on. All of this is important to me. It's important to my investment. Yes, it does require some of my time, but that's minimal. The real time demands in property management are on the site. Hiring that out makes sense under most circumstances. Off-site management is different. I feel that being my own off-site manager yields the greatest return for the time involved than anything else I might do in managing my rental properties.

Why not be your own property management company? Extend your shadow across your properties and watch them grow!

SHOULD YOU OWN UP TO BEING THE OWNER?

Shortly after I purchased my first fourplex, a friend mentioned in casual conversation that he knew a landlord who would never ever admit to his tenants that he was, in fact, the owner. He would always call himself the manager but never, never the owner. To someone who had just become a landlord, such a posture was inconceivable. I was proud of my units and denying ownership would have been tantamount to denying paternity of a first-born. Not only did I feel that I couldn't do it, but I couldn't really see the point of the ruse unless, perhaps, one owned tenements and didn't want to be bothered with all the attendant problems.

Years later, I came to understand the value of this polite fiction, and I have come to use it with some properties successfully myself. What it does, quite frankly, is enable you to pass the buck.

Invariably something will come up that a tenant wants to do which you know you don't like, but you're on the spot, and you can't think of a good reason for refusing the request outright. Tomorrow you will think of a good reason in hindsight, no doubt, and you'll kick yourself for not having thought of it when you needed it, but then it will be too late to do anything about it. If you are known as the "manager" or as one of the "partners," though, you merely say that you will have to consult with the owner or your partner. Then you will have the time necessary to think up a good excuse, or, if you wish, you can simply refuse the request after having consulted the "owner" and not offer any excuse at all for the refusal. When asked for detailed reasons, you simply say you're awfully sorry but there's nothing you can do about the matter. You tried, but your partner couldn't be budged.

It can even work when you live on the premises. You are the manager, aren't you?

SHOULD YOU RENT IT FURNISHED?

There is extra money to be made in renting furnished dwellings, no doubt about it, but it requires extra effort and investment, and sometimes it brings extra grief. Actually it adds yet another "business," furniture rental, to the one you're already in, so it should be thought of as a sideline which has certain advantages and disadvantages all its own.

Consider these advantages and disadvantages:

Advantages—
    —More income
    —Lower vacancy factor
    —Increased depreciation available for tax purposes
    —Less redecoration required when people move (furnished dwellings, when vacant, still look lived in and distract the eye from the walls)
    —Less wear and tear on the property caused by tenants' careless moving of their own heavy furniture

Disadvantages—
    —Greater investment required
    —More tenant turnover
    —Muscles needed for moving furniture about
    —More repairs
    —More maintenance (excluding redecorating)
    —Increased risk of damage
    —Greater theft potential
    —Storage area required for surplus furniture
    —Added recordkeeping and bookkeeping
    —Purchasing time needed (you have to select the furniture)
    —Obsolescence (furniture goes out of style)

Seemingly, the disadvantages of renting furnished dwellings outweigh the advantages. They certainly outnumber the advantages. What's more important, though, in this comparison is whether you would be adequately compensated for assuming the burden of all the disadvantages, and that comes down to numbers. If the added furnishings can produce, say, a 100% return on the investment over a twelve-month period without becoming trashed during that time, then renting furnished dwellings might actually be an attractive proposition. It can be done. Such a return can even be surpassed.

One landlord friend of mine has found that renting one-bedroom apartments furnished with his own sturdy homemade furniture, including waterbeds, yields him a 100% return in six months on the furniture and more than compensates him for the extra effort and investment. His turnover is slightly higher, but his vacancy factor is nil, and his cash flow is phenomenal. Renting furnished apartments has paid off handsomely for him.

If you are fully cognizant of both the advantages and disadvantages of renting furnished dwellings and if your own rentals lend themselves to being rented furnished, such as those catering to singles, armed services personnel, students, or vacationers, you might try furnishing one rental as an experiment before you furnish them all. See for yourself if you like the furniture rental business and see if you can make any money at it. Then either buy out Levitz or call the Salvation Army and have them haul the stuff away.

If you'd rather not experiment at all, recommend to those people who come to you to rent furnished dwellings that they contact a furniture rental company (listed in the Yellow Pages under "Furniture Renting & Leasing") and rent their furniture separately.

If you happen to acquire a building which has old furniture which obviously isn't adding enough income to compensate you for the trouble of looking after it, get rid of the furniture. Don't let the frustrations of handling a furniture rental business interfere with your more important activities. Give the furniture away to a charitable organization and deduct its agreed-upon value from your landlording income.

SHOULD YOU ALLOW YOUR TENANTS TO SLEEP ON WATER?

We landlords and landladies tend to be pretty protective of our property. We resist anybody and anything that might pose a threat. We don't want pets. We don't want teenagers. We don't want motorcyclists. We don't want children. We don't want attorneys. We don't want welfare recipients. We don't want students. We don't want musicians. And we certainly don't want waterbeds. We seem ornery, suspicious, misanthropic, negative.

Yet, we become that way honestly. We start out as innocents determined to be trusting and determined to be unlike any grouchy, greedy landlord or landlady we ever knew. Then we have experiences. We learn slowly, incredulously, but we learn. After we have cleaned up the filth and repaired the damage left behind by more than one unscrupulous tenant who has vacated owing us rent, we become less trusting of people and more protective of our property. We tend to regard people and things guilty until proven innocent.

So when waterbeds first swept into faddish favor in the late 60's, we landlords and landladies considered the perils of allowing one-ton water balloons to lie on the floors of our bedrooms, and we acted quickly to protect our interests. We banned them.

Inevitably some tenants sneaked them in, and just as inevitably our worst fears were realized. Those early waterbeds stained our carpets and buckled our hardwood floors, necessitating expensive repairs. We swore never to allow them, and we wrote into our rental agreements carefully worded clauses to cover future developments, too. We prohibited not only waterbeds but any and all liquid-filled furniture. We fought waterbeds in the courts, and, believe it or not, we won. Even today we do not have to rent to tenants with waterbeds (that might change soon if legislation proposed by the waterbed manufacturers ever passes).

But waterbeds are no longer a fad. They are here to stay, for there are many people who find them essential to a good night's sleep. Nor are waterbeds any longer the flimsy water bags they once were. They have become thick (20-mil; the toughest trash bags are only 5-mil) water containers adequately safeguarded against accidental spillage, so that today a properly designed and installed waterbed is perfectly safe for use in most rental dwellings.

What's a landlord or landlady to do then? Strike that "no liquid-filled furniture" clause from the contract and let the waterbeds pour in? Absolutely not!

Waterbeds are still capable of damaging your building. Flimsy waterbeds and waterbeds without frames or liners are still around, and they could cause you the same grief today that they caused people years ago.

What should you do? Above all, be protective. Either continue banning all liquid-filled furniture from your rentals (remember that you are well within your rights in doing so), or adopt a well-considered policy which will enable you to rent to waterbed tenants at minimum risk.

Communicate this decision, to ban waterbeds or to accept them on well-defined terms, clearly to both your prospective tenants and your existing tenants. Begin when you first qualify prospective tenants by determining whether they intend to have a waterbed or not. Make no assumptions about what they will be sleeping on. Bring the matter out into the open for frank discussion, and you will virtually eliminate unauthorized waterbeds that tenants try to sneak in, beds which expose you to damages you're not protected against.

Before you ever adopt a policy to admit waterbeds, if you choose to, you should determine whether your building can indeed support their weight structurally. Residential buildings built to current construction standards will withstand around 60 pounds per square foot on suspended floors and can safely support most any waterbed. Poured concrete floors, of course, pose no problem at all. If you have any doubts, first read the Waterbed Manufacturers' Association report called "An Analysis of Waterbed Floor Loading," which is available from the WMA, 1411 West Olympic Blvd., Los Angeles, CA 90015. Second, check with your local building department about the floor loading limits for your building. Third, if you still have reservations, hire a structural engineering firm (look in the Yellow Pages under "Engineers-Structural") to determine the weight per square foot which your building can safely support. Compare that with the weight per square foot of each waterbed in question, and you will be able to tell whether your building can take the weight.

Waterbeds vary significantly in total weight, from around 360 pounds for a twin-sized hybrid (urethane foam and water combination) bed to about 2,500 pounds for the large round all-water variety. You can estimate the total weight of any waterbed yourself by making some simple calculations. Multiply the water capacity in gallons by 8.33 pounds and then add 4% for the miscellaneous waterbed parts if it's an all-water type or 20% if it's a hybrid.

More important than total weight, though, is floor loading or weight per square foot, for these are the figures which structural engineers use to determine the stress the waterbed puts on the floor. Again, you can estimate the weight per square foot quite accurately yourself. Simply divide the total weight of the bed by the square footage of its base (unless the bed rests on a pedestal base which is smaller than the surface, the base and the surface dimensions will be the same).

Let's take, as an example, the most common size waterbed, the queen size (60" x 80"), and we'll figure its weight per square foot. The all-water type (9-inch fill) has a water capacity of 196 gallons; the hybrid, 72 gallons. 196 gallons times 8.33 pounds per gallon plus 4% equals 1698 pounds total weight for the all-water queen-size waterbed. 72 gallons times 8.33 pounds per gallon plus 20% equals 720 pounds, total weight for the queen-size hybrid. To find the pounds per square foot for a queen-size waterbed, assuming that the base and surface dimensions are the same, multiply the length (80") times the width (60") and divide by the number of square inches in one square foot (144). That's 80 x 60 or 4800 square inches; divided by 144, it's 35 square feet. Next, divide the weight, 1698 pounds, by 35 and you get 48.5 pounds, which is the weight per square foot of an all-water queen-size waterbed. Divide 720 pounds by 35 and you get 20.5 pounds, which is the weight per square foot of a hybrid queen-size waterbed. That wasn't hard, was it? You can do the same for any size waterbed.

Once the weight question is answered to your satisfaction and you know the floor loading limits for your building, you may want to consider renting to tenants who sleep on water. If so, take these seven items into consideration for each individual waterbed: specifications, components, installation, inspection, insurance, deposit, and agreement.

• SPECIFICATIONS—Waterbeds differ considerably. Learn the size, weight, and type of each waterbed your tenants wish to have. Using these specifications, calculate whether or not each bed falls within the floor loading limits for your building. Reject those which might seem perilous to you, and suggest that the tenants consider lighter beds.

• COMPONENTS—The minimum allowable components, as far as you are concerned, should be a mattress at least 20 mil thick with lap seams (preferably less than three years old so it has more flex-fatigue resistance), a safety liner at least 8 mil, and a frame enclosure which meets WMA standards. If made of wood, the frame should be at least 2" x 10", the deck should be at least 1/2" thick, and neither the deck nor the pedestal should have any particle-board components (plywood or solid natural wood only).

• INSTALLATION—To prevent floods and minor catastrophes when they are most likely to occur, insist that professional installers (every waterbed store has its own service department) do the installation, and insist that you be present to supervise the eventual dismantling. If, for some reason, professional help is unavailable and you feel confident enough in your own abilities, help the tenant yourself by overseeing the installation while you consult the manufacturer's printed instructions. Proper installation will validate the insurance policy and give you peace of mind.

• INSPECTION—Make your first inspection just after the waterbed has been installed. Check its location, which should be along a load-bearing wall and away from intense heat sources. Check its problem potential, which should include feeling the frame for protrusions which might puncture the mattress. Check for water spillage from the installation, and direct the tenant to clean up any water immediately. After that, you might wish to check the waterbed periodically, say, every six months or so, for possible damage and signs of potential damage.

• INSURANCE—Responding to popular demand, a number of insurance companies now write waterbed liability insurance designed specifically for tenants, and they make it available through agents and waterbed stores. The annual premium is minimal (around $25) for a policy with a $25 deductible clause and a liability limit of $100,000. Require your tenant to secure such a policy. It covers damage to the building and to the property of other tenants, but it specifically excludes fire damage; damage to buildings which do not conform to governing building codes; and damage resulting from failure to follow the manufacturer's spefitis for assembling, installing, filling, emptying, locating, and maintaining the waterbed. Because these policies expire after twelve months, make certain that the tenant renews for continuous coverage.

• DEPOSIT—Require at least an extra $25 deposit from the waterbed tenant to cover the deductible should the insurance policy have to cover damages. Add this deposit to the total security/cleaning deposit so it need not be restricted in use to waterbed damages

Waterbed Agreement

Dated **January 12, 1986**

(Addendum to Rental Agreement)

This agreement is attached to and forms a part of the Rental Agreement dated **January 12, 1986** between **Lester Landlord** , Owners, and **Richard Harvey & Mary Louise Renter** , Tenants.

Tenants desire to keep a waterbed described as **queen size, Combination, foam and water**

in the dwelling they occupy under the Rental Agreement referred to above, and because this agreement specifically prohibits keeping waterbeds without the Owners' permission, Tenants agree to the following terms and conditions in exchange for this permission:

1) Tenants agree to keep one waterbed approved by Owners for this dwelling. Waterbed shall consist of a mattress at least 20 mil thick with lap seams, a safety liner at least 8 mil, and a frame enclosure which meets the Waterbed Manufacturers' Association standards.

2) Tenants agree to consult with the Owners about the location of the waterbed. They agree to hire qualified professionals to install and dismantle the bed according to the manufacturer's specifications and further agree not to relocate it without the Owners' consent.

3) Tenants agree to allow Owners to inspect the waterbed installation at any and all reasonable times and Tenants agree to remedy any problems or potential problems immediately.

4) Tenants agree to furnish Owners with a copy of a valid liability insurance policy for at least $100,000 covering this waterbed installation and agree to renew the policy as necessary for continuous coverage.

5) Tenants agree to pay immediately for any damage caused by their waterbed, and in addition, they will add $ **25.00** to their security/cleaning deposit, any of which may be used for cleaning, repairs, or delinquent rent when Tenants vacate. This added deposit or what remains of it when waterbed damages have been assessed, will be returned to Tenants within **Seven** days after they prove that they no longer keep this waterbed.

6) In consideration of the additional time, effort, costs, and risks involved in this waterbed installation, Tenants agree to pay additional rent of $ **3.00** , which /includes/~~does not include~~/ the premium for the waterbed liability insurance policy referred to in item 4.

7) Tenants agree that the Owners reserve the right to revoke this permission to keep a waterbed should the Tenants break this agreement.

Owner _Lester Landlord_   Tenant _Richard Renter_

Tenant _Mary Renter_

By _____

Page **2** of **3**

alone. That way it's available to be used for any kind of damages, for cleaning, or for rent.

• AGREEMENT—Cross out and initial the liquid-filled furniture exclusion, if any, in the rental agreement you use, and add to the agreement the terms under which you are allowing the waterbed. These terms could be included in the remarks section of the agreement; they could be written or typed on the back of the agreement and signed by all parties concerned; or they could be written as a separate agreement and referenced to the main rental agreement. Written succinctly into the remarks section, the wording might be as follows: "Tenants have one waterbed approved by Owners for this dwelling. Waterbed shall consist of mattress, liner, and frame; shall be kept insured for liability of $100,000; and shall be installed according to manufacturer's specifications."

This entire waterbed-acceptance procedure involves additional time, effort, costs, and risks which other tenants should not have to subsidize. Therefore, consider adding a nominal sum to the waterbed tenant's rent to compensate you for all this, and consider including in the sum enough to pay the premium (a little more than $2 a month) yourself on the tenant's waterbed liability policy so you are certain the policy is kept current.

Waterbeds may not be what you want in your building, but if you do, and if you follow these guidelines, you will be able to rest well at night yourself no matter what you sleep on.

SHOULD YOU ALLOW PETS?

Just as there is no law yet compelling you to rent to tenants with waterbeds, there's none compelling you to rent to tenants with pets, seeing-eye dogs excepted, and you might be perfectly correct in excluding both waterbeds and pets from your rental property. It's your prerogative, your right, but in adopting a dogmatic, hidebound approach to these questions, you are excluding not just waterbeds and pets but also all of the people who go along with them, some of whom make very good tenants. By excluding pets, in fact, you are halving the number of people who can qualify to rent from you, for more than half of all American households have a dog or a cat. By excluding pets, you are making the task of finding good tenants that much more difficult because you have fewer people to choose from.

If finding good tenants without accepting pets is easy for you, then continue excluding pets altogether because pets undeniably do pose problems, but if you are having problems finding good tenants and if you have a building which is suitable for pets (buildings suitable for dogs and cats are those with yards or patios and with little or no carpeting), consider accepting good tenants who have good pets.

According to one university study, pet owners as a group are friendlier, richer, smarter, and more attractive than those who have no pets. Yet, when we think about pet owners as renters, we tend to think first about the stereotype of the inconsiderate pet owner who's never heard of pooper scoopers and doesn't believe in leashes. That's the same as people thinking first about unscrupulous landlords whenever they think about landlords. You're an example of a scrupulous landlord or landlady, aren't you? Well, there are lots of examples of scrupulous pet owners, too.

Scrupulous pet-owning tenants save you money because they tend to be more permanent residents, and they make you money because they will pay higher rent for their accommodations than will tenants without pets.

Whereas some landlords and landladies think that pets never add to the value of a rental dwelling, they're thinking with blinders on. They're thinking strictly about the pets of inconsiderate owners and about the additional management and maintenance problems such pets cause. That's one way to look at the situation. There is another way. Since pet owners will pay more rent and since higher rents translate into higher property values, pets can actually increase the value of a building. Did you ever think of that? Twenty dollars more per month for each unit in a six-plex adds up to additional income of $1,440 per year and equals an added property value of $10,080 at only seven times the gross income. That ain't pet feed!

Set the rent high, advertise that you accept pets, and you'll be inundated with applicants who have pets because pet owners' options are more limited. Avoid pet surcharges because they lead pet owners to believe that their pets' damages are already paid for; charge higher rents and higher deposits instead (higher deposits should not exceed the legal limits for all deposits which are set for your area, and they should not be designated as "pet deposits" because any deposit so designated must be used only for pet damages; they may not be applied to rent, cleaning, or breakage unrelated to the pet). My own experience with an admittedly small sample has shown that tenants with pets stay on average twice as long as those without and that they will pay $10 to $35 more per month for a place to live where they can keep their pets. They realize that finding another place which accepts pets is difficult at best and is sometimes altogether impossible, so once they move in, they tend to stay a long time and they will pay more in rent while they stay there.

Whether you choose to rent to people with pets or not, you must have a pet policy. Actually you have one already whether you realize it or not, but you may not have formalized it in writing. You may have been telling your tenants all along that you do not accept any pets, and they may be interpreting that to mean no fish, fowl, mammals, insects, or reptiles. Then again they may interpret it to mean that certain fish, fowl, and insects are acceptable, but not mammals or reptiles. Just what do you mean by "no pets" anyway? Would you allow someone to have a twenty-gallon aquarium or three parakeets in one cage? They're all pets. Would they violate your policy?

Spell out what you mean when you say "no pets" or "pets OK" by putting your policy in writing and making it fair to your tenants, their pets, the neighbors, and yourself. Specify in your policy the type, age, number, and reproductive capability (if appropriate) of the pets you will accept or not accept and outline these specifications clearly. Don't bother with size or weight limitations. They don't seem to be relevant to whether a certain pet will be a nuisance around the property. The age of a pet is far more important.

Take a look at these two pet policies—

PET POLICY

No pets of any kind may be harbored on the premises, even temporarily, no matter what they are and no matter who owns them.

If you should notice anyone with a pet on the premises, please report the sighting and its particulars to the management immediately.

PET POLICY

Subject to approval, tenants may have pets in any one of the following categories:
1. Caged birds (maximum of two)
2. Fish (as many as can survive happily in a fifty-five gallon aquarium)
3. House cats (one, spayed or neutered, at least three months old)
4. Dogs (one, spayed or neutered, at least nine months old)
5. Other animals (permitted only on a case-by-case basis)

Tenants shall bring all prospective pets to management for approval beforehand.
Tenants shall have a Pet Agreement covering the keeping of their pet.

You may wish to include in your list of acceptable pets only caged birds or only house cats, or you may wish to exclude every conceivable animal, no matter what it is. That's your decision to make. You have great flexibility in determining your policy and you have some flexibility in applying it, but you should be astute enough to recognize that whatever pet policy you adopt will have to apply equally to everyone in a building or at least to everyone in a very distinctly designated area. You cannot extend a privilege to some tenants and not to others. They won't stand for it.

As a consequence of buying a fourteen-unit complex some time ago, I happened to inherit a situation where an elderly lady had been allowed by the previous owner to have a small house dog. It was her constant companion, her security system, her confidant, and her first love, and I was averse to giving her the choice of dog or dwelling since that dog meant so much to her and since she had already lived there for fifteen years. Still, I was adamant about not allowing anyone else to keep a dog there because the building was being improved with new carpeting. Three of the thirteen other tenants who lived there defied me by getting their own dogs. When confronted with my no-pets policy, which I had already discussed with them, all three referred to the little old lady's dog. "If she can have one, why can't we?" they asked almost in unison. Indeed, why couldn't they?

The crucial difference between them and the little old lady as far as I was concerned was that she had had the dog long before I assumed ownership and before I instituted the no-pets policy. Her dog was "grandmothered" in. The other tenants couldn't have cared less how I rationalized the situation. As far as they were concerned, there was no difference whatsoever between her and them. If she were allowed a dog, then they should be as well. One of those tenants had to be evicted over this matter. The other two finally relented and gave their pets away, but they struggled hard. So did I.

By the way, if tenants ever do break your rental contract by acquiring a pet which you distinctly prohibit, you should confront them about the matter immediately and give them no more than three days to get rid of it. If you give them any more time, they will only dillydally in getting rid of the pet and become attached to it in the process, and you'll wind up having to evict them in the end. If you fail to approach them at all when you first learn about their pet, you have in effect given them your tacit approval, and you'd better

Pet Agreement

Dated **APRIL 26, 1987**

(Addendum to Rental Agreement)

This agreement is attached to and forms a part of the Rental Agreement dated **4-26-87** between **Leslie Landlady**, Owners, and **Tina Oldtimer**, Tenants.

Tenants desire to keep a pet named **Fang** and described as **Lhasa Apso** in the dwelling they occupy under the rental agreement referred to above, and because this agreement specifically prohibits keeping pets without the Owners' permission, Tenants agree to the following terms and conditions in exchange for this permission:

1) Tenants agree to keep their pet under control at all times.

2) Tenants agree to keep their pet restrained, but not tethered, when it is outside their dwelling.

3) Tenants agree not to leave their pet unattended for any unreasonable periods.

4) Tenants agree to dispose of their pet's droppings properly and quickly.

5) Tenants agree not to leave food or water for their pet or any other animal outside their dwelling.

6) Tenants agree to keep pet from causing any annoyance or discomfort to others and will remedy immediately any complaints made through the Owner or Manager.

7) Tenants agree to get rid of their pet's offspring within eight weeks of birth.

8) Tenants agree to pay immediately for any damage, loss, or expense caused by their pet, and in addition, they will add $ **75 -** to their security/cleaning deposit, any of which may be used for cleaning, repairs, or delinquent rent when Tenants vacate. This added deposit or what remains of it when pet damages have been assessed, will be returned to Tenants within **seven** days after they prove that they no longer keep this pet.

9) Tenants agree that Owners reserve the right to revoke permission to keep the pet should Tenants break this agreement.

Owner *Leslie Landlady*

By _____

Tenant *Tina Oldtimer*

Tenant _____

Page **4** of **4**

be prepared to fend off your other tenants. They'll want one, too. This is another one of those little landlording problems which only become more difficult to deal with if you procrastinate in handling them.

Having a pet policy which you can enforce when necessary is one thing, but finding good pet owners with good pets is another. It is a process for circumspection and deliberation. You will want to determine whether the pet owners you interview are devoted enough to their pet to care for it faithfully. Check them out by asking questions such as "Will you rent this place if we do not allow you to keep your pet?" and "Who will be taking care of your pet in your absence?" and "Will you pay a larger refundable security/cleaning deposit of $100?" and "Can you live by our pet agreement which says the following.....?" and "Who's your veterinarian?" and "Is your pet properly licensed?" Their answers to these questions will indicate fairly clearly how important their pet is to them and how faithfully they will care for it after they move in. The pet itself, which you ought to meet at some point before you agree to accept it, should fall within your pet policy guidelines and should be reasonably friendly, healthy, and well-behaved. If this preliminary screening of the owners and their pet raises any doubts in your mind about their ability and willingness to respect your property, refuse to rent to them. You have every right to be discriminating in this matter, and furthermore, you should be discriminating.

Refusing applicants with pets is pretty straightforward. Refusing existing tenants who want a pet is much the same, even when you suspect that they might prove to be indifferent toward the pet they choose. The only way to determine their attitude is to impose upon them the same set of conditions which you impose upon newcomers with pets. Caution your tenants that you will allow them to have a pet only if they discuss the matter with you in advance and only if you approve. When they approach you, review your pet policy with them first to make certain that they understand what kinds of pets you allow. Then go over the entire Pet Agreement item by item. Tell them that you treat all pet owners alike and that all of those tenants who now have pets have submitted their pets for approval, signed pet agreements, and increased their security/cleaning deposits. So long as your existing tenants will do likewise, they too will be allowed to have a pet. Emphasize that your refusal of any particular pet has nothing to do with their own tenancy but that keeping an unauthorized pet will certainly result in an eviction of both the tenants and the pet.

All of your tenants should understand that they have no right to have a pet on the premises unless you grant them the privilege under well-defined conditions. If they should fail to live up to those conditions, you will be forced to withdraw the privilege.

Should you allow pets? Considering your building, its vacancy factor, and your own inclinations, what do you think?

SHOULD YOU FURNISH THE MAJOR KITCHEN APPLIANCES?

You don't always have a choice about whether to supply your tenants with stoves and refrigerators in your unfurnished rentals because sometimes these appliances are already built in and sometimes the rental market is so fiercely competitive that you have to supply them if you want to keep your rentals occupied. When you do have a choice, however, either don't furnish them at all or tell your new tenants that you no longer supply these appliances in unfurnished rentals but that you would be willing as a favor to supply a stove or refrigerator on loan for a few months.

Tenants are far less likely to complain about the minor faults of their appliances when they are using a stove or refrigerator "on loan" than if you tell them the appliances are included in the rent. Tenants fear that each time you see the appliances you'll be reminded of the loan agreement and may ask for them back, so they keep mum about the little problems. Fiddling with temperamental stoves that bake lopsided cakes and explaining why milk freezes and ice cream melts in some crazy refrigerators takes far too much of your valuable time. Supplying these major appliances and providing what amounts to a full maintenance contract to boot doesn't pay off.

SHOULD YOU LEAVE THEM PLAIN OR FIX THEM FANCY?

Cosmetics people market hope. Automobile people market freedom. Wine people market status. Appliance people market convenience. Vitamin people market health. What do you market, landlord and landlady? A place to live with plain white walls. How pedestrian! Shame on you! You could do better, much better.

Don't get me wrong now. There's nothing wrong with renting out clean, functional dwellings with heating, electricity, carpets, drapes, and indoor plumbing, but it's just so, well, so practical. That's all. And "practical" doesn't sell for very much. Volkswagens are practical, too, but they don't sell for what Cadillac Sevilles do. People will rent your functional dwellings in tight housing markets no matter what, to be sure, but they will always pay more in any market if they believe they are getting more for their money, and you can give them more for their money without spending much of yours.

With a little extra work and very little investment, you could be marketing the same kinds of illusions that Seville customers so willingly pay extra money for. What illusions? Individuality, chic, warmth, luxury. "All that in my rental property, and with very little investment?" you ask? Yes! Here's how.

Hire yourself as an interior decorator and make these three alterations to your rental—wallpaper one wall, put up at least one woven shade, and mount a curtain rod valance over the shower bath. You could dream up other alterations if you wanted to, but they should be few, uncomplicated, inexpensive, and easy to care for.

Wallpapering only one prominent wall either opposite the front door or opposite the entrance to the kitchen makes a very big impression on prospective tenants as they walk in and begin visualizing themselves living there. Yet, vinyl-coated, prepasted wallpaper costs surprisingly little, is easy to apply, and is easy to care for, too.

A woven shade on any window which requires some kind of window covering anyway creates much the same impression as the wallpaper. It's an unexpected splash of color, a welcome departure from all those boring white walls so prevalent in rental dwellings, and it dazzles the beholders into believing that they are getting something special for their money. You don't even have to spend a lot on those Roman shades made of wood. They're costlier and no more decorative than the vinyl variety, which sell for approximately what you'd pay for ordinary window shades. Sears catalog offers both.

A shower-bath curtain-rod valance

made of 1" x 6" fir or pine and painted with a simple design or covered with fancy
Contact Paper spruces up drab bathrooms as if by magic. Mounted just in front of the rod
itself, the valance hides the curtain rod and lends a special illusion of warmth and luxury
to the place.

All three of these dazzlers together shouldn't cost the do-it-yourselfer any more than
$75, and yet they should yield around $10 more a month in increased rental income.
Think of what that does to the value of your property! At seven times the annual gross,
$10 of additional rental income increases the value by $840! That's a decent return on
your money, isn't it?

Try these dazzlers or be imaginative and think up others of your own and capitalize on
people's willingness to pay extra for illusions.

SHOULD YOU OUTFIT THE LAUNDRY?

An apartment-house laundry room can be a blessing or a curse. It can pay off as
handsomely as a small casino full of slot machines, or it can be simply another welfare
case for you to support. Mostly there are two factors which determine whether you will
win or lose in your laundry room—how much the machines are used and who owns them.

• USE—All things considered, your laundry room will pay off handsomely if it's used
frequently enough. Although you cannot tell for certain whether your tenants will indeed
do their laundry there or how many loads they will wash per week, you can make a good
educated usage guess based on the number of people or the number of bedrooms in the
building. If you have a fourplex, for example, and you have four families living there
with two children in each, you have sixteen people in all, and they will surely produce
enough dirty laundry to support one coin-operated washer and one dryer. On the other
hand, a fourplex tenanted by singles and couples, no matter how clean they happen to be,
just will not support a washer and dryer. The rule of thumb I use to determine whether I
ought to outfit a laundry room at all and, if so, with how many machines, is this—*Sixteen
people or twelve bedrooms (even the smallest dwelling counts as one bedroom) will
support one washer and one dryer*. If a building meets either of these minimums and if its
laundry machines are set to charge competitive rates, those machines should produce
liberal returns.

• OWNERSHIP—Some landlords and landladies feel that they have better things to
worry about than laundry machines and would rather let someone else handle them
completely. They have that choice and so do you if you have an apartment-house laundry
room. If you contract with a vendor to supply the machines on a lease or commission
basis, you will be relieved of all the ownership worries. The vendor will supply, insure,
and service the machines while you provide the wash house itself, the necessary
plumbing, hookups, and, of course, the utilities. He will write a one- to five-year contract
to assure himself a profit and then split the leavings with you.

If you supply the machines yourself, you will have to take care of the repairs and
maintenance, count the coins, worry about vandalism and other calamities, and you'll
have to pay for the machines with a sum of money which cannot be charged directly to
expenses, but you'll have the only access to the coin boxes, you will get to depreciate the
machines over a five-year period, and you'll get an investment tax credit to boot.

What choice should you make? That depends. If you are pretty clumsy or helpless
about maintenance matters, if you don't think you'd enjoy the business, if you own an
apartment building with fewer than sixteen occupants or twelve bedrooms, if your
building is located in an area prone to breakins and vandalism, *or* if you intend to dispose

of your building within three years, don't buy your own machines. Contract with someone else to supply them.

• DEALING WITH AN OUTSIDE VENDOR—Should you decide to permit someone else to supply the machines, ask other landlords and landladies for their recommendations of trustworthy companies and then shop around for the best available terms. They vary a lot. A straight commission should net you more than a lease-commission arrangement because some money will accrue to you with each load washed, regardless of how many. Under a lease-commission arrangement, the machine supplier retains a fixed sum each month and splits the balance with you, so if the machines produce only enough to cover the supplier's fixed sum, you get nothing, nothing but lemons, oranges, and grapes; no cherries. Tough luck. If yours is a small building, consider the laundry room more of an amenity than a moneymaker and hope that you'll be able to recover your utility costs.

Life with a laundry room vendor isn't all cherries, I can assure you. You have to be naturally suspicious when dealing with vendors because there's more than one way they and their employees can cheat you. Take a look at this one clause which appears in fine print at the end of a five-year laundry equipment lease I inherited from the previous owner of a property—"This lease shall be automatically renewed for the same period of time unless cancelled in writing by either party at least 90 days prior to expiration by registered mail." What's that verbiage mean? It means that if I fail to notify the vendor that I want to cancel the lease three months before it expires, I'll be stuck with it for another five years. Now that's what I call a cheater clause! Some wiley lawyer must be congratulating himself over sneaking that into the contract. It's entirely one-sided. The burden of cancelling the contract is mine, not the vendor's, and if I'm forgetful, I could have an unwanted contract on my hands forever. Read your laundry equipment lease carefully. Don't be caught without your reading specs at lease signing time, or you may be taken to the laundry.

Incidentally, every laundry equipment lease I have ever seen is automatically transferred to the new owner with a change of ownership. Selling a property releases the seller from the lease but binds the buyer exactly as it did the previous owner. Whenever you are negotiating to acquire a property with leased laundry equipment, review the lease, and if you find that it has restrictive terms, make them part of your negotiations.

The other primary way you might be cheated is through underreporting of income. If a vendor supplies you with laundry machines, the vendor also empties their coin boxes and counts the coins. The amount of income you receive depends upon how much income the vendor reports. Remember when several large oil companies were exposed on *Sixty Minutes* for underreporting the amount of oil they were pumping from Indian lands? It ran into the millions of barrels. Trucks were loading crude oil from wellhead sites at all hours and bypassing the flow meters. In comparison to that enormity, vendors' underreporting of laundry machine income is dime-and-quarter stuff, but the situation is no different. The potential for underreporting income is much same for laundry machines as it is for oil wells or a city's parking meters, for that matter. Only the amounts differ. Coins there for the taking are pretty tempting to some people, be they the vendors themselves, their employees, or your managers. And lest you think that those laundry coins don't amount to very much, get out your calculator and multiply the cost of one coin-machine wash and dry times the number of loads you do every month at your home times the number of families in your apartment house. Those are dollars, not pennies, you wind up with!

One response to this problem by at least one vendor is the non-resettable counter. Mounted directly inside the timer access plate, it tallies each actuation of the laundry machine's coin slide. When the machines are emptied, your manager or you accompany the vendor's route collector as he empties the coin boxes, and you both take the readings from the counters so you both know how much revenue the machines have generated. It's a good idea and appears to work pretty well.

Another response is what's known in the trade as "verified accounting." Your manager or you witness the collection and weighing of the coins on one of the new, highly sensitive, portable coin scales which give precise totals in dollars and cents of all the coins being weighed, even when they're mixed. The route collector then writes a receipt for the amount collected.

If your vendor offers neither of these verification methods, you will have to resort to a self-help method to keep from being cheated. Try one or both of these methods. The first one involves insisting that your manager or you be present when the coins are emptied, but that's not all. Because you can't know what sum of coins you're looking at unless you have some sort of quick-count method, get yourself a scale which will weigh as much as fifty pounds pretty accurately. Weigh the coins as they're emptied, write down the weights on a scratch pad, and later do the calculations to determine just how much the machines coughed up. If the coins are all quarters, as they frequently are nowadays, your calculations will be easy. If they're a mixture of quarters, dimes, and nickels, you'll have to work with the numbers a bit to come up with the right proportions, but when you do, you won't be far off.

The second method echoes one which is used by IRS agents to check false reporting of coin laundry income at launderettes. They call the washing machine manufacturer to find out how much water one wash load takes and then examine the launderette's water bill. After allowing for a certain margin of error, say 10%, they can calculate approximately what the launderette's income ought to be and compare that with what's being reported as income. You can do the same thing yourself even if your water in the laundry room is master metered along with the entire building's. Find out where the water line comes in to service your entire laundry room, and install a water meter right there. Yes, you as an individual may buy water meters, volt meters, watt meters, gas meters, light meters, practically any kind and size of a meter you might want. Unless it's particularly large, a water meter is reasonable, too. A 3/4" water meter in a quantity of one should cost less than $50. When you consider how much underreporting of income you might be suffering, that's nothing. Let your vendor know that you've installed a water meter, and watch your income post an immediate increase for some strange reason. In one instance, my laundry room income jumped around $200 per month after a water meter installation.

Perhaps the most important aspect of your efforts to be treated fairly by your laundry machine vendor is the interest you show in the whole operation. Too many apartment house owners regard their laundry rooms as beneath them. The laundry room is nickels, dimes, and quarters, and they're interested only in big bucks. They don't particularly care whether the laundry room is profitable or not. When the vendor recognizes this attitude and knows he's under no scrutiny, he'll do as he pleases, but when you've gone to all the trouble of installing a water meter in the laundry supply line and/or weighing coins as the machines are emptied, and the vendor knows you've gone to these lengths, he'll have to treat you honestly. He'll be afraid not to.

• GOING IT ALONE—If you are the least bit handy, if you believe you'd enjoy looking after your own coin-operated laundry machines, if you own an apartment building with at least sixteen occupants or twelve bedrooms, *and* if you intend to keep your building at least three years (naturally you can take them with you if you want to, but be sure you specify that in your property sales agreement), then, by all means install your own machines. You will be pleasantly surprised to see just how much money they can make, and soon you will understand why so many firms are in the business of supplying laundry machines on a commission basis, why they offer to paint laundry rooms for "free," why they invest in non-resettable load counters, why they buy expensive coin scales for account verification, why they advertise so heavily in apartment association publications, and why they offer various inducements to managers and owners of large complexes. It can be quite a lucrative proposition for them.

Should you decide after due consideration to install your own laundry machines in your apartment house, you need to know something about buying laundry machines, setting rates, changing rates, getting a decent return on your investment, and counting coins.

• BUYING COMMERCIAL LAUNDRY MACHINES—Consult *Consumer Reports* for the best information about the reliability and operating costs of various brands of domestic washers and dryers. Commercial machines, one old codger many years in the business told me, have innards exactly like the home machines. "Only the tops are different," he said. "When my bottoms wear out, I junk 'em and put my old tops on the cheapest new home machines made by the same manufacturer. They last just as long as new commercial models." I've never tried his junk-and-switch technique because my bottoms haven't worn out yet, but I will when they do.

If the two are that similar, then the manufacturers of good home machines also make good commercial machines, and you'll have no trouble finding the right machines for you.

My machines are all Kenmore commercial models purchased through Sears Contract Sales Department, which sells them for less than a regular Sears store's appliance department. In fact, Sears Contract Sales sells the machines for less than the wholesale price to my local Whirlpool dealer for commercial Whirlpool machines, and as you may know, Kenmore machines are made by Whirlpool.

Besides being inexpensive to purchase, Kenmores wash and dry well, are sparing on the utilities, are quite reliable, and are easy to repair. The one drawback they do have is that Sears' local parts cache for commercial machines is such slim pickin's that Sears usually has to send away for parts. Fortunately, however, the machines seldom need parts, and they seldom need repairs either.

Commercial Kenmores are not covered by lengthy guarantees as are the domestic models. Sears does sell maintenance contracts for nervous Nellies, but my own experience has shown that these contracts are priced higher than the repairs themselves would cost without a contract. I don't bother with maintenance contracts, and you shouldn't either. They're a ripoff, something you have to be sold, not something you'd buy.

My biggest problem with commercial laundry machines couldn't be solved with a maintenance contract anyway. Every so often I've gotten calls complaining that my washers or dryers weren't working and I've arrived with my tools only to find that the one thing wrong with them was that I had forgotten to empty the coinboxes, so I "fixed" them by emptying almost $200 from each pair of machines. That's what I call a jackpot!

One important consideration when you're selecting machines is whether to buy gas or electric dryers. In most areas, gas dryers are quite a bit less expensive to operate, so if you have natural gas available, you should give some thought to paying the little extra that gas dryers cost initially in order to save on operating costs over the years. Before making your final decision, however, be sure you check with your local utility companies about the relative costs of operating gas and electric dryers. They'll have the current, local information you need for making your decision.

By the way, don't bother looking around for used commercial laundry machines unless you know their complete history or don't mind rebuilding them yourself. Used machines are available, to be sure, but they're far more trouble than they're worth because most owners simply won't part with them unless they've been through the wringer.

• SETTING RATES—Since you with your laundry room are actually providing a convenience for your tenants rather than competing directly with coin-operated launderettes in the area, you should set your machines at rates slightly higher, say, 5 to 10 cents higher, than the prevailing scale for local launderettes. Your machines will need more repairs and wear out faster with frequent use, so you don't want to stimulate use too much by keeping the rates low. Keep them just low enough so the machines will be used fairly often, yet not so high that they won't be used often enough to justify your investment.

• CHANGING RATES—My first laundry machines had coin slides which were set to charge 25 cents to wash and 10 cents to dry. If I were to charge those rates today, I'd barely break even. As it was, I kept them much too long at those prices because the coin slides were fixed to accept only quarters and dimes, and finding adjustable coin slides took me a while. Adjustable slides enable you to change the rates to any one-, two-, three-, four-, or five-coin combination in minutes with only a screwdriver. These slides may be purchased by themselves and retrofitted to most existing machines. Sears now sells them, as do most other laundry machine suppliers. If you're ordering a new laundry machine, be sure you specify adjustable slides rather than fixed slides, to allow you the flexibility of adjusting your income to offset leaping utility costs.

• GETTING A DECENT RETURN ON INVESTMENT—Income from the machines should cover your utility costs, purchase of the machines, repair service, and a fair return on your investment. The return should be very fair, believe me. One of my eightplexes, all two-bedroom units, paid for its new washer and dryer and all its overhead in just eleven months. Ever since then, those machines have simply churned out profits, never missing a beat. Over a five-year period, the return on that investment has been in excess of 95% per year; not bad in anybody's book, I'd say.

Do keep an eye on your utility costs, though, for they can, in certain situations, gobble up all your profits and then some. I had one laundry room where the water heater and the dryers all operated on propane gas, and the gas bill alone each month amounted to more than the machines were grossing. I raised the rates, and that helped some, but then I hit upon the idea of shutting off the water heater entirely when I learned that the heat for hot water generally accounts for between 75% and 90% of all the energy used to wash clothes. After switching to cold-water washing only, I posted a sign to that effect, lowered the rates, and began enjoying a good return on my investment.

• COUNTING COINS—Those coins you remove from your laundry machines are all mixed up and require sorting, counting, and wrapping before being deposited. It's a pleasant chore, counting stacks of your very own coins, one which you can do almost without thinking while you watch TV, but if you find the laundry business profitable enough to install more than one washer and dryer, you will notice that counting coins becomes increasingly tedious. When that happens, buy a coin sorter for your counting house and restore some of the old pleasure to the chore.

There are coin sorters which whirl and tinkle and even tally their coins digitally, and they cost pretty pennies, too. You'd certainly need such a machine if you had a vending machine route or a casino, but you don't need the fanciest sorter available to help you count a few hundred dollars in coins every month. A simple, inexpensive sorter will handle the chore quite well.

Fortunately, there is one. It enables you to sort, count, and wrap coins quickly and accurately, and it works without moving a single part. Gravity makes it work. After you feed the coins in at the top, they sort themselves by following tracks of varying widths until they wind up sorted into calibrated stacks at the bottom. Little nubs in the stacking tubes raise the 41st or 51st coin, depending on the denomination, to mark full rolls, which can then be removed, checked with the instant count verifier, and wrapped (most banks provide coin wrappers free of charge as a service to their customers).

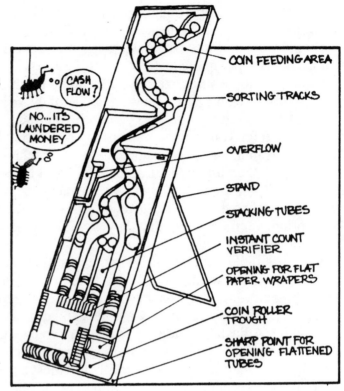

This marvel of simplicity and utility is called the Nadex Coin Sorter and Packager, Model 607. It's available through larger stationery and business supply stores or directly from the manufacturer, Nadex Industries, 220 Delaware, Buffalo, NY 14202. Telephone 716-845-6910.

SHOULD YOU PAY THE GARBAGE AND UTILITY BILLS?

Landlords and landladies frequently pay the garbage and water bills themselves for their single-family rental properties rather than leaving that responsibility to their tenants, and with good reason. Paying the garbage bill means that the garbage will positively be picked up and the property will be kept reasonably tidy. Paying the water bill means that the yard will probably be watered and the landscaping won't die of thirst. Paying both means that the tenant can offer no excuse for poor groundskeeping at least, and the place should look reasonably presentable when you drive by.

These arguments make sense for the house rental, but what about the apartment house which has no yard? Whenever I'm lucky enough to have separate water meters for each apartment, I require that the tenants pay their own bills. They should know what their water costs so they'll conserve more. Garbage is another matter altogether. Personally, I prefer to pay the garbage bill for all my rentals unless some other satisfactory precedent was established by a previous owner. Some tenants either forget to pay or discontinue service claiming that they would rather haul it to the dump themselves to save paying the bill, and then their cans begin to overflow and there's a constant mess for you to look after. Control of the garbage area is always easier if you pay. If you don't pay, there's bound to be friction caused by the invasion of one tenant's garbage can by strange garbage. It gets tossed aside and then begins a great garbage battle. Finally, there's more of a mess than you can cope with. You pay and you control. Make them pay, and you're likely to be plagued by a continuous garbage war.

SHOULD YOU CONVERT A MASTER-METERED BUILDING?

As for the utilities in an apartment house, my practice is to have the tenants pay for their own so long as they are on separate meters, and if they are not on separate meters, I try to effect a conversion.

Once situation that had me puzzled for a while involved a big, old fourplex with steam heat produced by one common boiler which was connected to a gas meter with dials that spun faster than a moon rocket's altimeter. I was paying the bill for that one meter myself, and with sharply rising utility rates, the bill soon rose to equal a fourth of the building's total rental income! As if that weren't bad enough, one tenant kept complaining that he never had enough heat, and I had to turn the controlling thermostat up to 80 degrees just to keep his place around 68. Every unit but one then had to keep the windows open night and day to avoid being bathed in steam heat. Consequently, much of the heat that I was paying so dearly for was literally going out those windows.

What could I do? I knew that I couldn't raise the rents to a level where the increased utility costs would be covered. That would have necessitated an increase substantially higher than market conditions warranted. Fortunately, because each unit already had its own gas meter for an individual kitchen stove and water heater, I could install new direct-vent heaters in each unit and connect them to the individual meters. So I went ahead and installed the heaters, and in less than twelve months, those heaters had paid for themselves in utility-bill savings, and my tenants' heating complaints evaporated into thin air that I wasn't paying to heat. Hooray and hallelujah!

Tenants are more interested in lower rent, I believe, than in the inclusion of utilities, and when they have to pay their own utility bills, they conserve energy as they should.

Fortunately for me, my fourplex was not a fully master-metered building. Fully master-metered buildings are dinosaurs, no longer being built today because they do not encourage utility conservation and because few owners want to speculate in gas and electricity futures. They require more work and more money to convert than my old fourplex did, but they may be worth converting all the same.

If you happen to be stuck with such an animal, seek out other owners who have already dealt with the problem themselves and learn what you can about their experience. Don't forget to confer with your utility company. Most offer their customers low-interest loans for energy conservation measures. Perhaps you can convince them that the conversion of your master-metered building qualifies.

Once you know what the conversion costs are, consider how long it will take to get your money back. Less than three years is very good; three years is good; more than three years is questionable. Also consider whether the conversion will make the building worth any more, and include that in your payback calculations as well. Don't just sit there fretting and sweating over the bills; do something.

SHOULD YOU ALLOW NAILS IN YOUR WALLS?

When you come across tenants who don't want to attach your walls to their pictures because they don't want to damage your wals, let me know, and I'll personally recommend that they be enshrined in the Tenants' Hall of Fame. The Hall still has lots of room.

For all those other tenants, you have several decisions to make. What should you allow them to use to attach your walls to their pictures, clocks, and other lightweight stuff? And should you let them hang the heavy stuff at all, stuff like birdcages, bookcases, lamps, planters, wall systems, and bulletin boards?

First, about the lightweight stuff—remember the olden days when tenants could cause their landlord or landlady to have a crying jag if they tried banging a nail into the wall and got caught? Why the concern? Because one nail in a plaster wall would sometimes cause a tiny crack which would grow into a fissure, and then chips and chunks of the plaster would start falling down, and finally there would be a lath wall showing where once there had been one of plaster. Fortunately, along came some nice person who invented stickem wall hangers, and the problem was solved. The stickem hangers would hold light burdens without disturbing the plaster wall at all. Landlords and landladies invariably recommended them and most tenants dutifully used them.

But things changed again with the advent of sheetrock, also known as plasterboard, wallboard, and gypsum board. A nail wouldn't crack the sheetrock as it would the plaster, but the stickem wall hangers, when removed, would peel off both the paint and the paper surface of the sheetrock, leaving a broad, ugly scar underneath which was difficult to conceal.

Since we now have both plaster and sheetrock walls in general use, landlords and landladies need to offer their tenants recommendations which vary according to wall type. Before you can make any recommendation, of course, you first must find out what kind of walls your building has. Don't be surprised if it has some walls of plaster and some of sheetrock. When older buildings are remodeled, the remodelers rarely replaster interior walls. They sheetrock 'em. Once you know what the walls are made of, you may confidently make your recommendations. For plaster walls, recommend that your tenants use stickem hangers whevever possible, and if they must use a nail, recommend that they drill a pilot hole first to avoid any cracking which might be caused by the impact of banging too hard on the wall. For sheetrock walls, recommend that your tenants use nails tapped in carefully and that they avoid using those stickem hangers or tapes altogether. Holes left by nails in sheetrock can be filled neatly with spackling compound and do not even have to be painted in most cases.

And now about the heavy stuff—here you should think as much about the psychological aspects of the heavy stuff as you should about the damage that hanging it could possibly cause. Because tenant turnover is costly, you want your tenants to feel well rooted in your units so that, all things being equal, they will stay a long time. If they are comfortably ensconced in one of your rentals midst all of their hanging plants, their swag lamps, their wall systems, and their pet parakeets, they likely will stay awhile. Swallow hard and let them hang these things.

There is always the danger in their hanging this heavy stuff from your walls, that they'll use an inadequate fastener and that chunks of your walls will come tumbling down when their heavies and your walls part company, but you may avoid this danger by recommending that they first try to find a concealed stud to screw or nail into. Show them how to do it with one of the new electronic stud finders (both Sears and K-Mart have them), and you might want to make one available to lend out for this very purpose. Attaching to a stud is by far the best way to hang heavy things from either plaster or sheetrock walls. If it's absolutely impossible to do, however, recommend that your tenants use an anchor (show them what you mean by an "anchor") designed to support at least twice the weight of what they're hanging.

By all means, discuss your "hanging policy" thoroughly with your tenants before they move in because few of them will approach you for permission or advice later on. They'll just go ahead and hang things any old way, but if you have discussed the matter with them in advance, most of them will try to follow your advice and hang their things your way. Let's hope so.

SHOULD YOU COVER THOSE NAKED WINDOWS WITH DRAPERIES, SHADES, BLINDS, OR BEDSHEETS?

Every type of window covering has its place, of course. A fancy dwelling which rents for a handsome sum should have handsome appointments, to include fine draperies, woven wood shades, vertical slat blinds, or wooden mini-blinds, whatever's in fashion, sometimes supplied by you and sometimes by your tenants. Neither you nor your tenants want anything but the best for those places. For average rentals, however, you may find that contract draperies work wonders to enhance appearances and keep tenants happy. They may be absolutely necessary if your competition is supplying them.

But don't overlook roller shades as a window covering possibility for any rental dwelling. They help to insulate. They are cheaper than drapes, longer lasting, easier to install, and easier to keep clean. They never need to be taken down for dry cleaning, they don't get threadbare, and except on sliding patio doors, shades and drapes can even fit on the same windows at the same time. You might consider supplying shades and drapery rods yourself and letting your tenants supply their own drapes, for those tenants who do supply their own draperies tend to stay put a lot longer.

Consider yourself lucky if you already have Venetian blinds in your rentals, and unless they are too dated, leave them right where they are because they should last a long time without requiring any further capital outlay. When kept cleaned and repaired by professionals, Venetians cost surprisingly little to keep up.

So-called mini-blinds have been popular with decorators for years, but they haven't always been as inexpensive, as available, or as durable as they are today. Many paint stores, department stores, hardware stores, and variety stores even have ready-made sizes in stock. Because they can be mounted either inside or outside window casements, stock mini-blinds can accommodate most window sizes. That's especially convenient for you when you need a window covering right away. Just go to a nearby store, buy one, and hang it. What could be simpler? Give mini-blinds a long, hard look as a window-covering alternative which will fit well into almost any rental unit. You'll find that they are more decorative, easier to clean, and easier to maintain than draperies, and they look every bit as good.

Above all, do use some kind of window covering when your rentals are vacant, yes, even if it has to be a bedsheet. The obviously vacant dwelling with naked windows is a prime target for vandals and squatters, both of whom seem to be on the increase these days.

SHOULD YOU MEASURE FOR AND INSTALL DRAPERIES YOURSELF?

Any time you require somebody to perform a service at your rental property site, you're going to pay dearly for that service.

You can measure for and install draperies yourself in a minimum amount of time, and you don't need to buy any expensive equipment to do it, so why should you pay somebody to come out to your rental property? Just take the following quick lesson before your first attempt.

• First, measure the distance across the front (face) of the installed rod or across where you want the rod installed. This measurement is called the drapery width and is always expressed first.

• Second, measure the distance from the top of the rod to one inch above the floor for floor-length draperies, or measure from the top of the rod to four inches below the window sill for apron-length draperies. This measurement is the drapery length and is always expressed second.

• Third, indicate whether the drapery is to be a panel (one-way draw opens from one side) or a pair (two-way draw opens from the middle).

Do not measure and include in your measurements either the rod projections (distance at each end between rod and wall) or the center overlap. Contract drapery shops make allowances for them.

Do not measure an old drapery's exact dimensions and submit them for duplication. Drapery sizes, strange as it seems, are not actual drapery measurements.

Do not add any height above the top of the rod up to that point where you think the drapery will extend.

Do not be afraid to inquire whether this is the very method used by your drapery supplier. Whereas contract drapery suppliers do use this method, suppliers who deal with the general public may use another. To find a contract drapery supplier, look under "Draperies-Whsle & Mfrs" in the Yellow Pages. Yes, they will sell to you. Give them one of your business cards, and they will probably even set you up with a billing account.

If there's no drapery rod in place and you have to install one, install it so you can take take advantage of the standard sizes which contract drapery shops keep in stock. Standard sizes will cost you much less and will not require you to wait those precious days while custom draperies are being made up to your specifications, something that is especially important when you have just finished redecorating a dwelling, have advertised it for rent, and then you learn that the draperies won't be ready for another two weeks. The bedsheets, old draperies, bedspeads, or drop cloths you'll then have to put on the windows will detract noticeably from that rental's appearance.

These are the standard contract sizes generally available (width x length), together with the common window openings they fit.

Two-Way Draw				One-Way Draw	
Window Opening	Drapery Size	Window Opening	Drapery Size	Window Opening	Drapery size
3' x 3'	42 x 44	6' x 6'8"	78 x 84	5' x 6'8"	64 x 84
4' x 3'	52 x 44	8' x 3'	102 x 44	6' x 6'8"	78 x 84
4' x 4'	52 x 56	8' x 4'	102 x 56	8' x 6'8"	102 x 84
4' x 6'8"	54 x 84	8' x 5'	102 x 68		
5' x 4'	64 x 56	8' x 6'8"	102 x 84		
6' x 3'	78 x 44	10' x 4'	126 x 56		
6' x 4'	78 x 56	10' x 6'8"	126 x 84		
6' x 5'	78 x 68				

As you can calculate from this table, the ends of the rod should normally extend three inches on either side of the window opening, and the top of the rod should be three and a half inches above the window opening. Such a rod installation will be firmly anchored in the wood of the window framing. If, because of an odd-sized window opening, you have to fudge a little to create a standard size, by all means, fudge. Use plastic or nylon anchors for mounting the rod brackets so you can avoid having to order a custom size.

Likewise, if there is a drapery rod already installed and it isn't exactly standard in length, don't despair. You can usually fit a drapery size which is an inch too big or too small without having to move the brackets. If, however, a standard-size drapery varies too much to fit your existing rod installation, just move the rod brackets so the standard size will fit and use anchors as necessary.

SHOULD YOU CARPET THOSE FLOORS?

Understand, first of all, that there is no such thing as a perfect floor covering for rental dwellings. Each one has its disadvantages, but there is one floor covering which has fewer disadvantages and more advantages for most rentals, excluding kitchen and bath areas, than any other floor coverings you might consider, and that one is wall-to-wall carpeting.

Besides the other attributes it has, carpeting adds tremendously to the soundproofing and income of any rental, and I can testify that it adds to the warmth and rentability as well. After working two weeks on one apartment unit, installing a new kitchen counter, sink, built-in oven, and vanity, and painting the walls and doors throughout, I thought I'd really made great changes, but all that work was nothing compared to the change that my carpet installer made in only three hours. Wowee! That apartment was transformed from stark, cold, colorless housing into an inviting, warm, cheerful place which someone would want to call "home," and it rented easily for a substantial sum. It's no wonder tenants prefer wall-to-wall carpeting and will pay more for it.

Before you buy any carpeting, however, make a few important approximations to determine whether you ought to make the investment at all. Consider roughly how much the carpeting will cost (draw and measure the floorplan, determine the yardage required, and multiply that by a telephone quote); consider how much additional rent you can expect if you add carpets (make a brief marketing survey); consider how much your income property will increase in value if you add carpets (use prevailing rules of thumb for determining the market value of income property and see whether the addition of carpets will more than offset the cost); and consider whether the condition of the present floors warrants either adding carpets or recarpeting right now (look them over carefully).

After you have considered those investment questions and have decided to go ahead with the carpeting, you'll still have decisions to make about areas, colors, patterns, piles, yarns, pads, prices, manufacturers, suppliers, and installers. Read on and then make your decisions with deliberation.

• AREAS—Since one of your major concerns is the overall expense, you might save by carpeting only a portion of a unit, perhaps just a living room, because it will cost a mere fraction of a fully carpeted installation and yet you will have "wall-to-wall carpet" to tout to prospective tenants. Another possibility for savings involves laying durable sheet goods (linoleum, tile, or vinyl) by entrances (usually in a three-foot square) and in hallways where traffic is heavy and the carpet tends to wear and spot quickly. You won't notice any savings by doing this right away, but you will in time because you won't have to replace an entire room full of carpeting to eliminate the eyesore of small worn areas.

• COLORS—Carpets come in all the colors God made and in some which only man could concoct, many of which you can summarily reject for rental units. No matter what color you choose, you'll manage to choose one that clashes with some tenant's taste, so don't worry too much about it. In general, avoid light and bright colors and choose those which are relatively neutral. Medium shades of gold and brown are the most neutral, but greens and blues work well, too. Darker colors naturally show less dirt and fewer spots, while lighter colors are more cheerful and make rooms look larger. Select darker colors for rentals where you can expect kids, pets, and less responsible tenants, and use lighter colors in places where you can expect sun fading and more responsible tenants.

• PATTERNS—There may be some doubts about what carpet color is best, but there's no doubt about what pattern of carpet is best for most rental units. Tweed is. Dirt, stains, wear areas, crumbs, toenail clippings, ashes, swatted flies, and swift cockroaches just don't show up as much on a tweed background. They blend right into its randomness.

• PILES—Carpets have piles, too. Carpet "pile" refers to the shape of the yarn. While the most durable carpet pile you can buy is level-loop, the most camouflaging is short shag (3/4-inch yarn), sometimes called cabled plush. Both are good for use in rentals. Short shag in solid colors, and especially in tweeds, will camouflage anything that tweeds will by themselves, and what's more, it will camouflage cigarette burns as well, but it shows traffic wear more than level-loops do. A 20-ounce (face weight measures the weight of the yarn in one square yard and determines, more than any other single factor, a carpet's price) level-loop will actually outwear a 50-ounce shag. Use shag in living rooms and bedrooms which have a moderate amount of traffic and avoid using it in heavy traffic areas like hallways. Those are best covered with sheet goods in shag installations (mixing carpet piles or colors within a single dwelling looks too tacky). Because they are so tightly woven, level-loop carpets wear well and should be installed in heavy traffic areas, but they will definitely show burns. If traffic wear is your primary concern, then choose either level-loop carpeting by itself or short shag combined with sheet goods. If burns are your primary concern, choose short shag.

• PADS—Remember that the pad you select is every bit as important as the carpet itself because it is the pad which gives carpeting that luxurious, substantial feeling underfoot and at the same time extends a carpet's life. Use a half-inch rebonded polyurethane pad or else a polymeric pad, and avoid jute, rubber, and light polyurethane pads. Rebonded and polymeric pads are in the lower, not the lowest, price range and are well worth the money. They will last through several changes of carpet.

• PRICES—Don't buy expensive carpet for rentals, no matter how much more wear the salesperson says you'll get from it. It will look just as shabby as any inexpensive carpet after tenants have used and abused it for five or six years. When combined with a good pad, nylon carpeting which sells in the lowest third of the price range will give at least as good service as expensive carpeting.

• SUPPLIERS—Carpet peddling is a very competitive business, and you can take advantage of this competition by shopping around for bids on your job. The biggest, most advertised retail supplier for the home market isn't necessarily the cheapest or the best source of carpets suitable for the rental market. Usually you will find better buys by trying small contract carpet firms which supply building contractors with lots of yardage and will deal fairly with you as a landlord or landlady because they consider you a businessperson and a source of repeat business. Ask several building contractors for the names of their carpet suppliers and then check the ads in publications from your rental property owners' association.

• INSTALLERS—If you can, get an itemized bid on your carpeting, at least for materials and labor, so you may hire your own installer if you wish. Many carpet installers moonlight, and you should be able to find a good one through "services offered" classified ads, one who will install your carpet for less than the price of the so-called "free installation" included in a package deal. Be sure you understand who's paying for the tackless strip and the metal threshold pieces, though. Some installers will quote you a price per yard which includes these items and others won't.

• SQUEAKS—Before you have anyone install carpeting for you, tread splayfooted, like Charlie Chaplin playing the little tramp, over every square foot of the installation area to find all the squeaks that have been caused over the years by loosening of the subflooring nails. Then nail the squeaks out with 2 1/2-inch cement-coated screw or ring nails placed strategically alongside the squeaky culprits. Squeaky floors annoy tenants upstairs and downstairs and detract from the image of your building.

SOME LAST WORDS

Hamlet, that Prince of Denmark, would have made a terrible landlord. He talked too much and he couldn't make decisions. The decisions in this chapter alone would have taken him dozens more plays just to contemplate. By then, his tenants would have either left in disgust, fallen fast asleep, or taken over. You can do better. You must.

Sure, the questions in this chapter themselves are mundane—To allow pets or not to allow pets? To carpet or not to carpet? These questions are not nearly as grandiose or poetic as Hamlet's "To be or not to be?" Are they? Nobody's going to write a play about real-world landlording decisions and the disturbing perplexity you go through whenever you make them, but you'll stay in this business a long, long time, and you'll prosper in it, too, so long as you can make prompt and mostly correct decisions about what will work and what won't.

Take enough time to think over the implications of your decisions, make up your mind, and then act.

HIRING HELP

Having decided to hire help to assist you in your landlording business (see "Should You Do It Yourself?" in Chapter 11), you become a boss, perhaps for the first time in your life.

Suffer no great trepidation over this new role. Simply prepare for it. You survived being called "landlord" or "landlady," didn't you? Surely, then, you will survive being called "boss." The truth is that as a landlord or landlady who hires help, you are more than just a boss supervising people. You're the personnel, accounting, payroll, legal, and executive departments of your business all rolled into one. Sounds impressive and also a little forbidding, doesn't it? It is, but don't worry. If you have shown yourself to be a competent landlord or landlady, you'll be a competent employer as well. It only takes some common sense, some understanding of people, and some acquaintance with the applicable laws, practices, procedures, and forms.

These next few pages are not meant to tell you all you need to know about hiring help. That is an enormous subject in itself, and there are numerous books devoted to it alone. The information provided here is intended merely to get you started in the right direction and to keep you out of trouble as you face a number of responsibilities and tasks which are altogether different from the usual ones involved in do-it-yourself landlording and probably altogether different from your normal workaday world, too, unless you already happen to be self-employed and have people working for you.

Although the information here pertains more to managers than to the other workers you might hire, it is, for the most part, relevant to both. Because residency on the premises is generally required of managers and because they aren't working under direct supervision, that is, they won't have you around to tell them what to do most of the time, the hiring process is somewhat more rigorous for them, but it can certainly be modified to suit the hiring of other workers as well, workers who are under direct supervision.

SETTLING THE INDEPENDENT CONTRACTOR-EMPLOYEE QUESTION

You have undoubtedly hired help in the past without even thinking much about it. You were hiring help when you hired a roofer to repair a leaky roof and when you called a plumber to install a new commode, but that was contractual hiring. In other words, those who did the work were not your employees. They were performing services for you while being either self-employed or employed by somebody else. You agreed to pay them a flat fee or an hourly rate, and they gave you a bill for their work. You may have blanched at those bills, but you had no hidden costs, no obligatory reports due governmental agencies, no increased insurance burden, and no extra bookkeeping chores, all of which you would have had if the roofer or plumber had been your employee.

Because of the benefits inherent in contractual employment and because contractual employees can be expected to do good work without requiring much supervision, many landlords and landladies prefer to hire only bonded contractual help—commercial gardeners, window washing specialists, artisan house painters, professional electricians, plumbing contractors, carpet cleaning services, and the like. They may pay more, but they avoid the hassles of being an employer, and independent contractors generally get the work done well and quickly.

Some landlords and landladies have tried to avoid the legal obligations and paperwork involved in being employers in another way, by drawing up contracts for those they employ and by calling their employees "independent contractors." Years ago that strategem worked satisfactorily, but it doesn't work so well any more, not since the government discovered that many so-called "independent contractors" had joined the underground economy. They weren't reporting any income, and naturally, because they weren't reporting any income, they weren't paying any income taxes. More than anything else, this increasingly widespread evasion of taxes by workers who were being paid their full wages, without any deductions being taken out, prompted a government crackdown on would-be independent contractors. Our government doesn't like to be cheated out of taxes any more than Mother Nature likes to be fooled. You may *avoid* paying taxes as we landlords and landladies do when we take advantage of the depreciation provisions in the tax law, but you may not *evade* paying taxes as some people do when they fail to report income. That's enough to get the government mad at you.

As employers, we don't particularly care whether the workers we hire pay their income taxes or not. We have our own concerns when we hire people to work for us. That's as much our concern as whether they say grace at the dinner table. Still, we cannot afford to overlook the government's distinction between employee and independent contractor unless we want to pay a penalty ourselves. When you hire an employee, then, don't try to convert that person into an independent contractor. It's not worth the trouble. Bite the bullet. Yes, you are saddled with the same burdens as any other employer. Yes, you do become an income tax collector for the government, and yes, you pay a premium for the privilege. Do it, whether you like it or not. It comes with the territory.

If you're ever wondering whether someone you hire is really an employee or an independent contractor, you may apply some simple tests. The primary one is this: If you control both *what* work is to be done and *how* it is to be done, then the person doing the work is your employee and not an independent contractor. Other tests to determine whether workers may be considered independent contractors are these—

Do the workers have a business license or a contractor's license?
Do they pay their own deductions, including self-employment tax?
Do they assume legal liability for their work?
Do they come and go whenever they want to?
Do they qualify as specialists who work without your having to supervise them?
Do they have a verbal or written contract for the work being performed?
Do they carry appropriate insurance?
Do they provide their own tools, equipment, and materials?
Do they work for other people?
Do they advertise their services?
Do they have business cards and stationery?

If the answers to these questions are mostly, if not entirely, affirmative, the workers could be considered independent contractors and your only responsibility would be to pay them. If not, you *must* consider them your employees, no matter what name you give them and no matter how carefully you draft a self-serving contract which both of you sign. The government has ruled, "An employee by any other name is still an employee."

As an employer, you assume a variety of attendant responsibilities, responsibilities which add approximately 30% to the actual wages you pay your employees, a heavy burden indeed. In other words, an employee whom you pay $5 an hour will really cost you $6.50. It's no wonder, then, that landlords and landladies try to interpret certain work relationships as contractual, and it's no wonder that the government has pursued the matter doggedly to recover taxes and protect the welfare of employees.

Should someone you hire as an independent contractor turn out to be using the status of "independent contractor" to evade taxes, you may be penalized for not having paid the employer's share of taxes for this "employee." To protect yourself from this possibility, submit a 1099-MISC form to the IRS, listing the independent contractor's name and how much you have paid him over the year. (For IRS forms, call 1-800-242-4585)

Should you ever force an employee to be an independent contractor in order to avoid the added expenses and responsibilities, you are exposing yourself to dire consequences, especially if that worker is injured on the job or wants to begin claiming social security benefits after having worked for you.

Keep in mind that apartment managers, the helpers you are most likely to hire, are *always* considered employees, no matter what ruse you use to metamorphose them into independent contractors. Therefore, you might as well resign yourself to having an extra paperwork and expense burden whenever you hire a manager. (Although local laws may require you to have on-site managers only for buildings with units above a certain number, having someone responsible on the premises of every multiple-family dwelling, even duplexes, is a worthwhile convenience.) You may get away without assuming this burden if you discount a tenant's rent a few dollars for doing yard maintenance around an apartment house or if you pay a few dollars every month to a resident who acts in your stead as, say, rent collector and resident keeper of the keys, but even then you should secure both workers' compensation and non-owned automobile insurance coverage. The potential liability for not having this minimal insurance when you hire help is too draconian for you to bear.

As for doing the burdensome paperwork involved in hiring employees, that will depend pretty much on whether you are hiring casual helpers or regular helpers and on how much money they are earning over a given period of time. If you wonder whether you ought to do the paperwork, call the governmental agencies involved with collecting taxes on wages and ask them.

COMPLYING WITH EMPLOYMENT LAWS

As an employer, you must comply with a variety of laws designed to protect employees and employ countless bureaucratic minions. To find out how these laws apply to you, contact your state department of employment. They will supply you with the proper instructions, employer numbers, tables, timetables, and forms necessary for complying with the laws.

Because rental property management work involves strange hours and sometimes long hours, what you decide to pay a manager may not comply with minimum wage standards. Should disgruntled former managers challenge you for having compensated them with something less than their entitlements, you may be forced to pay back wages and fines, that is, unless you can produce time sheets to prove that you did pay the minimum wage or more. The burden of proof is on you as the employer.

Keeping time sheets is a chore for your managers and for you, that's certain, but they will keep you from running afoul of the labor laws.

By the way, you needn't bother with time sheets for any manager earning more than $900 per month. Employees earning more than that amount are exempt from the laws governing minimum hourly wages and overtime.

SETTING THE PAY AND DEFINING THE JOB

Whenever people consider taking a job, they always have at least two questions in mind—"What's the pay?" and "What's required of me?" You should have the answers at the ready to both those questions and to others as well before you ever begin looking for help, casual or permanent, full- or part-time.

As for compensation, some landlords and landladies pay their managers a flat rate per unit per month, say, $20, and some pay a percentage of the rent collected, say, 5%, but neither of these methods for determining managerial compensation is fair to both landlord and manager because neither one reflects the time required to perform the tasks involved. I know some properties where $20 per unit per month would be a windfall for the manager because the properties practically run themselves and others with the same number of units where it would be a pittance because there's always something for the manager to do. Consider, for example, the difference between managing a complex tenanted mostly by retired adults which has no gardening to look after and managing another one tenanted mostly by working families who have up to three kids apiece. The manager of the adult complex may do little more than police a cement-covered courtyard and write rent receipts while the manager of the family units may have more to do than old Mother Hubbard. Neither a flat rate nor a percentage of the gross is fair compensation for management as far as I'm concerned.

Another, much fairer method of compensation involves paying for the work you can expect the manager to do at a particular property. The job might include as little as collecting rents when due, showing vacancies, and keeping the keys, or it might include all that plus pursuing late payers, checking applications, selecting tenants, banking, keeping records, doing minor maintenance and repairs, caring for the pool, cleaning, gardening, painting, and handling tenants' complaints.

List the tasks you expect your managers to perform and also try to establish the amount of time you think they should spend on those tasks during the average month. Collecting rents when due, you might figure, would average ten minutes per dwelling per month, and so on. Set the pay by multiplying an hourly rate, pegged somewhat above the minimum wage, times the anticipated number of hours you expect the managers to work, but guarantee to pay them a certain salary every month.

Review your time estimates after the managers have been on the job a while to make sure that you haven't underestimated or overestimated the time involved.

Here are some ideas about paying those you hire—

• Inquire into local practices for compensating full- and part-time managers. Ask your rental-property owners' association for some figures. If the association itself can't help you, its members can. Ask around.

• Never, ever, say that you are giving a manager "free rent"; the correct expression is "rental compensation." Rent is "free" only if you are giving it away, expecting nothing in return. If you are giving it away, you're a philanthropist, not a landlord or landlady.

• If you do compensate a manager by providing a residence, do not agree to pay the utilities, too. You cannot predict how much they will cost every month.

• Pay your helpers *after* they have done their work, not before.

• Compensating part-time managers in the form of rent constitutes advance payment. Collect full rent from them, the same as from other tenants, and then pay them a salary at the end of the month. Otherwise, being human, they will tend to regard their discounted rent after a while as a birthright and not as a compensation for services.

• Compensate full-time managers with salary and rent only if that is the accepted practice. Check into the special tax rules which apply to the portion of a manager's income attributable to the residence.

• Pay the members of a management couple separately for the work which each one performs so each of them will receive Social Security credits.

• Do not expect your employees to put forth a reasonable effort for unreasonable wages.

• Raise managers' compensation every time you raise rents.

• Do not give the manager so much to do that he cannot do it all adequately. If, in addition to everything else, you want your manager to paint and prepare every unit which becomes vacant, you may be saving money over hiring professionals to do the work, but you may be losing a lot more money by keeping your available rentals off the market while the work is either being done or waiting to be done. Pitch in yourself, or get some outside help.

ESTABLISHING A WORKER PROFILE

Recognizing that careless maintenance workers and bigoted, caustic, timid, or frenetic managers all will cost you time and money and good tenants, too, you should try to establish a profile of the ideal worker your job requires and then identify the categories of people who might most likely fit that profile.

Managers for multiple-family dwellings, for example, should be fair, honest, reliable, used to dealing with people, intelligent, self-assured, unflappable, willing to learn, handy, helpful, thrifty, neat, clean, inquisitive, organized, modest, pleasant, and patient homebodies who can speak with an air of authority and who resemble the residents of the property they manage.

Who is most likely to fit a profile like that? Few humans I know of. But those with service-oriented backgrounds would be the most likely to fit it. Some owners go out of their way to hire school teachers as managers because teachers know how to think on their feet, are accustomed to keeping records, are used to dealing with people, are used to disciplining, have spare time during the afternoon and summer, are "professional" in their outlook, work without close supervision, and could use the extra money. Other owners look for people who have a service-oriented background.

Chances are that you'll have to compromise in your choice, so decide which managerial qualities are most important for the job as you see it and which are the least important. Rank them.

Don't overlook the last criterion either, that the managers resemble the residents of the property they manage. Hiring a young couple to manage a building tenanted mostly by pensioners is courting trouble, just as hiring a pensioner to manage a student complex would be, or hiring a bigoted red-neck to manage a black-ghetto property. Managers who resemble their tenants can understand those tenant's unique problems and deal with them at the right level.

FINDING MANAGEMENT HELP

Whenever you're looking for management help, consider your existing tenants first. They already have a familiarity with the property and its occupants, and they are known to you, so you needn't be particularly apprehensive about their character. After all, you have already entrusted them with a dwelling worth $50,000 or so, and they have not been found wanting. The chances are good that they will be equally as reliable when looking after more of the same. Good tenants whom I have approached about becoming managers have invariably become good managers, even for as many as 113 units. (One good tenant I approached about managing an eightplex refused the job outright; he wanted to look after the building all right, but he didn't want tenants banging on his door at all hours. We made a deal that he would be called the "caretaker" rather than the "manager," and that he would keep the keys, show vacancies, and clean around the building, but that tenants would send their rent payments to me directly and call me with their complaints. The arrangement worked beautifully for both of us for years.) You might be surprised about the pool of talent that most residential income properties have, and you should not be averse to using it.

If you cannot identify one of your good tenants as a managerial candidate, advertise the position through the help-wanted classifieds, state employment offices, management schools' employment offices, agencies, and your rental property owners' association. You'll likely be besieged with applicants, for there seem to be many people who find the work agreeable. Even though this kind of work typically doesn't pay much, it offers certain advantages which many people prize: discounted housing, independence, autonomy, and a short commute.

INHERITING A MANAGER

Just as you will usually inherit tenants when you acquire a multiple-family dwelling, you will also frequently inherit managers, and you will be faced with the decision of whether to keep the old managers or find your own. (Because this takeover period is the perfect time for dishonest managers to abscond with funds, be sure you look very carefully through the rental payment records of any property you are acquiring which already has a manager. Ask plenty of questions until you understand precisely who owes what and when it is owed.) Unless there are obvious reasons to let them go right away, agree to keep them for a month or two until you become familiar with the place and can make an informed decision whether to keep them on a permanent basis or not.

Consider carefully how much the old manager is being paid. Talk over the job as it's being performed. Calculate the time involved and determine what the job is worth to you as the new owner. You may find that, based on the actual workload, the previous owner was overpaying the manager and couldn't tell the difference because he had owned the property a while and had had an easily assured and gradually increasing cash flow. Consequently, he may have been reluctant to upset the situation by reviewing the manager's pay. If that's the case, you'll probably have to begin looking around for a new manager. Not many people will accept a decrease in pay while continuing to do the same work they've been doing all along.

FINDING MAINTENANCE AND REPAIR HELP

When you're looking around for maintenance and repair help, consider your tenants second on your list of prospects. Whom should you consider first? Your relatives and friends, of course. Haven't you ever heard of nepotism? After eliminating your relatives and friends as prospects, look to your tenants for this kind of help, and only as a last resort should you have to advertise or call the local state employment office.

PREQUALIFYING

If you are considering relatives, friends, or acquaintances for a job, you have already prequalified them in your mind before you ever approach them about it, but if perfect strangers are inquiring about a particular job, you should take a little time to prequalify them first before going ahead with an interview. Otherwise, you'll be wasting their time and yours. At a minimum, each interview takes half an hour, so interviewing ten people will easily take a full day. That's much too much time. Unless you genuinely enjoy conducting interviews and have the time to do it, there's no reason for you to spend that much time at it. Shortcut the procedure by selecting two or three prime candidates to interview.

To select them, prequalify all the respondents by requesting written resumes. Read the resumes carefully and try to imagine each of these people working for you in the particular job you have available. Call only the ones who appear to be the most promising. If the position involves resident management, ask them the same questions you'd ask to prequalify tenant applicants. Then ask them the same questions you'd ask of any employee applicant, questions about their experience, salary requirements, and availability. If they appear worth pursuing, set up an interview. If not, tell them you'll "get back to them."

INTERVIEWING

Arrange employment interviews at the property itself preferably. Make note of anything which might provide clues as to the people's suitability for the job. Try to determine whether they might "have a drinking problem." Note especially their promptness, overall appearance, bearing, habits, sense of humor, odor, speech, smile, and hands. Outline the job first, including its responsibilities, its advantages, and its drawbacks. Tell applicants whether their living in a certain dwelling is a prerequisite for the position. Explain what the compensation is and when it's paid. Tell them whether there are raises which might be expected after a trial period, and so on.

Ask them whether the job appears attractive to them and whether they feel themselves capable of handling it. If so, proceed to ask them questions using the employment application as a guide, and transcribe the information yourself so you can measure their responses and let them talk freely. In addition to the questions on the application, you might want to ask such questions as how they feel about living in close proximity to people as manager and not being able to be good friends with anybody, how they would describe themselves to a stranger, what accomplishments they are most proud of, and why they feel they should be considered for the job. Establish good eye contact with them during the interview. Be friendly, attentive, and helpful, and encourage them to talk frankly about themselves while you take notes.

When you have finished the interview, show them around the property and make a promise to call them back within the next couple of days to inform them of your decision. It's only fair to let them know soon what you have decided so they can make other plans for themselves.

SELECTING

Call the employer references and try to verify the information you have on the applicants. Ask about the circumstances surrounding their departure from each job and ask quite frankly whether the employer would consider hiring them again.

After calling employers, run a credit check on the applicants, and also see what you can learn about their driving records through either your insurance company or your state's

Employment Application

Name Charley Goodfolks   Home Phone 555-0222   Work Phone 555-1981

Date of Birth 4/1/26   Social Security No. 198-83-6509   Driver's License No. Z900123

Own ___ Rent ✓ How long at address? 1 YR.

Present Add...

How many y... Present/La... Occupation...

Monthly Gross #13...

Spouse's Name O...

How many... Present/... Occupati...

Monthly Gross...

Depende... and age...

What s... have r...

What spous...

What you...

Are... Wher...

Sav... Ba...

Ch... Ba...

M... C...

O... F...

Management Agreement

Agreement between DUKE & LUCY MILQUETOAST   Dated APRIL 16, 1986

CHARLES & AGNES GOODFOLKS _____, Owners, and

_____, Managers, for management of property

located at 2100 MAIN ST., BIGTOWN

Compensation for Managers shall be $ 125.00 per month at a guaranteed minimum and shall be computed at an hourly rate of $ 5.00. Unless Managers obtain Owners' permission in advance or, in case of emergency, unless they notify Owners within 48 hours afterwards, Managers shall spend no more than 25 hours per month on managerial responsibilities. Managers shall record working hours on time sheets provided by Owners, one time sheet for each person exercising managerial responsibilities, and shall submit those time sheets at least once a month.

Other compensation shall be as follows: NONE; COMPENSATION ON AN HOURLY OR PER-JOB BASIS FOR ADDITIONAL TASKS.

Managers shall have days off as follows: TUESDAY & WEDNESDAY; vacation time as follows: ONE DAY PER MONTH (ACCUMULATING); sick leave as follows: ONE DAY PER MONTH (ACCUMULATING).

Managers' duties and responsibilities, which will be reviewed jointly in ninety days and annually after that, shall be as follows: KEEPING THE KEYS, COLLECTING RENTS WHEN DUE, PURSUING LATE PAYERS, SHOWING VACANCIES, MINOR MAINTENANCE (FIX LEAKY FAUCETS; REPLACE LIGHT SWITCHES AND LIGHT BULBS OUTSIDE), CLEAN GROUNDS AS NEEDED.

Managers shall receipt all monies collected on the Owners' behalf and shall deposit or transfer those monies within TWO DAYS of collection as follows: CALL OWNERS TO REPORT COLLECTIONS; DEPOSIT COLLECTIONS TO MILQUETOAST PROP. TWO.

Managers shall spend or commit to spend no more than $ 50.00 on the Owners' behalf without first obtaining permission.

Either Managers or Owners may cancel this agreement upon providing SEVEN days' written notice.

Managers hereby acknowledge that they have read this agreement, understand it, agree to it, and have been given a copy.

Owner Duke Milquetoast

By _____   Manager Charles Goodfolks

Manager Agnes Goodfolks

department of motor vehicles. Then, if everything appears satisfactory and you are still interested in hiring them, make an appointment to talk with them where they currently reside.

When you see where they live and how they live, you will be able to decide whether to hire them or not. If you don't like what you see, tell them you have other applicants to visit before you make your decision, and then leave. If you do like what you see, show them a blank copy of your management agreement and go over it with them. Be certain they understand those provisions in the agreement which call for them to submit their hours of work regularly on a time sheet. If the job means that they will be moving into a manager's dwelling, show them a copy of the Rental Agreement, too, and review it. Then complete both agreements.

Once you have made your decision, don't continue keeping the unsuccessful applicants in limbo. Send them a letter thanking them for their interest and wishing them good luck in finding an even better job.

SUPERVISING

If one of your employees were to discriminate against a prospective tenant illegally, give a tenant a black eye, fire another employee improperly, or even cause an automobile accident while on the way to the bank with your rent receipts, you as their employer would be held responsible. You can ill afford such problems. Managers should save you time and worry, not cost you both. Take the time, therefore, to let your managers know how much discretionary authority they have to act on their own, how much money they can spend without asking for your approval, which suppliers and service people you prefer them to patronize, what constitutes an emergency, what necessitates their calling you right away, how they should go about selecting new tenants, how you would like existing tenants to be treated, what your rent collection policy is, and how they should handle time sheets.

After you have told them what you want them to do and how you want them to do it, let them do it. Never undermine your manager's authority either by allowing tenants to approach you behind the manager's back or by making deals without the manager's knowledge. Tenants will try to divide and conquer. Don't let them get away with it. Sometimes they will have legitimate grievances which aren't being addressed by the manager, though, so at least listen closely to what they have to say whenever they take the trouble to contact you directly, but then talk with the manager and either let the manager reply to them or arrange a three-way discussion. Never go to see tenants by yourself without first consulting the manager. Work *with* your managers, not *around* them.

Since all people like to know that their work is being appreciated, show your employees that you like what they're doing for you. Praise them sincerely when they do good work, and remember them on their birthdays and during the holiday season.

If they are not handling the overall job as you wish it handled, tell them the source of your dissatisfaction and give them an opportunity to improve. Document what you say to them so you'll have ammunition to use in case any of your employees accuse you of terminating them illegally. If they don't improve, give them the opportunity to quit so they can save face by not getting fired.

TERMINATING

Sometimes a management arrangement just doesn't work out, and you find yourself faced with the unpleasant task of terminating managers, something rendered all the more awkward because they live on the premises as a condition of employment. You are not only terminating them; you are evicting them as well. Until they go, you don't even have a place for the new managers to live.

Under these circumstances, time is of the essence. You want them to vacate as quickly as possible. Offer them an incentive to leave within 24 hours, perhaps their accumulated vacation pay, and immediately reclaim the keys, bookkeeping records, equipment, and supplies. Ask a trusted tenant to look after things for the time being, but do not divulge to anyone the details surrounding the termination. If any announcement is in order, it might center around the transfer of managerial responsibilities and nothing more.

Believe it or not, I have acquired good properties at below-market prices from owners who sold out because they were unwilling or unable to terminate their incompetent managers, admittedly an unpleasant tast, but definitely achievable. When you have to do it, do it.

GIVING REFERENCES

From time to time, you will be called upon by other employers to furnish information about former or even current employees who are looking around for other employment. You'll want to give good employees a good recommendation, and giving them a good recommendation presents no problem at all. On the other hand, you'll want to give bad employees a bad recommendation, but doing so presents a definite problem. You leave yourself open to a lawsuit whenever you say anything bad about an employee which you couldn't prove conclusively in a court of law.

Go ahead and give concrete details about salary and length of employment whenever you're asked for that information legitimately. It can't be disputed and won't get you into any trouble. But whenever you're asked to give information which is subject to interpretation and which might be construed as negative, say "No comment!" It speaks volumes and won't get you into any trouble at all.

DOING PAYROLL

Using both the time sheets which your employees submit at least once a month and the figures for deductions provided by governmental agencies, calculate your employees' gross earnings and all their necessary deductions. Write those figures in duplicate on a statement of earnings and deductions form (Rediform 4H416 is one of several available for this purpose) for each employee. Tear out the original and give it to the employee along with your check for the employee's net earnings. Leave the copy of the statement attached to the pad as a record of payment and then transfer those figures to the Payroll Record sheet you keep for each employee (see sample in Chapter 17).

Do not deceive yourself into thinking that the employee's deductions are all you need to keep track of and pay to the government. You must contribute, too. Be sure to indicate in the shaded column the Social Security contribution you must make as an employer. This sum, almost equal to the employee's Social Security contribution, was not reflected in the statement given to the employee, but you must keep track of it nonetheless, and you must forward it, along with the monies collected, to the various governmental agencies involved at either monthly or quarterly intervals. Failure to do so will result in a response much swifter than any made to the person who fails to file an individual income tax return. For instructions about forwarding these monies, ask the IRS and your state tax collecting agency to send you their free employer booklets.

Time Sheet

CHARLEY GOODFOLKS
_____
Employee's Name

Charley Goodfolks
_____
Employee's Signature

456 SWEET ST.
_____
Property

Pay Period 3/1 to 3/15

DATE	TIMES		HOURS	DESCRIPTION OF WORK PERFORMED	CONTRACT AMOUNT
3/1	5:00 5:15 5:30 7:45		2½	groundskeeping; rent collection	
3/2	5	6	1	" "	
3/3	5:20	6:30	1⅙	" . "	
3/4	5	5:15	¼	" "	
3/5	12 3	1 5	3	groundskeeping & dumprun (with my truck)	5.00
3/9	5:15	6:00	¾	groundskeeping	
3/10	5	5:30	½	Plumbing repair, Apt 4	
3/12	10	11:30	1½	groundskeeping	
3/14	6	7:20	1⅓	"	

Total Hours   12
Rate   5.00
Hourly Gross   60.00
Contract   5.00
Total Gross   65.00

Total Contract   5.00

Duke
_____
Approved by

3/16
_____
Date

SOME LAST WORDS

In spite of all the complications involved in hiring help, you will find that your landlording business will prosper so much more with help than without it and that you will feel liberated enough to enjoy some of the advantages of the business. You cannot do all the work yourself. Don't die trying.

PARTICIPATING IN THE SECTION 8 SUBSIDIZED HOUSING PROGRAM

Inveterate M*A*S*H rerun watchers have heard the term "Section 8" often enough. Corporal Max Klinger keeps dressing up in outrageous female garb and concocting outlandish schemes to get out of the U.S. Army on a Section 8. That Section 8, a release for psychological reasons, bears scant resemblance to the Section 8 of this chapter. They just happen to share the same section numbers in their respective government documents. That's all. The Section 8 of this chapter does bear a remarkable resemblance to something else which has the stamp of government all over it, however, and that's the food stamp program.

The Section 8 Existing Housing Program is to rental housing what food stamps are to groceries. Both are federal government subsidy programs, and both enable the poor to live better than their incomes would otherwise allow them to. Through these programs, they get to taste meat, potatoes, milk, and indoor plumbing on a gruel, bread, water, and shantytown pocketbook.

Section 8 differs markedly from the other types of government housing programs which I maligned in the introduction to this book. Those are essentially housing-based subsidy programs. Tenants must live in a particular place to get their subsidies under those programs. Section 8 is a tenant-based program. It requires that tenants qualify financially just as the other programs do, but it doesn't restrict them to living in housing which is government-owned, government-financed, or government-operated. They could be living in rental housing belonging to anybody, even to you or to me. When they move from one rental dwelling to another, their subsidy goes with them.

Whereas the other government housing programs operate outside the competitive marketplace, the Section 8 program operates inside it. In fact, Section 8 involves a monitoring of the competitive rental housing market which makes its local administrators more informed about what's happening in the market than many rental property owners and managers. And whereas these other programs require government participation from a building's conception through its construction and on into its later stages, the Section 8 program covers only existing housing. Its full title actually is the "Section 8 Existing Housing Program," and in bureaucratic circles, it's referred to interchangeably as the "Section 8 Housing Program" or the "Existing Housing Program." Here it's simply called what the po' folks call it, Section 8.

Established by the 1974 Housing and Community Development Act, Section 8 is now a major federal program involving billions of dollars and thousands upon thousands of people. So far, it has had a salutary effect on the rental housing business, and though changes lie ahead for the program as legislators tinker with it, it likely will continue to have a salutary effect on the business for years to come.

As a free-enterprising rental property owner, you can be a key element in the program if you want to be, but you certainly don't have to be. Unlike poor, frustrated Klinger, you have a choice about whether to participate. Interested or not, you really ought to know something about this government program and how it operates in your community.

THE THREE PARTIES

Three parties make Section 8 work at the local level, and they are all three key parties. Without any one of them, there would be no local program. The three are tenants, rental property owners, and local public housing agencies. Tenants qualify to participate according to income and family size; owners qualify by having the right kind of rental housing available and by being willing to participate; and local public housing agencies "qualify" by having the necessary funds and personnel to run the program.

Qualified tenants may be young or old, normal or handicapped, active or lethargic, single or multiple, bright or dull, married or not married, but they may not be rich or poor. They may only be poor, not necessarily dirt poor, mind you, just poor according to the federal government's latest poverty level definition. Right now the so-called "truly needy" or very low income people who qualify for Section 8 subsidies must have an income amounting to less than half the median income for their given family size located in their particular part of the country. These figures vary from time to time, from family to family, and from place to place. Currently, a family of four in Oakland, California, will qualify if their yearly income is less than $16,700. That's not quite as poor as church mice, but it's at least as poor as the mice around my house.

As you might imagine, there are more people applying for Section 8 subsidies who actually qualify as truly needy than there are subsidies available, so the local housing agency gives preference to applicants according to various criteria. Those who are paying more than 50% of their income in rent, those who are living in substandard housing, those who are veterans, and those who are being displaced from their homes through some governmental action all receive preference.

For owners to qualify to participate in Section 8, they must have the right kind of housing available, must be willing to accept these particular tenants, must be willing to sign a year's lease with them and a year's assistance payments contract with the local public housing agency (may be up to three years), must be willing to have the property inspected by the housing agency, must be willing to maintain the property according to minimal standards, and must be willing to set the rent at or below the fair market value as determined by the U.S. Department of Housing and Urban Development for that county or metropolitan area.

The "right kind" of housing actually may take many forms, from tract houses to townhouses, from mobile homes to apartments. Just as there are no special "food stamp groceries" in the supermarket, there is no such thing as special Section 8 housing. Yet there are certain limits. The housing must meet minimal size, amenity, and condition requirements. At the very least, it must have a separate and private bathroom, a living room, and a separate kitchen or a kitchen area in the living room. In other words, a studio or efficiency apartment would do nicely. A hotel room without a private bath and facilities for food preparation would not. As a general rule, Section 8 housing must have one bedroom for every two people. It must have walls, floors, ceilings, windows, roof, wiring, plumbing, heating, and locks, all in good condition. And there must be no lead-pigmented paint anywhere about. That's one thing the government is adamant about in any residential housing it subsidizes. Simply put, it should be what the Section 8 materials repeatedly call "decent, safe, and sanitary" housing.

The third key party, the local public housing agency, is the local administrator of the program. It acts as the liaison with HUD, the conduit for the funds, and the inspector-general. It is directly responsible to the federal government and takes care of all the paperwork involved in making the program work at the local level. It qualifies the tenant-applicants, inspects the housing, negotiates the rent, signs the assistance payments agreement, calculates the tenants' contributions, collects the federal moneys, pays the owners, and polices the abuses. It has plenty to do.

HOW THE PROGRAM WORKS

All three parties have to be involved for Section 8 to work, but they don't all have to become involved at the same time. The housing authority is the first to become involved because it has to work together with HUD to set up the program at the local level. Once that's done, it solicits tenants to apply.

Tenants apply for admission to the program by proving that they're poor enough. If they can prove that, either they receive a certificate which entitles them to the subsidy or they receive a place on a waiting list with others who qualify for Section 8 assistance but can't get it just yet because there's none available.

For those lucky enough to receive a certificate, there's still more to do before they can move in somewhere and start using their subsidy. They have to go scouting for rental housing on the open market like everyone else. When they find something they like which would seem to fit the Section 8 guidelines for their family size, they must ask you as the owner whether you would be willing to accept them as tenants and whether you would be willing to participate in the Section 8 program. If you respond positively to both questions, you and the tenants sign a "Request for Lease Approval" form. Acting on the request, the housing authority dispatches an inspector to look the place over and negotiate lease terms. If the housing qualifies and you can agree on terms, you and the tenants sign a lease, which may be your own, so long as it conforms with certain guidelines, or one provided by the housing agency for this purpose. Then you and the housing agency sign the assistance payments contract. And finally, you collect the advance moneys, the tenants move in, and you all live happily ever after, well, for a year at least, you hope.

If your housing does not pass inspection, you may make the repairs and improvements to remedy its deficiencies and try again, or you may refuse to. That's up to you. No Section 8 tenants may move into any rental dwelling until it does pass inspection, though, and they aren't allowed to fix it up themselves so that it will comply. You must do the work.

As an owner-participant, you will receive directly from the tenants that portion of the rent which they are responsible for and directly from the housing agency that portion of the rent which Section 8 has promised to pay. Should your Section 8 tenants fail to pay you their share of the rent when it's due, you may still assess them late penalties and evict them if necessary, just as you would any other tenant.

If you as an owner wish to participate in the Section 8 subsidized housing program and you don't have a qualified tenant already lined up, you may contact your local housing agency and request that your name be placed on the referral list of available dwellings. Tenants who are looking for housing under Section 8 will know in advance that you are familiar with the program and are willing to participate. They will contact you directly about your vacancy.

THE ADVANTAGES AND DISADVANTAGES

There are certain advantages and disadvantages to your participating in Section 8, of course, and you'll have to weigh them against each other as you decide whether you want to participate.

The primary advantage is that you get to enjoy the benefits of having a strong co-signer, the federal government, on the hook for the tenants' unpaid rent, cleaning charges, and damage charges. This co-signer seldom has to step in and pay for the tenants' obligations, however, because subsidized tenants have more motivation to pay whatever they owe you than the average low-income tenant does. They know they're getting something for nothing, and they want to hold onto a good thing. They also know that big government is involved now. If they break their lease, not only is their landlord going to get mad, but big government is going to become aware of what's going on, too.

If Section 8 tenants don't pay and you have to evict them, the program will continue to pay its share of the rent during eviction proceedings and even afterward. It will pay 80% of the entire rent for a period of up to thirty days following the last time the rent was paid by the program. The same holds true if the tenants break their lease and vacate all of a sudden. You'll still be getting something from Section 8 after they leave. Should they damage your property, Section 8 will pay up to the equivalent of two months' rent for the repairs. In addition to those advantages, the program will also help to reduce your vacancy losses because you'll be able to rent to a greater number of potential tenants.

The primary disadvantage is that you're hampered somewhat more than otherwise. You're hampered because you have to commit your property to the program for at least a year, because you have to handle more paperwork and take the time to deal with a third party which isn't known for having a whole lot of common sense, and because you have to rent to low-income people who tend to be more ignorant and less responsible than tenants who can afford to pay the entire rent themselves.

You won't notice these disadvantages at all if you'd normally be plagued with vacancies, evictions, and damage losses, but you might notice them a lot if such woes have never bothered you.

SOME MISUNDERSTANDINGS

Rental property owners often misunderstand two aspects of the program: that a tenant who has qualified for assistance has also been qualified as an acceptable tenant by the public housing agency and that the "published" fair market rent figures are the rents they can charge. Neither happens to be true.

The housing agency qualifies tenants according to one criterion only—need. It takes a number of factors into consideration, but that's all it's trying to determine. That's all it may legally do. HUD specifically prohibits any further qualifying. Oddly enough, you're usually trying to determine exactly the opposite about your ordinary tenant applicants, that is, whether they can pay the rent. Section 8 tenants qualify for the program if they can't pay the rent. But financial responsibility isn't the only thing you consider when you're selecting tenants. You look at whether they're clean, cooperative, and generally responsible. The housing agency looks at none of these things. The owner must. The owner must qualify Section 8 tenants exactly like any other tenant on every account except financial responsibility. That's good management, and good management goes hand in hand with Section 8.

The other common misunderstanding involves the fair market rent figures which owners may see in their local newspapers. Don't get all excited when you see that Section 8 will pay $75 more for two bedrooms than what you're currently charging. Those figures can be misleading. For one thing, they include a utility allowance for water, garbage, electricity, and gas. When you eliminate payment for any of these services or utilities, the "fair-market rent" declines accordingly. For another thing, those published rents are the top rents approved for that category of bedroom size. The housing agency's inspector/negotiator will negotiate with you about the rent for your particular dwelling. You are not automatically assured that you will get the top rent allowed.

THE FUTURE

As an owner, you might be hesitant to participate in Section 8 because of its uncertain future as a federal government welfare program. Don't be. Future administrations aren't going to be any more successful in cutting back Section 8 funding than the current one has been. Its future is probably more assured than that of many of our industries. Do expect the program to change, though. Presumably it will become more like the food stamp program in that it will provide subsidies to tenants in the form of vouchers which they may spend on housing pretty much as they see fit. That prospect bodes well for the rental property owner.

SOME LAST WORDS

Face it. This is a welfare program, one of those government giveaway programs which some taxpayers resent and rail against. If you personally feel that welfare programs are wrong and that welfare recipients are lazy, good-for-nothing chiselers, then don't participate. Your attitude would surface eventually, and you'd probably find yourself saying or doing something which would put you behind the Section 8 eightball before long. If you're either ambivalent about or supportive of government welfare programs, consider participating, but don't commit yourself initially to more than one Section 8 tenant. Try one and get a feel for the operation of the program first. Then if you find you like the way it all works, commit yourself to more.

FATTENING THE BOTTOM LINE

Fattening your own bottom is a whole lot easier than fattening your bottom line in the landlording business, but no matter. The truth is that you can indeed fatten your bottom line in landlording. All you have to do is increase your income and decrease your expenses. It's that simple.

Simple? Ha! Only a simpleton would call it simple. It's simple to say but not quite so simple to do. It's like a presidential candidate saying he's going to balance the budget by lowering taxes and increasing defense spending. Wait a minute! That sounds simple all right, but it also sounds suspiciously like "voodoo economics," doesn't it? And we all know that that won't balance the budget, let alone fatten the government's bottom line.

Well, you don't have to practice any voodoo economics to fatten your bottom line in landlording, but you should be aware that fattening the bottom line in the landlording business is not only a matter of increasing income and decreasing expenses. That's just one of the ways. There are four all told, each tied to one of the four ways to make money in this business. Let's see, the other three are making your property worth more, saving more money on your income taxes, and paying off your loan with fewer dollars.

Each one of them has a bottom line of sorts, and all of them together contribute to the big bottom line, which is the sum of the differences between the following—net sales price and net purchase price, income tax savings and income tax penalties, positive cash flow and negative cash flow, original loan amount and payoff loan balance—over the entire period of ownership. That's the overall bottom line. That's the big picture.

Keep all of the bottom lines in mind. You can hardly do otherwise because they're so interrelated that you can scarcely do something about one of them without affecting another. Try to fatten all of them whever you can, but recognize that in this chapter we're referring to one bottom line primarily, the cash-flow bottom line. That means increasing income and decreasing expenses.

INCREASING INCOME

Other *Landlording* chapters mention only incidentally a variety of things you can do to increase a rental property's income, from raising rents to lowering rents (yes, lowering rents can actually increase your income), to outfitting the laundry room with your own machines, marketing illusions by installing dazzlers, setting up interest-bearing checking accounts, shortening turnover time by not trying to do everything yourself, adding furniture, infilling your land, and so forth. Those aren't the only things you might do. There are other ways to increase your income.

Some of these ways require a certain expertise to make them pay off best. Some require additional investments, which may not come easy. Some require certain existing facilites or space to work. Some require more labor and attention. But all of them yield a good return under the right circumstances.

If you're running on empty for ideas, think about these.

• DON'T GIVE AWAY THE SPACE YOU MIGHT BE CHARGING FOR.

As a landlord or landlady, you are renting out living space primarily, but you probably own other space which you consider so incidental to your primary business that you may be giving it away. This other space I'm referring to is parking and storage space.

Are you giving away parking and storage space to those who rent your living space whether they have any need for it or not? Parking and storage space has value no matter where it is. It's just more valuable in some places than it is in others, and it's more valuable to some people than it is to others.

Tenants with cars need garages more than tenants without them. Pack rats need storage space more than marsupials.

Look carefully at the allocation of the parking and storage space on your rental property. Try to determine how much rent you're getting from it now, even if it's bundled together with the rent you're charging for living space. Then try to determine how much you could get for it if you separated it out and rented it to either the same tenant who's using it now or to somebody else.

You may find that you could increase the income from your parking and storage space by charging separately for it. Why not do just that?

Lest you be reluctant to wrest space away from a tenant who's been "paying" for it all along and isn't using it, consider reducing that tenant's overall rent slightly. Then rent out the space to somebody else who's ready to pay you what it's really worth.

• CONVERT CARPORTS INTO GARAGES.

Most tenants will pay more for a carport than they will for a mere parking space, and they will pay more for a garage than they will for a carport. Take advantage of this potential for increasing your income and convert parking spaces into carports or garages, convert carports into garages.

Converting a carport into a one-car garage isn't much work and doesn't require much money. All this kind of conversion requires is four walls and a door. The roof's already in place. For less than $1000 in many cases, you can hire someone to do the converting and in the process create an income of $40-50 per month. That's a two-year payback and an increase in the value of your property of around $3500. That's what I'd call a good return on investment.

Before you pooh-pooh the idea, consider the phenomenal success of the mini-storage complexes which have sprung up across the country. Get with it!

• MAKE UNPRODUCTIVE SPACE PRODUCTIVE.

Have you ever stopped to consider how much rent you could be charging for those three garages you've reserved for yourself? They could be worth $50 per month per garage, $1,800 per year for all three.

Don't hog all the storage space yourself. People are willing to pay you for it. Consolidate in one garage all the things you've been hoarding in three garages. Hold a garage sale to dispose of the stuff you don't really need. Or, better still, call the Salvation Army to pick up the items they might be able to sell and get them to give you a receipt for your donation. Get the junk out of there. Organize the tools and supplies of your trade better. One garage is plenty for storing what you really need.

At the very least, realize how much those extra garages are costing you. Is that old bulky stuff you've been saving for years really worth all that much? Sure, you might have need for it someday, but remember that every month you keep it, you're adding onto its cost to you. You might think that your garage full of stuff which tenants left behind didn't

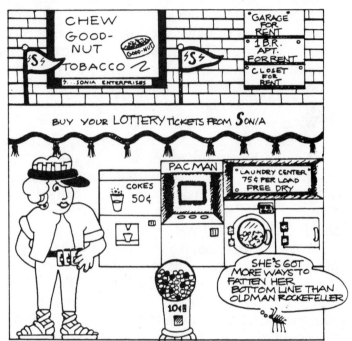

cost you anything. Well, it may not have to begin with, but now it's probably costing you $50 every month, and that mounts up in a hurry. The stuff had better be worth a lot because it's not free any longer.

Garages aren't the only unproductive space you might make productive. Offices and storage rooms have potential as well.

I'm always amazed at how many relatively small apartment complexes have large offices which some architect with no apartment management experience thought would be a good idea to include back when the building was still on the drawing board. Nobody questioned the space then and nobody questioned it for years afterward.

Ask yourself whether you really need an office at your complex? What are you using the office for? Might it be rented out as office space to an insurance agent or someone else, or might it be turned back into an apartment if that's what it once was? Do you really want employees of yours spending time in an office when they could be "on call" in their own home on the premises?

Just remember that office space is not free even to you as the owner, not when it could be generating income. As one room in the manager's apartment, an office makes sense, but as a totally separate space, and especially if it's a converted apartment, an office may not make any sense at all.

Is there any other room or space on the premises of your rental property which isn't getting the use it should? Might it be converted into rentable, productive space? That's your business, remember, renting out space.

• KEEP LOOKING WARILY AT OTHER INCOME POSSIBILITIES.

Vending machines, amusement machines, satellite television systems, car washing equipment, and billboards all offer other income possibilities to the apartment house owner. Many times they promise more than they produce, though, for all kinds of reasons, from unfavorable contracts to increased utility costs. Ask advice of others who have experience with such ventures in similar situations before you commit yourself.

DECREASING EXPENSES

Trying to fatten your bottom line by increasing income holds greater potential than trying to fatten it by decreasing expenses. There aren't that many things you can do to decrease expenses, and there's a limit beyond which you cannot go. That limit is zero.

You cannot save more than $22,213 in expenses on any property where the expenses are $22,213 per year. You'd be hard pressed to come anywhere near that, of course.

Nevertheless, you shouldn't overlook what opportunities there are to decrease expenses. There are almost always some.

Besides questioning your insurance coverage, picking the right things to do yourself while hiring out the others, implementing utility conservation measures, converting master-metered buildings, paying the manager according to some realistic measurement of the work involved, watching advertising costs, and the other ways to decrease expenses already mentioned in this book, here are a few more.

• TRANSFER COSTS.

When you rent out residences, you are furnishing your tenants with more than a roof over their heads. You are providing them with certain services, too, services which cost you money. Some of these services, such as maintenance and repairs, you absolutely have to provide and pay for because laws require you to, but that doesn't mean you have to provide and pay for maintenance and repairs when tenants are negligent or destructive. You don't. You may want to provide the service so the work gets done promptly, but you shouldn't be paying for it as well.

When a tenant shoots a shotgun through the ceiling and it blows a hole right through the roof, you go ahead and repair the damage, but you expect the tenant to pay for it, don't you? Sure, the tenant has damaged the building. The tenant should have to pay. If that roof had started to leak as a result of weathering or a windstorm, you would have paid for the repairs. That leak wouldn't be the tenant's fault, and repairing it is your responsibility under the warranty of habitability.

When a tenant plugs up a toilet or breaks a window, do you get it fixed and pay for the damage yourself, or do you make the tenant pay? Are plugged-up toilets and broken windows your responsibility or are they your tenant's? In my book, they're the tenant's responsibility, and the tenant should pay. You didn't plug up the toilet. You didn't break the window. No defect, no normal wear and tear caused the damage. It didn't happen through an act of God. It doesn't always happen through an act of your tenants, I'll grant you. It could be a neighbor's kid who put a rock through the window. But if you tell your tenants that they must pay for only those windows they break and that you will pay for the others, then you can be sure that no window broken in their place will ever be their fault, and they won't know who did it. You'll be paying for every broken window. Why should you pay automatically?

Sure, if there are special circumstances, then you can make a deal with your tenants. Get them to pay a portion and you pay the rest. That's reasonable. Just don't pay every time. Make your tenants responsible. Transfer the costs of dealing with these problems to them.

The rental agreement in this book does just that, and you should do the same. You don't have to switch rental agreements to make this change. All you have to do is give your tenants a "Notice of Change in Terms of Tenancy" which shifts the responsibility from you to them in 30 or 60 days, provided, of course, that your existing agreement and the landlord-tenant laws in your area allow you to.

Transferring these costs to your tenants will definitely decrease your expenses. Look around. Ask yourself whether there are any other services which cost you money but which you are providing free of charge to your tenants? Might you get them to pay for these services? Once they are, you've eliminated another expense and fattened your bottom line.

NOTICE OF CHANGE
IN TERMS OF TENANCY

TO ___HAROLD & MAUDE WEST___, Tenant in Possession

___1850 EAGLE BLVD., APT. 6___

___BIGCITY, CALIFORNIA___

YOU ARE HEREBY NOTIFIED that the terms of tenancy under which you occupy the above-described premises are to be changed.

Effective ___AUGUST 5___, 19_87_, there will be the following changes:

• ___Tenants must pay for repairs of all damage, including drain stoppages, which they or their guests have caused.___

• ___Tenants must pay for any windows broken in their dwelling while they live there.___

Dated this _2d_ day of ___July___, 19_87_.

___Jack Warren___
Owner/Manager

This Notice was served by the Owner/Manager in the following manner (check those which apply):
☑ by personal delivery to the tenant,
☐ by leaving a copy with someone on the premises other than the tenant,
☐ by mailing,
☐ by posting.

• QUESTION YOUR PROPERTY TAX BILL.

Perhaps you have seen one of those "QUESTION AUTHORITY" bumper stickers on an ancient, beat-up Volkswagen bus. You shake your head and lament the further decline of the old-fashioned values you were brought up with. Yet your own attitude toward authority could be costing you some big bucks.

You may be questioning all of your other landlording expenses and trying every which way to control them, but you may not even have thought about questioning your property taxes, and they're always a major expense. You may have thought your tax bill was sacrosanct because it comes to you on an official computer-printed form and appears to be based on a "Higher Authority" or at the very least upon some mandated formulas.

Whoa, don't get carried away now! That tax bill of yours may have some very exact figures on it, and it may be printed on an official form, but it is definitely subject to question. Go ahead and question it. Take the time once a year to examine your tax bill for each property. Make sure you understand it, first of all, and then see whether you agree with the figures. You want to be certain that the law is being applied to you fairly, that the formulas for calculating the value of your property are correct and that the tax rate has been applied to your property correctly.

If anything appears to be out of line, question the authorities. If you see the error of their ways but you can't quite convince them of their errors yourself, then consider whether the sums involved warrant your hiring an "authority" of your own to represent you. There are knowledgeable people who specialize in challenging property tax assessments. They expect to be paid well, of course, but what they expect for their efforts is a portion of your tax savings. They profit only if you profit.

• FOOL YOURSELF INTO THINKING YOUR CASH FLOW IS NEGATIVE.

Ordinarily you shouldn't be trying to fool yourself. Fooling oneself carries bad connotations. People say that you're only fooling yourself if you think you can keep up with the Joneses on half their income, if you think a movie star on location in your hometown is going to fall in love with you, if you think money buys happiness, if you think you're going to beat the odds in Atlantic City, or if you think your next cigarette is going to be your last. Those don't sound like good ways to fool yourself, do they?

They're not.

However, there is at least one good way to fool yourself that I know of, one which helps you watch your rental property expenses more carefully. Fool yourself into thinking that you have a negative cash flow. Some of you may not have to fool yourself. You already have a negative cash flow, and you'd be delighted just to break even. This method for decreasing your expenses won't help you in the least, but you can surely understand how it works.

If you have an honest-to-goodness negative-cash-flow property, you know how closely you watch your expenses. They're supremely important to you because you have to dip into your own pocket every month to support the property. You're depriving yourself of those funds. On the other hand, if your property is generating a positive cash flow, you don't pay nearly as much attention to the expenses. You pay them.

You can see how this attitudinal difference works whenever you buy a rental property which is either completely paid off or mostly paid off. You'll notice that the previous owners were lax in raising their rents and lax in controlling their expenses. "Easy-come-easy-go" seems to be their attitude. With a big new mortgage payment facing you every month, you'll be looking for all kinds of ways to make that property pay, and you'll discover them.

To keep yourself from becoming inattentive to your own expenses, fool yourself into thinking that your positive-cash-flow property is poorer than it actually is. It's a simple thing to do. You just transfer that property's excess funds out of its operations account once a month so the balance is never very high. That's all. You'll be fooling yourself into thinking that the property has little money available, and as a consequence, you'll watch those expenses a little more closely. It works for this old fool.

SOME LAST WORDS

Take neither your income nor your expenses for granted. Be alert to the opportunities which exist all around you for increasing your income and decreasing your expenses, but don't forget that your primary objective is to fatten your bottom line. It is not merely to increase income or decrease expenses, not when the one will have an adverse effect on the other. Increasing your monthly income by $5 while at the same time increasing your monthly expenses by $6 isn't any way to fatten your bottom line, not even when you multiply those numbers many times. Remember the old joke about the fellow who lost money on every sale but made it up on volume. Don't follow suit.

INSURANCE

Believe it or not, General Motors' biggest single expense is not payroll, steel, tires, aluminum, or even plastic. It's insurance, insurance of every kind imaginable. GM, with its considerable assets, has to proceed with caution in a society overrun with lawyers who are quick to place a highly inflated dollar value on stubbed toes and kinked necks and have convinced many people to pursue their fortunes through litigation.

As a rental property owner with assets somewhat less than GM's, you need not follow GM's example by spending more on insurance than anything else, but you should nevertheless be well covered with various kinds of insurance. You become increasingly vulnerable to losses, too, as you build your property assets, assets which look quite attractive to someone contemplating a lawsuit against you. Litigants and their legal counsel don't care how hard or how long you've worked to gather those assets. That's of no consequence. They show no mercy when they're fighting to get their hands on your money. They just want all they can get out of you, and, of course, they know you're wealthy because, after all, you own income property.

Because you do own income property, you have special insurance needs above and beyond those of people who don't. You should know something about the many kinds of insurance available to serve those needs and something about exercising prudence whenever you're thinking about insurance. That's what this chapter is all about.

BECOMING ACQUAINTED WITH THE MANY KINDS OF INSURANCE AVAILABLE

• FIRE

Lenders require you to protect their interest in your building with a fire insurance policy at the very least because they figure they cannot afford to risk a loss should the place go up in flames. Were that to happen, they'd lose the collateral for their loan and the income as well because you'd stop making the payments.

That's all understandable, but what about your share of your building? Shouldn't you have fire insurance on it, too? Absolutely yes! You should be even more cautious than your lender is because your equity in a building represents a much greater proportion of your total assets than what one building represents of a lender's assets. In addition, your interest in that building keeps growing as appreciation pushes the value up and your equity payments push the loan balance down. With more to protect virtually every month, you should be so cautious about your fire insurance that whenever your premium comes due, you make certain that your building is covered with a policy large enough to pay current replacement costs. Anything less, and you'd be playing with fire. Anything more, and you'd be wasting your money, for $110,000 worth of coverage on a building which costs $100,000 to replace will pay only $100,000, no matter what.

Note that you should insure only your building, its contents, and the other improvements on the property which might be damaged by fire. Do not insure the land. It'll still be there when the fire dies down.

Note also that you should insure your building for at least 80% of its replacement cost in order to comply with the standard policy's co-insurance clause. If your $100,000 building is insured for $50,000, and you have a loss of $25,000, the policy will pay only $12,500 (50% of the loss) even though you have $50,000 worth of coverage. Under the co-insurance clause, the *percentage* of coverage you have, not the amount, applies to losses. $50,000 of coverage on a $100,000 building translates into 50%. By insuring that $100,000 building for at least $80,000, you'd avoid being caught by the clause, and you'd receive a full $25,000 in the event of a $25,000 loss.

• EXTENDED COVERAGE

Most insurance companies offer what they call "extended coverage" (sometimes called "comprehensive coverage" or a "package policy") along with their standard fire insurance policies, and they price this coverage at very attractive rates. It may include damage caused by hail, explosions, windstorms, aircraft, vehicles, smoke, burst pipes, rioting, vandalism, falling trees, freezing, collapse, landslides, or accidental water discharge. Look into it.

• EARTHQUAKE

Extended coverage policies do not extend to include earthquake coverage. It's always a separate policy. Even with a high deductible and lots of exclusions, it's not cheap, but you shouldn't be without it in any area prone to earthquakes where you own improved property. One seconds-long earthquake could destroy your lifelong landlording work.

• FLOOD

Water damage is water damage, isn't it? Yes it is, but water damage has lots of causes, and as far as water damage and insurance coverage are concerned, what's most important is what causes the damage. You could find yourself "high and dry" one of these days upon discovering that your insurance policy covers only water damage caused by accidental leakage and not water damage caused by flooding, high water, or sewage backups. Ask for the coverage you want according to the likelihood of these calamities' occurring where your property is located, and don't assume that you have flood insurance unless you see it written in your policy. Like earthquake insurance, flood insurance doesn't come packaged with other coverage. It's separate.

In areas prone to flooding, which present too much risk for the average insurer, the National Flood Association will still provide coverage and at nominal rates.

• OTHER IMPROVEMENTS

Property improvements other than buildings, such as swimming pools, parking lots, walks, fences, and signs, may sustain direct damage from a flood, fire, ice storm, or other disaster, too, but they won't be covered by your standard building policy unless you include them specifically under extended coverage. Examine what your insurer offers for coverage and decide whether the peace of mind is worth the premiums. Many owners insure themselves ("insuring yourself" or "self-insurance" means that you act as your own insurer; you don't buy coverage from anyone else) for damage to their non-building property improvements because they regard the potential risk of damage, extent of damage, and consequences of damage to be minimal in relation to the other exposure they have.

• VANDALISM AND MALICIOUS MISCHIEF

Should anyone damage your property, say, by tearing your laundry machines apart for the coins or by laying waste a vacant apartment, your vandalism and malicious mischief insurance would pay to repair the damage. You hope you'll never have occasion to use such coverage because damage like this is pretty demoralizing to a conscientious owner, but if it should happen, you ought to have the right insurance to pay for the repairs. When included in a package policy, it can be quite inexpensive.

• LIABILITY

Even into the '70s, not every rental property owner bothered to obtain liability coverage because few people filed liability claims and even fewer collected. Today that's all changed. Today you can't afford to be without liability insurance any more than obstetricians can afford to be without malpractice insurance.

Now virtually anyone in business might be sued for "malpractice," from clergy to insurance agents to landlords. No longer does the age-old maxim, "Caveat emptor!" apply to business dealings. Now it's "Caveat venditor!" You are expected to be the perfect landlord or landlady and to supply the perfect rental property. That's quite a burden to bear, an impossible burden for any individual businessperson like yourself.

Both the number of liability cases and the types of cases have increased, as have the awards. It's not just the personal injury case caused by your supposed negligence that you have to worry about nowadays. It's the discrimination case, the wrongful eviction case, the invasion-of-privacy case, the failure-to-keep-me-happy case, the strict liability case. Those are ever-present worries.

The worries keep growing, too. "Strict liability" applied to landlording is something new. In case you haven't heard, courts are beginning to rule that tenants only have to prove that your "product" was defective and that as a result of the defect they were hurt. They do not have to prove that you were negligent in the least. This policy of strict liability has been applied to manufactured products for some years here in the U.S. It has caused some companies to go out of business entirely and others to stop making certain products. Cessna Aircraft, for example, stopped manufacturing the popular 152 trainer when its product liability insurance reached $17,000 for each one of these little $40,000 airplanes, the smallest of any they made and one of the safest airplanes ever built. At that rate (42.5%), your insurance bill on a $400-a-month apartment would be $170 a month, pretty high for only one type of coverage, wouldn't you say? We can only guess how the application of strict liability is going to affect the landlording business.

Don't go the self-insurance route for this risk. Buy insurance which will cover every liability you can think of, and while you're at it, buy enough. Buy the highest limits available. You will find that a million dollars' worth of coverage costs little more than a hundred thousand dollars' worth, and it could save you from the poorhouse, for the awards people manage to get in liability cases, especially when they involve a personal injury, tend to be high.

Expect your liability premiums to become a more noticeable expense than they have been in the past. Complain all you want to about the rising rates, but don't neglect paying them.

• LOSS OF RENTS

If a fire or some other mishap should render your rentals uninhabitable for a time, your tenants will stop paying you their rent all at once and you won't have any income to use for paying those fixed expenses which keep right on going. You'll have to pay those continuing bills out of your own savings unless you have loss-of-rents insurance coverage. In that case, your insurance company will compensate you for the loss of rental income over a reasonable period of time while your building is being repaired.

With all the other problems you're likely to have if a mishap should occur at your property, you don't need financial problems too, not when you can protect yourself for a small premium.

• CONTENTS

Your own belongings which you keep at your rental property, belongings such as mowers, tools, laundry machines, furniture, appliances, supplies, and the like, would be covered against a variety of losses by most comprehensive rental property owners' insurance policies (check yours to make sure), but your tenants' belongings would not be covered at all.

Because tenants frequently assume erroneously that your insurance does cover their possessions, you should mention when you first rent to them that they should secure their own tenants' insurance policy if they want coverage. You might even remind them of their exposure every so often in a note included with their rent receipt.

• WORKERS' COMPENSATION

Even though you may hire only casual help or deduct just a few dollars from a tenant's rent in exchange for minor management or maintenance services, you are an "employer" and you must have workers' compensation insurance. If that worker of yours were to require the slightest medical attention or become the least bit incapacitated while in your employ, you would be held liable. Don't assume this risk yourself. You know what medical bills can run nowadays, and you probably know what awards juries are making to people who become disabled on the job. You cannot afford to pay out such sums.

Most states require every employer to have workers' compensation insurance, and because it's required, the rates are reasonable. Groups usually offer the most attractive plans, so check to see what your rental property owners association is offering before you inquire elsewhere.

• MORTGAGE

Two completely different types of insurance coverage have come to be known as "mortgage insurance." The object of both types is the same, to pay off the balance of the outstanding mortgage when trouble strikes, but the beneficiaries are definitely not the same.

The first type benefits the property owner. It's pretty much the same as decreasing term life insurance, the decreasing sum being the mortgage balance. It's especially popular with homeowners because they want to protect themselves in case death or disability puts an end to some or all of the income used to make their house payments. The mortgage would then be paid off in full. Such insurance is available to cover rental property mortgages as well, and it may be just as important for some rental property owners to have as it is for homeowners, especially when a rental property is running a negative cash flow and one person is contributing income from a job to support it.

February 25, 1986

Dear *Richard and Mary Renter,*

     As we do every year, we have been reviewing our insurance policies, and we thought that you might like to know how you are affected by the insurance we carry.

     Basically, our policies cover only the building itself where you live. They do not cover any of your own belongings against damage or disappearance, nor do they cover you for negligence should you, for example, leave a burner going under a pan of grease and start a fire which damages the kitchen.

     To protect yourself against these calamities, you should get a tenant's insurance policy. Most insurance companies and agents will write such a policy for you, and we would strongly urge that you inquire about getting one.

     For the peace of mind that it gives, a tenant's insurance policy is reasonable indeed.

                Sincerely,

                Lester Landlord

When determining whether you should get this insurance coverage, consider both the salary and the time contributions of each person involved with the property because you may find that hired help would be needed to compensate for the work done by one of those people involved, and that, of course, would increase the negative cash flow still more. If you do choose to buy this kind of mortgage insurance for your income property, consult your tax adviser for advice on whether it is tax-deductible as a business expense in your situation. It may or may not be.

The other type of mortgage insurance will pay off the mortgage all right, but it won't benefit you as the property owner in the least. It protects your lender should you default on the mortgage and should the property be sold off for less than the balance owing. The policy would pay the lender the difference between the two.

Although your lender may require that you pay the premium on such a policy, don't suppose that you're getting the same coverage as the other kind of mortgage insurance. You're not. When the first one pays off, you or your heirs wind up with assistance in making your loan payments or with a property which is free and clear. When the second one pays off, neither you nor your heirs get a thing.

• FIDELITY

In some businesses where dishonest employees have the opportunity to steal cash and/or goods, wary employers buy fidelity insurance, that is, they "bond" their employees to protect themselves from pilferage and embezzlement. The employees you hire to manage and maintain your rental property have an opportunity to steal from you. Of that there is no doubt. They might appropriate your tools or supplies for their own use. They might under-report occupancies. They might charge higher rents than they report to you. They might withhold more from tenants' security deposits than they tell you about. They might find more than a few coins on the floor after they've counted the laundry money. They might be even more audacious and abscond with an entire month's rent receipts. All of these things have been known to happen to suspecting and unsuspecting owners alike. They could happen to you, too.

If you are inclined to put your properties on "automatic pilot," to let your manager run everything for months on end, checking only now and then to see whether there's any money in the property account down at the bank, you need fidelity insurance. You need it desperately. But if you are looking over your manager's shoulder on a random basis and you believe that you have a pretty good handle on your income, don't bother. The premiums for this kind of insurance are really much too high for the limited amount of exposure you will have.

Rather than pay fidelity insurance premiums for a policy which will pay careless employers for their carelessness, save the money and insure yourself by being careful. Reduce the opportunities managers have to steal from you. See that they handle little or no cash. See that they provide you with weekly income and occupancy reports. And see that you select your managers carefully in the first place.

Note that fidelity insurance covers losses you sustain as a result of your own employees' mishandling of funds. It would not cover losses caused by a manager working at your property if that manager were responsible to a property management company rather than to you. To protect yourself from that kind of loss, insist that any property management company you use, supply a bond of its own.

• AUTO

To protect your property assets, you should obtain the highest liability limits available for your own automobiles. Minimum liability insurance may be quite sufficient for your tenants. If they're hit with a $500,000 judgment, their insurance carrier would pay to the limits of the policy, their few assets would be liquidated, and they would simply declare bankruptcy. It's done every day. But what if you, a person of property, get hit with a $500,000 judgment, and you have only $100,000 in coverage? Kiss everything goodbye. Caveat, dear landlord and landlady!

• NON-OWNED AUTO

Non-owned auto liability insurance does not protect you from liability when you're driving a car other than your own. Your regular automobile policy should do that. No, non-owned auto protects you in case anyone you hire, even temporarily, is driving his own automobile and running errands for you when he becomes involved in an automobile accident. When the injured's attorney learns that your employee, while driving to the hardware store to pick up some more paint for you, caused the accident which injured his client, you will be added to the names of those being sued. Insurance to protect you under such circumstances is reasonably inexpensive and well worth the cost.

• UMBRELLA

Umbrella insurance coverage has nothing at all to do with those moveable tent tops we hold to keep raindrops from falling on our heads. No, umbrella insurance, which is also known as blanket or excess insurance, keeps covering us when we reach the limits of our other liability policies. These other policies cost more per dollar of coverage than an umbrella policy does because they pay off more. They pay the smaller claims. Umbrella policies pay only the larger claims and only the higher amounts of the larger claims. On a $665,000 claim, for example, the primary policy might pay the first $500,000, while the umbrella policy might pay the rest, $165,000.

To be most effective, your umbrella policy should leave no gaps between the upper limits of your various primary liability policies and the lower limit of the umbrella policy itself. It should also cover you for at least double the value of your personal assets. Buy it from the same company you bought most of your primary liability policies from, and you'll avoid potential squabbling between two companies which have different ideas for settling a single lawsuit.

• BOILER AND MACHINERY

You can imagine how horrendous the explosion of a boiler could be. The deaths, injuries, and property damage could result in some very costly claims. But the risk of claims isn't the only reason you should consider this type of insurance if you have the kind of equipment it covers: boilers, heavy machinery, pressure tanks, large air conditioners, or large compressors. You should consider it because the insurer becomes a partner with you in keeping losses to a minimum by inspecting the equipment regularly and making sure that it is well maintained and safe to operate.

Other insurers should spend as much of their premium dollars on loss prevention as boiler and machinery insurers do. They'd suffer fewer claims.

• WATERBED

Your tenants with waterbeds are the ones who ought to provide waterbed insurance, but face it, they're not going to remember to keep it in force. You'd be wise to charge them enough extra rent to pay for the policy, and then pay the premiums yourself if you want the coverage.

• TITLE

When you learn that title insurance companies pay out less than ten cents in claims out of every dollar they collect in premiums, you're inclined to think that you ought to stop whatever you're doing and become a title insurer yourself, whatever it is that title insurers do. After all, the house take in Vegas doesn't approach ninety cents out of a dollar. If it did, gamblers wouldn't return.

Well, then, should you buy title insurance yourself on your newly acquired properties? Why does title insurance pay out so little? And what is title insurance anyway?

First of all, title insurance protects buyers against other people's claims to a property which might result from any number of unexpected occurrences, such as forgeries, mistaken identical names, and undisclosed heirs. Title insurance guarantees that nothing out of a property's past will catch up with you and deny you ownership now or in the future. It guarantees that you have clear title, that you own the property.

Title insurance companies pay out so little in claims because they go to great lengths to discover problems with the title, and these protective measures are included in the price of the policy. If fire insurance companies operated similarly, they'd install an automatic sprinkler system in every building they cover and include the cost of the system in the price of the policy.

As to whether you should buy title insurance or not, in a way, you may not have much of a choice. Institutional lenders require you to buy enough title insurance to cover their loan. But the policy they require is strictly a lender's policy, not a buyer's policy. It's like the mortgage insurance which some lenders require borrowers to buy to protect the lenders. It doesn't pay you off at all. It does benefit you somewhat, however, because it pays for the insurer's exhaustive title search, and consequently, the buyer's title insurance premium, which you may choose to buy or not, is less expensive than it would otherwise be.

When you're trying to decide whether to buy a buyer's title insurance policy, you should remember that you pay for it only once, when you acquire the property, and then both you and your heirs are covered for as long as you or they own the property. You never pay another premium after that.

Whatever you do, don't acquire any property without having someone search the title at the very least, even if no lender's involved and you're paying for it in cash, yes, even if you win it in a poker game. That title search is an absolute must. It could reveal mechanics' liens, attachments, and old loans which the owner told you nothing about and which could trouble you for years to come.

EXERCISING PRUDENCE

Insurance is certainly available for every conceivable risk connected with landlording if you want to pay for it, and there are a great many insurance agents around who would be delighted to sell it to you, but since you surely don't want insurance to become your number-one expense as it is for General Motors, you should seize the opportunity to save money every time you review your insurance needs. Naturally you might be prudent in trying to save or you might be imprudent.

• *Here's how to be prudent:*

Select only the kinds of coverage you need for your location and situation. (Are there all that many hurricanes in Billings, Montana?)

Calculate carefully the amount of coverage you need. (Do you really need $380,000 worth of fire insurance for your $160,000 duplex?)

Shop around for coverage two months before the renewal date on your policy, and do it every time. ($285? Why, Gerry wants $450 for the very same thing!)

Price package policies. (You mean that fire, vandalism, liability, loss of rents, and contents coverage all together are only $20 more than fire insurance alone?)

Consider policies with deductibles. (Does earthquake insurance with a $5,000 deductible clause really have a premium $222 lower?)

• *Here's how to be imprudent:*

Buy only the kinds and amounts of coverage your lender and the law require. (The tenant in Apt. 112 wants how much for tripping on that broken step?)

Buy whatever coverage your agent sells you. (You think I need glacier coverage? OK, if you say so. The winters have been getting colder around here. Write it up.)

Buy only from your bridge partner who sells insurance on the side. (Can you get me a good deal, Gerry?)

Buy separate policies for each kind of peril. (Is it $85 more for contents and $18 for loss of rents or vice versa?)

Buy non-deductible coverage. (You want to settle my claim about the dent in my commercial washing machine for $12?)

RESPONDING TO AN ACCIDENT

Whenever an accident on your property results in an injury, see that the injured party receives proper medical attention right away. Immediately after that, contact your insurance agent and complete an accident report. As time goes by, the witnesses and the injured party tend to forget what actually happened, and you can be sure that their muddled memories are not going to favor their landlord or landlady as they struggle to reconstruct the accident.

GETTING YOUR FAIR SETTLEMENT

Some insurance companies don't pay claims very willingly or fairly. They make you jump through their flaming hoops before they will pay you even a pittance. Should you suspect that your insurance company won't treat you equitably when handling your claim, secure the services of a public insurance adjuster. Their business is to represent policyholders. They know how much claims are worth because they're involved with them all the time. For a percentage of your claim, they get bids, do the paperwork, make the phone calls, and argue on your behalf. They will make sure that you get every cent your insurance company owes you and that you get it promptly. You'll find them listed in the Yellow Pages under "Adjusters."

SOME LAST WORDS

Be prudent whenever you buy insurance affecting your income property business. You'll save on the premiums and you'll protect your assets so that someday you'll be able to enjoy them yourself.

PROVIDING SECURITY

True security, absolute security, is utterly impossible in this world. It always has been and it always will be. Metal detectors, luggage X-ray machines, and sharp-eyed security people at airline passenger terminals have helped to curtail, but not eliminate, airplane hijackings. Even the most sophisticated electronic alarm systems and round-the-clock Secret Service agents cannot protect the President of the United States from harm. All we landlords and landladies can hope to do is provide a modicum of security for our tenants and ourselves by taking reasonable precautions. That's what this chapter is about, reasonable security precautions.

PICKING AND PLACING FIRE EXTINGUISHERS

Why it is that insurance companies don't absolutely require fire extinguishers for all the buildings they insure, I certainly don't know. I do know that no rental building I have ever purchased has had them, and now they all do. Whether your insurance company cares enough about your having fire extinguishers available to require them shouldn't matter. You need them. Your tenants need them. All us sinners need them.

Although you are undoubtedly violating local fire ordinances if you do not have extinguishers available at your rental properties, enforcement of those ordinances is so lax that the chances are good you won't be fined or even warned if you don't have them. But why should you wait for a fire safety inspector to tell you to install extinguishers before you buy them? They are so important that you should go out to buy and install them as soon as you have read this section on fire extinguishers. Remember that your property and your tenants' lives and their property are all endangered if there's no extinguisher available when needed.

You need witness only one fire in your rentals to become convinced that you need extinguishers, but by then, of course, it's too late. If you haven't witnessed any fires in your rentals lately, consider the following scenario.

After cooking a big breakfast for her family, your tenant is cleaning up the kitchen when she hears familiar music introducing her favorite morning television program. In her haste to watch, she inadvertently turns the electric burner beneath the pan of bacon grease to high heat, one click from off, and rushes into the living room. Ten minutes later, all of a sudden, the grease ignites into flames high enough to scorch the kitchen cabinets and set the walls on fire. The tenant rushes about looking for an extinguisher nearby, and finding none, she tries dousing the flames with water. Naturally, that only feeds the inferno. Finally realizing her plight, the woman grabs her portable TV, scrambles out, and screams "FIRE!" Someone calls the fire department, but by the time the fire trucks arrive and fire fighters can put out the blaze, the entire apartment, as well as the one next to it, are rendered uninhabitable.

Then what happens? The insurance adjuster surveys the damage. You get estimates for repairs, and sometime later the work begins. Three months after the fire, you're looking around for new tenants to move into the two repaired apartments. You have lost three months' rent on the two apartments, spent hours of your own time planning and supervising, and gone through the uncertainties again of selecting more new tenants. In other words, you're out of pocket considerable money for expenses and you've wasted a considerable amount of time. Even if you do have a rent-loss coverage provision in your insurance policy, you still suffer a loss because you've had to spend so much time on the project, time you cannot possibly be compensated for.

As a landlord or landlady, you need fire extinguishers. There's no doubt about it. The only question is what type should you buy?

The extinguisher you buy should be effective in fighting all kinds of fires, it should be easy to carry and use, it should not leave a catastrophe to clean up after, it should be durable, it should be rechargeable, and it should be modestly priced.

There is one type which fits these guidelines fairly well, but first let me warn you about two types of extinguishers which are still found around rental properties and should be avoided as if they were incendiary bombs. Soda-acid and pressurized water extinguishers they're called. They are easy to recognize because they both come in shiny chrome or brass cylinders about two feet tall and eight inches in diameter. You'll notice them around many older apartment houses. I suppose they're still used because grandpa used to use them, and I suppose they're still all right if you happen to have a stationery store, a lumber yard, or a yardage shop because they're great for putting out paper, wood, and natural fiber fires, but they're as messy as untrained quintuplets to clean up after. They're also heavy, and they only aggravate other types of fires because they shoot water, hardly the best extinguishing agent for a small electrical fire or a small grease fire.

Around your rental properties, you should use dry chemical fire extinguishers exclusively, ones which are filled with a mono-ammonium-phosphate-base dry chemical or its equivalent as an extinguishing agent and will work on any class of fire. These extinguishers fit the guidelines well. The five-pounder, rated 2A, 40B, and C is ideally suited for rental property installations. It's called a five-pounder because the fire-fighting chemicals inside it weigh just that. Its total weight is around ten pounds, still light enough so almost any tenant can wield it.

Check the letters and numbers on any extinguisher you are considering in order to determine the class and size of fire it can effectively extinguish. The letters stand for classes of fire. "A" firefighting agents will put out fires fed by wood, paper, cloth, rubbish, and some plastics. "B" firefighting agents will put out fires fed by flammable liquids, paint, grease, or cooking oil. "C" firefighting agents will put out live-wire electrical fires. The number appearing before each class was assigned by Underwriters' Laboratories (UL) and indicates the size fire in that class which the extinguisher will put out. The larger the number, the larger the fire it will put out, and hence the greater is the extinguisher's effectiveness. A "1A" extinguisher, for example, will put out 50 burning pieces of wood which are 2" x 2" and 20" long; a "2A" extinguisher will put out a fire twice that size, and so on. A "1B" extinguisher will put out 3.25 gallons of naphtha (a solvent) blazing away in a 2.5 square-foot pan, and, likewise, a "2B" extinguisher will extinguish a blaze twice that size. Only the "C" class has no numerical rating. "C" means that the chemical in the extinguisher does not conduct electricity and is therefore safe to be used on electrical fires. The big soda-acid and pressurized water extinguishers have a "2A" rating, and that's all. They're totally worthless on flammable liquids and on electrical fires, whereas the five pounder is just as effective on Class "A" fires as the water monsters are, besides having a "40B" and a "C" rating, too.

Having selected a suitable type, you will still have to decide where to place your extinguishers, what size to buy, what brand to buy, and whether or not to house them in glass-fronted boxes which require either a key or breakage of the glass for access. Generally speaking, one five-pounder is enough for four to five single-story apartments if their doors are within thirty feet of the extinguisher's location. If you have a fourplex with entrances on two levels, install two extinguishers, one on each level, and be safe. If you can't decide where to place them outside, try mounting one two-pounder in every kitchen. Sometimes this course is more economical anyway because you don't then have to buy glass-fronted boxes (around $20 apiece), something I always do when mounting extinguishers outside. Two-pounders with a rating of "1A:10BC" run somewhere between $12 and $30 each, while the five-pounders with a rating of "2A:40BC" are $20 to $40. Shop around and compare prices because extinguishers are often discounted.

The cautions which follow all resulted from costly or painful experiences I have had with fire extinguishers myself. I hope you may learn the lessons involved without having to repeat the experiences.

Caution ONE—You would think that extinguishers which are labeled "rechargeable" are, in fact, rechargeable. Well, technically they may be, but in a practical sense they may not be rechargeable at all because they may be able to hold only their original factory charge and not one they get in the field. When their contents has been spent on a fire or they have lost their pressure spontaneously over time, you might try to have them recharged at an extinguisher service shop only to learn that what you purchased are disposable extinguishers rather than rechargeable ones. If you expect your extinguishers to last a long time and take recharging, then before you buy, ask the advice of someone trustworthy who recharges extinguishers for a living, preferably someone who does not also sell extinguishers.

Caution TWO—If you do buy the smaller extinguishers, be wary about placing them in any exposed areas, including shared laundry facilities. They're the perfect size for use in cars, trucks, boats, and recreational vehicles, and they sometimes mysteriously develop legs. Engrave them with your name and a distinguishing number, such as the address of your rental property, so you can identify them positively when necessary.

Caution THREE—Heads, bare fists, and feet were not made to break glass, TV barroom brawls notwithstanding. Instruct your tenants to use a shod foot or any hard object that doesn't bleed when they have to break glass in an emergency to get to an extinguisher.

Caution FOUR—No extinguisher lasts very long. Nine to twelve seconds is all that a five-pounder will last in a sustained blast. It's made to be used in short two-second bursts rather than all at once, and though it certainly will not extinguish a burning house, it should extinguish any small fire your tenants are apt to have.

SUPPLYING SMOKE DETECTORS

Some landlord or landlady must have invented paint rollers and smoke detectors because both of these devices are so tailor-made for use in rental properties—the one to minimize endless painting work, the other to minimize exposure to fire damage.

Even if you do hang fire extinguishers on every wall, you're still exposed to fire damage, for someone has to act fast and use those extinguishers when they're needed. If no one acts fast enough, an entire building could quickly become a midden of ashes with some brand-new, unused extinguishers down near the bottom.

Along with your carefully selected fire extinguishers, therefore, you should provide carefully selected smoke detectors, passive devices to warn tenants of any impending fire

danger which they can act upon before it gets out of control. Because tenants tend to be a little more careless about handling fire-causing agents than you would be in your own home and because you can't possibly keep watch over them constantly, smoke detectors are ideal watchdogs to protect life, limb, and property. They aren't fire sprinklers, mind you. They can't put out fires, but they do do a good job of warning the living that there is a fire.

Now that so many manufacturers make them, perfectly adequate smoke detectors are available for as little as $10 and as much as $35. At such prices, there's no reason for any rental dwelling to be without them.

There are two techniques of fire detection used in the smoke detectors readily available today, ionization and photocell. Each has definite advantages. Ionization detectors are good at detecting rapidly burning, flaming fires. Photocell detectors are good at sensing slow, smoldering fires.

In order to detect both types of fires in their earliest stages, you need to have both types of smoke detection. Sears lists one detector in the big catalog which combines both ionization and photocell detection in a single unit. It sells for $29.99.

A reasonable alternative to the two-in-one detector would be two different types of detectors in two different locations. The photocell detector might be located near bedroom areas because that's where smoky fires tend to start, and the ionization type might be located near the kitchen because that's where blazing fires tend to start.

All detectors require an electrical power source. Some run on house current and some run on batteries. Those which run on house current are preferable because they don't depend upon the uncertain reliability of a battery and they're less likely to be disabled by tenants who are tired of hearing their burning steaks sound the alarm. Unless your building is being constructed or rewired, however, you might as well forget about installing a detector which runs on house current. Retrofitting new electrical outlets in the unusual locations which are best suited for detectors is simply too expensive. On the other hand, battery-operated detectors can be mounted practically anywhere.

Select a detector which uses a readily available battery like the standard 9-volt battery used in transistor radios. They're a whole lot cheaper to replace than uncommon types.

Before you buy any detector, familiarize yourself with your community's recommendations and/or regulations. Some require a particular type and some require a certain number to be installed in certain locations. Find out what those regulations are and comply.

While you're conducting orientation for new tenants, give instructions in smoke detector care. Show them where each detector is, tell them why each was located there, show them how to conduct a functional test, explain to them how to shut it off, and demonstrate how to replace the battery. Make sure that each detector is in working order when they move in, and have them initial the smoke detector paragraph on the Condition & Inventory Checksheet, but don't rely entirely on them to check the functioning of each detector. Do it yourself periodically.

CHANGING LOCKS

Give your new tenants the assurance that the locks on their dwellings have been changed so that previous tenants couldn't possibly use old keys for access. You needn't hire a locksmith for this job either. You can do it yourself. If you can turn a screwdriver, you can change locks.

The simplest way to make this change if you lack the expertise and equipment to rekey lock cylinders is to keep several spare locksets on hand. They should be exactly like the old ones if possible (locks from the same manufacturer shouldn't require changing either the spring-loaded latches or the striker plates, nor should you have to worry about adjusting the door cutout sizes). You can change locks quite simply by zipping out two screws with a Yankee screwdriver, removing the old lock, putting a new one in its place, and securing it by zipping the two screws back in again. That's all there is to it. (To keep dust and water from settling inside the pin chambers and gumming up the works, always install locks so the flat edge of the keyway is on the bottom. In other words, the key cuts should point up whenever a key is inserted. To reverse their keyways, Kwikset locks require a special cylinder removing tool, an inexpensive item available from your hardware store or locksmith shop.) What do you do with the old locks? Play "musical locks" with them, of course. No one need know where they went. If people ask, tell them they went to "Lock Heaven."

Whether you install new or resurrected locks doesn't seem to matter at all. What is most important to tenants' feeling of security is knowing that no former tenants have keys.

While you're changing the locks on their doors, you might want to inform your tenants exactly who does have access to their home.

SELECTING PADLOCKS

To gain access with just one key to all the padlocked garages and storage enclosures where you keep your landlording equipment and supplies, buy padlocks which are keyed alike. All padlock manufacturers make them and most regular hardware stores carry them in stock. Just ask.

Don't use keyed-alike padlocks for those applications at multiple-family dwellings where every tenant needs access, applications such as gates and common storage areas. You don't want to have to issue still another key to each of your tenants. For those applications, use a special kind of combination padlock called the Sesamee Keyless Padlock. It can be set to any of 10,000 combinations and can be reset very simply at any time. Set it to an easily remembered number like a building address or the current year, and your tenants will all have access when they need it without having to fumble for keys.

Any padlock which is used by more than one tenant will soon disappear, however, unless you attach a chain to its shackle. Ask at your hardware store for a special padlock chain restraint made by the Master Lock Company which fits most padlocks and eliminates this lost-padlock problem.

INSTALLING PEEPSCOPES

Some entrances to dwellings are blind, that is, there's no way for the occupants to see who's at the door. Occupants have to either talk through the door or open it a crack to answer. Sometimes people attach security chains to their doors and door jambs to limit the door's movement and hence restrict access, but these chains provide more psychological than physical security because they pull loose from their mountings in response to the slightest blow and expose the occupants immediately to outside danger.

A far better way to solve this problem is to install a peepscope right in the door itself so that occupants can see who's out there knocking on the door without jeopardizing their own safety. Peepscopes cost less than $5 each and take less than five minutes to install. Take care to install yours low enough, say around four and a half feet from the door bottom, so most anybody will be able to peep through. Tenants appreciate peepscopes.

HELPING TO PREVENT BURGLARIES

You will want to try what you can to prevent burglaries from occurring at your rental property because every burglary reflects negatively on the property itself and scares off better tenants, but you hardly have unlimited funds to spend for prevention and you must recognize that no measure you take will be 100% effective, no matter what it costs. Before you go out and spend the big bucks to hire a guard service or install decorative iron grillwork all around your building, try taking other much less expensive measures which your tenants would surely appreciate, measures like strategically located outside lighting, "Operation Identification," and the closet safe.

• OUTSIDE LIGHTING—When the sun goes down, criminals come to life. They use darkness as a shield to protect themselves from being noticed while doing their dastardly deeds. They're the antithesis of the stage performers who live for being in the spotlight and seeing their names up in lights. Criminals much prefer anonymity, staying in the shadows and out of sight so they cannot be identified.

Because burglars, robbers, muggers, rapists, and vandals tend to avoid well-lit areas, you have to provide good lighting to keep them at bay. If you don't and a crime should occur on your property where you "should have installed lighting," you will be held responsible for the crime just as surely as if you had slipped on your black T-shirt and panty hose (over your face, of course) and taken up your Saturday night special to go out and do some wrongs.

You're left with no choice but to provide good lighting and maintain it. Light as much outside area as you can with energy-efficient fluorescent or sodium-vapor lamps, and you'll be marking your building as a poor target for nighttime burglars, as well as assisting your tenants in their nocturnal peregrinations.

• "OPERATION IDENTIFICATION"—"Operation Identification" involves engraving every item of value with the owner's name and driver's license number to prevent burglars from fencing it easily. Burglars might be able to keep this marked booty for their own use and have no problems, but whenever they try to convert it into cash, they encounter difficulties. Fences certainly don't want stuff which is plainly identified because it is just too easy to trace. Burglars can try to eradicate the engraved marks by grinding them off, but that's too much like work and it leaves marks which diminish the item's value to anyone buying stolen goods. Whenever they come upon engraved goods, then, burglars tend to leave them behind because there's plenty of other stuff around for the taking that won't cause them a bit of trouble.

Many urban police departments lend engravers and supply warning decals which can be placed near every likely burglary access to strike the fear of "Operation

Identification" into any burglar who's casing the joint. You might consider buying an engraver yourself (they're less than $15), identifying all of your own tools and valuables, and then lending it to your tenants. They'll appreciate it, and you'll all find that it works. By the way, for less laborious, better-looking engraving, try using cursive script rather than printing each letter separately.

• PADLOCK EYES—The other burglary prevention measure is one designed more to lessen the impact of burglaries than to prevent them from happening altogether. It involves creating a closet safe where tenants can secure their valuables right at home. A closet safe is merely a closet with a lock on it which is intended to delay burglars, forcing them to spend more time and make more noise than they would like to, many times frustrating them completely and causing them to leave with far less than what they came for. The lock on a closet safe might be a doorknob or deadbolt lock keyed like the entrance locks or it might be a padlock which the tenants supply themselves.

Having tenants supply their own padlocks is preferable, of course, because it relieves you of the responsibility of looking after still another lock and key. The usual padlock hardware is a little unsightly, I know, and you might shake your head at the thought of installing it on an inside door, but Master No. 60 Padlock Eyes, which are designed to be used on any ordinary household door, are almost unnoticeable. Yet they, together with a good door and a strong padlock, make a fairly invulnerable closet safe and provide excellent protection for valuables.

Whatever else you can do to thwart burglars and give your tenants a sense of security will help you keep good tenants longer, and that's good business.

NEUTERING TENANT IDENTIFICATION

To thwart the criminal types who prey on single, defenseless people, identify tenants on mail boxes, bell buttons, and tenant directories with their last names only or with their last names and first initials only. Do not give would-be intruders a clue as to the sex or number of people living in any dwelling.

TAKING SAFETY PRECAUTIONS FOR HANDLING RENT

You are a wise landlord or landlady to insist on cash, a money order, or a cashier's check for a tenant's initial rental payment. You have to be absolutely certain that you're not giving a new tenant the keys to a $50,000 dwelling in exchange for a bum check or some worthless collateral. After that, however, you should be more concerned about the risk involved in handling cash, for you could lose your property's entire monthly income all too easily by misplacing it or getting robbed, and since there's no commercially available and affordable insurance policy to protect you from the loss, it would be yours alone to bear. Take the precaution, therefore, of refusing to accept cash.

Some tenants will want to pay you their rent in cash, and since cash is legal tender for all money transactions, you will have to take it unless you stipulate with adequate notice in advance that you won't. State in your rental agreement or takeover letter that rent must be paid by check or money order and insist on it! Some contrary tenants who deal strictly in cash may wave a fistful of greenbacks in your face and say, "Take it or leave it," and you'll have to weigh all the factors of the situation before deciding what to do. If you accept it, they will probably continue trying to pay you in cash month after month, and if you decline it, you may never collect their rent at all. I usually accept their cash and patiently explain each time why I prefer rents to be paid by check or money order, until they finally tire of hearing my repeated explanations and give in.

Even though you are resolute about not accepting cash, you may face a loss if someone robs you and gets away with your rent checks and money orders, because even stolen checks and money orders can be negotiated by a thief who knows how. Add one extra safety precaution—the "Little Old Rubber Stamp Trick."

Invest a few dollars in deposit stamps for yourself and any manager who handles rent for you so that stolen checks and money orders cannot be negotiated easily, if at all. As soon as a tenant hands you a check or money order, stamp the back with a rubber stamp which might read like one of these—

FOR DEPOSIT ONLY
to the account of
Lester Landlord

or

PAY TO THE ORDER OF
BIG BANK
Lester Landlord
011-123456
FOR DEPOSIT ONLY

Stamped on the backs of your checks and money orders, such a deposit stamp renders them virtually worthless except as deposits to your own bank account. No one can cash them by trying to impersonate you at the corner liquor store or delicatessen. They can only be put into your account.

These same deposit stamps are also handy for marking the coin wrappers you use for rolling all those quarters, dimes, and nickels generated by your coin-operated laundry machines. Banks usually insist that rolls of coins be identified in case they're found wanting.

If using the "Little Old Rubber Stamp Trick" saves you just one unauthorized check cashing, it's well worth the small cost.

SOME LAST WORDS

Go ahead and provide every security precaution in the book which appears reasonable for the kind of property you have, but do not advertise your property's security features. You don't want to be sued by a tenant who becomes the victim of a crime and claims to have been misled by your advertising. Let tenants make up their own minds as to the security of the property.

KEEPING RECORDS

For some people the most onerous chore of landlording is keeping records. They'll look after their properties with great vigor and delight, but speak to them about keeping records and they'll laugh nervously, perhaps they'll point to a dog-eared, old rent receipt book and a stack of shoeboxes stuffed with miscellaneous slips of paper, and they'll say they just haven't got the time to sit down and shuffle papers. They have much more important work to do. Besides, they have an accountant who does it all for them. Sound familiar? Have any more excuses to add?

Unfortunately those people who neglect recordkeeping don't recognize what's truly important in this business. Since they keep their records haphazardly, they don't really know what's happening at all and they can't make good decisions. They don't know whether their rents are covering their expenses, so they haven't a clue whether a rent raise is warranted. They don't know how much they're now spending on utilities compared to previous periods, so they have yet to consider conserving utilities as a cost-saving measure. They don't keep any figures on their coin-operated laundry machines, so they're still charging 25 cents to wash and 10 cents to dry. They don't even know when they'll be making the final payment on a second mortgage. Consequently, they can't know when to expect an increase in cash flow. When can they plan to buy their new Cadillac Seville? They can't say.

These things are truly important in this business. Sure, you have to do a great many other important things, but few are ever quite so important as recordkeeping, and none will assist you in both managing your property day by day and satisfying the requirements of the IRS. You cannot afford to neglect it.

Landlording without recordkeeping is like trying to play football without keeping score. Nobody would know what was going on. If the teams didn't know their scores and the time remaining, they couldn't adjust their strategies, and the fans wouldn't know whether to get excited or not. Bashing heads is only part of the game.

To do recordkeeping right, you may use a quill pen, ink pot, eye shade, sleeve garters, and leather ledger if you want to, or a fancy computer with two floppies, a 20mb hard disk, and more RAM than ewes ever see. That doesn't matter. What does is that you have a system, preferably one which you can understand yourself. The one outlined in this chapter might be considered rudimentary by some standards, but it is wholly sufficient for landlords and landladies who do their own recordkeeping. Some people have used it for just one rental house, and others have used it for more than three hundred rentals. It's a flexible system, simple to follow, easy to crosscheck, and exhaustive enough to lead into tax preparations. It's based on forms which are designed to be read vertically and to fit into a standard 8 1/2" x 11" binder. Best of all, it's all right here in your hands. You can get started using it right away by making copies of the forms included in the back of the book.

Before we get to the forms themselves, though, let's consider a way to keep those miscellaneous slips of paper out of your old shoeboxes.

FILING

You handle so many important written records in your landlording business that you have to organize them so they are readily accessible when needed or you will become hopelessly bogged down in unnecessary searches for lost records now and then. A simple filing system will help.

For each property, make up three file folders (you might want to use folders of a different color for each property). Label each folder with the property's address or some other designation and "RECORDS," "TENANT RECORDS," or "RECEIPTS."

• In the RECORDS file folder, keep the property's insurance policies, title papers, termite reports, tax information, deeds, notes, loan records, and anything else pertaining to the property as a whole that you're not already keeping in your safety deposit box.

• In the TENANT RECORDS file folder, keep completed Rental Applications, Rental Agreements, Leases, Condition and Inventory Checksheets, and any other papers pertaining to the property's tenants, including those tenants who have moved out.

• In the RECEIPTS file folder, keep the paid receipts for expenses related to the property. As soon as you get a receipt, circle the amount paid and mark it with the date of payment, the method of payment ("$" for cash, check mark and number for a check, and a "CC" for credit cards), and the property's address, so you'll be able to identify it easily if it happens to be mislaid. If the receipt does not include a description of the item or service paid for, write a description on it.

Prorate on an itemized or percentage basis those receipts which

cover expenses for more than one property so that each property pays its own share. If two properties are involved, make a duplicate receipt for
one property's share and reference it to the original bill, which should be adjusted and then inserted into the other property's file. For unreceipted expenses, such as casual labor, make up your own receipt with the important information, get a signature if you can, and file it with the other expense receipts.

Arrange all receipts chronologically in the file folder so they will be easier to post. Arranging them is easy to do unless you get very far behind and your receipts become mixed up. Just put the most recent receipt face up and in the back of the folder, and you won't have to bother about sorting them later. All the receipts for one month should be kept together and slipped into a folded sheet of paper which is identified with the month and the year. When you finish recording the receipts for the month, staple them together inside the folded sheet and leave them in the folder.

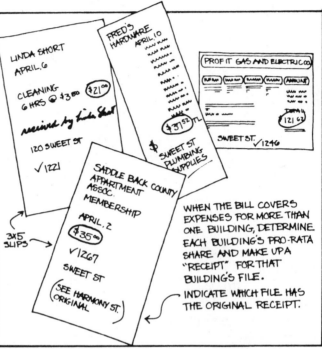

At the end of the year, empty the RECEIPTS folder of that year's receipts and put them, along with the year's income and expense sheets referred to later, into a large envelope for storage. Because you never can tell when the tax collector will request an audit of your books, you would be wise to keep them for a long time to come (ever since some seven-year-old records helped to net me a $20,000 tax refund windfall, I recommend keeping them seven years at least).

If you begin accumulating more and more properties, you will probably want to add more folders to your filing system to accommodate the greater volume of paperwork. The following might prove useful—INCOMING, UNPAID BILLS, BANKING, LOANS, and PAYROLL. You'll surely find plenty of stray items to keep safely and neatly tucked away inside these folders.

That's all there is to keeping your written records organized. Read on to learn how to use these records in doing your bookkeeping.

BOOKKEEPING

Basically, the loose-leaf book kept for recording purposes has five sections— TENANTS, INCOME, EXPENSES, SUMMARIES, and LOANS/INSURANCE. Properly filled out and kept up to date, the forms in these sections will give you quick access to most of the information you need to operate rental property.

Blanks for every sheet used in these sections appear in the back of the book. Use the blanks as originals and copy them for your own loose-leaf book. Do not write on the original forms themselves. Write only on the copies.

• TENANTS—Tenant Record

The first section, the one for tenant information, has only one form. It's called the Tenant Record. Record information on it which you'll need to refer to occasionally, information such as rent due dates and tenants' telephone numbers.

Nowadays so many people have unlisted phones that you may not be able to get your tenants' numbers from a directory or from the information operator. Having the numbers handy will save you lots of fumbling, frustration, and wasted trips.

Although you hope that you won't ever have to take advantage of such information, you may use the Tenant Record form to keep track of your tenants' current checking and savings account numbers so you'll know where to go to attach these assets if you have to collect a money judgment against them. The savings account number should be on the Rental Application, and the checking account number will be written in those funny-looking magnetic numbers at the bottom of the tenant's rent check. Be prepared!

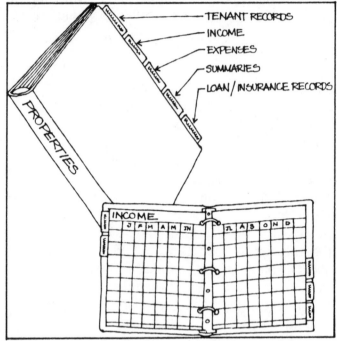

Because you will refer to the Tenant Record repeatedly and because these sheets should last for years, you may wish to keep them clean with a transparent page protector which slips on and off easily and is available in most stationery stores. When tenants move, cross them off the Tenant Record using a yellow or pink highlighter felt pen which does a neat job and still gives you access to the old information if you need it.

Add new tenants to the bottom of the list. Even though they won't be in order according to their dwelling number or letter designation, their information will be readily accessible.

Use a separate Tenant Record sheet for each multiple-family property. One will do adequately for a small collection of rental houses.

Tenant Record

Location 456 SWEET ST.

	Unit	Tenant	Phone	Moved In	Moved Out	Rent Date/Rent	Deposit/Less Rent	Bank/Ckg. Acct. Nos.
● 1	456	RICHARD & MARY RENTER	555-1280	1/84		1ST	720/478	BIG BANK ✓ 040 39586-04
2	458	AMELIA GILTRONG	557-4672	3/83		✓	678/450	CENTRAL BANK ✓ 1074372
3	460	CHESTER & CATHY CAREFEE	555-2845	1/85		✓	762/506	BIG BANK ✓ 04040853-07 SAV 04067125
4	462	ERNIE PEABODY	557-4343	7/81	3/85	✓	651/432	
5	464	SONDRA FREELY	557-6258	5/79		✓	453/402	1ST NATL BANK ✓ 11803582
6	462	HENRY & GLADYS ANGEL	557-8442	4/85		✓	720/478	STAGE COACH BANK ✓ 12011790
7								

• INCOME—Monthly Rental Income Record

The second bookkeeping section, INCOME, includes three different forms—Monthly Rental Income Record, Laundry Income, and Other Receipts and Income.

Unless you have quite a few properties, one of each form should suffice. For example, if you are Lester Landlord and you have one duplex, half of which you occupy yourself, and one fiveplex, you can easily list both properties on a single Monthly Rental Income Record.

If you do enter more than one property on a form, use a highligher pen to mark "TOTAL" lines all the way across both sheets, and you'll find that the totals are easier to see.

If you have room, you can even use the same record sheets for subsequent years by listing the properties again further down the sheets and indicating on each "TOTAL" line which year you are recording. One advantage in recording your rental income this way is that you have instant access to past years' rental income for comparison purposes. You'll know when you last raised rents and how much of a vacancy factor you created by doing so. You can use this information to help you prepare for the next raise rent increase.

After using these sheets to record rental income for a full year, calculate the total year's income for each dwelling and enter it in the "Year's Totals" column. Total that column so you can crosscheck the monthly totals for all buildings on the sheets. If your figures don't match, find out why they don't and correct your error.

This kind of crosschecking is easy work with an electronic calculator. Get yourself a printing calculator which produces a paper tape record of its entries. Sometimes just one slightly incorrect entry will cause an error and you can find it without painstakingly adding each item again merely by comparing the tape, item for item, with the Income Record figures.

MONTHLY RENTAL INCOME RECORD

Page ___1___
Location(s) _SWEET ST & NEAT ST._
Period ___1985___

	Unit	Jan.	Feb.	Mar.	Apr.	May	
1	456 SWEET ST.	458 -	458 -	458 ·	458 -	458 -	1
2	458 " "	430 -	430 -	430 -	430 -	430 -	2
3	460 " "	586 -	486 -	486 -	486 -	486 -	3
4	462 " "	412 -	412 -	206 -	558 -	458 -	4
5	464 " "	382 -	382 -	382 -	382 -	382 -	5
6	TOTAL	2268 -	2168 -	1962 -	2314 -	2214 -	6
7							7
8							8
9	125 NEAT ST	350 -	350 -	378 -	378 -	378 -	9
10							10
11	TOTAL BOTH BLDGS	2618 -	2518 -	2340 -	2692 -	2592 -	11
12							12
13							13
14							14
15							15

• INCOME—Other Receipts & Income

The last of the income forms, called Other Receipts & Income, uses two sheets to span a full year and is used to record whatever doesn't count as rental income.

Income items which may be included are added appliances or furniture, deposit forfeits, interest on deposits, late charges (unless you use the discounted rent policy, in which case both gross and net rents could be recorded as regular rental income), laundry collections, laundry commissions, garages, etc. Those income items which are normally included in the rent should be recorded as rental income and not here. Rents for furnished apartments, for example, need not be itemized separately, nor should a garage rent be recorded separately if it's normally included in the rent. If, however, you bill tenants separately for their garage, air conditioner, or anything else, then you may wish to include those separate amounts here.

Still, don't worry yourself much about where to include an item. Worry instead about whether you have inadvertently recorded any income on both the Monthly Rental Income Record and the Other Receipts & Income record. Do avoid that! Only the laundry income should be recorded in two places, the Laundry Income sheet and the Other Receipts sheets.

Although tenants' deposits may be treated as income when received and may be recorded here as other income, you're wise not to do so. Instead of handling them that way and being taxed on them just as if they were rent, do not record them anywhere as income. Record them on the Tenant Record and list as income only what you do not return to the tenants after they move. That, after all, is when the deposits do become income, not before.

Last month's rent and other rents paid in advance are another story. The IRS tells us that they must be considered as income when received. There's no choice.

One Other Receipts & Income form may last you a year or it may last you several, depending on the number of properties you have. Fill it out pretty much the same way you do the Monthly Rental Income Record, grouping all the items for one building together.

OTHER RECEIPTS & INCOME

Added Appliances or Furniture, Deposits, Interest on Deposits, Late Charges, Laundry, Garages, etc.

Page ___1___
Location(s) _SWEET ST. & NEAT ST._
Period _____1985_____

#	Description of Income	Jan.	Feb.	Mar.	Apr.	May	#
1	SWEET ST.						1
2	LAUNDRY	86 75	85 50	92 25	78 75	86 75	2
3	GARAGES	45 -	45 -	30 -	45 -	45 -	3
4	INTEREST ON DEPOSITS/ACCTS				18 80		4
5							5
6	TOTAL	131 75	130 50	122 25	142 61	131 75	6
7							7
8	NEAT ST.						8
9	LATE RENTS						9
10	INTEREST ON DEPOSITS/ACCTS				3 90		10
11							11
12	TOTAL	0	0	0	3 90	0	12
13							13
14							

• INCOME—Laundry Income

If you own coin-operated laundry machines, use the Laundry Income sheet to record every collection before you post the monthly totals to the Other Receipts & Income sheets. Otherwise you'll be saving little scraps of paper, each representing one collection, until you have a full month's collections and can make the monthly entry. Those scraps may very well get lost in the wash.

There are seven columns on the Laundry Income sheet, but you need not use every one. If you don't wish to compare washer and dryer receipts and you're not interested in cumulative totals, don't bother with those things. Use only the columns you want, the bare minimum being a "Date" entry and a "Both" entry. The "Both" entry, of course, would be your total for each collection.

The other columns will provide quite useful information to anyone who bothers to take the time to complete them, though. The separate washer and dryer columns tell you how much use each machine is getting. From these figures you can determine each machines's exact number of loads. Use this information to check on a machine's reliability whenever it needs repair. Perhaps, because of this information, you'll want to change makes of machines when they need replacement or when you purchase a set for another location. The separate washer-dryer columns also provide a revealing ratio of use for the machines. If a tenant claims that the dryer is requiring twice as many coins to dry each load as it used to, you can calculate whether it is or not by checking for a change in the income ratio between the machines. You'll find out whether the machine really does need repair or whether the tenant is testing your gullibility.

The "Cumulative Totals" column tells you at a glance whether your investment is paying off. Let's say your machines cost you $1,000 and you take in $200 in the first six months. At that rate, just recouping your investment would take two and a half years, and that's not including the utilities it takes to run them or the cost of the repairs. But if the machines last ten years and on a projected basis take in $70 a month or $8,400 in all, $2,500 of which goes for utilities and $800 for repairs, you'll make a return on your investment of 41% per year simple interest. That's not bad! I'll take that kind of a return any old time. The "Cumulative Totals" column will also help you decide whether to increase or decrease the amount you're charging per load.

The "Monthly Totals" column is a convenience expressly for the purpose of entering the necessary figures on the Other Receipts & Income sheets, but these figures will also let you compare month-by-month laundry receipts if your collection dates are fairly consistent and frequent. Remember that not every line requires a monthly entry, only those which represent the last collection for the month.

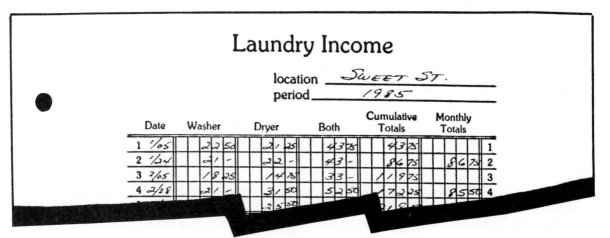

Laundry Income

location _Sweet St._

period _1985_

	Date	Washer	Dryer	Both	Cumulative Totals	Monthly Totals	
1	1/05	22 50	21 25	43 75	43 75		1
2	1/24	21 -	22 -	43 -	86 75	86 75	2
3	2/05	18 25	14 75	33 -	119 75		3
4	2/28	21 -	31 50	52 50	172 25	85 50	4
			25 50				

• EXPENSES—Expense and Payment Record

There are three forms in the expense section of the loose-leaf record book—the Expense and Payment Record, Payroll Record, and Depreciation Record.

The first one, the Expense and Payment Record, is probably the most used of all the forms in the book. Remember all those receipts you moved from your shoeboxes and shopping bags into a neat file folder labeled "RECEIPTS," which you then organized by date of payment? Well, here's where you record them all.

The entries are made chronologically and should include all the expense receipts in the RECEIPTS folder, plus the payroll expenses from the Payroll Record and the loan payments which are recorded on the Loan & Note Record sheets.

Besides being chronological, the entries are separated into eleven categories which enable you to refer easily to certain kinds of expenses whenever you want to find out where all your money's going. You may find some surprises when you examine the categories, surprises that appear only when you examine a series of similar expenditures rather than just one bill. Might you, for example, have inadvertently paid your property taxes or your insurance twice? Don't laugh. It happens. Here's where you can check on your own absentmindedness.

If it weren't for the loan payments, filling out expense sheets would be idiot's play. What makes the loan payment entries a little tricky are those portions of the payments which aren't actually expenses. Column 11, which is the amount you pay on the principal of your loan, represents an increase in your net worth rather than an expense. Yet, since it is definitely money paid out, it should be recorded as such. Likewise, an impound account, which should be posted to Column 12 as a non-deductible item, is a savings account, forced savings, to be sure, but still a savings account. The mortgagor uses an impound account to pay taxes and insurance, and the funds you pay into an impound account are not an expense, strictly speaking, until they're actually used.

EXPENSE AND PAYMENT RECORD

Page __3__

Location(s) __Sweet St__

Period __1985__

	Date	How Paid	To Whom Paid	For	1 Total Paid Out	2 Interest	3 Taxes. Licenses	4 Insurance	
1			BAL FWD		3054 32	160 439	24 80	∅	1
2	4/02	267	BIG BANK	1ST MORTGAGE	579 03	311 42			2
3	✓	268	S. HONEYBAGS	2ND "	122 -	53 34			3
4	4/06	269	LITTLE TOWN HDWE	MISC HOME MECH	43 29				4
5	4/07	270	SADDLEBACK CNTY	PROP TAXES	674 31		674 31		5
6	4/10	271	MONOPOLY GAS ELEC	3/1 – 4/1	57 12				6
7	4/11	272	K-MART	SHADES	12 26				7
8	4/12	273	LITTLETOWN WTR DIST	MARCH WTR	41 30				8
9	✓	274	MONOPOLY GARBAGE	" SVC	22 50				9
10	4/15	275	PHOENIX PAINTS	PNTNG SUPP	32 64				10
11	✓	276	LESTER LANDLORD	PERSONAL DRAW	280 00				11
12	✓	277	C. GOODFOLKS	PAYROLL	56 32				12
13	4/19	278	" " P/C	STAMPS, MISC HOME	14 32				13
14	4/20	279	USA INSURANCE	ANNUAL PREM	286 54			286 54	14
15	4/21	280	LITTLETWN OFF SUPP	ENVELOPES, COPIES	5 47				15
16	4/25	281	SEERES CO.	WATER HEATER	443 64				16
				ROLL	47 54				

When the mortgagor uses your impounded funds to pay taxes or insurance, record the payment like any other and stipulate in the "How Paid" column that funds for payment came out of the impounds account. I know, I know, this means that the amount in the "Total Paid Out" column is actually more than what you will have paid out. Trust me, though, and I'll show you on the Summary of Business and Statement of Income form how everything evens out again. Just don't worry about it now, and don't worry about the matter at all if you're not even paying into an impounds account with your mortgage payment. That's just fine.

Now let's take a look at the procedure for normal entries. After you fill in the information called for in the first five columns, you come to the columns with the eleven different headings. Choose whichever one best fits each expense and put the amount in that column. Be sure, however, that it's all on the same horizontal line. Even though the lines are numbered four times on the two sheets, sometimes your eyes will play tricks on you and you may wind up using the wrong line. Use a ruler as a guide if you have to.

Don't deliberate too much about the proper categories for ambiguous expenses. If you can't easily decide whether something should be called a "service" or not, then it can't matter too much, and since you identify each item in the "For" column anyway, you always have backup information in case you want to change categories later for some reason or other.

If you find that you have no use for a certain column heading, if, for example, you have no payroll to enter, change the heading to something more useful to you. Other possibilities are travel/telephone, advertising/rental fees, and non-employee labor.

Now look again at the sample Expense and Payment Record for Lester Landlord's fiveplex. Note that the distribution of the mortgage payments is broken into three categories—interest, mortgage payment, and non-deductible (impounds). Note also that the first line of these sample sheets has the totals brought forward from the previous

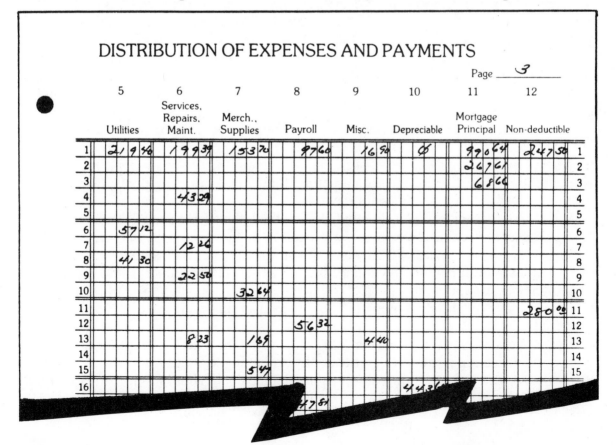

sheets. You must do this on every page except the first one for the year (corresponding left and right sheets should have the same page numbers).

After you have entered your final expenditure for the year, total the last sheet and you'll have your annual expenditures for the property.

Let me caution you here, though, about two important no-no's related to your Expense and Payment Record sheets. Never include as a regular, deductible expense either the items which the government requires you to depreciate or the money you pay yourself.

"Depreciable items" are either personal property used in your landlording business (a utility trailer, for example) or replacements (new roof) or improvements (new patio) to your real property. You have to "depreciate" these things, that is, you have to write them off little by little over a period of years. You might think that a new stove or a new water heater is an item which you should be able to charge off against this year's income. After all, you had to pay for the whole thing this year, didn't you? (Even if you didn't pay for it entirely this year, having borrowed the money instead, that wouldn't make any difference as far as depreciation is concern) Shouldn't you be able to write it all off this year, too? Sorry, scrupulous landlord and landlady, but you can't write a depreciable item off as an expense during a single year. And because you can't list it as an expense, you'll have to enter it in column 10 so you can keep track of it in a special way. You'll see.

Money which you pay yourself from your property's income is called a personal draw, which is definitely not an expense and is not the least bit deductible. It's personal income withdrawn from the business. If you wish to keep track of any money you pay yourself out of your property account, and you would be wise to do so, enter it on the Expense and Payment Record, but be sure to list it as a non-deductible item in column 12.

• EXPENSES—Depreciation Record

The Depreciation Record is a worksheet which enables you to keep track of the amount of depreciation available to you for every year you own something which is depreciable. It will serve to remind you years after you have paid for something depreciable whether you still have some depreciation coming to you and precisely how much it is. It will also help you calculate your adjusted basis when you dispose of a piece of real property, for the depreciable balance of everything you include in a transfer of real property should be added to the depreciable balance of the property itself in order to calculate your capital gain for tax purposes.

As mentioned already, depreciable items are personal property used in your landlording business, as well as replacements and improvements made to your real property. Here are some examples of depreciable items—major equipment, appliances, air conditioners, roof replacements, carpeting, linoleum, swimming pools, laundry machines, wiring, remodeling, and draperies.

With these depreciable items in mind, do you think that either an $80 sander or a $30 kitchen faucet replacement would be depreciable? No, they wouldn't. They're not expensive enough to bother with. In general, you should depreciate an item only if it costs more than two- or three-hundred dollars and has a useful life of more than a year or two. Painting is one exception, though. Even if an exterior paint job costs $3,500, improves the appearance of your rental property 100%, and lasts six years, you can and should expense it.

Remember that expensing is better than depreciating because it allows you an immediate deduction from income instead of your having to wait for it. You don't get any larger deduction by depreciating, so if you have some doubt about whether to expense or

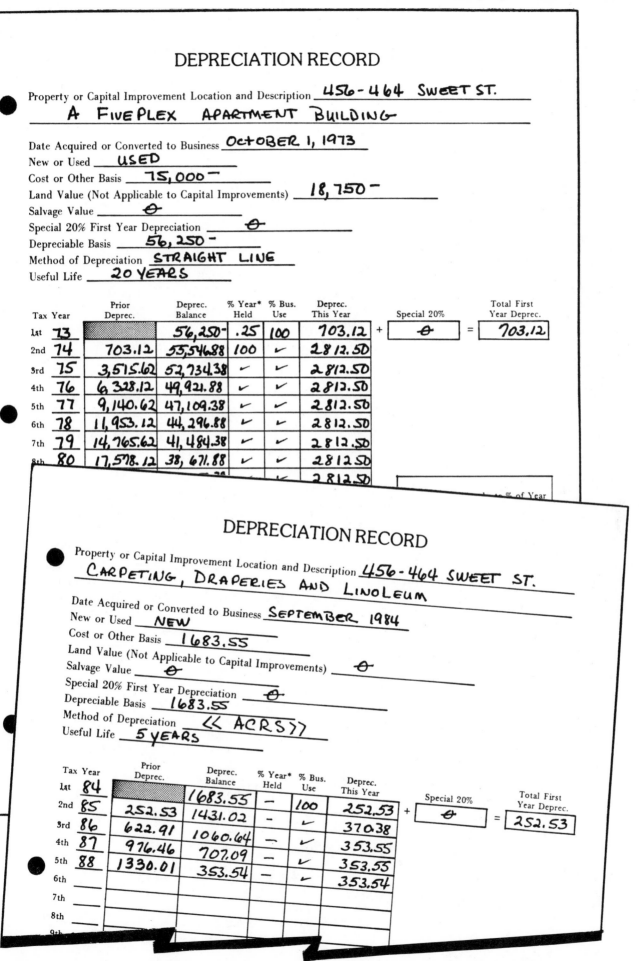

DEPRECIATION RECORD

Property or Capital Improvement Location and Description __456-464 SWEET ST.__

__A FIVEPLEX APARTMENT BUILDING__

Date Acquired or Converted to Business __October 1, 1973__

New or Used __USED__

Cost or Other Basis __75,000 –__

Land Value (Not Applicable to Capital Improvements) __18,750 –__

Salvage Value __0__

Special 20% First Year Depreciation __0__

Depreciable Basis __56,250 –__

Method of Depreciation __STRAIGHT LINE__

Useful Life __20 YEARS__

Tax Year	Prior Deprec.	Deprec. Balance	% Year* Held	% Bus. Use	Deprec. This Year		Special 20%		Total First Year Deprec.
1st 73		56,250 –	.25	100	703.12	+	0	=	703.12
2nd 74	703.12	55,546.88	100	✓	2812.50				
3rd 75	3,515.62	52,734.38	✓	✓	2812.50				
4th 76	6,328.12	49,921.88	✓	✓	2812.50				
5th 77	9,140.62	47,109.38	✓	✓	2812.50				
6th 78	11,953.12	44,296.88	✓	✓	2812.50				
7th 79	14,765.62	41,484.38	✓	✓	2812.50				
8th 80	17,578.12	38,671.88	✓	✓	2812.50				
			✓	2812.50					

DEPRECIATION RECORD

Property or Capital Improvement Location and Description __456-464 SWEET ST.__

__CARPETING, DRAPERIES AND LINOLEUM__

Date Acquired or Converted to Business __SEPTEMBER 1984__

New or Used __NEW__

Cost or Other Basis __1683.55__

Land Value (Not Applicable to Capital Improvements) __0__

Salvage Value __0__

Special 20% First Year Depreciation __0__

Depreciable Basis __1683.55__

Method of Depreciation __<< ACRS >>__

Useful Life __5 YEARS__

Tax Year	Prior Deprec.	Deprec. Balance	% Year* Held	% Bus. Use	Deprec. This Year		Special 20%		Total First Year Deprec.
1st 84		1683.55	–	100	252.53	+	0	=	252.53
2nd 85	252.53	1431.02	–	✓	252.53				
3rd 86	622.91	1060.64	–	✓	370.38				
4th 87	976.46	707.09	–	✓	353.55				
5th 88	1330.01	353.54	–	✓	353.55				
6th				✓	353.54				
7th									
8th									
9th									

depreciate an item because of its cost or useful life, go ahead and expense it. For example, carpet that costs you $189 ought to be expensed, as should an $86 replacement drapery.

On the other hand, $189 worth of carpet which is part of a larger carpet replacement totaling $736 ought to be depreciated.

Before you fill out a Depreciation Record, you will have to know the particulars about the expenditure and the IRS classification it falls under, and then you will have to decide which depreciation method to use. Since the Economic Recovery Tax Act of 1981 took effect, the classifications have been both rigidified and simplified, and the recovery periods (useful lives) have been shortened. Now there are four classifications—3-year property (autos, light trucks), 5-year property (water heaters, carpeting), 10-year property (residential mobile homes), and 18-year property (buildings and building components such as roofs), and the depreciation rates are simple to calculate from the prescribed percentages for each classification. For 5-year property, you deduct 15% the first year (no matter which month of the year you acquired the property; this so-called "half-year convention" does not apply to real property, which is still prorated), 22% the second, and 21% for the third through the fifth years. That's a whole lot simpler than trying to decide upon the useful life and the salvage value of a depreciable item and then trying to pick a depreciation method from a considerable array of them, hoping that your decisions won't trigger a dispute with the IRS.

As for methods, now there are essentially only two to concern yourself with, ACRS and straight line. "ACRS" stands for Accelerated Cost Recovery System, and it may be applied only to those depreciable expenditures made during 1981 and after. There's no other accelerated depreciation available in most situations, but that's nothing to lament because ACRS is generous in terms of both recovery periods and rates. The sample Depreciation Record for Lester Landlord's carpeting, draperies, and linoleum illustrates how ACRS works on 5-year property. One of the more important things to note about this example is that all of Lester's 5-year depreciable expenditures made during the year for his five-plex are lumped together on one Depreciation Record sheet. No longer need you fill out a separate sheet for each one and do separate calculations. In addition, there is no longer a 20% special first-year write-off or a salvage value to be determined. To learn more about the specifics of ACRS, read IRS Publication 534 or the latest edition of *Your Income Tax*.

The straight line method is virtually the same as always. It lets you write off something depreciable at a constant rate and, if you prefer, over a longer period of time as well. The sample Depreciation Record for Lester Landlord's fiveplex acquired in October, 1973, illustrates how straight line works when applied to real property. He deducted the presumed land value from the acquisition cost and got his depreciable basis. Then he divided his basis by 20, the useful life he selected back then, and multiplied that by 25%, the percentage of the first year he held the property, and he came up with his depreciation for 1973. For 1974 and all successive years, except the final one, his depreciation equals 1/20th or 5% of the original basis. The final year picks up the balance for those months he didn't own the property during the first year. That's pretty easy, isn't it?

Because your familiarity with depreciation will help you make good decisions affecting the profitability of your landlording business, try your best to understand how depreciation works and try to make the calculations yourself before you consult a tax oracle for advice. To become as knowledgeable as you should be about depreciation and other tax matters, read *Aggressive Tax Avoidance for Real Estate Investors* (see Sources & Resources for particulars).

• EXPENSES—Payroll Record

For each employee you hire, you will have to keep a Payroll Record. It's absolutely essential. Fortunately, it's a relatively simple form to use.

Once you have calculated the employee's various payroll deductions and have prepared the statement-of-earnings-and-deductions form to accompany each payroll check (see chapter 12), post those figures onto the Payroll Record, and then add to all that the employer's contribution to Social Security (shaded column). Refer to this form whenever you have to prepare monthly, quarterly, or annual reports for the government agencies involved.

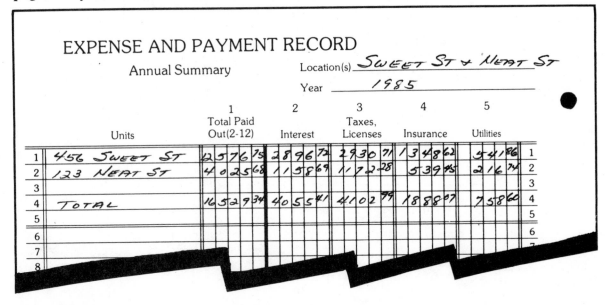

PAYROLL RECORD

Property: 456 SWEET ST
Employee: CHARLES GOODFOLKS
Social Security No.: 198-83-6509
Pay Rate: $5.00/HR
Exemptions: 2
☒ Married
☐ Single

	Period	Gross	Federal Withholding Tax	State Disability	Employee FICA	Employer FICA	State Withholding Tax	Other	Net	Ck No.	
1	1/01 - 1/15	55.00	Ø	.50	3.88		Ø		50.62	211	1
2	1/16 - 1/31	40.00	Ø	.36	2.82		Ø		36.82	220	2
3	2/01 - 2/15	50.00	Ø	.45	3.53		Ø		46.02	229	3
4	2/16 - 2/28	36.00	Ø	.32	2.47		Ø		32.21	235	4
5	3/01 - 3/15	65.00	Ø	.59	4.58		Ø		59.83	246	5
6	3/16 - 3/31	45.00	Ø	.41	3.17		Ø		41.42	259	6
7											7
8	1ST QTR	290.00	Ø	2.63	20.45		Ø		266.92		8
9	1ST QTR TAX DEP				20.45	20.45			40.90	261	9
10											

• SUMMARIES—Annual Summary of Expenses and Payments

The summaries section includes two different forms. The first one closely parallels the Expense and Payment Record and is solely for the purpose of gathering together the expenditures for several properties. If you have only one property, you would already have figured your expenditures for the year on the final Expense and Payment Record page, and you would not need to use this form.

EXPENSE AND PAYMENT RECORD

Annual Summary

Location(s): SWEET ST & NEAT ST
Year: 1985

	Units	1 Total Paid Out (2-12)	2 Interest	3 Taxes, Licenses	4 Insurance	5 Utilities	
1	456 SWEET ST	12576.75	2896.72	2930.71	1348.62	541.86	1
2	123 NEAT ST	4025.68	1158.69	1172.28	539.45	216.74	2
3							3
4	TOTAL	16529.34	4055.41	4102.99	1888.07	758.60	4
5							5
6							6
7							7
8							

The only difference between the regular Expense and Payment Record form and this Annual Summary of Expenses and Payments form is that "Unit(s)" takes the place of the first four columns, "Date," "How Paid," "To Whom Paid," and "For," and there's a thirteenth column for recording both regular and supplemental depreciation.

List each property's location on the form first and then record the total expenses just as you have calculated them on the final Expense and Payment Record sheets for each property. That accomplished, you will be prepared with the figures needed for the next form.

• SUMMARIES—Summary of Business and Statement of Income

The Summary of Business and Statement of Income form brings together all income and all expenses for a final reckoning. Use them monthly if you want to and you'll be exceedingly well informed about the financial status of your property. Though desirable, monthly summaries are hardly indispensible, however, and most landlords and landladies use them just once a year unless they're using a computer bookkeeping system such as the

Summary of Business and Statement of Income

Location(s) ___SWEET STREET___

Year/Month ___1985 / APRIL___

		Totals	
1			1
2			2
3	INCOME:		3
4	Rental	2314 00	4
5	Other	142 61	5
6	TOTAL INCOME	2456 61	6
7			7
8			8
9			9
10			10
11			11
12	EXPENSES & PAYMENTS		12
13	Interest	364 76	13
14	Taxes, Licenses	674 31	14
15	Insurance	286 54	15
16	Utilities	98 42	16
17	Services, Repairs, Maintenance	74 02	17
18	Merchandise, Supplies	63 41	18
19	Payroll	104 13	19
20	Miscellaneous Expenses	10 90	20
21	Depreciable	443 64	21
22	Mortgage Principal	336 27	22
23	Non-deductible	280 00	23
24			24
25			25
26	TOTAL EXPENSES & PAYMENTS	2736 40	26
27	less Non-deductible	280 00	27
28	TOTAL	2456 40	28

one shown in Chapter 20. It gives monthly and year-to-date totals automatically.

Whether you use this summary form on an annual or a monthly basis, you will make some important calculations using it. Here's where you subtract from your expense totals the depreciable items you paid for this year, the amounts credited to your loan principals, as well as your sundry non-deductibles (including impounds). And if you haven't done so already, here's where you have the opportunity to deduct as business expenses your telephone, the office space used in your home (use great discretion with this one; be prepared with proof), and your mileage (log your landlording trips for substantiation). When you have completed all of these calculations, you'll have a net expense figure ready for your income tax return.

What's more, when you take the difference between your total expenditures and your non-deductibles and you subtract this figure from your total income, you will know what your actual cash flow is, that is, what you actually took in minus what you actually paid out.

(Note that this cash flow figure includes as "expenses" what you paid out for both mortgage principal and depreciable items. Even though what you paid toward mortgage principal represents a kind of forced savings account and what you paid for depreciable items will be deducted for tax purposes over a number of years, you still had to pay out that money this year. What's left over for spending, saving, or investing after you've paid all your expenses is in one sense the true cash flow produced by the property. But it's not the same as the "cash flow" which has been referred to elsewhere in this book along with the other three ways to make money in the landlording business. If you want to calculate that cash flow, you don't include either the mortgage principal payments or the cost of the depreciable items. You include among the ordinary expenses only the amount of this year's depreciation on the depreciable items you paid for during this year and prior years. That's the classic way to calculate cash flow, but it results in an unreal figure, if you ask me. It's not really the money you get to pocket. Personally, I think the other figure is more meaningful. Use whichever one makes more sense to you.)

• LOANS/INSURANCE—Loan & Note Record

The Loan & Note Record form enables you to keep tabs on your loans, an activity some might say is akin to the miser's counting his stacks of gold eagles and silver dollars. It ain't necessarily so. Actually, this form provides you with information which is very useful when you're renegotiating a loan, when you're double-checking a lender's interest calculations, or when your payment book is lost in the mail. Everything's here, the

LOAN & NOTE RECORD   Page 3

Property: 456 - 464 SWEET ST., LITTLETOWN
Noteholder & Address: BIG BANK, P.O. BOX 678, LITTLETOWN
Loan Number: 01-4321   Original Loan: 60,000
Interest: 10%   Payment: $579.03   Due Date: 8/01/93

	Payment Date Paid / If Changed	Principal	Interest	Impounds & (Imp. Disb.)	Impound Balance	Principal Balance	
1	BAL FWD					38160.-	1
2	1/01	261.03	318.00			37898.97	2
3	2/01	263.20	315.83			37635.77	3
4	3/01	265.40	313.63			37370.37	4
5	4/01	267.61	311.42			37102.76	5
6	5/01		309.19			36837.79	6

original amount of the loan, the interest rate, payment, principal balance, etc., and filling it out takes just a moment after you receive your payment book back from the lender.

Come to think of it, filling out this record is kind of fun, too, because you can see the equity in your property gradually build up each time you fill another line with figures. Maybe misers do have more fun. Well, in this business you'd better take your fun when and where you can get it.

• LOANS/INSURANCE—Insurance Record

This last form may be used to keep track of your insurance policies. It's not an absolutely essential part of your records, and you won't get any jollies out of it, but you will find that having all of your insurance information in one place is surely convenient when you begin wondering how soon a policy's due or what coverage you still have on a certain property. Insurance policies themselves are not written to yield that kind of information quickly.

Insurance Record

Property 456 SWEET ST.

Company / Agent	Type of Policy	Policy Number	Limits	Premium	Expiration Date
• USA INSURANCE	APT OWNERS	FI-778-1101	215,000	$286.54	4/30/86
(AMOS BEER BARREL 555-1068)					
• UMBRELLA EARTHQUAKE		699837	165,000	$317.00	12/02/86
(JOE ROGER 557-11__)					

SOME LAST WORDS

Do your recordkeeping regularly at least once a month, and you'll find that it's practically tolerable.

Better still, get yourself a microcomputer and follow the suggestions in Chapter 20 for computerizing your operations. Even a home-grown computer bookkeeping system will save you lots of drudgery and time, and it should motivate you enough to keep on top of all your recordkeeping instead of sinking beneath it.

DOING TAXES

During the first two weeks of April every year, most adults seem to suffer from the same malady, the dreaded DT's. They wobble a little and complain a lot, and their eyes grow bug-eyed and red. They start imagining all sorts of devils and demons and beastly beasties, and it isn't until after the fifteenth of the month that the symptoms finally disappear, because not until then do they finish Doing Taxes.

Landlord and landlady, if you're among those seasonal sufferers, you should be ashamed of yourself! Income tax time is an especially good time for you, and you should enjoy the opportunity to snicker a little over your good fortune. Don't wait until April 15th to file your return. Do it as soon as you can, so you'll have your income tax refund check in hand when everyone else is suffering those dreaded DT's. Besides, you need that check by April to help pay your property taxes.

You get to snicker over your income taxes because at tax time you may take advantage of one of the more important ways to make money in landlording—depreciation.

Every year, little by little, you get to depreciate the value of the capital improvements on your property, and then you get to deduct this amount from your income. After you have enjoyed the depreciation deduction for a few years and you decide to sell the property, you'll have to pay income taxes all right, but you'll have to pay them on only a portion of the difference between the selling price and the depreciated value. This amount is known as a "capital gain" and much of it is tax free or subject to only a minimum tax.

For example, if you bought a used fourplex ten years ago for $40,000 and you depreciated it down to $25,000 over ten years (using the straight-line method and a useful life of 20 years), that means you saved paying income taxes on an average of $1,500 of your income every year, a total of $15,000. If you now sell the property for $100,000 (to learn about the impending tax consequences every time you plan to acquire or dispose of income property, spend a few bucks and consult an aggressive accountant or tax attorney), you have a capital gain of $75,000, the difference between the sales price and the depreciated value (frequently referred to as the "depreciable balance"), but you have to pay income taxes on only 40% of this capital gain, or $30,000. In other words, you keep all of $45,000 completely out of the tax collector's hands. It's nontaxable. Even if you're in the highest personal income tax bracket, the 50% bracket, your tax liability wouldn't exceed $15,000 on the entire $75,000 capital gain. Pretty neat, huh?

It's still better if you exchange your property. In most cases you pay no income taxes on your capital gains at all when you exchange. You may defer the payment of taxes until you finally do sell off your properties, or you may keep exchanging properties and keep avoiding the payment of taxes forever. When your heirs assume the ownership of your property, they do so at its then current value, not at its old basis or depreciable balance.

By exchanging, therefore, you avoid paying the capital gains tax while you are alive, and so do your heirs when they acquire it upon your death. It's mindboggling to think that you might be increasing your own net worth by leaps and bounds year after year and yet be liable for minimal income taxes, if any! Don't you wish you could retrieve all you've ever paid in income taxes and could use it for property acquisitions? By making the right investments, some people have been doing that all along, paying no taxes year after year. That's how they become millionaires.

Ah, but you say, "I've only got a fourplex, and I just want to know how to prepare the tax forms I need to submit with my income tax return. I can't be wasting my time dreaming about owning more property and becoming a millionaire. I have all I can handle right now. One place is plenty."

Okay, okay. Here's how to do your return, and here are some sample tax form sheets completed for Lester Landlord (he's no millionaire either), who has a duplex he bought in 1977, half of which he occupies himself, and a fiveplex he bought in 1983.

DOING YOUR OWN TAXES BY HAND AND CALCULATOR

Begin preparing your taxes by completing a "Depreciation Record" sheet (see Chapter 17) for each building and for the various depreciable expenditures you have made. Use the same form for all of them, but use one sheet for each building and one sheet for each classification of depreciable expenditures made for a particular building. For example, Lester should have one sheet for the new roof he put on his duplex in 1980 and another one for the new roof he put on his fiveplex in 1984. He should have one sheet for all the five-year items he bought for his duplex in 1985 and another sheet for all the five-year items he bought for his fiveplex in 1985. All of these *Depreciation Records* should remain in his three-hole recordkeeping binder for reference whenever it's time to do taxes.

Next comes the biggest job of all for procrastinators, completion of the annual summary sheets for all rental property held. These you may do manually with the forms provided in Chapter 17 or you may use your computer and a spreadsheet template like the one shown in Chapter 20. How you arrive at the summaries doesn't matter so long as they're accurate. Once you have completed these summaries, keep them close at hand. Together with the depreciation sheets, they comprise the primary source of data essential from here on.

Now make blank copies of tax forms E-3, D-1, and SD in the forms section of this book (these forms, by the way, could be made into computer spreadsheet templates as well), and using applicable information from your *Depreciation Records*, fill out D-1 and SD. Use D-1 for buildings only and SD for anything else depreciable, from furnaces to roofs. Also, list your non-ACRS and your ACRS items separately. Print "Non-ACRS" in

FORM E-3	RENTAL INCOME AND EXPENSE	YEAR 19 _85_

NAME(S) OF TAXPAYERS _LESTER LANDLORD_   **SOC. SEC. NUMBER** | 123 | 45 | 6789

PROPERTY LOCATION & DESCRIPTION

		GROSS INCOME
PROPERTY A	_123 NEAT ST._	3,495.60
PROPERTY B	_456-464 SWEET ST._	16,040.45
PROPERTY C		
PROPERTY D		
PROPERTY E		
PROPERTY F		
PROPERTY G		

Total Income (to Schedule E, line 3) **19,536.05**

EXPENSES

	A	B	C	D	E	F	G	TOTALS
Interest	1172.28	2930.71						
Taxes, Licenses	539.45	1341.62						
Insurance	216.74	541.86						
Utilities	169.08	422.69						
Service, Repairs, Maintenance	64.90	162.31						
Merchandise, Supplies	221.57	553.92						
Payroll	∅	∅						
Miscellaneous Expenses	49.88	124.72						
Other: Tel	∅	144.48						
Travel	∅	169.70						
Subtotal	2433.90							
% Bus. Use	50%							
Subtotals (Total to Schedule E)	1216.95	6349.01						7615.96
Depreciation (Form D-1)	553.12	2812.50						3365.62
Supp. Depreciation (Form SD)	48.33	715.18						763.51
Totals	1818.40	9926.69						11,745.09

*Sum of depreciation and supplemental depreciation totals (to Schedule E)   **4129.13**

large letters on the D-1 and SD forms for depreciable items acquired before 1981 and "ACRS" on the D-1 and SD forms for depreciable items acquired during 1981 and after.

Enter the appropriate property location and description information on form E-3 and post each building's depreciation for the year from form D-1 to E-3. Add all the supplemental depreciation as noted on SD for each property and post these figures onto E-3 in the space marked "Supp. Depreciation." Remember that all the supplemental depreciation for each building must be added together before it is posted.

After you post both regular and supplemental depreciaton for your properties onto E-3, enter the gross income as calculated on the *Expense and Payment Record Annual Summary*. Then post all the expenses from the summary sheet to E-3 and calculate the totals. Remember to add the two asterisked boxes and post their sum in the bottommost box on the form.

Using all of this information, you can easily fill out Form 1040, Schedule E. In Part I of Schedule E, simply write "see attached form E-3" across the columns. Check the notes in the parentheses on E-3 for posting locations and then post the totals from E-3 to the corresponding "Totals" lines of Schedule E. Now, add lines 18 and 19 on Schedule E and deduct their sum from line 3. Put the difference, be it positive or negative, on line 24 (parenthesize the number if it's negative), and combine that with whatever amount you put on line 25 (farm income) to get a total for line 26. Look at Parts II and III on Page 2 of Schedule E next and see whether they apply to you. Also at this time, write "see forms E-3 and SD" through the "Property A" section of Part V to advise the reviewer of your return where to look for your depreciation information. If the other parts on page 2 do apply to you, include their totals with your line 26 total in the summary under Part IV; if they don't, merely transfer the total on line 26 to Form 1040, line 18.

From this point on, just go ahead and finish your tax computations as you normally do, snickering as you go, and remember to attach forms E-3, D-1, and SD to Schedule E when you send in your return.

DOING YOUR OWN TAXES BY COMPUTER

What would you say if I told you there's a computer program available which automatically transfers the total on line 26, Schedule E, to line 18 on your 1040? What's more, it calculates your taxes any which way you want; it prints out the very forms you sign and submit to the IRS; and it won't let you forget to check a box you're supposed to check. What's that? Did you say you'd sell your shares in H. & R. Block? I would, too.

Well, there is such a program. It's called MacInTax™, and there's nothing else like it. It does all the above and a whole lot more (see Sources & Resources). It makes manual tax preparation seem like washboard laundering.

No longer do you have to concentrate so intently on making sure you do every calculation on your return correctly, that you post the total from one box on one form to the right box on another form, and that you are consistent with the names and social security numbers on every form you submit. No longer do you have to redo your return when you discover belatedly that you forgot to include the second payment you made on the property taxes for one of your rental houses. Add that figure into the expenses for that house, and MacInTax takes care of all the recalculations down the line.

MacInTax removes most of the grunt work from tax preparation and gives you the opportunity to analyze your return to see whether you might save on your taxes by readjusting your investments.

The only thing the program doesn't do is sign the return. You still have to do that.

FORM D-1	DEPRECIATION WORKSHEET						YEAR 19 85

NAME(S) OF TAXPAYERS **LESTER LANDLORD**   SOC. SEC. NUMBER **123 45 6789**

PROPERTY LOCATION & DESCRIPTION

PROPERTY A   123 NEAT ST.

PROPERTY B   456-464 SWEET ST.

PROPERTY C

PROPERTY D

PROPERTY E

PROPERTY F

PROPERTY G

	A	B	C	D	E	F	G	TOTALS
Date Acq'd or Conv. to Bus.	3/67	10/73						
New or Used	USED	USED						
Cost or Other Basis	29,500	75,000						
Land Value	7375	18,750						
Salvage Value	0	0						
20% 1st Year Deprec.	0	0						0
Deprec. Basis	22125	56,250						
Prior Deprec.	18,621.87	28,828.12						
Deprec. Balance	3,503.13	27,421.88						
Method of Deprec.	S.L.	S.L.						
Useful Life	20	20						
Full Year Deprec.	1106.25	2812.50						
% Year Held	100	100						
% Bus. Use	50	—						
Deprec. This Year	553.12	2812.50						3365.62

PAGE TOTAL   3365.62

⟨⟨ACRS⟩⟩

FORM SD	SUPPLEMENTAL DEPRECIATION	YEAR 19 85

NAME(S) OF TAXPAYERS	LESTER LANDLORD	SOC. SEC. NUMBER	123	45	6789

CAPITAL IMPROVEMENT LOCATION & DESCRIPTION

1   123 NEAT ST. — LAWNMOWER.

2   456-464 SWEET ST. - WATER HEATER

3   " " ' " - CARPETING, DRAPERIES, LINOLEUM

4

5

6

7

	1	2	3	4	5	6	7	TOTALS
Date Acq'd or Conv. to Bus.	2/81	6/81	9/84					
New or Used	NEW	NEW	NEW					
Cost or Other Basis	230.14	444.00	1683.55					
Salvage Value	0	0	0					
20% 1st Year Deprec.	0	0	0					N.A.
Deprec. Basis	230.14	444.00	1683.55					
Prior Deprec.	133.48	257.52	0					
Deprec. Balance	96.66	186.48	1683.55					
Method of Deprec.	ACRS	ACRS	ACRS					
Useful Life	5	5	5					
Full Year Deprec.	—	—	—					
% Year Held	—	—	—					
% Bus. Use	50	100	100					
Deprec. This Year	48.33	93.24	252.53					394.10

PAGE TOTAL   394.10

MacInTax sells for less than $100 (updates for succeeding years are about half the original cost) and runs only on the Apple Macintosh. It's such a good program that even though you have no intention of buying a Mac, you might want to think about buying the program anyway and giving it away to a friend who does have a Mac in exchange for computer time. Then both of you could use the program to do your returns.

Lacking a friend with a Mac, you could buy both the program and some computer time. Macs are available for rent from certain computer stores, especially those near college campuses.

Another way to enlist the aid of a computer, virtually any computer, for doing your taxes is to use an electronic spreadsheet program like Visicalc, Supercalc, Lotus, Multiplan, or Excel to create your own spreadsheets according to the patterns of the forms shown in this chapter. Once you have them set up to your liking, you can use them year after year with little alteration. They're not nearly as automated as MacInTax, but they are very useful.

SOME LAST WORDS

There are those naysayers you'll encounter in this world who will say you're a pig-headed fool for doing your own taxes. They'll say you should have a sorcerer in money matters do them for you, someone who's thoroughly experienced in doing income taxes for propertied folk, someone who knows all the latest loopholes applicable to your situation, and those naysayers may be right. It all depends on your ability and your inclination. Some people have the good sense to invest in rental property, but they lack the capacity to deal with numerical data and somewhat complicated instructions. People like that should leave their taxes to experts.

If you happen to be a landlord or landlady who possesses the ability and inclination to prepare your own taxes, however, do them yourself, by all means, but once you have finished with them, get a second opinion from a specialist by buying an hour or two of professional advice. You cannot possibly keep abreast of the volumes of current tax laws, and you could unknowingly be throwing money away by overlooking perfectly legitimate tax angles.

Whether you have your taxes prepared for you or whether you do them yourself, try to get a feel for the tax principles which affect your landlording business. Read about taxes in periodicals and jot down questions for your consultant. A capable professional will save you money and give you a tax education at the same time.

Whereas you may not be foolish for preparing your tax return yourself, you certainly would be foolish for submitting it to the tax collector without first reviewing it with someone who knows the subject intimately.

HOW WILL YOU KNOW WHEN YOU'RE A MILLIONAIRE?

You already know that there are four ways to make money in this business, but you won't know whether you're actually making money at any of them unless you sharpen your pencil or power up your computer and have a session with the numbers now and then. Naturally you only have to keep up with your regular bookkeeping to know whether you're getting any cash flow or equity buildup, and you only have to do your income tax return every year to know whether you're getting any tax shelter, but you won't know whether you're getting any appreciation and you won't know whether you're getting any closer to becoming a millionaire unless you complete a financial statement. It alone can tell you whether you've really "made it." It alone can tell you whether you're a pauper, a thousandaire, a millionaire, or a billionaire.

If you haven't been keeping track of your financial health with a financial statement, shame on you. It's one of the more agreeable undertakings in this entire business.

You're in good company if you don't have a clue what your financial health is, though. While being escorted around the newly opened Disneyland by Walt Disney, one foreign potentate, suitably impressed, remarked that Disney must be a very wealthy man, whereupon Disney replied, "I guess I am. They tell me I owe ten million dollars." He honestly had no idea what he was worth! He never realized he could walk into an automobile showroom and drive out in a snazzy little sportscar until he did just that on a whim sometime later. Fortunately for him, Walt Disney had a brother who kept track of the finances, and he had a banker, A.P. Giannini himself (founder of Bank of America), who kept an eye on the company's fortunes.

Lacking a devoted brother and an astute banker to look after your financial health, you're left to do the job yourself. Great! It's not something you ought to have somebody else do for you anyway. Nobody else is going to find the special pleasure in preparing your financial statement that you are. It's more fun than watching the World Series or the Super Bowl. It's kind of like participating in them. This really and truly is your life, your financial life. Indulge yourself. Do yours yourself.

What you may not realize is that you have probably been doing financial statements for years without even thinking much about them, certainly without enjoying them. That's right! Every time you've applied for a loan and filled out a loan application, you've actually made up a financial statement. That's mostly what loan applications are, you see. They're a picture of your financial health. They tell the lender how much you're worth and whether you have enough income to repay the loan. You haven't been enjoying them because you were forced into doing them. They were required "homework." Ugh!

Go on. Go to your files and get the last loan application form you filled out. See. You had to list your assets and your liabilities, your income and your expenses, and somewhere on that form you had to calculate what your net worth was at the time. That's

```
------------------------------------------------------------
            * * PERSONAL FINANCIAL STATEMENT * *
------------------------------------------------------------

LESTER & MARGARET LANDLORD
123 Neat Street, Littletown        (999) 557-4715

              B A L A N C E   S H E E T
                     ASSETS

CASH: Big Bank, Checking (0134-673209), Svngs (569-35355)    21,440
IRA's: Lester (Ferrell/Finch), Margaret (USA S & L)          12,000
PERSONAL RECEIVABLE:  Loan to brother-in-law                  4,356
BOAT: 1982 Bayliner 700                                       6,300
VEHICLES:  1984 Buick Regal                                   9,700
           1980 Ford Pickup                                   5,200
REAL ESTATE (see page 3)                                    415,400
Gotcha Mutual Funds                                           7,000
HOUSEHOLD GOODS                                              12,356
STAMP COLLECTION                                              1,525
                                                            -------
TOTAL ASSETS                                                495,277


                    LIABILITIES

Real Estate Indebtedness (see page 4)                       120,527
Personal Improvement Loan                                     3,500

                                                            -------
TOTAL LIABILITIES                                           124,027

NET WORTH (assets minus liabilities)                        371,250

       I N C O M E   &   E X P E N S E   S T A T E M E N T

Net Income for 1984
           Rental Properties (Depreciation Excluded)         17,779
           Interest                                           1,036
           Littletown School District                       24,751
           Hair Crafters                                     14,236
                                                            -------
Total Net Income                                             57,802

Personal Expenses (1985)
           Domicile                                          11,489
           Other                                             7,264
                                                            -------
Total Personal Expenses                                     18,753

Net Spendable Income (1985)                                 39,049

December 31, 1985
```

```
Lester & Margaret Landlord    PERSONAL FINANCIAL STATEMENT    page 2
------------------------------------------------------------------
                      GENERAL INFORMATION

Ages:   Lester 48;  Margaret 45

Soc. Sec. Nos. (Lester) 555-55-5555;  (Margaret) 999-99-9999

Martial Status:  Married, June 5, 1963

Credit Cards (entire balance of each paid monthly):
          Vista Charge             123-45678-910
          Seeres                   9876543-21
          Littletown Emporium      456-123-789
          Chevell Gas              58-5735-659

Insurance:
          Health:   Full Coverage, Frazier
          Life:     Good Hands Mutual (term)
          Auto:     USA Insurance
          Personal Umbrella Policy:  Totes Co., $2,000,000


Lester has been employed in the maintenance department of the Littletown
School District for 20 years.  Currently, he is the maintenance supervisor.
Margaret is a beauty operator at Hair Crafters, a beauty salon in Littletown.

We have never failed in business or compromised debts with our creditors.

There are no suits, judgments, or executions of attachments pending against
us.

We have recently drawn wills.

To the best of our knowledge, the information given in this Personal Financial
Statement is true and correct as of December 31, 1985.


Signed  _Lester Landlord_              _Margaret Landlord_
```

```
Lester & Margaret Landlord    PERSONAL FINANCIAL STATEMENT    Page 3
------------------------------------------------------------------
                     R E A L   E S T A T E

ADDRESS, TYPE, WHEN       TITLE IN NAME OF      COST    ESTIMATED
ACQUIRED                                                MKT VALUE


1) 123-125 Neat St.       Lester & Margaret Landlord  31,500   74,200
   Littletown, USA
   Duplex
   February, 1973

2) 256-264 Sweet St.      Lester & Margaret Landlord  75,000  211,200
   Littletown, USA
   Fiveplex
   October, 1973

3) 786 Treat Ave.         Lester & Margaret Landlord  27,500  130,000
   Littletown, USA
   House
   August, 1965
                                          -------------------------
                              TOTALS     130,000   415,400

Estimated market values of rental properties 1 and 2 were based on a Gross
Rent Multiplier of 8, using current rental income.


December 31, 1985
```

```
Lester & Margaret Landlord    PERSONAL FINANCIAL STATEMENT    Page 4
------------------------------------------------------------------
              R E A L   E S T A T E   M O R T G A G E S
   (numbers in first column refer to property numbers on page 3)

HELD BY               NOTE      ORIGINAL   PRESENT   MONTHLY  PAST
                      NUMBER    DEBT       BALANCE   PAYMENT  DUE

1) Sam Moneybags      7$$11     8,000      4,356     122      no
   590 Park Ave.
   Bigtown, USA

2) Big Bank           01-4321   60,000     38,160    579      no
   P.O. Box 678
   Littletown, USA

3) Little S & L       ZT38-21   80,000     78,011    799      no
   432 Main St.
   Middletown, USA
   (refinancing of property 3)
                              --------------------------------
               TOTALS         148,000     120,527   1,500

******************************************************************

              I N C O M E   P R O P E R T I E S '   A N N U A L
                    I N C O M E   A N D   E X P E N S E S

                         GROSS      GROSS      NET
PROPERTY                 INCOME*    EXP**      INCOME

123-125 Neat Street      9,279      3,428      5,851

256-264 Sweet Street     27,717     15,789     11,928
                       --------------------------------
               TOTALS    36,996     19,217     17,779

*Figures based on current income schedules.
**Debt service is included in these figures; depreciation is not.


December 31, 1985
```

all a financial statement is. It's two basic parts—a balance sheet, which is comprised of your assets and liabilities, and an income and expense statement, which is comprised of your annual income and your annual expenses. Subtract your liabilities from your assets and you can tell whether you're a millionaire. Subtract your annual expenses from your annual income and you can tell whether you're going to be a millionaire for long.

If you don't particularly care what you're worth or you just don't want to know, then continue doing what you've been doing all along. Complete your latest "financial statement" only when you're applying for a loan to buy some more rental property. Don't think much about it, and above all, don't enjoy doing it. In-betweentimes, go about your business oblivious of your financial health. Press your nose to the window of that Cadillac showroom and keep on dreaming of the day when you can afford to walk in there and buy one with cash.

Oh, come on! Let a little joy into your life while you can still enjoy it! There's more to life as a rental property owner than ignorance and dreams and temperamental toilets. There's no bliss in that. You don't really want to be oblivious of your financial health and spend your time dreaming about a rosy future while you're out fixing tenants' stinky toilets, do you?

That sort of plodding, mindless approach to one's lot in life may work for those people who juggle their income and expenses one week at a time and buy lottery tickets with their every spare dollar, but that's not a good approach for anyone who's regularly accumulating assets. That's not a good approach for you. It's chancey and unbusinesslike, and it's terribly shortsighted. You cannot make informed business decisions unless you are informed about your own affairs, and your financial statement is a large part of what makes you informed.

Convinced? Good, good, good! Go to the head of the class!

Now take a look at Lester Landlord's financial statement shown here. Notice how it's laid out. It's arranged something like an income tax return with the summary page first and all the supporting "schedules" following behind. Notice how clear and readable it is. He's included plenty of information to substantiate what appears on that all-important first page. You don't have to guess where his cash is or who his creditors are and how much he owes each one of them. You don't have to guess where his real estate is located or how he determined what his property is worth. He bares it all.

You can tell as much about him from looking over this one financial statement as you could from sifting though his trash can every week. Don't laugh. That's how archaeologists reconstruct early civilizations. Every arrow head, every copper coin, every lead pot, every jar fragment reveals something. Had early people kept financial statements like Lester's, archaeologists would have much cleaner jobs today.

Some types of information included in Lester's financial statement may seem unnecessary to include in your own statement, especially when you're making it up just to please yourself. That's true. They aren't necessary. But sometime you may want to use your financial statement to help you qualify for a loan. Then you'll wish you had included your credit card numbers, insurance particulars, employment history, and so on. Make that statement show a complete financial profile right from the start, and you'll have no regrets later.

GETTING STARTED

After looking over Lester's financial statement, you might be wondering where you'd start in making up your own. Well, you can start by surrounding yourself with whatever records you have of your investments. Beyond that, where you start is going to depend entirely on the number and variety of the items you have to list in the four information categories. Conceivably, you could start with the first page and end there, so long as you could explain fully what everything means, but that's not likely.

You can find out for sure by starting with the first page. Soon you'll see whether you need to add more pages to list all your stocks and bonds, all your cash accounts, all your real estate, all your indebtedness, all your partnerships, all your business endeavors, and so on. List them on separate pages only if they overflow the first page. You don't need a separate page to list just two or three stocks, but for ten or fifteen, you certainly do.

Let your financial statement grow naturally to accommodate whatever items you have to include. My own used to take three pages; now it takes nine. Whenever I update it, I start with the back page and work toward the front.

CALCULATING YOUR ASSETS

As far as your personal financial statement is concerned, your assets are your rental properties, your house, vehicles, stocks, bonds, mutual funds, cash accounts, precious metals, livestock, raw land, partnerships, business interests, personal goods, vested pensions, notes receivable, trusts, and the cash surrender value of your life insurance. They all have a value. They're all worth something if they have to be liquidated, perhaps what you have in them, perhaps less, perhaps a lot more.

You may think you have other assets, such as straight teeth and a trim figure, but they're figurative assets as opposed to hard, literal assets. Like family photo albums and bronzed baby shoes, they have personal value but no market value. They can't be converted into cash. No one would pay you anything for them, so don't list them here.

Establishing the value of all your assets which do have a market value does take some effort, especially since you as a real estate investor have certain assets which are bought and sold in what's called a disorderly market. Stocks, bonds, and commodities are sold in orderly markets. They're easy to set a value on. You can look up yesterday's sales transactions of AT&T common stock in your daily newspaper, for example, and you will know exactly what your 122 shares were worth as of the previous day, but there's no place where you can go to look up yesterday's value of your real estate holdings. You can't know exactly what they're worth unless they're actually sold in the disorderly real estate marketplace, and even then, those sales figures can be deceptive because of the eagerness of the principals and the details of the financing. Properties which sellers want to get rid of quickly are going to sell for less than their market value as are those which have high-cost financing and require a high down payment. Sales prices alone don't tell all there is to tell about market values. There are many, many factors involved.

Whenever possible, professional appraisers base their appraisals on several approaches, most commonly, replacement cost (how much the property improvements would cost to build today, plus a certain market value for the land), income (how much the property produces in income times an accepted multiplier which would depend upon property type and whether the income were net or gross), and comparable sales (how much other similar properties have sold for recently). Not one of these three can yield an exact figure. Each is merely an approximation, and the final appraisal figure is merely a composite of these approximations.

Property appraisal is part science, part art, part sorcery. Because of the large sums of money involved in real estate, professional appraisers must appear methodical and exhaustive in their research and competent in their skills. They must be able to give their clients some assurance that a property has a certain value so that a money transaction can take place which is fair to all concerned.

Appraisers spend a lot of effort trying to justify their conclusions. Their amply documented reports please their clients and necessitate hefty fees, but because there are so many elusive variables in real estate valuation, appraisers aren't going to come up with property values which are much more accurate than yours done quickly. When you're just trying to figure out approximately what your real estate is worth so you can include it among your assets, you needn't go to all the trouble they do. You're going to be reasonably accurate a large percentage of the time with just a cursory appraisal using any one of the approaches they use. You won't be right on the money, but then, neither would they.

When you're appraising your own property for your financial statement, try to detach yourself from it if you can. Think of yourself as a potential buyer of the property, not as the owner. Look the numbers over, perform some calculations, make a few telephone calls, close your eyes, and ask yourself what you'd pay for the property realistically yourself if it belonged to someone else. Be honest. Base your appraisal on something you can justify.

If it's multiple-family rental property you're appraising, some sort of income formula like a gross rent multiplier will do, whatever applies to your type of rental property. Don't go overboard and value it at ten or twelve times the annual gross income when it ought to be seven either. That will make a substantial difference in the property's value and will distort your balance sheet and resultant net worth. Find out what the commonly used yardstick is for your type of multiple-family rental property and use it.

If it's a single-family rental property or the house you occupy, comparable sales figures will do well enough. Remember that sales figures are different from listing figures. Sellers may list their properties at whatever price they want to list them for. They don't sell their properties at whatever price they want to sell them for. Properties sell for whatever a buyer is willing to pay and a seller is willing to take. You want sales figures to help you establish the fair market value of your property, and you can get them from a cooperative real estate agent or from county records.

The trouble is that even if you were able to peg the price of your property correctly and a buyer were to give you that price, you wouldn't net that amount in crisp cash money. You'd net something less. Commissions, prepayment penalties, transaction fees, transfer taxes, legal fees, and other costs would reduce the net proceeds you'd realize from the sale. Be that as it may, don't discount your holdings to reflect these costs. A lender might do that a second time upon looking at your figures, and you don't want it deducted twice. You don't need a liquidated cash value for your holdings anyway. All you need is a market value.

You might want to do a little research to learn the market value of your other assets, but that'll be easy compared to putting a value on your real estate, and it's not so consequential. Whether your Ford truck is worth $6,500 or $5,800 isn't going to make all that big a difference in your financial statement when you're dealing with thousands upon thousands of dollars.

In calculating your assets, be most concerned about remembering to include everything you own which is of any significant value. That is important.

CALCULATING YOUR LIABILITIES

Whereas your assets may take a little time to calculate, your liabilities won't, so long as there's a semblance of order in your recordkeeping system. The mortgages, loans, and credit card balances you owe are all liabilities, and they all have definite dollar figures attached. They're solid figures, but you must remember that they change every day because the interest on your liabilities is accruing daily, and the loan balances are changing as well. Also remember that there can be some liabilities you might overlook, such as taxes you owe but haven't paid yet, a mechanics lien on your property, an old school loan, or an interest-free loan from a trusting family member. They're liabilities, too. They detract from your assets. Estimate what they are and include them among your liabilities.

CALCULATING YOUR NET WORTH

Calculating your net worth is the easiest part of all. Simply subtract your liabilities from your assets and presto, you have the tell-tale figure. That's it. That's your momentous net worth figure.

If it's in seven figures or more, then you're a millionaire. Congratulations! You've arrived at an important milestone in your life! You've learned a lot from playing Monopoly all those years, haven't you? If it's in four, five, or even six figures, you're still a lowly thousandaire. Keep working. If it's in three figures and you've been landlording for more than a year, you'd better think about raising your rents and getting a copy of *How I*

Turned $1,000 into Six Million in Real Estate in My Spare Time. You need help!

MAKING UP YOUR INCOME AND EXPENSE STATEMENT

Once you've calculated your net worth, you're more than halfway to completing your financial statement, but you still need to indicate how much you're taking in and how much you're spending. You might have a net worth of $1 million and think that you've done pretty well for yourself until you find out that you actually have more money going out every month than you have coming in. Negative-cash-flow properties can put you in that position, you know. One or two such properties may not affect you very much if you have substantial earned income that you want to protect from taxes and if you feel that the properties have good upside potential, but more than that and you could begin to have problems. Watch those properties. They have been known to eat their owners out of houses and homes. Ask yourself why you're investing in negative-cash-flow properties anyway when you could be investing in something known as *income* property and still get the same tax advantages.

In order for you to be able to analyze each of your properties separately, you really should show the income and expenses for each one separately. Whether you include an extra sheet to show the income and expenses for each property as Lester did or whether you break them down on the final balance sheet doesn't matter. The important thing is that you show them separately so that you can judge the consequences of owning each one by itself.

MAKING FINANCIAL STATEMENTS USEFUL

Once you've completed your financial statement and you know how close you are to that magic millionaire status, what do you do with it? Frame it if you want to or file it away, but take the time to study it first. Ask yourself some questions about your investments. What's the equity in each of your properties yielding in terms of cash flow and appreciation? Is that yield plus the equity buildup and tax shelter good enough? Should you think about selling certain properties which have already yielded most of their potential? Should you be buying more properties? Are your properties worth all the trouble? At least you can think about such questions when you have some pertinent information readily available.

When you've analyzed your financial statement and feel you know it well, give a copy to that banker with whom you're trying to establish a working relationship. It'll be essential to your getting a line of credit when you want one.

Keep an extra copy on hand for those times when you have to fill out one of those many loan applications you always seem to be filling out as a real estate investor. Write "see attached financial statement" in the appropriate sections of the loan application, and you'll be able to fill them out in a hurry. You'll be able to enjoy loan applications. Fancy that!

Put one copy of your financial statement away with your will so your heirs will know what your assets are and where they're located.

Keep another copy with your rental property records so you'll be able to get to it easily when you need the information. And don't throw the outdated ones away. They enable you to track the progress of a given asset over a period of time, and they tell the interesting story of your financial growth.

For better and for worse, the information in your financial statement is not good forever. In fact, it's one of those things which is obsolete the day after you complete it, but you don't really need to complete a new one every week. Once every six months is often enough unless your financial status changes radically during the interval.

If you should ever be inclined to take back a note in lieu of cash for a property you sell, get a copy of the buyers' most recent financial statement. You need it more than you need a rental application from a tenant because you're giving the buyers greater control over the property than you're giving a tenant and you still have a stake in what they do with it. You need the buyers' financial statement even more than an institutional lender needs it because you're going to be in the most vulnerable position as a lender. You'll have the most junior mortgage. If there's a foreclosure, you'll be the last lender to be paid. You'll get the leavings. You need to know how these people pay their bills and whether they have enough income and assets to repay the loan in case the property can't pay its own way. Like any other lender, you don't want to have to foreclose. That's a messy and expensive procedure which you want to avoid if you can. By looking at the buyers' financial statement and verifying certain items, you could be avoiding a potential foreclosure. Other lenders request financial information on borrowers. You should, too. You have every right to request it.

SOME LAST WORDS

As of 1986, the United States has one million millionaires, almost one person in every 200. Seven out of ten of those millionaires made their fortunes by investing in real estate. If you're not one of them yet, be patient. You'll get there. By updating your financial statement regularly, at least you'll know when the big moment arrives.

USING A COMPUTER

If you have a computer system already, you may find in this chapter several ways to put that system to good use.

If you don't have a computer system, you may find in this chapter some reasons why you might want to consider buying one.

BUT, just as it's all right not to drink alcohol, it's all right not to have a computer. Really, it is! In spite of what those clever television ads say, or your neighbors, or your kid's teachers, or the media, or the computer store salesperson, there's nothing a computer can do for you that you can't also do by hand without one. It's just that a computer will save you time, and it will motivate you to do some of those things you don't do at all or don't do when you should because they're so tedious and take so much time.

Few Americans nowadays would exchange their Buick for a horse and buggy. They've gotten so used to the advantages of an automobile that getting along with anything less would be unthinkable. Automobiles have been around a long time, and their advantages are pretty obvious. In comparison, computers haven't been around long at all, and their advantages are not so obvious.

When the first edition of this book appeared back in 1975, which was the same year, believe it or not, that Volkswagen stopped selling "beetles" in the U.S. and America got out of Vietnam, there was no such thing as a personal computer. Computers were monstrosities which cost a small fortune to acquire, a small staff to operate, a small priesthood to program, a small utility company to power, and a small throne room to house. They weren't available to mere mortals. The closest thing to a personal computer then were word processing machines which cost around $15,000 apiece and were little more than the electronic typewriters of today.

In the years since then, a lot has happened in the computer world. Fortunes have been made and lost, companies have come and gone, reputations have waxed and waned, but now, if you want to, you can enjoy the fruits of many creative people's labors. We have available to us today some very powerful and inexpensive computers.

The trouble is that many people bought one of these very powerful and inexpensive computers as a status symbol, something they thought they had to have, without thinking much about what they were going to do with it. They bought a computer for as little as possible, fiddled with it awhile, played some games on it, tried filing some kitchen recipes, and then parked it in a closet when the novelty wore off and they couldn't think of anything else to do with it. There's a lot of computer power languishing in people's closets in the U.S.A. today. That's too bad because even inexpensive home computers have amazingly useful capabilities.

You, landlord and landlady, are fortunate. You don't have to think very hard about what to do with a computer. There's plenty you can do with one, from creating your own forms and letters to doing your own bookkeeping and financial statements. Like never before, you can keep track of your business with accuracy and currency, detail and ease.

Useful though they are in rental property management, computers still require a certain initial commitment in time and resources. With better computers and better programs to make them work, however, that commitment isn't so great anymore, but it's still a commitment you have to make unless you want to fill your own closet space with more flea market fodder.

If you're the type of person who balked at automating with a rubber stamp and a hand-cranked adding machine, then you definitely shouldn't computerize. Stick with what you've been doing all along. Don't change. If you're the type who hates to spend time or resources on anything without getting an immediate reward, then you shouldn't computerize either. But if you're the type who is always looking for better ways to do things, and you recognize that you're going to have to commit some time and some resources up-front to make your landlording business run better in the future, then you should definitely computerize. Not doing so wouldn't make any sense.

Am I a proselytizer of computers in landlording? You bet. As far as I'm concerned, they're as useful in landlording as they are in conquering space. As far as you are concerned, well, you have to make that decision.

Should you have fears and doubts, should you wonder what language some of these computer people are talking, should you wonder how a computer might help you, read on.

FEAR NOT

Computers are stupid. When tested, they always reveal I.Q.'s of either 0 or 1. You're much smarter than that. I know you are. Why, computers are so stupid, so obedient, that they will do exactly what you tell them to every time! Be honest now. When was the last time you got a tenant to do that? So why be afraid of computers?

Computers are passive, too. In spite of what you may have seen in some science-fiction movie or other, computers have never been known to attack people. Why be afraid of them? There's nothing they can do to hurt you or you to hurt them.

You can hit every key on a computer's keyboard all day long and in every conceivable combination, and you won't get executed, you won't start a nuclear war, you won't even break into American Airline's reservation system or a Citibank payroll file, not accidentally you won't. Have no fear of that.

Ordinary people did have something to fear about computers a few years ago. Computers were different then. They were primitive beasts, tough to tame, and requiring lots of patience, technical knowledge, concentration, and logical thinking to operate. They could do a lot of work for you, but often as not, they would make work for you.

All that's changed now. Now they come pretty much tame and housebroken, and you have nothing to fear from having them around. You don't have to spend all that much time learning how to use one anymore.

If you haven't taken a look at the new breed of computer yet, visit a computer store and take a look at the Apple Macintosh, the Atari 520ST, and the Commodore Amiga. They are truly different. You can be fearless around them.

If you're embarrassed to learn about computers because you don't want to appear ignorant around little kids who seem to grasp these new-fangled machines so quickly, don't be. Most kids and most adults, too, who are computer junkies, love to show others what they can make their computers do.

Remember that everybody's been a computer beginner sometime. If you don't know diddlysquat about computers right now, so what? Now's the time to get started, no matter how young you are.

BUT WHAT CAN I REALLY DO WITH ONE?

What can you, dear landlord or landlady, do with a computer? Let me count the ways.

You can handle your normal bookkeeping chores as usual, but you can also analyze your bookkeeping data with percentages and graphs. Are you spending too high a percentage of your expenses on insurance, for example? You can't tell that without using a computer unless you take a lot of extra time to produce comparable figures. A computer can do it in a jiffy.

You can analyze the occupancy rates of your various-sized dwellings so you can tell whether the rents for your one-bedroom units are two high or too low. If they're showing an 80% occupancy rate over the same period of time that your two-bedroom units are showing a 96% rate, your one-bedroom rents are probably too high and should be adjusted.

You can set up a year's budget in advance and try to stay within it. When have you ever been able to do that before?

You can analyze the potential of a property which is being offered for sale and calculate a fair offer. When you get ready to sell your own property, you can calculate a fair sales price based upon the detailed operational figures you've assembled.

You can complete your own tax return almost painlessly. You won't need an eraser or a calculator or any midnight oil to help you do it either.

You can produce loan payment schedules for all your loans, including those held by private parties and those with balloon payments.

You can make up your financial statements so you'll understand full well how you're doing in your financial dealings and know when you've joined the Millionaire Club of America.

You can create letters and forms as fast and as perfectly as the best legal secretary who's still using an ordinary typewriter.

You can keep track of your tenants' addresses, phone numbers, bank account numbers, birthdays, rents, deposits, payment history, and rent raise anniversaries.

That's pretty heady stuff, isn't it? Believe it or not, you can do all of these tasks with the various programs mentioned in this chapter.

A LITTLE JARGON

Before you start thinking much about using a computer in landlording, you really ought to learn a little computer jargon, "tech talk."

Jargon helps people engaged in similar pursuits to understand each other quickly. As a real estate investor, you unwittingly use jargon sometimes, and few outsiders would understand what in the world you're talking about. "COE" (close of escrow), "REO" (real estate owned by note holders who have foreclosed), "paper" (mortgages or notes in lieu of cash), "points" (percentage points charged by lenders), "boot" (difference between equities involved in a trade), "DOS" (due on sale), "recording" (placing a document on file with the county for all to see), "wrap" (a combination of existing loans and a new one carried by the seller), and "title" (evidence of someone's right to a property) are all terms which mean something special to you, something quite different from what they mean to the woman in the street.

Computer people use jargon just as you unwittingly do. They use so much of it that one group of computer people using one type of computer frequently cannot understand their colleagues who use another type of computer. Four words they all understand, though, are "hardware," "software," "programs," and "files," and you should understand what they mean, too. They're essential terms.

"Hardware" in computer jargon is anything you can see and touch. That includes the computer which sits on your desk, the keyboard your fingers tap on, the screen you look at, and the printer which gives you print on paper. "Hardware" also includes the disk drives which store information on disks much as videotape machines store information on tape cassettes.

"Software" in computer jargon is anything you can't see or touch. Computer programs which do word or number processing are "software" as are instructions which tell the computer where to find what's stored in its memory. Software is essential to making hardware work the way you want it to. A movie stored on a videocassette is software. You can't see it unless the videotape player interprets it for you and you can't touch it. Yet you know the movie is there. The same is true with computer software. You know that something is in there interpreting your commands. You just can't see it. That's the software at work.

"Programs" are software. You can't see them or touch them. They're stored on magnetic disks, magnetic tape, or on computer memory "chips." They are very detailed instructions written by computer programmers to make computers act in certain ways in response to your user commands. Programs turn computers into many different things. There are programs which make personal computers act like calculators, flight simulators, electronic typewriters, speed reading machines, filing cabinets, telephone dialers, and arcade machines.

"Files" are software, too. They're what you as a computer user save your own information in. When you write a letter on a computer or enter a whole series of numbers that you want to save, you save them on a magnetic disk as a file. Once they're on disk, you can retrieve them whenever you want.

Whew, that's enough jargon!

Let's take a look at how you might use computer programs for word processing, number handling, data management, and other specialized uses.

THE POWER PROGRAMS
• WORD PROCESSING

Word processing programs enable you to manipulate words easily and quickly. With a word processor, you may type away on your computer's keyboard to your imagination's content and then move those words around to suit your second thoughts.

The two primary uses for word processing in landlording are correspondence and forms creation.

Correspondence is obvious enough. Whenever you "feel a letter coming on," you sit down at your computer and bang away on the keyboard. When the letter looks pretty good to you on the screen, you tell the program to print it out on paper. If it looks good to you on paper, you send it. If it doesn't, you go back to the same letter on the computer screen and adjust it to your liking without having to type it all over again or use Liquid Paper as a cover up. You add a comma, move a paragraph, delete a word, change a name. Then you print the letter-perfect version. That done, you save the letter in a file on your computer's disk if you think you might want to use parts of that same letter again sometime, or else you go ahead and eliminate it. Stored as a word processing file on your disk, the letter does take up storage space, remember, so you must be sure you have the space.

Forms creation isn't that much different from correspondence. It involves either making up your own forms from scratch or using someone else's like those in this book. All you do is create a word processing file for each form you want to use. You may take a "standard" rental application and adapt it to fit your locale, the type of tenant you cater to, the type of dwelling you rent out, and the times. Or you may take a standard rental contract and do the same with it, adding or deleting a word here, a paragraph there, according to your needs. You can also personalize your agreements for yourself and each of your tenants if you want to, using the computer printout as your original agreement. That way, instead of numerous blanks on the form, there would be only the signature blanks. The computer would "fill in the blanks" with your name, your tenants' names, their address, and the other particulars.

• SPREADSHEET PROGRAMS

Spreadsheet programs are not the only computer programs which process numbers, but they're the easiest for ordinary people like us to learn and use. Usually the second business application program mastered by the personal computer user, they do more to justify the use of a computer by landlords and landladies than any other program because they're not only easy to learn and use, they're versatile and powerful as well.

What's surprising is that computer spreadsheet programs are such a recent innovation that even my unabridged edition of *The Random House Dictionary of the English Language*, which was copyrighted in 1971, lacks an entry for the word "spreadsheet." The first spreadsheet program available for microcomputers, VisiCalc®, appeared on the scene in the mid-70s and worked only on the Apple II computer. Because so many businesspeople recognized its potential right away, that program alone sold thousands upon thousands of Apple II's and helped to establish Apple Computer as a company. Today, computer spreadsheet programs run on almost every microcomputer, and they are so much improved that they make the first version of VisiCalc seem as crude as a crystal set.

A computer spreadsheet program consists of what resembles a large piece of graph paper inside the computer. Each one of the graph paper's little boxes, or "cells," as they're called, can be addressed individually with a column and row designation, like every good seat in a college football stadium. The very first cell in the upper left-hand corner of a spreadsheet is A1 ("A" is the column and "1" is the row). The very last one in the bottom right-hand corner, depending on how many cells your spreadsheet program has, might be BK63 ("BK" is the column and "63" is the row).

```
  : A ::B ::   D   ::    F    ::    G    :: H  ::  I  :: J :: K :: L  ::  M  ::  N  :
1:========================================================================================
2:SWEET STREET              INCOME AND EXPENSES - 1985              MONTH:   April
3:========================================================================================
4:Date  Ck #  Paid To       For            Total  Adver BnkChgs Car Exp Dues&Pub Garbage Insurance Interest
5:
6:4/2   267 Big Bank       1st mortgage    579.03                                          311.42
7: "    268 S. Moneybags   2nd mortgage    122.00                                           53.34
8:4/6   269 Littletown Hdwe misc hdwe acct  43.29
9:4/7   270 Saddleback Cnty prop taxes     674.31
10:4/10 271 MonopolyGas&Elec 3/1-4/1        57.12
11:4/11 272 K-Mart          shades
12:4/12 273 Lttletwn WtrDist April water
13: "   274 Monopoly Garbage April service
14:4/15 275 Phoenix Paints  paint & suppli
15: "   276 Lester Landlord personal draw
16: "   277 C. Goodfolks    payroll
17:4/19 278  "    "    P/C  plumbsupp,post
18:4/20 279 USA Insurance   annual premiu
19:4/21 280 LttltwnOffSupp  envelopes,copy
20:4/25 281 Seeres Co.      water heater
21:4/31 282 C. Goodfolks    payroll
22:
23:4/15     $$$ Mtn Oaks Hdwe  pnt brushes,sw
24:4/22     $$$ Littletown Rag ad to rent apt
25:
26:
27:
28:
29:
30:
31:
32:
33:
34:
35:
36:
37:
38:
39:
40:
41:
42:
43:
44:
45:
46:
47:
48:
49:
50:
51:
52:
53:
54:
55:
56:
```

```
   :  O  :: P :: Q :: R   :: S  ::  T   :: U  :: V   :: W  :: X  ::  Y  :: Z :: AA :: AB :
1:========================================================================================
2:SW ST 4/85 PAGE 2
3:========================================================================================
4:Lgl&Prof Lic/Perm OfcSupls Out Srvs Pstg&Frt Promo Repairs Sewer Supplies Txs,EPT Txs,Pay Txs,Prop Tel Trv&Ent
5:----------------------------------------------------------------------------------------
6:
7:
8:                                                   43.29
9:                                                                                    674.31
```

```
    : AC :: AD :: AE :: AF :: AG :: AH  ::      AI       :: AJ  :: AK  ::  AL   :: AM :
1:========================================================================================
2:SW ST 4/85 PAGE 3                                          S U M M A R Y
3:========================================================================================
4: Util  Wages  Deprec  Princpl Non-Ded           Prior Months This Month Yr to Date % of Totals
5:----------------------------------------------------------------------------------------
6:                267.61           Income:
7:                 68.66             Rental        6,398.00   2,314.00   8,712.00    94%
8:                                   Laundry         264.50      78.75     343.25     4%
9:                                   Storage/Garages 120.00      45.00     165.00     2%
10: 57.12                            Other             .00      18.86      18.86      0%
11:                                 ------------------------------------------------
12: 41.30                          TOTAL INCOME    6,782.50   2,456.61   9,239.11   100%
13:
14:                                 Expenses:
15:                       280.00     Advertising      12.50       6.50      19.00     0%
16:       56.32                      Bank Charges       .00        .00        .00     0%
17:                                   Car Expenses      .00        .00        .00     0%
18:                                   Dues&Publications .00        .00        .00     0%
19:                                   Garbage         90.00      22.50     112.50     2%
20:              443.64               Insurance         .00     286.54     286.54     5%
21:       47.81                       Interest      1,104.39     364.76   1,469.15    28%
22:                                   Lgl&Prof          .00        .00        .00     0%
23:                                   Licenses&Permits 10.00       .00      10.00     0%
24:                                   Office Supplies   1.37       5.47       6.84     0%
25:                                   Outside Services 35.00       .00      35.00     1%
26:                                   Postage&Freight   4.40       4.40       8.80     0%
27:                                   Promotion         .00        .00        .00     0%
28:                                   Repairs         74.39      51.52     125.91     2%
29:                                   Sewer             .00        .00        .00     0%
30:                                   Supplies       152.33      57.94     210.27     4%
31:                                   Taxes, EPT       7.40        .00       7.40     0%
32:                                   Taxes,Payroll    7.40        .00       7.40     0%
33:                                   Taxes,Property    .00     674.31     674.31    13%
34:                                   Telephone       25.67        .00      25.67     0%
35:                                   Trvl&Entrnmnt     .00        .00        .00     0%
36:                                   Utilities      193.73      98.42     292.15     6%
37:                                   Wages           97.60     104.13     201.73     4%
38:                                   Depreciable       .00     443.64     443.64     8%
39:                                   Mortgage Prncple 990.64    336.27   1,326.91    25%
40:                                   Non-Deductible  247.50     280.00     527.50
41:                                 ------------------------------------------------
42:                                 TOTAL          3,054.32   2,736.40   5,790.72
43:                                   Less Non-Deduct 247.50     280.00     527.50
44:                                 ------------------------------------------------
45:                                 TOTAL EXPENDITURES 2,806.82 2,456.40  5,263.22  100%
46:
47:                                 Income         6,782.50   2,456.61   9,239.11
48:                                   Less Expenditures 2,806.82 2,456.40 5,263.22
49:                                 ------------------------------------------------
50:                                 $ $ CASH FLOW $ $ 3,975.68     .21    3,975.89
51:
52:                                 Tot Exp less Debt
53:                                   Serv & Deprec as  .27       .68        .38
54:                                 % of Tot Income
55:                                 ------------------------------------------------
56:  98.42 104.13 443.64 336.27 280.00 Checkbook Balance         359.14
```

(page 2 lower-right fragment)
```
674.31    .00    .00
```

Now, if these carefully identified cells could hold only numbers, they'd be about as useful as a curl of calculator tape in a wastebasket. We'd have to keep asking ourselves what the numbers meant, just as we'd be asking ourselves what a radio sportscaster meant in announcing, "We have two great basketball scores for you, folks, 89 to 88 and 106 to 104!" You'd have to admit that those were great scores. But they wouldn't mean anything without team names next to them.

So, spreadsheet programs allow you to put words into their cells as well as numbers, but what's more important, they allow you to put formulas (add up what's in cells A6 through AH6 and put the sum in cell G6) and cell references (look at another cell and put its value or formula in this one) there, too. These formulas and cell references are what make spreadsheet programs versatile and powerful.

Because a blank computer spreadsheet has so many cells waiting to be filled and so many capabilities waiting to be used, it has tremendous potential in and of itself, but you won't see the true extent of that potential until you have filled some of those cells with a carefully prepared layout which you can use over and over again. These cell layouts are called "templates." They're actually nothing more than words and formulas which you use frequently.

Rather than begin each computer spreadsheet session with a blank spreadsheet and put into it the same words and formulas you've used before and know you'll use again, you use a template, one you make up yourself or one you buy from someone else (ExPress sells them; see Sources & Resources).

Except for one essential difference, a spreadsheet template is much like any of the bookkeeping forms in this book. The big difference is that the spreadsheet template has a "calculator" built right into it and that this calculator performs its mathematical calculations automatically.

Were you manually posting a series of numbers on a paper bookkeeping form, you'd first have to enter the numbers on the form and then you'd have to run a calculator tape to total them. You'd be entering every number twice and doubling your odds for making errors. Using a spreadsheet program and a template, you'd be entering the numbers only once. The built-in calculator would take over from there, so you'd have fewer opportunities to make mistakes.

Is it any wonder, then, that accounting firms today, which have to be extremely accurate in their calculations, wouldn't be without their personal computers, spreadsheet programs, and templates?

You could create all sorts of these templates for yourself if you wanted to. Lester Landlord's financial statement in the previous chapter was made with one. You could make up something similar without too much trouble. And you could make up others for loan tables, property analyses, tax schedules, bookkeeping, or anything else which involves numbers, too.

The three-page expense-and-payments-record template shown here is a good example of a useful template which you could use with most any spreadsheet program. This one happens to have been prepared using SuperCalc™. It is printed here with number-and-letter borders so you can identify each individual cell. It also includes a month's data so you can see what it looks like when it's in use.

To create this template yourself, you'd enter into your spreadsheet program what appears in the five-column listing of cell contents. Doing so is not as hard as it may first appear because many of the cell entries are repeated with slight modifications. Enter one of them, and command your spreadsheet genie to replicate that one in other cells. G56, for example, is replicated with adjustments in all the cells from H56 through AG56.

```
SuperCalc                               AI9    = "  Storage            AM22    = AL22/AL45
=                                       AL9    = SUM(AJ9:AK9)         G23     = SUM(H23:AG23)
A1      = '=                            AM9    = AL9/AL12             AI23    = "  Licenses&Permits
A2      = "PROPERTY NAME                G10    = SUM(H10:AG10)        AK23    = P56
F2      = "INCOME AND EXPENSES - YEAR   AI10   = "  Other             AL23    = SUM(AJ23:AK23)
I2      = "MONTH:                       AL10   = SUM(AJ10:AK10)       AM23    = AL23/AL45
O2      = "PROP NAME/MONTH/YEAR/PAGE 2  AM10   = AL10/AL12            G24     = SUM(H24:AG24)
AC2     = "PROP NAME/MONTH/YEAR/PAGE 3  G11    = SUM(H11:AG11)        AI24    = "  Office Supplies
AJ2     = "       S U M M A R Y         AI11   = '-                   AK24    = Q56
A3      = '=                            G12    = SUM(H12:AG12)        AL24    = SUM(AJ24:AK24)
A4 TL   = "Date                         AI12   = "TOTAL INCOME        AM24    = AL24/AL45
B4      = "Ck #                         AJ12   = SUM(AJ7:AJ10)        G25     = SUM(H25:AG25)
D4 TL   = "Paid To                      AK12   = SUM(AK7:AK10)        AI25    = "  Outside Services
F4 TL   = "For                          AL12   = SUM(AL7:AL10)        AK25    = R56
G4      = "Total                        AM12   = AL12/AL12            AL25    = SUM(AJ25:AK25)
H4 TR   = "Adver                        G13    = SUM(H13:AG13)        AM25    = AL25/AL45
I4      = " BnkChgs                     G14    = SUM(H14:AG14)        G26     = SUM(H26:AG26)
J4      = "Car Exp                      AI14   = "Expenses:           AI26    = "  Postage&Freight
K4      = "Dues&Pub                     G15    = SUM(H15:AG15)        AK26    = S56
L4      = "Garbage                      AI15   = "  Advertising       AL26    = SUM(AJ26:AK26)
M4      = "Insurance                    AK15   = H56                  AM26    = AL26/AL45
N4      = "Interest                     AL15   = SUM(AJ15:AK15)       G27     = SUM(H27:AG27)
O4      = "Lgl&Prof                     AM15   = AL15/AL45            AI27    = "  Promotion
P4      = "Lic/Perm                     G16    = SUM(H16:AG16)        AK27    = T56
Q4      = "OfcSupls                     AI16   = "  Bank Charges      AL27    = SUM(AJ27:AK27)
R4      = "Out Srvs                     AK16   = I56                  AM27    = AL27/AL45
S4      = "Pstg&Frt                     AL16   = SUM(AJ16:AK16)       G28     = SUM(H28:AG28)
T4      = " Promo                       AM16   = AL16/AL45            AI28    = "  Repairs
U4      = "Repairs                      G17    = SUM(H17:AG17)        AK28    = U56
V4      = " Sewer                       AI17   = "  Car Expenses      AL28    = SUM(AJ28:AK28)
W4      = "Supplies                     AK17   = J56                  AM28    = AL28/AL45
X4      = "Txs,EPT                      AL17   = SUM(AJ17:AK17)       B29     =
Y4      = "Txs,Pay                      AM17   = AL17/AL45            G29     = SUM(H29:AG29)
Z4      = "Txs,Prop                     G18    = SUM(H18:AG18)        AI29    = "  Sewer
AA4     = "  Tel                        AI18   = "  Dues&Publications  AK29    = V56
AB4     = "Trv&Ent                      AK18   = K56                  AL29    = SUM(AJ29:AK29)
AC4     = "  Util                       AL18   = SUM(AJ18:AK18)       AM29    = AL29/AL45
AD4     = "  Wages                      AM18   = AL18/AL45            G30     = SUM(H30:AG30)
AE4     = "Deprec                       G19    = SUM(H19:AG19)        AI30    = "  Supplies
AF4     = "Princpl                      AI19   = "  Garbage           AK30    = W56
AG4     = "Non-Ded                      AK19   = L56                  AL30    = SUM(AJ30:AK30)
AJ4     = "Prior Months                 AL19   = SUM(AJ19:AK19)       AM30    = AL30/AL45
AK4     = " This Month                  AM19   = AL19/AL45            G31     = SUM(H31:AG31)
AL4     = "Yr to Date                   G20    = SUM(H20:AG20)        AI31    = "  Taxes, EPT
AM4     = "% of Totals                  AI20   = "  Insurance         AK31    = X56
A5      = '-                            AK20   = M56                  AL31    = SUM(AJ31:AK31)
G6      = SUM(H6:AG6)                    AL20   = SUM(AJ20:AK20)       AM31    = AL31/AL45
AI6     = "Income:                      AM20   = AL20/AL45            G32     = SUM(H32:AG32)
G7      = SUM(H7:AG7)                    G21    = SUM(H21:AG21)        AI32    = "  Taxes,Payroll
AI7     = "  Rental                     AI21   = "  Interest          AK32    = Y56
AL7     = SUM(AJ7:AK7)                   AK21   = N56                  AL32    = SUM(AJ32:AK32)
AM7     = AL7/AL12                       AL21   = SUM(AJ21:AK21)       AM32    = AL32/AL45
G8      = SUM(H8:AG8)                    AM21   = AL21/AL45            G33     = SUM(H33:AG33)
AI8     = "  Laundry                     G22    = SUM(H22:AG22)        AI33    = "  Taxes,Property
AL8     = SUM(AJ8:AK8)                   AI22   = "  Lgl&Prof          AK33    = Z56
AM8     = AL8/AL12                       AK22   = O56                  AL33    = SUM(AJ33:AK33)
G9      = SUM(H9:AG9)                    AL22   = SUM(AJ22:AK22)       AM33    = AL33/AL45
```

```
G34       = SUM(H34:AG34)              AJ47        = AJ12
AI34      = " Telephone               AK47        = AK12
AK34      = AA56                       AL47        = AL12
AL34      = SUM(AJ34:AK34)             G48        = SUM(H48:AG48)
AM34      = AL34/AL45                  AI48        = " Less Expenditures
G35       = SUM(H35:AG35)              AJ48        = AJ45
AI35      = " Trvl&Entrnmnt            AK48        = AK45
AK35      = AB56                       AL48        = AL45
AL35      = SUM(AJ35:AK35)             G49        = SUM(H49:AG49)
AM35      = AL35/AL45                  AI49        = '-
G36       = SUM(H36:AG36)              G50        = SUM(H50:AG50)
AI36      = " Utilities                AI50        = "# # CASH FLOW # #
AK36      = AC56                       AJ50        = AJ47-AJ48
AL36      = SUM(AJ36:AK36)             AK50        = AK47-AK48
AM36      = AL36/AL45                  AL50        = AL47-AL48
G37       = SUM(H37:AG37)              G51        = SUM(H51:AG51)
AI37      = " Wages                    AI51        = '-
AK37      = AD56                       G52        = SUM(H52:AG52)
AL37      = SUM(AJ37:AK37)             AI52        = "Tot Exp less Debt
AM37      = AL37/AL45                  G53        = SUM(H53:AG53)
G38       = SUM(H38:AG38)              AI53        = " Serv & Deprec as
AI38      = " Depreciable              AJ53 1      = (AJ45-(AJ38+AJ39))/AJ12
AK38      = AE56                       AK53 1      = (AK45-(AK38+AK39))/AK12
AL38      = SUM(AJ38:AK38)             AL53 1      = (AL45-(AL38+AL39))/AL12
AM38      = AL38/AL45                  G54        = SUM(H54:AG54)
G39       = SUM(H39:AG39)              AI54        = " % of Tot Income
AI39      = " Mortgage Prncple         A55        = '-
AK39      = AF56                       D56        = "THIS MONTH'S TOTALS
AL39      = SUM(AJ39:AK39)             G56        = SUM(G6:G54)
AM39      = AL39/AL45                  H56        = SUM(H6:H54)
G40       = SUM(H40:AG40)              I56        = SUM(I6:I54)
AI40      = " Non-Deductible           J56        = SUM(J6:J54)
AK40      = AG56                        K56        = SUM(K6:K54)
AL40      = SUM(AJ40:AK40)             L56        = SUM(L6:L54)
G41       = SUM(H41:AG41)              M56        = SUM(M6:M54)
AI41      = '-                         N56        = SUM(N6:N54)
G42       = SUM(H42:AG42)              O56        = SUM(O6:O54)
AI42      = "TOTAL                     P56        = SUM(P6:P54)
AJ42      = SUM(AJ15:AJ40)             Q56        = SUM(Q6:Q54)
AK42      = SUM(AK15:AK40)             R56        = SUM(R6:R54)
AL42      = SUM(AL15:AL40)             S56        = SUM(S6:S54)
G43       = SUM(H43:AG43)              T56        = SUM(T6:T54)
AI43      = " Less Non-Deduct          U56        = SUM(U6:U54)
AJ43      = AJ40                       V56        = SUM(V6:V54)
AK43      = AK40                       W56        = SUM(W6:W54)
AL43      = AL40                       X56        = SUM(X6:X54)
G44       = SUM(H44:AG44)              Y56        = SUM(Y6:Y54)
AI44      = '-                         Z56        = SUM(Z6:Z54)
G45       = SUM(H45:AG45)              AA56        = SUM(AA6:AA54)
AI45      = "TOTAL EXPENDITURES        AB56        = SUM(AB6:AB54)
AJ45      = AJ42-AJ43                  AC56        = SUM(AC6:AC54)
AK45      = AK42-AK43                  AD56        = SUM(AD6:AD54)
AL45      = AL42-AL43                  AE56        = SUM(AE6:AE54)
AM45      = AL45/AL45                  AF56        = SUM(AF6:AF54)
G46       = SUM(H46:AG46)              AG56        = SUM(AG6:AG54)
G47       = SUM(H47:AG47)              AI56        = "Checkbook Balance
AI47      = "Income                    AK56        = 0000
```

Once you set up an expense and payment record template like this one, you don't have to do it again. That's the beauty of it. All you do after that is call up the template. Then you start with cell A6 and enter the date, the check number, the payee, and a description of the expense or payment item itself; you select the column heading which best describes the item you're posting and enter the dollar amount there. When you've done that for all the month's entries, the spreadsheet program will insert the totals for each line into column "G," total the columns, and place these column totals into the proper positions for the cumulative summary over in the "This Month" column (AK), all automatically.

But wait, there are several more steps you need to take to get full advantage of the really important information the template can provide for you. After you've posted all expenditure entries as outlined, enter the income for the current month in cells AK7 through AK10. Then you load the "Year to Date" column from the previous month's spreadsheet into the "Prior Months" column (AJ) on this month's spreadsheet, and the program will figure everything else out for you, right down to cash flow and percentages. That's what I call useful information, easily produced!

I would like to caution you here to examine closely every spreadsheet template you create (once you've created a template and are using it, you needn't worry much about entry errors because they'll be noticeable). A simple formula error in one cell will be magnified whenever that formula affects any other cell. The error will just keep being repeated. Neither the computer nor the program knows any better. If, for example, you inadvertently tell the program to put the sum of every cell from H7 through H54 into cell H56, when you meant to include cell H6, too, you're going to have a problem. The problem may not surface for a while if you seldom enter a number in cell H6, and even when you do enter a number in H6, you may not notice what's wrong in H56. There won't be any bells blowing or error messages appearing on your viewing screen. The error will just creep in quietly, on little rat feet.

If that ever happens, you'll know why computer people are so mindful of the phrase, "Garbage in, garbage out!" Do be careful. Spreadsheets are powerful, but they're also unforgiving.

• DATA BASE MANAGEMENT PROGRAMS

Data base management programs are essentially filing programs but with math functions added. Your telephone book is a large database, and all the names in it are filed alphabetically according to last names. If you wanted a list of all the people who have a certain telephone prefix or live on a certain street, you'd have to sit down and laboriously make a list of them. Ah, but if you had your whole telephone book entered into a data base management program, all you'd have to do to get a list of the people who live on Tewkesbury Street and have a 555 prefix is ask for it. The program would then sort through everyone looking for those two things in combination and it would print you a list.

Data base management programs are powerful, but they have been difficult to master in the past. Without attending a weekend seminar or pouring over some fairly technical material and learning some cryptic commands, you couldn't become proficient in using most data base management programs.

Fortunately, the newer data base management programs like Helix™ (see Sources & Resources) are much easier to learn and use, and they're far more versatile. With Helix, you as a non-programmer could design an entire recordkeeping system to keep track of just about everything for your rental properties. Ultimately, it would be even easier to use on a monthly basis than a spreadsheet template, but it would take more time to design.

• CANNED PROGRAMS

So-called "canned programs" are different from word processing, spreadsheet, and data base management programs. Canned programs are not nearly so flexible as the others. They are not written to be flexible; they're written to perform specific tasks. In that, they might be said to resemble the combination of a spreadsheet program *and* a particular spreadsheet template. They do one thing and they should do it well because they can't be modified to do anything else.

An excellent example of a canned program is MacInTax, which was mentioned in Chapter 18. It's easy to master, and it does a great deal with a minimum amount of input from you.

There are, however, a lot of canned business programs on the market which are, quite simply, terrible because they take a long time to learn or because they don't do very much of what you want them to. Buyer of canned programs, beware.

Be wary, by all means, of the program which is sold as the complete property management software package. First, they're not going to be cheap. Second, they're not going to do all that you want them to do. And third, they're going to be difficult or impossible to change. They're set up one way and that's it.

If you are inclined to purchase any canned program for more than $200, make arrangements to try it out first before you buy. I have one which cost over $2,000 sitting on a shelf. It didn't work out for me, and I couldn't get my money back when I discovered that it wouldn't. That expensive lesson from Hard Knocks College you needn't learn the expensive way.

GENERAL RECOMMENDATIONS

• Read hardware and software reviews in *Consumer Reports*, *Infoworld*, and the *Whole Earth Review* before you buy. These three periodicals (see Sources & Resources) publish reasonably unbiased reviews of the computer items they test.

• Try to find someone who's using the hardware or software you're interested in acquiring and ask them how they like it. For contacts, call your local rental property owners' association, your area's high school or college computer department or attend a meeting of a local computer club.

• Try a computer club. They're great support groups where you can find all kinds of help. You're welcome whether you own a computer or merely have an interest in using one. Some clubs are for people who happen to live in a particular geographic area and want to get together to talk computers. Some are for people who have one specific type of computer or computer operating system (like IBM-PC compatibles, Apple Macintosh, or CPM). Some are for people who are using a particular type of software (Lotus 1-2-3®, Wordstar®, or dBase®). And some are for people who have similar business uses for their computers (real estate appraisers or lawyers).

• Do not buy any piece of computer hardware or software until you can see an immediate need for it. There's not one computer or computer-related purchase I have ever made, whether it's been on sale or not when I bought it, which I couldn't buy today for less money than what I originally paid for it. Because you have to spend some time learning how to use each new piece of software for your computer, buying a whole batch of software which you can't use right away is foolish. By the time you get around to using all that you bought, there will be newer, improved versions available, and you'll have to pay extra for the updates.

• Do not overlook public-domain software (free to everybody) and what's called shareware (software intended for free distribution among users who are under no obligation to pay for it unless they find it useful). You may obtain this software through user groups or over the telephone from computer bulletin boards or information services like CompuServe. (You might wonder why anyone would make software available for little or nothing. Here's why. Writing computer programs is one thing. Writing extensive documentation, packaging the program, marketing it, and supporting it are something else again. Some programmers like to write programs but hate to write documentation. They're similar to those rental property owners who like to buy property but hate to manage it. These programmers consider themselves non-commercial types and would rather make their work available for little or nothing than either put themselves at the mercy of software publishers or not make their software available to the public at all.)

• Although the biggest complaint computer owners have is that they bought too early, don't wait for that right moment to buy the right computer at the right price. That time will simply never come.

• Do not buy any hardware, new or used, unless you know where you can have it repaired. Although it requires repair much too seldom to justify a maintenance contract, it sometimes does require repair, and when it does, you should know where to take it.

• To avoid many frustrations, buy a hardware configuration with these *minimums*: a typewriter-like keyboard with the keys located where you're used to finding them, a clear monitor with sharp definition, 64K of random-access memory (RAM) with an 8-bit system (CPM and Apple II systems), 256K with a 16-bit system (IBM-PC-compatible systems), and 512K with a 32-bit system (Apple Macintosh, Atari 520ST, and Commodore Amiga systems), one disk drive (preferably two), and a printer.

• Consider buying a used computer. Even the newer computer models appear for sale used, sold presumably by those who have to try the latest of everything without thinking about how they're going to use it. Used computers are available through your daily newspaper's classified ads, through computer flea markets, and through ads in a tabloid called *Computer Shopper*, which is available at many computer stores. A used computer is much less expensive than new equipment, and the seller usually throws in some disks, accessories, and software at no extra charge. Because of software piracy (unauthorized copying), so-called "used" software doesn't have much market value. Yet, new software costs plenty if you have to go out and buy it. Not only do you generally get valuable software for nothing with a used machine, but you get the computer hardware for much less than its new cost.

• Do not buy any used computer which lacks the manufacturer's serial number. Serial numbers on computer equipment are printed on adhesive labels which get peeled off when the equipment changes hands illegitimately. If you can't find a serial number on the equipment, it's probably stolen, and you'll have to do some mighty fast talking whenever you take it in for repair. You may have to do that fast talking down at the police station, and you may even have your computer equipment confiscated as stolen property if you're not careful. The first thing a computer repairer looks for is that serial number, so it should be one of the first things you look for when you're contemplating the purchase of a used system; no serial number, no purchase.

• To foil those who traffic in stolen equipment, engrave the serial number, your name, and your driver's license number on the chassis and case of every separate piece of computer equipment you own.

• If you already have a computer, so long as it can run a word processing program and a spreadsheet program and so long as you feel comfortable with it, use it. Don't run out and buy something else which is new and improved.

• Check your homeowners' insurance policy to make sure it specifically includes your personal computer. Some don't. If your insurance agent doesn't write computer insurance, ask other computer owners who writes theirs.

• Always "back up" your work, that is, make duplicate copies of it on another disk. Power outages, magnetic fields, defective disks, operator error, disk drive problems, software worms, static electricity, and coffee spills all conspire now and then to cause you to lose the work which you spent hours doing. The loony bins are full of people who didn't back up their work. Don't join them.

SOME LAST WORDS

Someday there will be computers available which will repair leaky roofs, collect the rents, do all your bookkeeping chores, discipline your tenants, draw your bathwater, and read you bedtime stories. While you're waiting for that day to arrive, consider using a computer to assist you in handling some of your more mundane landlording chores. That kind of computer and the programs to run it are available right now, today.

FORMS

The forms in this section have been introduced in the text, all, that is, except the bulk of the rent reminders (only two of the twelve reminders appeared in the text). The forms are all included here so you may reproduce them on any copier according to your needs.* If you do plan to copy them, keep them clean and free of marks. These are your originals, remember, and any marks on them will show up on your copies.

All told, there are five forms categories in this section:

1) Tenants
2) Rent Reminders and Notices
3) Employees
4) Records
5) Taxes

A title page precedes each category and lists the forms which follow, as well as where they were introduced in the text.

To assist you in finding the blank forms you seek, we put small page numbers in the upper corners. When you go to copy these forms, either white-out the page numbers, cut them off, or fold the corner of the page over so the number will not show up on your copies.

*The author hereby grants permission to the purchaser of this book to copy any or all of these forms for personal use. Their reproduction for sale or distribution shall constitute an infringement of copyright.

The author assumes no responsibility for the legality or currency of these forms. Before using them, check with your local housing authorities, your local rental property owners' association, and/or an attorney knowledgeable about real estate law to determine whether they are appropriate for your use.

TENANTS

Rental Application

for (address)_____

	Home	Work
	Phone	Phone

Name_____Phone_____Phone_____

Social Security No._____Driver's License No._____

Present Address_____
How long at   Reason for
this address?_____ Rent $_____ moving_____

Owner/Manager_____Phone_____

Previous Address_____
How long at   Reason for
this address?_____ Rent $_____ moving_____

Owner/Manager_____Phone_____

Name and relationship of every person to live with you (include ages of minor children)

_____

Any pets?_____ Describe_____ Waterbed?_____
Present
Occupation_____ Employer_____ Phone_____
How long with
this employer?_____ Supervisor_____ Phone_____
Previous
Occupation_____ Employer_____ Phone_____
How long with
this employer?_____ Supervisor_____ Phone_____

Current Gross Income Per Month (before deductions) $_____

List sources of income (other than present employment listed above)_____

_____

Savings
Account: Bank_____ Branch_____ Acct. No._____
Checking
Account: Bank_____ Branch_____ Acct. No._____

Major Credit Card_____ Acct. No._____

Credit		Balance	Monthly
Reference_____	Acct. No._____	Owed_____	Payment_____
Credit		Balance	Monthly
Reference_____	Acct. No._____	Owed_____	Payment_____

Have you ever filed bankruptcy?_____ Have you ever been evicted?_____
Vehicle(s)
Make(s)_____ Model(s)_____ Year(s)_____ License(s)_____
Personal
Reference_____ Address_____ Phone_____
Contact
in Emergency_____ Address_____ Phone_____

I declare that the statements above are true and correct, and I hereby authorize
verification of references given and a credit check.

Date_____ Signed_____

Rental Agreement

Dated_____

Agreement between_____, Owners, and
_____, Tenants, for a dwelling located at
_____.
Tenants agree to rent this dwelling on a month-to-month basis for $_____ per
month, payable in advance on the _____ day of every calendar month to Owners or
their Agent,_____. When rent is paid on or before the
_____ day of the calendar month, Tenants may take a $_____ discount.
   The first month's rent for this dwelling is $_____.
   The security/cleaning deposit on this dwelling is $_____. It is refundable
if Tenants leave the dwelling reasonably clean and undamaged.
   A deposit of $_____ for _____ keys will be refunded after the keys have
been returned.
   Tenants will give _____ days' notice in writing before they move and will
be responsible for paying rent through the end of this notice period or until
another tenant approved by the Owners has moved in, whichever comes first.
   Owners will refund all deposits due within _____ days after Tenants have
moved out completely and returned their keys.
   Only the following persons and pets are to live in this dwelling:

_____
Without Owners' prior written permission, no other persons may live there, and
no other pets may stay there, even temporarily. It may not be sublet or used for
business purposes.
   Use of the following is included in the rent:_____
_____
   Remarks:_____
_____
   Tenants agree to the following:
1) to keep yards and garbage areas clean.
2) to keep from making loud noises and disturbances and to play music and
   broadcast programs at all times so as not to disturb other people's peace
   and quiet.
3) not to paint or alter their dwelling without first getting Owners' written
   permission.
4) to park their motor vehicle in assigned space and to keep that space clean
   of oil drippings.
5) not to repair their motor vehicle on the premises (unless it is in an
   enclosed garage) if such repairs will take longer than a single day.
6) to allow Owners to inspect the dwelling or show it to prospective at any and
   all reasonable times.
7) not to keep any liquid-filled furniture in this dwelling.
8) to pay rent by check or money order made out to Owners. (Checks must be
   good when paid or Owners will not grant discount.)
9) to pay for repairs of all damage, including drain stoppages, they or their
   guests have caused.
10) to pay for any windows broken in their dwelling while they live there.

   Violation of any part of this agreement or nonpayment of rent when due shall
be cause for eviction under appropriate sections of the applicable code. The
prevailing party shall _____ recover reasonable attorney's fees involved.

   Tenants hereby acknowledge that they have read this agreement, understand
it, agree to it, and have been given a copy.

Owner_____   Tenant_____

*By_____   Tenant_____
*Person authorized to accept legal service on Owners' behalf

Lease

Agreement between_____, Owners, and
_____, Tenants, for a dwelling located at
_____.

Tenants agree to lease this dwelling for a term of _____, beginning
_____ and ending _____ for $_____ per month, payable
in advance on the _____ day of every calendar month to Owners or their Agent,
_____. When rent is paid on or before the _____ day of
the calendar month, Tenants may take a $_____ discount.

The first month's rent for this dwelling is $_____.

The entire sum of this lease is $_____.

The security/cleaning deposit on this dwelling is $_____. It is refundable
if Tenants leave the dwelling reasonably clean and undamaged.

If Tenants intend to move at the end of this lease, they agree to give
Owners notice in writing at least 30 days before the lease runs out. Otherwise
they will be regarded as automatically switching over to a month-to-month tenancy.

A deposit of $_____ for _____ keys will be refunded after the keys have
been returned.

Owners will refund all deposits due within _____ days after Tenants have
moved out completely and returned their keys.

Only the following persons and pets are to live in this dwelling:

_____

Without Owners' prior written permission, no other persons may live there, and
no other pets may stay there, even temporarily. It may not be sublet or used for
business purposes.

Use of the following is included in the rent:_____

_____

Remarks:_____

_____

Tenants agree to the following:
1) to keep yards and garbage areas clean.
2) to keep from making loud noises and disturbances and to play music and
   broadcast programs at all times so as not to disturb other people's peace
   and quiet.
3) not to paint or alter their dwelling without first getting Owners' written
   permission.
4) to park their motor vehicle in assigned space and to keep that space clean
   of oil drippings.
5) not to repair their motor vehicle on the premises (unless it is in an
   enclosed garage) if such repairs will take longer than a single day.
6) to allow Owners to inspect the dwelling or show it to prospective at any and
   all reasonable times.
7) not to keep any liquid-filled furniture in this dwelling.
8) to pay rent by check or money order made out to Owners. (Checks must be
   good when paid or Owners will not grant discount.)
9) to pay for repairs of all damage, including drain stoppages, they or their
   guests have caused.
10) to pay for any windows broken in their dwelling while they live there.

Violation of any part of this agreement or nonpayment of rent when due shall
be cause for eviction under appropriate sections of the applicable code. The
prevailing party shall _____ recover reasonable attorney's fees involved.

Tenants hereby acknowledge that they have read this agreement, understand
it, agree to it, and have been given a copy.

Owner_____ Tenant_____

*By_____ Tenant_____
*Person authorized to accept legal service on Owners' behalf

Co-Signer Agreement

Dated_____

(Addendum to Rental Agreement)

    This agreement is attached to and forms a part of the Rental Agreement between _____,
Owners, and _____, Tenants, which is
dated _____.

    My name is

_____.

    I have completed a Rental Application for the express purpose of enabling the Owners to check my credit. I have no intention of occupying the dwelling referred to in the Rental Agreement above.

    I have read the Rental Agreement referred to above, and I promise to guarantee the Tenants' compliance with the financial obligations of this Agreement.

    I understand that I may be required to pay for rent, cleaning charges, or damage assessments in such amounts as are incurred by the Tenants under the terms of this Agreement if, and only if, the Tenants fail to pay.

        Signed:

_____

Condition & Inventory Checksheet

Dated _____

Tenant Name _____ Address _____

Date Moved In _____ Date Notice Given _____ Date Moved Out _____

Abbreviations:

Air Conditioner, A/C	Clean, Cl	Drapes, Drp	Hood, Hd	OK, OK	Table, Tbl
Bed, Bd	Cracked, Cr	Dryer, Dry	Just Painted, JP	Poor, P	Tile, Tl
Broken, Brk	Curtains, Ctn	Fair, F	Lamp, Lmp	Refrigerator, Ref	Venetian Blinds, VB
Carpet, Cpt	Dinette, Din	Good, G	Lightbulbs, LtB	Shades, Sh	Washer, Wsh
Chair, Ch	Dishwasher, Dish	Heater, Htr	Linoleum, Lino	Sofa, Sfa	Waxed, Wxt
Chest, Chst	Disposer, Disp	Hole, H	Nightstand, Ntst	Stove, Stv	Wood, Wd

Circle applicable rooms; enter abbreviations	Walls, Doors		Floors		Windows		Light Fixtures		Inventory: Appliances, Furniture		
	cond.	chgs.	cond.	chgs.	cond.	chgs.	cond.	chgs.	Item	cond.	chgs.
Living Room											
Dining											
Kitchen											
Bath 1											
Bath 2											
Bedroom 1											
Bedroom 2											
Bedroom 3											
Other											

Charges _____ _____ _____ _____ _____

Total Itemized Charges _____

Other Charges Not Itemized
   (Broken Locks, Dirty Garage, etc.
    Explain on Backside) _____

Total Deposits _____

Deduction for Improper Notice _____

Less Total Deductions _____

Deduction for Missing Keys _____

Deposit Refund or
Amount Owed _____

Total Deductions _____

☐ Tenants acknowledge that the smoke detector was tested in their presence and found to be in working order and that its operation was explained to them. Tenants agree to test the detector at least every other week and to report any problems to the Owner in writing. If the smoke detector is battery operated, Tenants agree to replace the battery as necessary (unless laws require otherwise).

Tenants hereby acknowledge that that they have read this Condition & Inventory Checksheet, agree that the condition and contents of the above-mentioned rental dwelling are without exception as represented herein, understand that they are liable for any damage done to this dwelling as outlined in their Lease or Rental Agreement, and have received a copy of this checksheet.

Owner _____ Tenant _____

By _____ Tenant _____

BANK INFORMATION AUTHORIZATION

BANK: This request to report your direct experience and transactions is for the purpose of establishing your customer's ability to pay rent to the landlord or landlady whose name appears below. It is understood that this report is a business courtesy and is strictly confidential. Its authorship will not be disclosed nor will your bank assume any obligation for errors, omissions, or changes in this information.

	Savings	*Commercial (Checking)*		*Loans*
Date Opened	_____	_____	No Experience	_____
High	_____	_____	Date Opened	_____
Medium	_____	_____	Open Balance	_____
Low	_____	_____	Date Closed	_____
Date Closed	_____	_____	How Paid	_____
			Satisfactory____ Unsatisfactory____	

Remarks _____

Authorized Signature _____ Bank Stamp:

TENANT-CUSTOMER: Please complete all information in this section and forward to your bank along with a stamped envelope addressed to the landlord or landlady whose name appears below.

Last Name (Print)	Husband (First Name)	Wife (First Name)

Address _____

Bank _____ Savings Account No. _____

Address _____ Checking Account No. _____

_____ Loans _____

_____

Tenant-Customer Signatures (His & Hers)

LANDLORD/LANDLADY: Print your name and address in the blanks provided, sign your name as acceptance of the above statement to bank, and give this form to the tenant who has applied to rent from you.

Name _____

Address _____

_____ _____
                                                 Signature

Pet Agreement

Dated_____

(Addendum to Rental Agreement)

This agreement is attached to and forms a part of the Rental Agreement

dated_____between_____, Owners,

and_____, Tenants.

Tenants desire to keep a pet named_____and described

as_____in the dwelling they occupy under the

rental agreement referred to above, and because this agreement specifically

prohibits keeping pets without the Owners' permission, Tenants agree to the

following terms and conditions in exchange for this permission:

1) Tenants agree to keep their pet under control at all times.

2) Tenants agree to keep their pet restrained, but not tethered, when
   it is outside their dwelling.

3) Tenants agree not to leave their pet unattended for any unreasonable
   periods.

4) Tenants agree to dispose of their pet's droppings properly and quickly.

5) Tenants agree not to leave food or water for their pet or any other
   animal outside their dwelling.

6) Tenants agree to keep pet from causing any annoyance or discomfort to
   others and will remedy immediately any complaints made through the
   Owner or Manager.

7) Tenants agree to get rid of their pet's offspring within eight weeks
   of birth.

8) Tenants agree to pay immediately for any damage, loss, or expense
   caused by their pet, and in addition, they will add $_____ to
   their security/cleaning deposit, any of which may be used for cleaning,
   repairs, or delinquent rent when Tenants vacate. This added deposit
   or what remains of it when pet damages have been assessed, will be
   returned to Tenants within _____ days after they prove that they
   no longer keep this pet.

9) Tenants agree that Owners reserve the right to revoke permission to
   keep the pet should Tenants break this agreement.

Owner_____   Tenant_____

By_____   Tenant_____

Page_____ of _____

Waterbed Agreement

Dated_____

(Addendum to Rental Agreement)

    This agreement is attached to and forms a part of the Rental Agreement dated

_____ between_____, Owners,

and_____, Tenants.

    Tenants desire to keep a waterbed described as_____

_____

in the dwelling they occupy under the Rental Agreement referred to above, and because

this agreement specifically prohibits keeping waterbeds without the Owners' permission,

Tenants agree to the following terms and conditions in exchange for this permission:

1)   Tenants agree to keep one waterbed approved by Owners for this dwelling. Waterbed shall consist of a mattress at least 20 mil thick with lap seams, a safety liner at least 8 mil, and a frame enclosure which meets the Waterbed Manufacturers' Association standards.

2)   Tenants agree to consult with the Owners about the location of the waterbed. They agree to hire qualified professionals to install and dismantle the bed according to the manufacturer's specifications and further agree not to relocate it without the Owners' consent.

3)   Tenants agree to allow Owners to inspect the waterbed installation at any and all reasonable times and Tenants agree to remedy any problems or potential problems immediately.

4)   Tenants agree to furnish Owners with a copy of a valid liability insurance policy for at least $100,000 covering this waterbed installation and agree to renew the policy as necessary for continuous coverage.

5)   Tenants agree to pay immediately for any damage caused by their waterbed, and in addition, they will add $_____ to their security/cleaning deposit, any of which may be used for cleaning, repairs, or delinquent rent when Tenants vacate. This added deposit or what remains of it when waterbed damages have been assessed, will be returned to Tenants within _____ days after they prove that they no longer keep this waterbed.

6)   In consideration of the additional time, effort, costs, and risks involved in this waterbed installation, Tenants agree to pay additional rent of $_____, which /includes/does not include/ the premium for the waterbed liability insurance policy referred to in item 4.

7)   Tenants agree that the Owners reserve the right to revoke this permission to keep a waterbed should the Tenants break this agreement.

Owner_____   Tenant_____

By_____   Tenant_____

Page_____ of _____

Dear

You probably know already that the building where you live has changed hands. Because tenants usually feel some apprehension every time such a changeover occurs, we would like to take this opportunity to clear the air by letting you know just what you can expect in the future about a few things.

DEPOSITS...One special concern you must have is your deposits. We are concerned, too, and we want to make absolutely certain that all of your deposits are credited to you. To avoid any misunderstandings about your deposits and other matters related to your living here, we would like you to answer the questions on the sheet attached. They are questions which you should be able to answer quickly from memory or by referring to information readily available to you. Please do so as soon as possible and return your answers to us in the envelope provided.

PAYMENT BY CHECK OR MONEY ORDER...Since it is unwise for anyone to keep or carry cash around in quantities, we request that you pay your rent by check or money order (made payable to us exactly as underlined below). You will be protected and so will we.

PROMPT PAYMENT...You are expected to pay your rent within three days after the due date. For example, rent due on the first must be paid by the fourth at the very latest. If you anticipate being late beyond that for any reason whatsoever, please let us know beforehand. If you don't, we will assume that you are deliberately avoiding payment, and we will immediately serve you with the notice which starts eviction proceedings.

MAINTENANCE...We expect you to pay your rent promptly, and you can expect us to respond promptly to maintenance problems. Sometime within the next week, we will visit you to inspect for any building maintenance work that should be taken care of. You can help by starting now to make a list of such work which you notice around the house.

RENTAL AGREEMENT...We will also stop by soon to explain to you the standard rental agreement we use, and we will leave you with a copy of your own.

We are reasonable people and we will try anything within reason to make living here enjoyable for you, but naturally we need your cooperation. If we have it, we will get along well together and we can all take pride in this place that you call home.

Sincerely,

Tenant Information:

Your Name_____

Your Address_____

Your Home Telephone Number_____Your Work Phone_____

Who lives with you? (Include ages of the children, please)_____

_____

What pet(s) do you have?_____

Do you have a waterbed?_____

What vehicle(s) do you have? Make(s)_____License(s)_____

Where do you work? (Company name)_____

Where does your co-tenant work? (Company name)_____

When did you move in?_____

What is your current rent per month?_____

What date is your rent paid up to right now?_____

When is your rent due each month?_____

What refundable deposits have you paid? Keys $_____Security $_____

Cleaning $_____ Other (please explain) $_____

When you moved in, you paid your first month's rent. Did you also then pay your last

month's rent? _____ If so, how much was it? $_____

Which of the following furnishings belong to the owners of the building? (Please give
room locations where appropriate.)

Carpets_____Drapes_____

Shades_____Blinds_____

Stove_____Refrigerator_____

Other appliances? (Please list)_____

Other furniture? (Please list)_____

Do you have a rental agreement or lease in writing? _____

If so, what is the date of the latest one? _____

In case of an emergency, what friend or relative of yours should we contact?

Name_____Telephone Number_____

Date_____ Your Signature_____

FOR YOUR INFORMATION:

Important Numbers:

Police_____   Telephone Co._____

Fire_____   Gas Co._____

Ambulance_____   Electric Co._____

Paramedic_____   Water Co._____

Doctor_____   Manager_____

The best time to contact the manager is _____.

In an emergency, when you cannot get hold of the manager, call

_____.

Helpful Hints:

1) A fire extinguisher is located _____.
Use short bursts aimed at the base of the fire. Never use water
on a grease fire; either use the extinguisher provided or throw
baking soda on it.

2) The electrical shutoff for your dwelling is located
_____.
Check there to see whether a fuse has blown (have an extra on
hand) or a circuit breaker has tripped. Restore service by
replacing any fuse which appears to be blown (use one with the
same number on it) or by flipping the circuit breaker switch back
and forth once.

3) The gas shutoff for your dwelling is located
_____,
but there may be an individual valve on the line supplying each
appliance as well. Shut off the gas by turning the valve 90
degrees, that is, so it crosses the direction of the supply line.

4) The water shutoff for your dwelling is located
_____,
but you may be able to shut off the water to an individual faucet
by turning off the supply valve below your sink or toilet (not
your tub or shower). If hot water is leaking anywhere, shut off
the valve on top of the hot water heater.

5) Whenever you defrost the refrigerator, turn it off or set
the control knob to defrost. Place a pan to catch the water and
empty it when necessary. Do not try to break up the ice with any
implement like a knife or an ice pick. Let it melt on its own or
speed it up by placing a pot of hot water in the freezing
compartment. Dry the floor thoroughly when you have finished.

FOR YOUR INFORMATION - Page 2

6) Whenever you use the garbage disposer, if you have one, feed garbage in gradually along with lots of cold water, and let the water run for half a minute after you turn off the switch. Use the disposer only for those things which are edible, but don't put either cooking oil and grease down it; put them and everything else except toxic liquids in the trash. Keep metal objects out of the sink while using the disposer and turn off the switch immediately if you hear any loud metallic noises. Do not put your hand into the disposer (use tongs to retrieve objects) and do not use any chemical drain openers. If the disposer stops running on its own and you haven't heard it make any strange noises, something may have gotten stuck. Try turning the blades with a disposer wrench. Then push the reset button. After you have tried all this and you find that it still doesn't work, call the manager.

7) Whenever you want to dispose of any liquids which aren't edible, please see the manager. Many liquids are toxic and should not be put down the drain or in the trash. They must be disposed of carefully so they will not contaminate the soil or the water supply in this area. Included in this list of hazardous household wastes are the following: oven cleaners, ammonia-based cleaners, drain cleaners, floor wax, furniture polish, deodorizers, spot removers, medicines, paint, thinners, paint removers, wood preservatives, art supplies, photographic chemicals, antifreeze, car waxes, crankcase oil, fuels, radiator flushes, rust inhibitors, engine cleaners, insect sprays, weed killers, and swimming pool chemicals.

8) Whenever water rises in the toilet bowl, do not try flushing the toilet again. The bowl can hold just one tank of water at a time. More water from the tank will only cause the bowl to flow over. Use a plunger first, and then try flushing it again. Do not try to flush feminine napkins or paper diapers down the toilet. They may disappear from the toilet bowl, but that's no guarantee they'll clear the sewer pipes completely. They could require a plumber's visit, and that'll cost you money.

9) Whenever you have showered or bathed, please take a moment to mop up the excess water on the bathroom floor. A dry floor is a safe floor.

10) Whenever you want to hang anything from, or stick anything to, the walls or ceilings in your dwelling, please ask the manager to explain how to do it acceptably.

11) Whenever you want to remove the screens from your windows, please ask the manager how to do it properly. Some screens have to be removed from the inside and some from the outside. The manager will show you how.

Dear

    Moving time is always a busy time, and you will have lots of things on your mind now that you have given notice you are moving. One of those things undoubtedly is how to get your deposits back promptly. In your case, they amount to $_____.

    Contrary to what some tenants believe, we WANT to return your deposits, and we WILL return them to you so long as you leave your place "reasonably clean and undamaged." That's what your rental agreement says and that's what we will do. You're probably wondering, however, what "reasonably clean and undamaged" means, so we'd like to tell you how we interpret it and tell you also what you should do to get your deposits back.

    "Reasonably clean" to us means as clean as you would leave your dwelling if you knew your best friend or favorite aunt were going to move in after you. To get it that clean, we expect you to clean the appliances, stove hood, and cabinets (under sinks, too) both inside and out; remove all non-adhesive shelf paper; use an appropriate cleanser on the showers, tubs, toilets, sinks, mirrors, and medicine cabinets (inside as well); dust the ceilings (for cobwebs), baseboards, window sills, and closet shelving; wash the kitchen and bathroom walls, and spot-clean the walls in other rooms; wash the light fixtures and windows inside and out; vacuum the floors; scrub the floor tile or linoleum; sweep the entry, patio, storage enclosure, and garage; remove all personal belongings (including clothes hangers and cleaning supplies); and dispose of all trash. PLEASE DO NOT CLEAN THE DRAPERIES, SHAMPOO THE CARPETS, OR WAX THE FLOORS. We prefer to do those cleaning chores ourselves, and you will not be charged for our doing them.

    "Reasonably undamaged" to us means that items which we have supplied should not be missing (including light bulbs) or broken; that there should be no new burns, cracks, chips, or holes in the dwelling or its furnishings; and that the paint on the walls should be sufficient to last at least two years from the time they were last painted. PLEASE DO NOT REMOVE ANYTHING YOU HAVE ATTACHED TO THE WALLS OR CEILINGS WITHOUT FIRST TALKING TO US, and please try to avoid nicking the paint in the halls and doorways as you move things out.

    After you have returned the keys, we would like to inspect your dwelling with you to check it for cleanliness and damage, and unless we have to get prices on special work or replacements, we will refund all deposits owed to you at that time.

    We expect you to have moved out completely by _____. Because we are making arrangements for new tenants to move in soon after that, we would appreciate hearing from you immediately if your moving plans should change.

    We hope your moving goes smoothly, and we wish you happiness in your new home.

               Sincerely,

Dear

    As we do every year, we have been reviewing our insurance policies, and we thought that you might like to know how you are affected by the insurance we carry.

    Basically, our policies cover only the building itself where you live. They do not cover any of your own belongings against damage or disappearance, nor do they cover you for negligence should you, for example, leave a burner going under a pan of grease and start a fire which damages the kitchen.

    To protect yourself against these calamities, you should get a tenant's insurance policy. Most insurance companies and agents will write such a policy for you, and we would strongly urge that you inquire about getting one.

    For the peace of mind that it gives, a tenant's insurance policy is reasonable indeed.

                Sincerely,

Dear

We want to make the place where you live as safe as it can be.
We are constantly on the lookout for anything around your home
which might prove hazardous to life, limb, or property. But hard
as we try, we cannot uncover every potential danger all by
ourselves. We need your help.

Because you are around your home much more than we are, you have
a greater opportunity to notice hazards. Please report to us
anything you notice which you think might prove hazardous to you
or anyone else. We promise that we will investigate the
hazardous condition and remedy it if we possibly can.

Please complete the bottom section of this letter and return it
to us with your next rent payment.

Thank you for your cooperation in making your home a safer place
to live.

                    Sincerely,

= =

☐ We know of nothing which appears to be unsafe in or around our
home, but we will alert you whenever we do notice something.

☐ We would like to call your attention to the following unsafe
conditions in or around our home:

_____

_____

_____

_____

We suggest that you take the following corrective action:

_____

_____

_____

_____

Signed _____ Dated _____

RENT REMINDERS & NOTICES

	Blank Form on Page Number	Example Form on Page Number
Rent Reminders	291-6	86
Notice of Intention to Vacate	297	108
Notice of Change in Terms of Tenancy	298	34, 201
Notice of Change in Terms of Tenancy (Rent)	299	93
Notice to Pay Rent or Quit	300	85
Notice to Perform Covenant	301	118
Notice to Terminate Tenancy	302	120

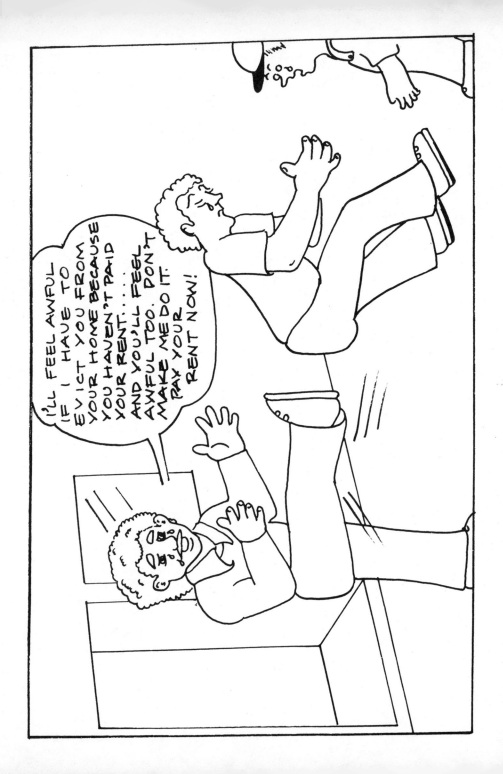

NOTICE OF INTENTION TO VACATE   Date _____

TO:_____

FROM:_____

    Please be advised that on _____ we intend to
move from our residence at _____.

    We understand that our rental agreement calls for _____ days'
notice before we move and that this is _____ days' notice. We understand that we are responsible for paying rent through the end of
the notice period called for in the rental agreement or until another
tenant approved by the management has moved in, whichever comes first.

    We understand that our deposits will be refunded within _____
days after we have moved out completely and returned our keys to the
management, so long as we leave our dwelling reasonably clean and undamaged.

    Reasons for leaving: _____
_____

    Forwarding address: _____

    In accordance with our rental agreement, we agree to allow the
management to show our dwelling to prospective tenants at any and all
reasonable times.

                        Tenant _____

                        Tenant _____

NOTICE OF CHANGE
IN TERMS OF TENANCY

TO _____, Tenant in Possession

_____

_____

YOU ARE HEREBY NOTIFIED that the terms of tenancy under which you occupy the above-described premises are to be changed.

Effective _____, 19_____, there will be the following changes:

_____

_____

_____

_____

Dated this _____ day of _____, 19_____.

_____
Owner/Manager

This Notice was served by the Owner/Manager in the following manner (check those which apply):
    ☐ by personal delivery to the tenant,
    ☐ by leaving a copy with someone on the premises other than the tenant,
    ☐ by mailing,
    ☐ by posting.

NOTICE OF CHANGE
IN TERMS OF TENANCY
(Rent)

TO _____, Tenant in Possession

_____

_____

YOU ARE HEREBY NOTIFIED that the terms of tenancy under which you occupy the above-described premises are to be changed.

Effective _____, 19_____, your rent will be increased by _____ per month, from _____ per month to _____ per month, payable in advance.

Dated this _____ day of _____, 19_____.

_____
Owner/Manager

This Notice was served by the Owner/Manager in the following manner (check those which apply):
☐ by personal delivery,
☐ by leaving a copy with someone on the premises other than the tenant,
☐ by mailing,
☐ by posting.

NOTICE
to Pay Rent or Quit

TO _____, TENANT IN POSSESSION:

You are hereby notified that the rent is now due and payable on the premises now held and occupied by you, being those premises situated in the

City of _____, County of _____,

State of _____, commonly known as

_____

Your account is delinquent in the amount of $_____, being the rent for the period from _____ to _____.

You are hereby required to pay said rent in full within _____ days or to remove from and deliver up possession of the above-mentioned premises, or legal proceedings will be instituted against you to recover possession of said premises, to declare the forfeiture of the Lease or Rental Agreement under which you occupy said premises and to recover rents and damages, together with court costs and attorney's fees, according to the terms of your Lease or Rental Agreement.

Dated this _____ day of _____, 19 _____.

_____
Owner/Manager

PROOF OF SERVICE

I, the undersigned, being at least 18 years of age, declare under penalty of perjury that I served the Notice to Pay Rent or Quit, of which this is a true copy, on the above-mentioned Tenant in Possession in the manner(s) indicated below:

☐ On _____, 19 _____, I handed the Notice to the tenant.

☐ I handed the Notice to a person of suitable age and discretion at the tenant's residence/business on _____, 19 _____.

☐ I posted the Notice in a conspicuous place at the tenant's residence on _____, 19 _____.

☐ I sent by certified mail a true copy of the Notice to the tenant at his place of residence on _____, 19 _____.

Executed on _____, 19 _____, at _____.

_____

NOTICE
to Perform Covenant

TO _____, TENANT IN POSSESSION:

PLEASE TAKE NOTICE that you have violated the following covenant(s) in your Lease or Rental Agreement:

_____

_____

_____

You are hereby required within _____ days to perform the aforesaid covenant(s) or to deliver up possession of the premises now held and occupied by you, being those premises situated in the City of _____, County of _____, State of _____, commonly known as _____.

If you fail to do so, legal proceedings will be instituted against you to recover said premises and such damages as the law allows.

This notice is intended to be a _____ day notice to perform the aforesaid covenant. It is not intended to terminate or forfeit the Lease or Rental Agreement under which you occupy said premises. If, after legal proceedings, said premises are recovered from you, the owners will try to rent said premises for the best possible rent, giving you credit for sums received and holding you liable for any deficiencies arising during the term of said Lease or Rental Agreement.

Dated this _____ day of _____, 19 _____.

_____
Owner/Manager

PROOF OF SERVICE

I, the undersigned, being at least 18 years of age, declare under penalty of perjury that I served the Notice to Perform Covenant, of which this is a true copy, on the above-mentioned Tenant in Possession in the manner(s) indicated below:

☐ On _____, 19 _____, I handed the Notice to the tenant.
☐ I handed the Notice to a person of suitable age and discretion at the tenant's residence/business on _____, 19 _____.
☐ I posted the Notice in a conspicuous place at the tenant's residence on _____, 19 _____.
☐ I sent by certified mail a true copy of the Notice to the tenant at his place of residence on _____, 19 _____.

Executed on _____, 19 _____, at _____.

_____

30-DAY NOTICE
to Terminate Tenancy

TO _____, TENANT IN POSSESSION:

PLEASE TAKE NOTICE that you are hereby required within 30 days to remove from and deliver up possession of the premises now held and occupied by you, being those premises situated in the

City of _____, County of _____,

State of _____, commonly known as

_____.

This notice is intended for the purpose of terminating the Rental Agreement by which you now hold possession of the above-described premises, and should you fail to comply, legal proceedings will be instituted against you to recover possession, to declare said Rental Agreement forfeited, and to recover rents and damages for the period of the unlawful detention.

Please be advised that your rent on said premises is due and payable up to and including the date of termination of your tenancy under this notice.

Dated this _____ day of _____, 19 _____.

_____
Owner/Manager

PROOF OF SERVICE

I, the undersigned, being at least 18 years of age, declare under penalty of perjury that I served the 30-Day Notice to Terminate Tenancy, of which this is a true copy, on the above-mentioned Tenant in Possession in the manner(s) indicated below:

☐ On _____, 19 _____, I handed the Notice to the tenant.

☐ I handed the Notice to a person of suitable age and discretion at the tenant's residence/business on _____, 19 _____.

☐ I posted the Notice in a conspicuous place at the tenant's residence on _____, 19 _____.

☐ I sent by certified mail a true copy of the Notice to the tenant at his place of residence on _____, 19 _____.

Executed on _____, 19 _____, at _____.

_____

EMPLOYEES

Employment Application

Name_____ Home Phone_____ Work Phone_____

Date of Birth_____ Social Security No._____ Driver's License No._____

Present Address_____ Own____ Rent____ How long at address?_____

How many years of schooling have you had?_____

Present/Last Occupation_____ Employer_____ Phone_____

Monthly Gross_____ How long with this employer?_____ Name of Supervisor_____ May we contact?____ Phone_____

Spouse's Name_____ Date of Birth_____ Social Security No._____ Driver's License No._____

How many years of schooling has your spouse had?_____

Present/Last Occupation_____ Employer_____ Phone_____

Monthly Gross_____ How long with this employer?_____ Name of Supervisor_____ May we contact?____ Phone_____

Dependents' names and ages_____

What skills do you or your spouse have related to this job?_____

What experience have you or your spouse had related to this job?_____

What physical handicaps do you or your spouse have?_____

Are you and your spouse bondable?_____ Previous bonding?_____

When are you available for this job?___ _____

Savings Account Bank Name_____ Branch_____ Account Number_____

Checking Account Bank Name_____ Branch_____ Account Number_____

Major Credit Card Name_____ Account Number_____

Credit Reference_____ Account Number_____ Balance Owed_____ Monthly Payment_____

Personal Reference_____ Address_____ Phone ( )_____

Personal Reference_____ Address_____ Phone ( )_____

Contact in Emergency_____ Address_____ Phone ( )_____

　　I/we declare that the statements above are true and correct, and I/we hereby authorize verification of those statements.

Date_____ Signed_____

Management Agreement

Dated _____

Agreement between _____, Owners, and

_____, Managers, for management of property

located at _____.

    Compensation for Managers shall be $_____ per month at a guaranteed minimum and shall be computed at an hourly rate of $_____. Unless Managers obtain Owners' permission in advance or, in case of emergency, unless they notify Owners within 48 hours afterwards, Managers shall spend no more than _____ hours per month on managerial responsibilities. Managers shall record working hours on time sheets provided by Owners, one time sheet for each person exercising managerial responsibilities, and shall submit those time sheets at least once a month.

    Other compensation shall be as follows:_____

_____

    Managers shall have days off as follows:_____;

vacation time as follows:_____;

sick leave as follows:_____.

    Managers' duties and responsibilities, which will be reviewed jointly in ninety days and annually after that, shall be as follows:_____

_____

_____

_____

    Managers shall receipt all monies collected on the Owners' behalf and shall deposit or transfer those monies within_____ of collection as follows:_____

_____

    Managers shall spend or commit to spend no more than $_____ on the Owners' behalf without first obtaining permission.

    Either Managers or Owners may cancel this agreement upon providing _____ days' written notice.

    Managers hereby acknowledge that they have read this agreement, understand it, agree to it, and have been given a copy.

Owner_____   Manager_____

By_____   Manager_____

Time Sheet

_____
Employee's Name

_____
Employee's Signature

Property

Pay Period_____to_____

DATE	TIMES		HOURS	DESCRIPTION OF WORK PERFORMED	CONTRACT AMOUNT

Total Hours _____   Total Contract _____

Rate _____

Hourly Gross _____

Contract _____   _____
                                 Approved by   Date

Total Gross _____

RECORDS

	Blank Form on Page Number	Example Form on Page Number
Tenant Record	311	226
Monthly Rental Income Record	312-3	227
Laundry Income	314	229
Depreciation Record	315	233
Other Receipts & Income	316-7	228
Expense and Payment Record	318-9	230-1
Expense and Payment Record (Annual Summary)	320-1	235
Payroll	322	235
Summary of Business and Statement of Income	323	236
Loan & Note Record	324	237
Insurance Record	325	238

Tenant Record

Location _____

Unit	Tenant	Phone	Moved In	Moved Out	Rent Date	Deposit/ Rent	Bank/Ckg. Acct. Nos.
1							
2							
3							
4							
5							
6							
7							
8							
9							
10							
11							
12							
13							
14							
15							
16							
17							
18							
19							
20							
21							
22							
23							
24							
25							
26							
27							
28							
29							
30							

MONTHLY RENTAL INCOME RECORD

Page _____

Location(s) _____

Period _____

Unit	Jan.	Feb.	Mar.	Apr.	May	
1						1
2						2
3						3
4						4
5						5
6						6
7						7
8						8
9						9
10						10
11						11
12						12
13						13
14						14
15						15
16						16
17						17
18						18
19						19
20						20
21						21
22						22
23						23
24						24
25						25
26						26
27						27
28						28
29						29
30						30
31						31
32						32
33						33
34						34
35						35
36						36
37						37
38						38
39						39
40						40
41						41

MONTHLY RENTAL INCOME RECORD

Page _____

	Jun.	Jul.	Aug.	Sep.	Oct.	Nov.	Dec.	Year's Totals	
1									1
2									2
3									3
4									4
5									5
6									6
7									7
8									8
9									9
10									10
11									11
12									12
13									13
14									14
15									15
16									16
17									17
18									18
19									19
20									20
21									21
22									22
23									23
24									24
25									25
26									26
27									27
28									28
29									29
30									30
31									31
32									32
33									33
34									34
35									35
36									36
37									37
38									38
39									39
40									40
41									41

Laundry Income

location _____

period _____

Date	Washer	Dryer	Both	Cumulative Totals	Monthly Totals	
1						1
2						2
3						3
4						4
5						5
6						6
7						7
8						8
9						9
10						10
11						11
12						12
13						13
14						14
15						15
16						16
17						17
18						18
19						19
20						20
21						21
22						22
23						23
24						24
25						25
26						26
27						27
28						28
29						29
30						30
31						31
32						32
33						33
34						34
35						35
36						36
37						37
38						38
39						39
40						40
41						41

DEPRECIATION RECORD

Property or Capital Improvement Location and Description _____

_____

Date Acquired or Converted to Business _____

New or Used _____

Cost or Other Basis _____

Land Value (Not Applicable to Capital Improvements) _____

Salvage Value _____

Special 20% First Year Depreciation _____

Depreciable Basis _____

Method of Depreciation _____

Useful Life _____

Tax Year	Prior Deprec.	Deprec. Balance	% Year* Held	% Bus. Use	Deprec. This Year	Special 20%	Total First Year Deprec.
1st						+	=
2nd							
3rd							
4th							
5th							
6th							
7th							
8th							
9th							
10th							
11th							
12th							
13th							
14th							
15th							
16th							
17th							
18th							
19th							
20th							
21st							
22nd							
23rd							
24th							
25th							

*Conversion: Months to % of Year

Months	% of Year
1	8.3
1.5	12.5
2	16.7
2.5	20.8
3	25
3.5	29.2
4	33.3
4.5	37.5
5	41.7
5.5	45.8
6	50
6.5	54.2
7	58.3
7.5	62.5
8	66.7
8.5	70.8
9	75
9.5	79.2
10	83.3
10.5	87.5
11	91.7
11.5	95.8
12	100

OTHER RECEIPTS & INCOME

Added Appliances or Furniture,
Deposits, Interest on Deposits,
Late Charges, Laundry, Garages, etc.

Page _____

Location(s) _____

Period _____

	Description of Income	Jan.	Feb.	Mar.	Apr.	May	
1							1
2							2
3							3
4							4
5							5
6							6
7							7
8							8
9							9
10							10
11							11
12							12
13							13
14							14
15							15
16							16
17							17
18							18
19							19
20							20
21							21
22							22
23							23
24							24
25							25
26							26
27							27
28							28
29							29
30							30
31							31
32							32
33							33
34							34
35							35
36							36
37							37
38							38
39							39
40							40
41	Totals						41

OTHER RECEIPTS & INCOME

Page_____

	Jun.	Jul.	Aug.	Sep.	Oct.	Nov.	Dec.	Year's Totals	
1									1
2									2
3									3
4									4
5									5
6									6
7									7
8									8
9									9
10									10
11									11
12									12
13									13
14									14
15									15
16									16
17									17
18									18
19									19
20									20
21									21
22									22
23									23
24									24
25									25
26									26
27									27
28									28
29									29
30									30
31									31
32									32
33									33
34									34
35									35
36									36
37									37
38									38
39									39
40									40
41									41

318

EXPENSE AND PAYMENT RECORD

Page _____

Location(s) _____

Period _____

Date	How Paid	To Whom Paid	For	1 Total Paid Out	2 Interest	3 Taxes, Licenses	4 Insurance	
1								1
2								2
3								3
4								4
5								5
6								6
7								7
8								8
9								9
10								10
11								11
12								12
13								13
14								14
15								15
16								16
17								17
18								18
19								19
20								20
21								21
22								22
23								23
24								24
25								25
26								26
27								27
28								28
29								29
30								30
31								31
32								32
33								33
34								34
35								35
36								36
37								37
38								38
39								39
40								40
41		Totals						41

DISTRIBUTION OF EXPENSES AND PAYMENTS

Page _____

	5	6	7	8	9	10	11	12	
	Utilities	Services, Repairs, Maint.	Merch., Supplies	Payroll	Misc.	Depreciable	Mortgage Principal	Non-deductible	
1									1
2									2
3									3
4									4
5									5
6									6
7									7
8									8
9									9
10									10
11									11
12									12
13									13
14									14
15									15
16									16
17									17
18									18
19									19
20									20
21									21
22									22
23									23
24									24
25									25
26									26
27									27
28									28
29									29
30									30
31									31
32									32
33									33
34									34
35									35
36									36
37									37
38									38
39									39
40									40
41									41

EXPENSE AND PAYMENT RECORD

Annual Summary

Location(s) _____

Year _____

	Units	1 Total Paid Out(2-12)	2 Interest	3 Taxes, Licenses	4 Insurance	5 Utilities	
1							1
2							2
3							3
4							4
5							5
6							6
7							7
8							8
9							9
10							10
11							11
12							12
13							13
14							14
15							15
16							16
17							17
18							18
19							19
20							20
21							21
22							22
23							23
24							24
25							25
26							26
27							27
28							28
29							29
30							30
31							31
32							32
33							33
34							34
35							35
36							36
37							37
38							38
39							39
40							40
41	Totals						41

DISTRIBUTION OF EXPENSES AND PAYMENTS
Annual Summary

	6 Services, Repairs, Maint.	7 Merch., Supplies	8 Payroll	9 Misc.	10 Depreciable	11 Mortgage Principal	12 Non-deductible	13 All Depreciation	
1									1
2									2
3									3
4									4
5									5
6									6
7									7
8									8
9									9
10									10
11									11
12									12
13									13
14									14
15									15
16									16
17									17
18									18
19									19
20									20
21									21
22									22
23									23
24									24
25									25
26									26
27									27
28									28
29									29
30									30
31									31
32									32
33									33
34									34
35									35
36									36
37									37
38									38
39									39
40									40
41									41

PAYROLL RECORD

Property _____ Social Security No. _____ Exemptions _____

Employee _____ Pay Rate _____ ☐ Married   ☐ Single

	Period	Gross	Federal Withholding Tax	State Disability	Employee FICA	Employer FICA	State Withhding Tax	Other	Net	Ck No.	
1											1
2											2
3											3
4											4
5											5
6											6
7											7
8											8
9											9
10											10
11											11
12											12
13											13
14											14
15											15
16											16
17											17
18											18
19											19
20											20
21	Qtr. Totals										21
22											22
23											23
24											24
25											25
26											26
27											27
28											28
29											29
30											30
31											31
32											32
33											33
34											34
35											35
36											36
37											37
38											38
39											39
40											40
41	Qtr. Totals										41

Summary of Business and Statement of Income

Location(s) _____

Year / Month _____

Totals

1									1
2									2
3	INCOME:								3
4	Rental								4
5	Other								5
6	TOTAL INCOME								6
7									7
8									8
9									9
10									10
11									11
12	EXPENSES & PAYMENTS								12
13	Interest								13
14	Taxes, Licenses								14
15	Insurance								15
16	Utilities								16
17	Services, Repairs, Maintenance								17
18	Merchandise, Supplies								18
19	Payroll								19
20	Miscellaneous Expenses								20
21	Depreciable								21
22	Mortgage Principal								22
23	Non-deductible								23
24									24
25									25
26	TOTAL EXPENSES & PAYMENTS								26
27	less Non-deductible								27
28	TOTAL								28
29	less Depreciable								29
30	TOTAL								30
31	less Mortgage Principal								31
32	TOTAL NET EXPENSES (for tax purposes)								32
33									33
34	TOTAL INCOME (line 6)								34
35	less line 28								35
36	CASH FLOW								36
37									37
38									38
39									39
40									40
41									41

LOAN & NOTE RECORD

Page _____

Property _____

Noteholder & Address _____

Loan Number_____ Original Loan_____

Interest _____ Payment _____ Due Date _____

	Payment Date Paid / If Changed	Principal	Interest	Impounds & (Imp. Disb.)	Impound Balance	Principal Balance	
1							1
2							2
3							3
4							4
5							5
6							6
7							7
8							8
9							9
10							10
11							11
12							12
13							13
14							14
15							15
16							16
17							17
18							18
19							19
20							20
21							21
22							22
23							23
24							24
25							25
26							26
27							27
28							28
29							29
30							30
31							31
32							32
33							33
34							34
35							35
36							36
37							37
38							38
39							39
40							40
41							41

Insurance Record

Property_____

Company Agent	Type of Policy	Policy Number	Limits	Premium	Expiration Date

TAXES

FORM E-3	RENTAL INCOME AND EXPENSE		YEAR 19

NAME(S) OF TAXPAYERS		SOC. SEC. NUMBER			

PROPERTY LOCATION & DESCRIPTION

GROSS INCOME

PROPERTY A _____

PROPERTY B _____

PROPERTY C _____

PROPERTY D _____

PROPERTY E _____

PROPERTY F _____

PROPERTY G _____

Total Income (to Schedule E, line 3)

EXPENSES

	A	B	C	D	E	F	G	TOTALS
Interest								
Taxes, Licenses								
Insurance								
Utilities								
Service, Repairs, Maintenance								
Merchandise, Supplies								
Payroll								
Miscellaneous Expenses								
Other:								
Subtotal								
% Bus. Use								
Subtotals (Total to Schedule E)								
Depreciation (Form D-1)								*
Supp. Depreciation (Form SD)								*
Totals								

*Sum of depreciation and supplemental depreciation totals (to Schedule E)

| FORM D-1 | DEPRECIATION WORKSHEET | YEAR 19 |

NAME(S) OF TAXPAYERS

SOC. SEC. NUMBER

PROPERTY LOCATION & DESCRIPTION

PROPERTY A _____

PROPERTY B _____

PROPERTY C _____

PROPERTY D _____

PROPERTY E _____

PROPERTY F _____

PROPERTY G _____

	A	B	C	D	E	F	G	TOTALS
Date Acq'd or Conv. to Bus.								
New or Used								
Cost or Other Basis								
Land Value								
Salvage Value								
20% 1st Year Deprec.								
Deprec. Basis								
Prior Deprec.								
Deprec. Balance								
Method of Deprec.								
Useful Life								
Full Year Deprec.								
% Year Held								
% Bus. Use								
Deprec. This Year								

PAGE TOTAL

FORM SD	SUPPLEMENTAL DEPRECIATION	YEAR 19

NAME(S) OF TAXPAYERS	SOC. SEC. NUMBER			

CAPITAL IMPROVEMENT LOCATION & DESCRIPTION

1 _____

2 _____

3 _____

4 _____

5 _____

6 _____

7 _____

	1	2	3	4	5	6	7	TOTALS
Date Acq'd or Conv. to Bus.								
New or Used								
Cost or Other Basis								
Salvage Value								
20% 1st Year Deprec.								
Deprec. Basis								
Prior Deprec.								
Deprec. Balance								
Method of Deprec.								
Useful Life								
Full Year Deprec.								
% Year Held								
% Bus. Use								
Deprec. This Year								

PAGE TOTAL

SOURCES & RESOURCES

The names, addresses, telephone numbers, and dates given here were checked for accuracy when *Landlording* went to press. By the time it came off the press, some of them were probably already outdated. If you have trouble locating any of these sources or resources, consult the reference librarian at your local public library. Reference librarians are outstanding resources in themselves.

ASSOCIATIONS

HALT, 201 Massachusetts Ave., N.E., Suite 312, Washington, D.C. 20002. Telephone 202-546-4258.

HALT stands for "Help Abolish Legal Tyrrany." It's a non-partisan membership organization which was founded in 1977 to reduce the cost and improve the quality of legal services in America. Such modest goals! Researchers will find cures for cancer and heart trouble long before legal services improve in this country. We've got to start sometime somewhere, though. Included with membership are a number of what HALT calls *Citizens Legal Manuals*, one of which is about real estate and another of which is about shopping for a lawyer. They're useful, and, in my opinion, so is the organization.

National Apartment Association, 1101 14th St., N.W., Suite 804, Washington, DC 20005. Telephone 202-842-4050.

Most state and local rental property owners' associations are affiliated with the National Apartment Association. Contact the NAA to find an association near you.

CATALOGS FROM VARIOUS SUPPLIERS

Catalog shopping used to mean Sears Roebuck and Montgomery Ward. Not any more! Catalog shopping has become increasingly popular since the first big gas crisis. Even now that gas is cheap, when adjusted for inflation, and readily available once more, catalog shopping is still growing in popularity, and no wonder. It's fun. It's convenient. It saves time. It saves fuel. It offers wide variety. It offers value. And it allows for easy comparison shopping.

Each of the companies listed here publishes a catalog which you may use no matter where you or your rental property happens to be, but most of them also have various locations scattered about the country. Except as noted, the offices listed here are main offices. Contact that office to learn whether there is a location near you.

*Brookstone.*127 Vose Farm Rd., Peterborough, NH 03458. Telephone 603-924-9541.

Brookstone publishes tool, garden, and kitchen catalogs, all chock full of top-quality merchandise and all sold at regular retail prices. They carry unusual items which are hard to find elsewhere, such as a completely enclosed electric extension-cord reel which will hold up to one hundred feet of 12-gauge, 3-wire cord; virtually indestructible 100-year-life screwdrivers which will take any sort of physical or verbal abuse; and an assortment of 200 O-rings which will save any landlord or landlady plumber many trips to the hardware store. They fill orders promptly and stand behind their merchandise.

Garon. 1924 Highway 35 CN 20, Wall, NJ 07719. Telephone 1-800-631-5380 except in New Jersey, where the number is 201-449-1776.

This building-and-grounds-maintenance catalog lists a wide variety of caulks, cements, cleaners, coatings, compounds, mortars, and sealers, together with the equipment used for their application.

Grainger's. 5959 W. Howard St., Chicago, IL 60648. Telephone 312-647-8900.

This thick catalog lists almost every electric motor known to man for both general and specialized applications. In addition, it includes compressors, pumps, light fixtures, carpet steam cleaners, electric drain augers, hand tools, testing devices, and so on and so on.

Maintenance Warehouse. P.O. Box 20037, San Diego, CA 92120. Telephone 1-800-431-3000 nationwide except from Alaska and Hawaii, where you should call 619-286-2222 collect.

This rapidly growing company specializes in providing most of the tools, equipment, materials, and supplies we landlords and landladies use in our rounds. In fact, Maintenance Warehouse sells only to the owners and managers of rental housing. Were you to make a list of the many things you use most often and replace most often around your rental property, chances are good that you'd find them all in this catalog. It has faucet parts, locksmithing supplies, ganged mailboxes, paint, appliance dollies, cleaning supplies, and more, lots more. Their 800 number automatically connects you with the warehouse nearest to you to guarantee speedy service. With minimum orders, shipping is included in the prices, that is, except for very heavy or bulky items. Get one of these wonderful catalogs. It offers a truly unique service, one-call shopping for landlording necessities. It's a must!

Pier-Angelli Company. 3866 Providence Rd., Edgemont, PA 19028. Telephone 1-800-523-7120 except in Pennsylvania, where the number is 215-359-1100.

This is probably the best source for hard-to-find plumbing parts and hardware. Their catalog has lots of actual-size illustrations which make the positive identification of parts as easy as it can be.

Sears, Roebuck and Co. Check the white pages of your telephone book for your nearest catalog sales store.

If you haven't heard of the Sears Catalog, you must be a time traveler or a refugee from the second or third world, but you may not have heard of Sears' specialized catalogs. They expand on the big book's listings, featuring, for example, power and hand tools in one catalog and office equipment and supplies in another. All the Sears catalogs are especially useful for price comparisons at home. Don't buy coin-operated laundry machines out of the big catalog, though. Buy them from your local Sears Contract Sales Office. It sells the same machines for less.

Seton Name Plate Corporation. P.O. Drawer EA-1331, New Haven, CT 06505. Telephone 1-800-243-6624 except in Connecticut, where the number is 203-488-0085.

In this catalog you'll find in-stock and custom-order signs, stickers, labels, markers, tags, name plates, badges, and decals of all kinds. Need a fire extinguisher sign, a graphic sign, an OSHA sign, or a "NO PARKING ANY TIME" sign? Seton has 'em. It also has spray-can graffiti remover and changeable-letter boards which make fine tenant directories.

Standard Appliance Parts Co. 1820 "S" St., Sacramento, CA 95814. Telephone 1-800-251-3671 except in California, where the number is 1-800-722-1831.

Most larger cities have appliance parts supply houses which maintain a parts inventory for all the local appliance repairers. Their entry doors may be marked "Wholesale to the Trade," but don't be intimidated; go in anyway and tell them the truth about what you do. They'll sell to you, and they'll probably press one of their catalogs into your hands as you leave. If not, ask Standard for a catalog and order by telephone from them whenever you need a thingamawhatsit for your air conditioners, heaters, dishwashers, refrigerators, stoves, ovens, water heaters, or laundry machines.

The Streamliners. 5 Pleasant View Dr., Box 480, Mechanicsburg, PA 17055. Telephone 1-800-544-5779 except in Pennsylvania, where the number is 1-800-257-6800.

Streamliners sells real estate forms, imprinted stationery, business cards, pegboard systems, rent payment envelopes, parking stickers, and the like.

U.S. General Supply Company. 100 Commercial St., Plainview, NY 11803. Telephone 1-800-645-7077.

This is supposed to be America's largest catalog of brand-name tools and hardware. Send them a dollar, and they will send you their latest full-sized catalog and numerous small sale catalogs over a twelve-month period, whether you buy anything from them or not. They will also send you a one-dollar credit certificate which you may apply to your very first order. U.S. General lists a complete range of tools, from homeowner quality (useful life—minutes) to industrial quality (useful life—years), and they discount all their tools from list prices. The outstanding Porter-Cable Speed-Bloc sander, for example, is discounted approximately 25% off the list price.

COMPUTER BOOKS

Brand, Stewart (ed.). *Whole Earth Software Catalog.* Garden City, New York: Quantum Press/Doubleday, 1985.

Computer books don't wear their age very well, especially if they try to review what's happening in the computer business. It's a business which changes so rapidly that a book published last week may be obsolete this. Such is the case with the first edition of this book, a gargantuan effort to analyze and critique computer products of all sorts, many of which are no longer on the market. Get the very latest version of this book. You'll find it jam-packed with good information about buying computers and software in general, as well as about a particular computer or software product.

COMPUTER PROGRAMS

Electric Checkbook™. State of the Art, 3191-C Airport Loop, Costa Mesa, CA 92626-4618. Telephone 714-850-0111.

Writing checks and reconciling your bank statement was never easier. This program handles your bookkeeping almost entirely through your checkbook. Write a check and the amount is automatically deducted from your checking account register and from the bank balance shown in your financial statement. It prints checks and categorized year-to-date statements of expenses as well as financial statements. Although written for "home use," the program can be adapted to work satisfactorily as a bookkeeping system for a small-time landlording business. It runs only on the Macintosh.

Excel™. Microsoft, 10700 Northup Way, Bellevue, WA 98004. Telephone 206-828-8088.

What Lotus 1-2-3 is for the IBM-PC and its compatibles, Excel is for the Macintosh, only more so. It is awesome! As a recent arrival on the computer spreadsheet scene, Excel incorporates the best features of its predecessors and allows easy movement of data to and from the popular spreadsheet programs. Because it makes full use of the Macintosh user commands, it takes less time to learn than spreadsheets which run on other machines. Yet, it is more powerful, if you can believe that! It runs only on the Macintosh.

Helix™. Odesta, 4084 Commercial Ave., Northbrook, IL 60062. Telephone 312-498-5615.

Anyone who has ever attempted to learn how to use a computerized data-base management system such as dBASE™ will recognize with even a cursory glance just how much of a quantum leap forward Helix is. It's not only easy to learn, set up, and use, but it does things that other fully relational data-base management systems cannot. It stores and sorts graphic images as well as alphanumeric data. You could use it for keeping track of your bookkeeping, your buildings (including pictures), your various types of units (including floor plans), your vacancy statistics, your tenants, your loan schedules, your paint cans, your rental furniture, your competition, your ships as they come in, or your cows as they come home. It runs only on the Macintosh.

Landlording™ (The Forms). ExPress, P.O. Box 1639, El Cerrito, CA 94530-4639. Telephone 415-236-5496.

There's nothing fancy or mindblowing here. This "computer program" consists of some of the *Landlording* forms which appear here in the back of the book plus some spreadsheet templates. They're available on disk so you won't have to spend hours entering them into your computer yourself if you're so inclined. Once you have the forms and templates in your own computer, you may tailor them to meet your needs, and you may merge into them your own specific data about tenants and dwellings. Various computer formats are available.

MacInTax™. Softview, 315 Arneill Road, Suite 215, Camarillo, CA 93010. Telephone 1-800-MACNTAX except in California, where the number is 1-800-MACVIEW.

Seeing this program for the first time is like seeing color TV after a lifetime of viewing black-and-white. Right on the computer's screen are facsimiles of the familiar IRS forms themselves. You enter the appropriate figures *once* in the same boxes you'd be using if you were filling out the forms manually, and the program does all the calculations for you. All of the forms are linked, too; complete Schedule E, and the appropriate figures are posted automatically to your 1040. Change something on Schedule E, and everything which is related to it throughout your return will be changed as well. Do "what if" calculations on any part of your return and you'll know instantly how they affect the results. In addition, the entire IRS instruction booklet is "on-line," that is, it's inside the computer, available for retrieval on command. Want information about a particular item on an IRS form? Point to that line and click. Presto, the IRS helps appear. No IRS agent could possibly be any faster! Want to print out your return? Well, how do you want it? On blank paper or on the actual IRS pre-printed forms? You make the choice. The IRS will accept either one. If the IRS were sending U.S. taxpayers a manual version and a computer version of its 1040 tax reporting package, this would be the computer version. I can't imagine a better one. It reduces this onerous chore from days to hours, and it's totally accurate. Currently, it runs only on the Macintosh, and, in my opinion, it alone is reason enough to buy a Mac. What's more, it's inexpensive, and you needn't spend a week studying a New-York-City-telephone-directory-sized manual trying to learn how to run the darn thing. It uses standard Mac commands, so if you know how to run other Mac programs, you already know how to run MacInTax. The latest version becomes available every January.

Supercalc®. Computer Associates International, 2310 Fortune Drive, San Jose, CA 95131. Telephone 408-942-1727.

On the market a long time, first for computers running the CPM-80 operating system and then for the IBM-PC and compatibles, Supercalc is a super spreadsheet program which has been carefully improved over the years. It is second to Lotus 1-2-3 in sales but not in power, features, or value.

INVESTMENT BOOKS

Allen, Robert. *Nothing Down*. New York: Simon and Schuster, 1984.

This has to be the bestselling real estate book of all time. It's been on the non-fiction bestseller lists not for weeks or months, but for years. I can see why. It's a readable introduction to the wonders of real estate investing, a heady world which offers the financial independence of a big lottery win to Bob and Betty Brown-Bag if only they'll spend some time working real estate deals instead of waiting around for one-in-ten-million luck to strike. It has helped to contribute to a change in many people's thinking about the financing of real estate. Still, you should be aware that some of the book's techniques rely upon high inflation for their success, and they won't work during periods of low inflation. The book has been updated and improved.

Bruss, Robert. *The Smart Investor's Guide to Real Estate*. New York: Crown, 1985.

Real estate's "Answer Man," the syndicated columnist who answers everybody's real estate questions in his "Real Estate Mailbag" column, has gathered all his sound advice together here in this one place. To make the book especially understandable, he has spiced his advice with numerous practical examples showing how real estate ideas apply to real-world situations. He has also included selected answers to the many questions asked of him over the years.

Cain, Christopher. *Maximize Your Resort Property Investment Business*. P.O. Box 2669, Columbia, MD 21045: Christopher Communications, 1985.

For anyone who rents out a vacation home by the week or weekend and wants help in making it pay, this book is a treasure-trove of good ideas. There are ideas for finding renters on your own, dealing with management companies (if you must), handling emergencies from a distance, and keeping people coming back year after year. Be forewarned that if you use all of this book's good ideas, your vacation home will be so booked up that you won't be able to find accommodations there for yourself. You'll have to rent someone else's. That, I suppose, is the epitome of success in the vacation home rental business.

de Heer, Robert. *Realty Bluebook*. 122 Paul Drive, San Rafael, CA 94903: Professional Publishing Corporation, 1984.

It's written primarily for real estate sales people and includes some stuff you probably wouldn't be interested in, but it does have some most useful loan tables and tax information, as well as helpful explanations of real estate contract clauses. A newly revised edition comes available every November.

Gadow, Sandy. *All About Escrow or How to Buy the Brooklyn Bridge and Have the Last Laugh!* Box 1639, El Cerrito, CA 94530-4639: ExPress, 1984.

This guide to the arcane rite of real estate passage called escrow clarifies the terminology and parts the waters. If you live in a state which uses escrow procedures, you ought to have this book handy so you won't feel like a knotty-pine dummy as you go through escrow, wondering whether you're being manipulated by the other party; wondering what the difference is between a deed of trust, a grant deed, and a quit-claim deed; wondering how to shop for the best financing; or wondering whether there's some way you might save money on your title insurance premium.

Glubetich, Dave. *Double Your Money in Real Estate Every 2 Years*. 2110 Omega Rd., Suite. A, San Ramon, CA 94583: Impact Publishing Company, 1980.

Let's see, if you can double your money in real estate every two years and you start out with $2000 and you don't add one more dollar of your own money along the way, you'll have over a million dollars in twenty years and over two million in twenty-two years. That's not bad! You've heard of compound interest. Glubetich's book is about compound investing. It continues the lessons begun in his popular book, *The Monopoly Game*, which has shown thousands how to make money investing in single-family houses. This later book provides answers to the negative thinkers' questions and the negative-cash-flow questions as well.

Lowry, Albert. *How You Can Become Financially Independent by Investing in Real Estate*. New York: Simon and Schuster, 1982.

The Lowry-Nickerson Real Estate Investors Seminar has been a fixture on the American scene for years. I'd be willing to bet that it has produced more graduates who went on to become millionaires than the nation's leading school of business has since the year it was founded. Whenever someone has been involved with a successful teaching program as long as Lowry has, you know he has a lot to say about the subject matter. You also know that the subject matter is going to be pretty well organized. You're right on both counts. Lowry's book summarizes on half a page his tested, foolproof formula for becoming financially independent; then it goes on to detail the many do's and don'ts involved in making that formula work.

Maloney, Roy. *Real Estate Quick & Easy*. P.O. Box 882222, San Francisco, CA 94188: Dropzone Press, 1983.

Ever have somebody sit down with you and explain patiently and concisely just what a "cap rate," "internal rate of return," "gross rent multiplier," "prescriptive easement," and the "Rule of 72" are? That's what this book does. It explains hundreds of real estate terms and concepts in the simplest way possible, through illustrations, graphs, and a highly condensed text.

Nickerson, William. *How I Turned $1,000 into Five Million in Real Estate in My Spare Time*. New York: Simon and Schuster, 1980.

This book is classic enough so that most buyers of rental property know what a "Nickerson" is (it's a fixer-upper with potential for forced appreciation, yielding at least two dollars of added value for every dollar spent on fixing it up). The book is loaded with sage advice and good information about purchasing, improving, managing, and trading rental properties. Although it has been updated, the techniques it espouses for pyramiding your real estate wealth remain the same today as they did when it was first published in 1959, when you could buy rental properties any day for $5,000 a unit. Anyone who bought the book back then and bought properties according to Nickerson's 20-year plan couldn't fail to have become a millionaire by 1979. Any edition of the book will do. Just roll your eyes at the numbers in the early editions and pay attention to the formulas.

Scher, Les. *Finding and Buying Your Place in the Country*. New York, NY: Collier Books, 1974.

This book does cover country property, but there's so much that urban and suburban property have in common with country property that you'll want to examine a copy of this book even though you never plan to leave West 89th Street. It's very thorough. It tells about dealing with insurance agents, lawyers, lenders, neighbors, partners, real estate agents, sellers, and tax assessors, not so that you can take advantage of them, but so that they won't take advantage of you, whether you're a city hick or a country slicker.

Tappan, William. *Real Estate Exchange and Acquisition Techniques*. Englewood Cliffs, NJ: Prentice-Hall, 1978.

If you are to preserve your capital in real estate transactions, you must understand how exchanges work. This book explains the mechanics of exchanging, both two- and three-way. It also provides information about the benefits of exchanging (tax benefits aren't the only ones), the special techniques which help to consummate exchanges, and the legal basis for exchanging. That's all in Part One. Part Two consists of a listing of 169 different acquisition techniques divided into seven categories. Some are far out and some aren't; a careful reading of all 169 should get you thinking.

LAW & EVICTION BOOKS

These books are intended for use in California. Ask your local apartment association whether there's something similar for your state.

Brown, David; Ralph Warner. *The Landlord's Law Book*. 950 Parker St., Berkeley, CA 94710: Nolo Press, 1985.

This is not one of those impressively bound tomes which line the walls of attorneys' offices and are dusted more often than they're consulted. This is a frank and friendly law book written by two attorneys who are committed to making accurate legal information available to the uninitiated.

California Apartment Association. *California Rental Housing Reference Book*. 1107 9th St., Suite 1010, Sacramento, CA 95814: California Apartment Association, 1985.

This extensive compilation of "official" residential rental property information includes some text about tenancies, portions of the California Civil Code pertaining to rental dwellings, some legal case citings, a batch of attorney-reviewed forms which have been approved by the CAA, and short explanations of how the forms are to be used. Unfortunately the book is marred in two respects: 1) Because the compilers do not want you to photocopy the forms, they have overprinted each one with a large "SAMPLE" in shaded letters. You must either buy the forms from your local apartment association or type them out yourself. 2) I can imagine several good reasons they might have for rendering the forms impossible to photocopy, but I can't imagine one good reason for their neglecting to include an index. After all, this is a *reference* work, not a work of fiction. People consult it to find something in particular. Instead of being directed to what you're looking for by an alphabetized index, you have to go to the trouble of checking the table of contents and thumbing through the book. In spite of these shortcomings, however, I recommend it as an indispensable reference work for California landlords and landladies.

Moskovitz, Myron; Ralph Warner; and Charles Sherman. *California Tenants' Handbook*. 950 Parker St., Berkeley, CA 94710: Nolo Press, 1985.

Some landlords and landladies might think it's the enemy's battle plan and might even regard it offensive. Some of it is. But it is primarily defensive, and it gives you a chance to consider the tenant's point of view for a change.

Robinson, Leigh. *The Eviction Book for California*. Box 1639, El Cerrito, CA 94530-4639: ExPress, 1984.

It details each step of the entire legal eviction process in California and includes the forms necessary to do an eviction yourself. When you've exhausted every possible method for getting problem tenants to move without resorting to the courts, find a copy of this book and get them out by going into court.

MAINTENANCE BOOKS

Ebeling, Walter. *Urban Entomology*. 1422 Harbour Way South, Richmond, CA 94804: University of California, Division of Agricultural Sciences, Publications Office, 1975.

More than a big book about city bugs, it's over six hundred pages of detailed, factual information about all kinds of cosmopolitan pests, from cockroaches to snakes. It explains where they come from, how they live, and how they die. It may save you from having to hire a professional exterminator.

How Things Work in Your Home (and What to Do When They Don't). Alexandria, VA: Time-Life Books, 1975.

In clear illustrations and tight prose, this book outlines how plumbing, electrical, heating, and cooling systems work. It explains how the various components of these systems operate, and it details ways to troubleshoot malfunctioning heaters, appliances, septic tanks, faucets, and the like.

Reader's Digest Complete Do-It-Yourself Manual. Pleasantville, NY: The Reader's Digest Association, 1973.

It's a valuable book full of good illustrations and photographs. If you have a job to do, like pouring a cement walkway or repairing a decayed threshold, you can look it up in the index and then turn to practical hints for doing it right.

Reader's Digest Fix-It-Yourself Manual. Pleasantville, NY: The Reader's Digest Association, 1977.

Shhh, don't tell anybody, but the "complete" manual above wasn't 100% complete. Here's more of the same, just as good.

Robinson, Robert. *Complete Course in Professional Locksmithing*. 111 N. Canal St., Chicago, IL 60606: Nelson-Hall Co. 1973.

As the title indicates, this is a training manual for professionals, and it includes much more than you'll ever want or need to know about locksmithing, but it also includes the basics which you may want to familiarize yourself with.

MANAGEMENT BOOKS

Bierbrier, Doreen. *Managing Your Rental House for Increased Income*. New York: McGraw-Hill. 1985.

Here's a thorough presentation of a novel way to squeeze positive cash flow out of rental houses, written by someone who is out there in the rough-and-tumble world doing it herself and making it pay off. Bierbrier tenants her houses with single people whose aggregate rent is greater than what a single family would pay. She reveals exactly how she does it, too, from acquiring the houses to acquiring the tenants and keeping them in line.

Kelley, Edward. *Practical Apartment Management*. 430 No. Michigan Ave., Chicago, IL 60611-4090: Institute of Real Estate Management. 1984.

This is a somewhat pedantic, but competent, treatment of the subject, written primarily for the managers of large apartment complexes.

Lowry, Albert. *How to Manage Real Estate Successfully in Your Spare Time*. New York: Simon & Schuster. 1980.

This book's strong suit is sales, finding warm bodies and getting them to rent empty apartments. It should be particularly helpful to anyone who's trying to fill a new apartment building in an area where others are trying to do the same.

Reed, John. *How to Manage Apartments for Maximum Cash Flow and Resale Value*. 342 Bryan Dr., Danville, CA 94526: Reed Publishing. 1985.

Should you suspect that you're becoming soft in the heart, read this book. It's written by someone who's hard-hearted, hard-headed, and hard-nosed about rental properties. He's the kind whose heart is eagerly sought after for transplants. It's been so little used. Contrary to what you might think, the book does not come with a black cape, glue-on handlebar moustache, and braided cowhide whip. They're extras.

PERIODICALS

The addresses and telephone numbers given here are those of the subscription offices and not necessarily those of the business, editorial, or advertising offices. Most of these periodicals carry no advertising and hence have no biases except those of their writers, editors, and publishers, which may in themselves be considerable.

Consumer Reports. Consumer Reports, Box 2480, Boulder, CO 80321. 11 issues a year, plus a buyer's guide in lieu of a December issue, no advertising.

This trustworthy magazine publishes the results of the tests and studies conducted in its own fiercely independent testing laboratories. Although it is obviously pro-consumer, supposing that *Consumer Reports* is therefore anti-business would be a true non-sequitur. Expect it to publish articles written from a tenant's perspective (they're the "consumers" in our business, remember) from time to time, but also remember that you in your role as landlord or landlady are a consumer of various goods and services, too. Look to it for forthright evaluations of fire extinguishers, smoke alarms, ladders, paints, cleaning agents, carpets, computers, appliances, locks, telephones, and tools. You'll even find informative articles on mortgages, wills, banks, and insurance companies. Don't buy a thing without consulting it. Each issue includes a handy index of the previous eleven issues. The annual buyer's guide, published as the December issue, summarizes earlier articles and runs to almost 400 pages. It's well organized and available separately from newsstands and bookstores.

Impact Reports. Impact Publishing Company, 2110 Omega Rd., Suite. A, San Ramon, CA 94583. 1-800-446-7228. 10 issues a year, no advertising.

Each report (6,000-10,000 words) is devoted to a single subject of interest to the small real estate investor. Subjects covered have ranged from options to foreclosures and exchanges. An eight-page newsletter called *Winning with Real Estate*, which consists of articles written by a variety of real estate investment advisers, accompanies each report. There is a full money-back guarantee for those who are dissatisfied after two issues.

InfoWorld. InfoWorld, P.O. Box 1018, Southeastern, PA 19398. 1-800-544-3712 or 215-768-0388 in Pennsylvania. 52 issues a year, advertising.

You could be living isolated on Walden Pond and still feel current about the rapidly changing world of microcomputers if you were keeping up with your *InfoWorld* reading. Avoid reading the tabloid-like gossip if you can and concentrate on the reviews of hardware and software. They're generally good and they're generally useful. You may need to reserve a corner of your house for your stack of rapidly accumulating issues because you won't want to toss 'em.

Journal of Property Management. Institute of Real Estate Management, 430 N. Michigan Ave., Chicago, IL 60611. 312-661-1930. 6 issues a year, advertising.

This bimonthly journal is written by and for the managers of large apartment complexes. It's somewhat high fallutin and includes some articles, such as those about elevators and mainframe-computer bookkeeping systems, which are of no practical value to the do-it-yourself landlord or landlady, but every so often it does have articles which are of great practical value, such as those on painting and energy conservation. They're worth the cost of subscribing.

Landlord-Tenant Law Bulletin. Quinlan Publishing Co., 131 Beverly St., Boston, MA 02114. 12 issues a year, no advertising.

This monthly eight-page bulletin summarizes recent court decisions involving landlord-tenant disputes from around the country. Written for the attorney and interested layman, it makes for very instructive reading. It should help you understand your rights and potential liabilities more fully and should help you avoid needless litigation.

Real Estate Investing Letter. HBJ Newsletter Bureau, 50 Washington St., Norwalk, CT 06854. 203-853-0400. 12 issues a year, no advertising.

This lively publication is subtitled "A Guide to Prudent Investing," and it is just that, investment- rather than speculation-oriented. The articles run the gamut from investing in small town property to evaluating older houses and using a mortgage broker.

The Robert Bruss Real Estate Newsletter. Tribune Media Services, P.O. Box 534, Palmyra, NJ 08065. 12 issues a year, no advertising.

In his popular newspaper column, Mr. Bruss limits himself to answering his readers' questions, and each newspaper's real estate editor limits the column to whatever space is available after all the advertising has been set in place; sometimes there's no space for Bruss at all. This monthly newsletter might be called *Bruss Unbound* or *Bruss Unlimited* because he chooses the real estate subjects himself, and he has eight full pages to develop them in, without ever being squeezed out by advertising layouts. The subjects are topical and what he says about them is useful and well researched. Subjects he has covered so far include negotiation strategies, equity sharing, tax-deferred exchanges, distress property acquisition, due-on-sale clauses, lease options, tax law changes, and lots more, one in each issue. Don't own real estate without it.

Whole Earth Review. POINT, 27 Gate Five Road, Sausalito, CA 94965. 6 issues a year, no advertising.

A combination of *CoEvolution Quarterly* and *Whole Earth Software Review, Whole Earth Review* is published by the same people who have given us the *Whole Earth Catalog* in its various renditions and the *Whole Earth Software Catalog.* Don't bother to read it unless you think of yourself as open-minded because you are sure to find something in it which will offend your political or moral sensibilities. Nonetheless, it's an eye-opener sometimes, and it's a great source of information on books, tools, and computer goodies. Among what it calls its maniacal subscribers, those coughing up $1,000 or more, are Marlon Brando and Bamboo Flying Water. You don't have to be a maniac to read it. The maniacs I know who do, say that being a maniac doesn't help in the least.

TAX BOOKS

Lasser Tax Institute. *Your Income Tax*. New York: Simon and Schuster. 1985.

The newsprint and small type used in this book make it look distinctly like a dull IRS publication, but then, maybe federal tax rules are always dull, no matter who publishes the information. It has concise explanations of the tax laws and practices which you should be familiar with, even if someone else prepares your taxes. It also has a good index and good cross references.

Reed, John. *Aggressive Tax Avoidance for Real Estate Investors*. 342 Bryan Dr., Danville, CA 94526: Reed Publishing. 1985.

This "English-language translation" of income tax laws affecting real estate investors minces no words. With mathematical proof, it explains why you should be aggressive in those many gray areas of tax law, and then it shows you how to be aggressive. The book's rules for understanding income taxes may surprise you, but unless you follow them, you're paying more taxes than the law requires. It explains depreciation and exchanging clearly and also tells how to find a good, aggressive tax adviser. It's revised annually to reflect changes in the tax laws themselves and in their interpretation.

INDEX

WORDS IN EDGEWISE

Yours is a thankless job, dear landlord and landlady. Just remember that landlording is a business. People are not going to commend you for your efforts, but neither are they going to stop depending on you. People who are too timid, too transient, too insolvent, too young, too feeble, too smart, too stupid, or otherwise too indisposed to own their own housing are all depending on you to provide them with housing. Do just that, and do it as best you can.

There will be times when you will feel distraught over your landlording troubles and trials, times when you will have tried your best and yet you find yourself on the short end. Don't show your anger. Keep a punching bag at home for that. But if you cannot get along with a tenant or a tenant with you, get the tenant out. You know how to do it. Run your business yourself. Don't let your tenants run it for you.

ORDER FORMS

EXPRESS, P.O. BOX 1639, EL CERRITO, CA 94530-4639

Dear EXPRESS:

   I'm not a property owner yet, but I'd like to be one someday, and I think I'd like to know what I'm doing. Show me.

Please send me _____copies of *Landlording*   @$17.95 $ _____
                 _____copies of *The Eviction Book for California*   @$14.95 $ _____
                 _____copies of *All About Escrow*   @$10.95 $ _____
               California residents add 6% sales tax (6½% in transit counties) $ _____
                                  Shipping and handling $ _2.00_
Make check or money order payable to EXPRESS.   TOTAL DUE $ _____

SEND TO _____
_____
_____ ZIP _____

EXPRESS, P.O. BOX 1639, EL CERRITO, CA 94530-4639

Dear EXPRESS:

   I'm an unscrupulous property owner who's merciless, lowdown, and greedy, and I'll pay double the usual price for your books just to lay my hands on all that great information. It may even reform me, who knows?

Please send me _____copies of *Landlording*   @35.90 _____
                 _____copies of *The Eviction Book for California*   @29.90 _____
                 _____copies of *All About Escrow*   @21.90 _____
               California residents add 6% sales tax (6½% in transit counties) $ _____
                                  Shipping and handling $ _2.00_
Make check or money order payable to EXPRESS.   TOTAL DUE $ _____

SEND TO _____
_____
_____ ZIP _____

EXPRESS, P.O. BOX 1639, EL CERRITO, CA 94530-4639

Dear EXPRESS:

   I'm a scrupulous property owner and I'd like copies of your books for my very own. Hurry up with my order. I need all the help I can get right now.

Please send me _____copies of *Landlording*   @$17.95 $ _____
                 _____copies of *The Eviction Book for California*   @$14.95 $ _____
                 _____copies of *All About Escrow*   @$10.95 $ _____
               California residents add 6% sales tax (6½% in transit counties) $ _____
                                  Shipping and handling $ _2.00_
Make check or money order payable to EXPRESS.   TOTAL DUE $ _____

SEND TO _____
_____
_____ ZIP _____